THE EPISTLE TO THE
HEBREWS

Other works by Dr. Surrendra Gangadean & The Logos Foundation:

Philosophical Foundation: A Critical Analysis of Basic Beliefs

History of Philosophy: A Critical Analysis of Unresolved Disputes

Theological Foundation: A Critical Analysis of Christian Belief

Philosophical Foundation: Trivium Study Guide

The Logos Papers: To Make the Logos Known

The Westminster Confession: A Doxological Understanding

The Westminster Shorter and Larger Catechisms: A Doxological Understanding

On Natural and Revealed Theology: Collected Essays of Surrendra Gangadean

The Logos Curriculum: Grammar Catechisms: Philosophical, Theological, and Historical Foundations

The Contradictoriness of Sin: A Reading of Paradise Lost

Fundación Filosofica: Un Análisis Crítico de Creencias Básicas

DOXOLOGICAL REFORMED SERMON SERIES:

The Biblical Worldview: Creation, Fall, Redemption— Genesis 1–3: Scripture in Organic Seed Form

The Unity of the Church: That They May Be One That the World May Believe

The Person and Work of Christ: To Undo What Adam Did and To Do What Adam Failed to Do—A Summary Exposition

The Gospel of Matthew: The Person and Work of Christ— The Fulfillment of Redemption Through the One to Come

The Epistle to the Romans: The Righteousness of God Revealed from Faith to Faith—The Gospel According to St. Paul

The Book of Revelation: What Must Soon Take Place— Doxological Postmillennialism

The Natural Moral Law: The Foundation for Lasting Culture, Volumes 1–5

PHILOSOPHICAL FOUNDATION DIALOGUE SERIES:

Introduction to Philosophy: The Basic Things Are Clear to Reason

DOXOLOGICAL REFORMED SERMON SERIES

THE EPISTLE TO THE
HEBREWS

Christ Is Superior in Every Way

Foundation to Persevere in Biblical Faith

SURRENDRA GANGADEAN

LOGOS
PRESS
PAPERS

◆

λ
LOGOS

A DIVISION OF THE LOGOS FOUNDATION
Phoenix, Arizona

Cover design: Beth Ellen Nagle
Typesetting: Matthew P. Hicks & Brian J. Phelps

Library of Congress Cataloging-in-Publication Data pending

Gangadean, Surrendra, 1943–2022.
    The epistle to the Hebrews: Christ is superior in every way—
    foundation to persevere in biblical faith
    Includes Index
    ISBN: 979-8-9910952-0-4 (hbk.)
    ISBN: 979-8-9910952-1-1 (pbk.)
    ISBN: 979-8-9910952-2-8 (e-book)

1. The Book of Hebrews 2. Superiority of Christ 3. Foundational Doctrine 4. Persevering in Biblical Faith 5. Doxological Reformed I. Title

For those looking for
the city whose architect
and builder is God

CONTENTS

Series Preface   ix

Introduction   xiii

PART I: THE EPISTLE TO THE HEBREWS
2001 SERMON SERIES

1. The Superiority of the Son (Hebrews 1)   3

2. Jesus: The Merciful and Faithful High Priest (Hebrews 2)   19

3. Fix Your Thoughts on Jesus (Hebrews 3)   35

4. Dividing Soul and Spirit (Hebrews 4)   51

5. Perfect Through Suffering (Hebrews 5)   67

6. Hope: An Anchor for the Soul (Hebrews 6)   83

7. Christ: A Priest Forever (Hebrews 7)   99

8. The New Covenant (Hebrews 8)   115

9. The Contrast Between the Old and the New (Hebrews 9)   131

10. Christ: The Lasting Sacrifice (Hebrews 10)   149

11. The Commendation of Faith: Part I (Hebrews 11:1–19)   167

12. The Commendation of Faith: Part II (Hebrews 11:17–39)   185

13. Discipline for Holiness (Hebrews 12:1–13)   203

14. No Turning Back (Hebrews 12:14–19)   219

15. Exhortations to Life (Hebrews 13:1–25)   235

PART II: THE FOUNDATION
2001 SERMON SERIES

16. Sin and the Need for Christ (Hebrews 6:1–3)   253

17. Repentance and Faith (Hebrews 5:11–6:3, 11:1–6)   271

18. The Doctrine of Baptism: Part I (Matthew 28:16–20)   287

19. The Doctrine of Baptism: Part II (Acts 1–2; Ephesians 4)   303

20. Laying on of Hands (John 2:12–22)   321

21. Resurrection of the Dead (1 Corinthians 15:12–28)   339

22. Eternal Judgment (John 15:1–8)   355

About the Author   379

SERIES PREFACE

T HE *DOXOLOGICAL REFORMED SERMON SERIES*[1] is a collection of
Pastor Surrendra Gangadean's sermons during his over two-de-
cade tenure as the founder and senior pastor of Westminster Fellowship Church. During this period, he delivered over 1,000 sermons,
preserved through audio recordings, handwritten outlines, and congregants' notes. These sermons now form the basis of dozens of books,
offering a Doxological Reformed exposition of the Scripture, the moral
law, and foundational theological doctrines.

The significance of this collection lies in its pioneering nature—in
seeking to advance the kingdom of God—providing the groundwork
for future hermeneutical works. Pastor Gangadean developed and
applied Rational Presuppositionalism[2] to general revelation in his
work *Philosophical Foundation*,[3] addressing enduring challenges of the
modern and postmodern world. Similarly, he tackled central questions
concerning the content and application of Scripture. Recognizing the
impracticality of writing full commentaries, Pastor Gangadean used
sermons to engage the meaning of Scripture, foundational doctrines,
and the moral law as applied to all of life.

Consequently, The Logos Foundation Editorial Board has unani-
mously decided to present the sermon series in its original form. Minor
grammatical changes aside, the content remains untouched, accurately
reflecting Pastor Gangadean's ongoing thought process. We aim to
prepare the way for future generations to connect directly with the
mind that shaped these doctrines. Preservation of the original will also

---

1. Surrendra Gangadean, *The Westminster Shorter and Larger Catechisms: A Doxological Under-standing* (Phoenix: Logos Papers Press, 2023), xv-xxxii.

2. Surrendra Gangadean, "Paper No. 101: Rational Presuppositionalism: Critically Examin-ing Assumptions for Meaning," in *The Logos Papers: To Make the Logos Known* (Phoenix: Logos Papers Press, 2022), 521–526; "Paper No. 52: Common Ground (Part III)," 281–282; "Paper No. 2: Common Ground," 9–13; "Paper No. 95: Rational Presuppositional Apologetics," 503–506; "Paper No. 96: The Project of Rational Presuppositional Apologet-ics," in *The Logos Papers*, 507–508.

3. Surrendra Gangadean, *Philosophical Foundation: A Critical Analysis of Basic Beliefs*, Second Edition (Phoenix: Public Philosophy Press, 2022).

aid the Editorial Board in capturing the diverse contexts in which his ideas were expounded. These sermons, coupled with foundational work in philosophy, theology, the humanities, and history, form the basis for forthcoming biblical commentaries. While each book is not exhaustive in itself, the series collectively reflects Pastor Gangadean's distilled wisdom throughout his body of work. As more books are published, a complete tapestry of his understanding will gradually unfold.

We regard the content of these sermons as invaluable contributions to the Next Reformation.[4] They illustrate how contextual thinking can illuminate the organic content of Scripture, reaching across every book and addressing even the most disputed passages that have troubled the Church throughout history. Through these sermons, the perspicuity of Scripture is meticulously brought into focus, shedding light on the clarity derived from general revelation, special revelation, and the cumulative insights of the Historic Christian Faith.[5] The convergence of the doxological focus, the doctrine of clarity and inexcusability, the knowledge of God as the good, and Rational Presuppositionalism collectively work to unveil the profound meaning of Scripture and encapsulate the essence of its truth.

Pastor Gangadean's preaching approach unfolds with a discernible progression. In the earlier sermons from 1993 to 2004, the emphasis rests on biblical exposition of the books of Scripture, laying a robust foundation by elucidating fundamental doctrines such as clarity and inexcusability, the divine image in man, the knowledge of God, church authority, and worship. Delivered with rapidity, these sermons were densely packed with content aimed at a comprehensive exposition.

From 2005 to 2014, a pronounced shift occurred in Pastor Ganga-dean's sermons, with a heightened focus on the need for sanctification within the context of discipleship. This period aimed to equip the congregation to grasp the interplay between foundational truths and personal application, fostering maturity. These sermons naturally evolved from the preceding foundational exposition of Scripture. After a decade of delving into the objective and subjective facets of biblical truths and

---

4. Gangadean, "Paper No. 62: The Next Reformation," in *The Logos Papers*, 335–337.

5. Surrendra Gangadean, *The Westminster Confession of Faith: A Doxological Understanding* (Phoenix: Logos Papers Press, 2023); Surrendra Gangadean, *The Westminster Shorter and Larger Catechisms: A Doxological Understanding* (Phoenix: Logos Papers Press, 2023).

their integration, the imperative to address remaining sin within the congregation became increasingly apparent.

The subsequent phase of preaching, spanning 2015 to 2022, witnessed a shift towards existential hermeneutics, emphasizing the moral law, the unity of the Church, public witness, and adopting a more deliberate and rhetorical expository style. While his pace slowed, his focus intensified on discerning how to apply truths to dismantle self-deception and self-justification among congregants and within the broader Church. The doctrine of repentance of root sin and an in-depth analysis of the doctrine of clarity and inexcusability assumed central significance.

The essence of these sermons constitutes the most profound exposition of the Word of God in its fullness to date. The expositor lived an exemplary life, building upon the cumulative insights from the three foundations, and endeavored to equip God's people with a clear understanding of Scripture amidst its myriad challenges, facilitating enduring responses.

Anticipating that this sermon series will serve as an essential source for crafting a biographical account of Pastor Gangadean's life and work, it becomes evident in these sermons how providence in his life, the challenges inherent in shepherding the flock, the practical application of doctrinal principles to the life of the Church, and a continuous response to the prevailing state of the Church and culture are interwoven. They stand as a testament to the life of a faithful servant who fought the good fight, finished the race, and kept the faith.[6]

These sermons, given initially to the congregants of Westminster Fellowship over the years, are deemed blessings that must be shared with the broader body of Christ. We consider it imperative to extend these blessings to our fellow brothers and sisters, and view it as our duty to contribute to the spiritual enrichment of the larger Christian community.

May the Lord bless the preaching and hearing of His Word, and may this compilation serve as the foundation for the contextual interpretation of Scripture for generations to come, and persist until the fulfillment

---

6. *2 Timothy 4:7–8.*

of the dominion[7] and mission[8] mandates in the earth being filled with the knowledge of the glory of the Lord as the waters cover the sea.

—THE LOGOS FOUNDATION
EDITORIAL BOARD
Phoenix, Arizona
February 2024

---

7. *Genesis 1:26–28.*
8. *Matthew 28:18–20.*

INTRODUCTION

2 Peter 3:15–16

¹⁵Bear in mind that our Lord's patience means salvation, just as our dear brother Paul also wrote you with the wisdom that God gave him. ¹⁶He writes the same way in all his letters, speaking in them of these matters. His letters contain some things that are hard to understand, which ignorant and unstable people distort, as they do the other Scriptures, to their own destruction.

THE EPISTLE TO THE HEBREWS: *Christ Is Superior in Every Way—Foundation to Persevere in Biblical Faith* is a Doxological Reformed exposition of the central themes of Hebrews and the hope of salvation in its fullest sense. The superiority of Christ in every way is the acknowledged central theme by all Reformed commentators and interpreters. Among them, John Owen's masterful, seven-volume *An Exposition of the Epistle to the Hebrews* stands out for its comprehensiveness, depth, and soundness of Reformed theology. His work extensively addresses the epistle's covenantal, soteriological, and Christocentric themes. Pastor Surrendra Gangadean accepted the content regarding the authorship, dating, occasion, and circumstances of the Book of Hebrews as consistent with tradition and the result of John Owen's careful efforts in reaching those conclusions. Having found no sufficient basis to question John Owen's findings, Pastor Gangadean built upon his work to focus on areas central to strengthening and deepening the content of Hebrews and, by implication, strengthening the foundation. This expository sermon series should be seen as complementary to the theological themes already developed by John Owen; it is not intended as a displacement or rejection.

Since John Owen's publication over 300 years ago, the Church has faced enormous challenges from without—Modernity and Postmodernity—and increased divisions and apostasy within. The current divisions in the Church and decay in the culture show a longstanding lack of foundation and the need to get the foundation more firmly established. In Scripture, foundation is called for as the first principles,[1] for endurance against tempests,[2] for lasting fruit,[3] for unity of the faith and fullness,[4] and for a lasting culture in the City of God.[5] Foundation is needed to attain to *maturity* in one's own understanding, *fruitfulness* in the increase of understanding in others, *unity* in all relations in every sphere of life, and *fullness* in all the riches of knowledge and understanding. It is by spiritual maturity in the foundation that one goes from infancy in understanding to taking every thought (raised against the knowledge of God) captive to the obedience of Christ.[6] Only through spiritual maturity attained by building on the foundation can believers be brought to proclaim the lordship of Christ over all things. The foundation cannot be bypassed.

Foundation is necessary for maturity in the faith. Through it, ignorance is rendered inexcusable and distortions incoherent. Foundation restrains what **"ignorant and unstable people distort."** It sets contextual boundaries to the possible meanings to interpret a passage; the more basic provides the basis for the meaning of the less basic. As such, the foundation is to be built to withstand challenges against the coherence of the faith. Pastor Gangadean can be characterized as a theologian focused on foundation—a foundational theologian. His work encompasses philosophical, theological, and historical foundations. Hebrews is concerned with theological foundation, and this topic is exposited in several sermon series and classes that will be made available in four additional volumes spanning from 1992–2022.[7] It can be properly said that Pastor Gangadean **"writes the same way in all his letters** [books]," with a keen eye on foundation to secure the basis for a lasting work.

---

1. *Hebrews 5:12–6:1* KJV.

2. *Matthew 7:24–29*.

3. *1 Corinthians 3:10–15*.

4. *Ephesians 4*.

5. *Hebrews 11:10; Revelation 21*.

6. *2 Corinthians 10:4–5*.

7. (1) *The Biblical Worldview: Creation, Fall, Redemption—Genesis 1–3: Scripture in Organic Seed Form* (2024); (2) *Biblical Foundation: In Narrative and Theological Form* (forthcoming); (3) *Theological Foundation: The Seven Pillars of the Faith* (forthcoming); (4) *Theological Foundation: The Knowledge of God and Man* (forthcoming).

The challenge of addressing the **"things that are hard to understand"** and making them intelligible to the reader is where Pastor Gangadean's focus comes in through Rational Presuppositionalism.[8] The things that are hard to understand (subjectively) are so because the more basic/ elementary things are not in place (objectively).[9] "Though by this time you ought to be teachers, you need someone to teach you the elementary truths of God's word all over again" (Heb. 5:12a). He took upon making the less basic understandable by addressing the content of the foundation, which is more basic. A truth can be objectively clear and yet subjectively difficult, especially when the more basic is not in place. To overcome the subjective difficulty, the reader needs to be prepared to hear;[10] the more basic will render the less basic intelligible. This is part of preparing the way of the Lord, to make a highway for our God.[11] Through a clearer and fuller foundation, believers are prepared to press ahead and become established in discerning the will of God in their lives and the culture at large.

Having the foundation explained is different from building on it. Foundation provides the basis to persevere, pay more careful attention,[12] hold firmly,[13] show diligence to the very end,[14] and run with perseverance[15] to overcome challenges to the faith. Persevering postmillennialism is required for doxological postmillennialism to be realized.[16] Diligently seeking God by making use of the ordinary means and getting the foundation laid in our lives is necessary to make disciples of all the nations—teaching them to obey all that Christ has commanded.[17]

---

8. Gangadean, *Philosophical Foundation*, 19–23; Gangadean, "Paper No. 101: Rational Presuppositionalism," 521–526; "Paper No. 52: Common Ground (Part III)," in *The Logos Papers*, 281–282; Gangadean, *On Natural and Revealed Theology*, 59–66.

9. *Hebrews 5:11–14.*

10. *Matthew 11:15, 13:9.*

11. *Isaiah 40:1–5.*

12. *Hebrews 2:1.*

13. *Hebrews 3:14.*

14. *Hebrews 6:11.*

15. *Hebrews 12:1–2.*

16. Gangadean, "Paper No. 49: Eschatology (FAQ)," 271–274; "Paper No. 104: Eschatology (Twelve Points)," 539–544; "Paper No. 118: Eschatology (Seven Points)," 603–607; "Paper No. 119: Pauline Eschatology," in *The Logos Papers*, 609–610.

17. *Matthew 28:18–20.*

The need for building on foundation begins with believers in the house of God; then it is to go out from Zion to all the families of the earth—teaching the nations, transforming culture, and overcoming in the spiritual conflict between belief and unbelief.[18]

Perseverance requires biblical faith. Biblical faith involves a worldview held with understanding, built consistently in light of the foundation summed up in Hebrews 6:1–2 with its assumptions and implications. Biblical faith has content; it understands the nature of God and man, and good and evil. Biblical faith is pleasing to God; it entails diligently seeking.[19] Biblical faith is having certainty and proof of what is not seen;[20] God's eternal power and divine nature are clearly seen from the things that are made.[21] Biblical faith reasons when tested and overcomes challenges in providence.[22] Biblical faith passes on the blessing—the promise.[23] Biblical faith values and evaluates consistently with the promise.[24] Biblical faith fights the good fight—the spiritual war.[25] Biblical faith is necessary to inherit the promise of God—all the families of the earth being blessed.[26] Biblical faith is long-term; it sees the distant future and works with perseverance for it. Biblical faith is what is needed to understand the things that are **"hard to understand"** and to build on the foundation until we attain the fullness that there is in Christ. Biblical faith awaits the consummation of the promise beyond death.[27] By faith we understand; faith understands the basic things: the foundation and all that is built upon it.

This commentary on Hebrews is written for those seeking to build on a strong and lasting foundation to advance the work of the kingdom. It is for those who understand the good as the knowledge of God through the work of dominion in providence. It will press the reader

---

18. *Isaiah 2:1–5.*

19. *Hebrews 11:6* KJV.

20. *Hebrews 11:1–3.*

21. *Romans 1:18–20.*

22. *Hebrews 11:17–19.*

23. *Hebrews 11:21–22.*

24. *Hebrews 11:24–26.*

25. *Hebrews 11:32–34.*

26. *Genesis 12:1–3.*

27. *Hebrews 11:39–40.*

to understand the centrality of foundation, perseverance, and biblical faith to engage in the work of the kingdom as co-heirs with Christ. The exposition of Hebrews, along with the seven added sermons on foundation, will enable the reader to see the majesty of the rule of Christ in completing the eschatological work of filling the earth with the knowledge of God.

—THE LOGOS FOUNDATION
EDITORIAL BOARD
Phoenix, Arizona
October 2024

———

PART I

THE EPISTLE TO THE
HEBREWS
2001 SERMON SERIES

———

1

THE SUPERIORITY
OF THE SON

Hebrews 1

¹In the past God spoke to our forefathers through the prophets at many times and in various ways, ²but in these last days he has spoken to us by his Son, whom he appointed heir of all things, and through whom he made the universe. ³The Son is the radiance of God's glory and the exact representation of his being, sustaining all things by his powerful word. After he had provided purification for sins, he sat down at the right hand of the Majesty in heaven. ⁴So he became as much superior to the angels as the name he has inherited is superior to theirs.

⁵For to which of the angels did God ever say,
　"You are my Son;
　　today I have become your Father"?

Or again,
　"I will be his Father,
　　and he will be my Son"?

⁶And again, when God brings his firstborn into the world, he says,
　"Let all God's angels worship him."

⁷In speaking of the angels he says,
　"He makes his angels winds,
　　his servants flames of fire."

⁸But about the Son he says,
　"Your throne, O God, will last for ever and ever,
　　and righteousness will be the scepter of your kingdom.

⁹You have loved righteousness and hated wickedness;

therefore God, your God, has set you above your companions
by anointing you with the oil of joy."

[10]He also says,
  "In the beginning, O Lord, you laid the foundations of the earth,
    and the heavens are the work of your hands.

[11]They will perish, but you remain;
    they will all wear out like a garment.

[12]You will roll them up like a robe;
    like a garment they will be changed.
  But you remain the same,
    and your years will never end."

[13]To which of the angels did God ever say,
  "Sit at my right hand
until I make your enemies
  a footstool for your feet"?

[14]Are not all angels ministering spirits sent to serve those who will inherit salvation?

WE WILL BE GOING THROUGH A STUDY of the Book of Hebrews.
We have not done this before. We have done several other
books, but we have not done Hebrews. It is a difficult book to tackle.
It is the second major epistle in the New Testament. There are things in
it that are hard to understand.[1] We have often heard messages from the
Book of Hebrews, portions here and there. In the *Foundation Study*,[2]
which we did for several weeks, the beginning was from the Book of
Hebrews. There is teaching in this book that we need to hear, and by
the grace of God, we hope to hear this teaching.

INTRODUCTION

By way of introduction, we should say: *To* whom the book was written,
when it was written, *by* whom it was written, and *what* the occasion
was for writing it. We should know that there are a lot of questions that
have existed in the history of the Church concerning this book. I have

---

1. *2 Peter 3:16.*

2. The Foundations Sermon Series has been added to the latter part of this work to comple-
ment the exposition of the Book of Hebrews.

studied some of these discussions and have, upon reflection, weighed the arguments and reasonings back and forth and have come to a certain conclusion that is in keeping with the main belief of the Church historically. There are notable persons who have taken different positions.

I have followed the teaching and the writing of John Owen, who wrote an extensive commentary on the Book of Hebrews[3] around 1668. He comes after many others in the Reformed position, and he benefits from them and responds to them. His learning is enormous. I believe, at one point, he was probably the head of the University of Oxford at the tail end of the Puritan period.[4] Remember, the Westminster Confession was written between 1643 and 1648. In 1660, there was a great ejection of the Puritan ministers, but his influence has continued and has been significant.

Pauline Authorship

The book, by common agreement, is written to the Hebrews and so carries the name Hebrews. This book does not have an author explicitly attached to it. There has been an author named in other places, and Paul identifies himself in the Epistles, but neither at the beginning nor at the end is there any author's name affixed to this book. For that reason, it has caused questions to be raised. The majority opinion in the history of the Church is that Paul wrote Hebrews, but others have thought otherwise. I think the majority opinion is to be heeded and used for several reasons, and we will mention just a few.

There is a testimony in 2 Peter 3:15–16, where Peter speaks about Paul *writing* to the Hebrews because he uses the word *us*. He uses the word *us* referring to the fact that he himself is a Hebrew and is writing to the Hebrews, to the 12 tribes scattered abroad, the diaspora that remained after the Babylonian captivity. There, he speaks about things which are "hard to understand" (2 Pet. 3:16), and in Hebrews, Paul also speaks about the Melchizedekian priesthood, which is *hard* to be

---

3. John Owen, *An Exposition of Hebrews* (Marshallton, DE: The National Foundation of Christian Education, 1969).

4. "In 1651, John Owen became Dean of Christ Church College, Oxford and eighteen months later was made vice-chancellor of Oxford University, under the chancellorship of Cromwell" (458). Joel R. Beeke and Randall J. Peterson, *Meet the Puritans: With a Guide to Modern Reprints* (Grand Rapids, MI: Reformation Heritage Books, 2006), 458.

spoken of because they were slow of hearing.[5] This element certainly comes through. We should not think there is some other letter Paul had written to the Hebrews which has been lost.

There may be questions raised on the fringes of the discussion, but we are saying that Peter's testimony is one reason to believe Paul is the author of Hebrews. The fact that there is no name attached to the letter can be explained because of the context of to whom it was being written. When Paul writes to the Gentiles, his apostolic authority is more to the fore, so he speaks of himself writing in his apostolic authority. Hebrews is written to the Jewish Christians who recognize, not apostolic authority, but the authority of Scripture. From the very beginning of Hebrews, Paul gives scriptural references and relies upon the Scriptures rather than his apostolic authority. For this reason, the authorship is not stated.

Some have said that the writing style is not Pauline. By that, they do not mean the content of it because the content is certainly like Paul (although some things are different because he is writing to a different group of people and approaching it in a different way). Some have said the Greek style, the very diction and the words, shows an elegance that may not be characteristic of Paul. Some others have said, 'We do believe Paul wrote the words in Hebrew and then it was translated into Greek.' A close study examined the writing and concluded that there is no translation here. First of all, there is no Hebrew letter for which there is any existing testimony (manuscript or report) from which it was translated—and Paul was one of the most learned men in his day, perhaps the most learned man in his day. In the same way, Calvin was perhaps the most learned man in his day and had acquaintance with the writings of the Greeks. Likewise, Paul was certainly capable of writing in this way. This objection is not weighty.

Last, there are certain particulars about persons and circumstances mentioned at the end of the book, particularly about Timothy. Some say, in Hebrews, Timothy is called "my brother" (Heb. 13:23), and elsewhere, Paul calls him "my son" (1 Tim. 1:2). If it says 'my son,' it is clearly Paul writing. No one else is father to Timothy in the faith but Paul. Why is it that the author of Hebrews is calling him 'my brother?' Owen's answer is that when Paul addresses Timothy *directly*, he speaks

---

5. *Hebrews 5:10–11.*

to him as 'my son.' When he writes *about* Timothy to others, he speaks of him as 'my brother.'[6] These objections that have been raised can be answered, and we believe that it is Paul who is writing. There are other reasons we will see as we go along.

Time

Paul had a burden for his people; we will look at this. Before we go further into Paul as the author and Paul's heart in this matter, we should say at what time Paul is writing. Again, from the details of this letter, at the end,[7] he writes, "I particularly urge you to pray so that I may be restored to you soon" (Heb. 13:19). Paul was in prison and was set free, and Timothy was also released from prison. We put those together, and we find that the time was about A.D. 61, perhaps A.D. 63.

Occasion and Circumstance

The occasion is that Paul is writing to the Hebrews, particularly those in Judea, but it is not limited to them. He is writing to the Jewish believers. He is not writing to the Jews in general, but to the Jewish believers, those Jews who had come to acknowledge Christ as Savior. There is a great urgency in this letter, and something that still stays with us is this: Tumults, seditions, and troubles of all sorts were arising in Judea. These were the things that our Lord spoke about: "You will hear of wars and rumors of wars, but see to it that you are not alarmed. Such things must happen, but the end is still to come" (Matt. 24:6). These are the birth pains, just before the birth of the Church, where the Church becomes fully separated from the Jewish community. They have been brought forth from that community. The bringing forth of the child—the Church—is going to be the death of the one that brings it forth—the community that brings it forth. Jesus had said that Jerusalem would be destroyed.[8] In Judea, there were many who believed in Christ and were very zealous for the law. These persons were in particular danger. What was the danger? The danger was that they would

---

6. For a defense of Paul's authorship, see: John Owen, *An Exposition of Hebrews: Volume I* (Marshallton, DE: The National Foundation for Christian Education, 1969), 83–95.

7. *Hebrews 13:19–25.*

8. *Matthew 24.*

continue to hold to the temple, the worship, and the priesthood that they had been attached to according to the law, and that they would perish in the judgment that was to come upon the nation.

For they would, more and more, under trouble, go back to the old way and find comfort in the old way. They would have apostatized to Judaism if they continued and did not separate themselves. On the other hand, if they did separate themselves and yet continued to believe in the law as they had believed, they would be disconsolate, discouraged, cast out, and burdened. These believers were in a difficult situation, and it was an urgent matter. Paul is writing to them to speak to them about Christ, who is superior, and introduces a way that is superior to that for which they were so zealous.

All through this book, this one thing comes about: *Christ is superior*, and the way introduced by Christ is the superior way. We need not fear; we need to let go of the old tradition and the particulars of the old economy, and there were two factors operating there. One, the Old Testament economy (the Mosaic law), and two, a certain amount of tradition; you might say a great deal of tradition that was brought in in connection with the law and often supplanted the law.

For us, you might say, 'We are not caught in an old tradition.' Oh, yes, we are. Not in that particular way, but we are caught in the same struggle with our past, our tradition, our comfort zone, our holding back, our settling down, and our not going forward in the same way these believers were struggling.

In the Book of Acts, we find the character of Paul, his heart, and his concern for his people. In Acts 21:13–23, we are told that he was going up to Jerusalem to minister to his people and bring material help in the difficulties they were having, and the prophecy through Agabus came that he would be bound there. The people pleaded with Paul not to go up to Jerusalem. "Then Paul answered, 'Why are you weeping and breaking my heart? I am ready not only to be bound, but also to die in Jerusalem for the name of the Lord Jesus.' When he would not be dissuaded, we gave up and said, 'The Lord's will be done'" (Acts 21:13–14). And Paul goes up to Jerusalem.

When we arrived at Jerusalem, the brothers received us warmly. The next day Paul and the rest of us went to see James, and all the elders were present. Paul greeted them and reported in detail what

God had done among the Gentiles through his ministry. When they heard this, they praised God. Then they said to Paul: "You see, brother, how many thousands of Jews have believed, and all of them are zealous for the law. They have been informed that you teach all the Jews who live among the Gentiles [this is where the letter is also going] to turn away from Moses, telling them not to circumcise their children or live according to our customs. What shall we do? They will certainly hear that you have come, so do what we tell you. There are four men with us who have made a vow. Take these men, join in their purification rites and pay their expenses, so that they can have their heads shaved. Then everybody will know there is no truth in these reports about you, but that you yourself are living in obedience to the law" (Acts 21:17–24).

This is the law. The Jewish Christians had zeal for the law. I want to, at some point, stop using the phrase *Jewish Christians*. I want to simply use the word *Christians* because the former phrase perpetuates something that is not to be perpetuated. We have to rethink this whole question about our background, our tradition, and our identity. We need to learn to think in a godly way about what our identity is to be. We have all kinds of antinomies in mind when we think, 'Do I want to give up my identity?' In philosophy class, we are dealing with the question of personal identity, the memories of that, and what our identity is. It is connected with our history in a certain way, but we will see that there is a history. It is not a matter of giving up one's identity/tradition for another mere tradition. There is a new way to think about identity. A way that is glorious, liberating, and that will truly satisfy the deepest longings of our hearts.

There were Jewish Christians who were very zealous for the law. There are, to this day, Jewish Christians who are still zealous for the law. There are many who affirm Christ as Savior and yet have a particular separate identity. Some are called *Messianic Jews*. There has been a continuing struggle with this. There is a witness to Jewish people who are not believers, and then there is a witness to Jewish people who are believers. We have to learn how to bring this witness, the witness of God. In the Book of Hebrews, Paul will inform us, tell us how, and show us how. He tells us how we are to deal with our tradition that we hold to, by which we come short of the fullness that there is in Jesus

Christ our Lord. God wants us to have the fullness that is in Him. Paul also says in Romans 9 about his concern and longing for his people:

> I speak the truth in Christ—I am not lying, my conscience confirms it in the Holy Spirit—I have great sorrow and unceasing anguish in my heart. For I could wish that I myself were cursed and cut off from Christ for the sake of my brothers, those of my own race, the people of Israel. Theirs is the adoption as sons; theirs the divine glory, the covenants, the receiving of the law, the temple worship and the promises. Theirs are the patriarchs, and from them is traced the human ancestry of Christ, who is God over all, forever praised! Amen (Rom. 9:1–5).

In Galatians, Paul speaks about how zealous he was for the law. Galatians 1:13–14 says, "For you have heard of my previous way of life in Judaism, how intensely I persecuted the church of God and tried to destroy it. I was advancing in Judaism beyond many Jews of my own age and was extremely zealous for the traditions of my fathers." This is part of what Paul is dealing with. He is speaking as one who longs for his brothers and one who himself has been in the position of having zeal for the law. He is one who, by the grace of God, in coming to see Christ, was brought out of Judaism. This is the Paul who is writing to these people. This is the occasion.

CONCERN FOR THE LAW AND TRADITION

There is a whole question about the law and tradition. In Matthew 5:17–20, Jesus said about those who would keep the law, "For I tell you that unless your righteousness surpasses that of the Pharisees and the teachers of the law, you will certainly not enter the kingdom of heaven" (Matt. 5:20). Do you want law? Are you zealous for the law? I will tell you about zealousness for the law. Those who are the most zealous for the law still come short. So short, in fact, that unless your righteousness exceeds theirs, you will certainly not enter the kingdom of heaven.

Even in that in which we glory, that zealousness for the law, we may come short. The question is, should we be zealous for the law as we understand it—in terms of the ceremonial laws that were given in the Old Testament? All of these ceremonial laws were pointing to

Christ who was to come.[9] When Christ, who is the reality, comes, the types and shadows fade away. As John the Baptist said, "He must become greater; I must become less" (Jn. 3:30); likewise, Jesus spoke of the law. In this section, He speaks about how the law is to be properly understood. There are a number of references where we see how the tradition has set aside the law.

In Matthew 15:1–20, Jesus spoke regarding washing hands and the Sabbath and many other references.

> Then some Pharisees and teachers of the law came to Jesus from Jerusalem and asked, "Why do your disciples break the tradition of the elders? They don't wash their hands before they eat!" Jesus replied, "And why do you break the command of God for the sake of your tradition?" (Matt. 15:1–3).

We have to understand what the word "tradition" is referring to. Some of you know this word tradition from *Fiddler on the Roof*[10] and the rejoicing and the comfort that there was for Tevye and his family in the tradition. The tradition was set up side by side with the law, and it came to overshadow and replace the law as what the true, full law was to be. It was supposed to go back to the days of Moses and was thought to be handed down by word of mouth. It came to be written and summarized in the teachings of the Talmud and the Mishnah on how we are to live. Even later, it came to be embodied in the rabbi's life. He was the living Torah. 'If you want to know how you are to live, how you are to eat, how you are to hold your spoon, if you want the fullness, look at the rabbi. Go to the rabbi. Talk to the rabbi. He has that living tradition within him.'

We should remember that this tendency toward tradition is recurrent. What has happened in the history of Christianity is similar; it involves *enormous* departure from the faith in the name of tradition. In the Roman Catholic Church, tradition has been placed on par with and has supplanted Christ. Mary is worshiped more than Christ. He is in the background, but Mary is co-mediatrix with Christ, and blessings flow from her. Devotions go to her. Tradition is in the Church of the Old Testament and in the Church of the New Testament. Tradition

---

9. Gangadean, *The Westminster Confession*, 207–221.

10. *Fiddler on the Roof*, Norman Jewison and Joseph Stein (The Mirisch Company, 1971).

comes from the human heart that fails to see God. We, too, have our traditions. There is such a thing as a *Reformed tradition* and being *traditionally Reformed,*[11] which in the name of what has gone before, will not look at what is coming and what needs to come, and will also dig in, oppose, and exclude those who would reach for fullness in Jesus Christ. Tradition: No one is exempt from it. Let us give heed to this word so we do not come short.

SPIRITUAL IDENTITY:
Children by Faith

There is a third background factor in thinking about Paul's authorship: a deeper reason and deeper sense of identity of what it is to be in a tradition, and what it is to be a Jewish person. The identity was found in terms of being the seed of Abraham and being a physical descendant of Abraham. This is so emphasized (and to this day it continues), that one may be a Jewish person if they are physically descended from Abraham, even if they do not believe in God. It came about that the physical connection had replaced the spiritual connection.

What we are taught in Scripture is that the promise was to Abraham and to his seed, and in Abraham, all the families of the earth would be blessed.[12] This is his seed, which is Christ. It was promised, concerning the seed, that Christ would come from Abraham in his physical seed by promise. And this has been fulfilled. Those who inherit the promise are those who are like Abraham—those who have faith. Abraham believed God and it was counted to him for righteousness.[13]

So here we have our tradition. There is Irish tradition, Indian tradition, Hispanic tradition, Canadian tradition, German tradition, you name it. We are often connected to this by way of our physical descent. We feel connected, it is very powerful, and it is very deep. Yet we inherit the promises *only by faith*. Esau was born of Rebecca and was twin brother to Jacob. They were both equally, physically descended from Abraham. Yet Esau showed he lacked faith in how he sold his birthright

---

11. Gangadean, *The Westminster Catechisms*, xxviii-xxxii.

12. *Genesis 12:1–3.*

13. *Genesis 15:6; Romans 4:1–22; Galatians 3:6–9; Hebrews 11:8–10, 17–19.*

and married women outside of the faith. Jacob, by the grace of God, held to the faith and received the promise.

We are inclined to think about identity in physical terms, whereas we should think about identity in spiritual terms. The Jews argued with Jesus about this often. "Abraham is our father." Christ was not doubting Abraham was their father physically. "'If you were Abraham's children,' said Jesus, 'then you would do the things Abraham did'" (Jn. 8:39). "'We are not illegitimate children,' they protested. 'The only Father we have is God himself'" (Jn. 8:41). Christ responded that they would not do these things and oppose Him if God were their father.[14] When they do try to come to a more spiritual connection, the question was to remain: Did they have faith? Did they understand? Or did the tradition, for which they were so zealous, blind and hinder them from hearing, seeing, and understanding the true work of God?

The idea of physical descent has always been a sticking point: when Jesus spoke about the widow in Elijah's day, or Naaman the leper, or when Christ was in contact with the Samaritan woman, or with His disciples. It always raised questions and caused concerns and sometimes opposition. It is as if the privilege of being a physical descendant, the chosen of Jewish descent, was being taken away. The promise was *always* to those who had faith; it was *not* being taken away. It was always, always, always to those who had faith as Abraham did. No one has *ever* participated in the promise on the basis of mere physical descent—*no one*. They must be born again.[15] They must have faith.

We have to be careful not to slip back into the state of looking to our tradition, our forebearers, our fathers, our past, and try to connect in that way. We must have faith and connect with our Lord Jesus. More could be said, but this is enough for now. Let us say this: Our tradition and our lineage are to be traced *spiritually*. This is how we form our identity. Our lineage is to be traced in connection with that great cloud of witnesses spoken of in Hebrews 11. These persons are our fathers. These persons are our forebearers. These are the ones we connect with. These are the ones we feel at home with. These are the ones we are looking forward to seeing. I look forward to seeing Job, and Jacob, and Abel, and Abraham, and Moses, and Samson, and David,

---

14. *John 8:42–47.*

15. *John 3.*

and Tertullian, and Augustine, and Chrysostom, and Luther, and Calvin, and B. B. Warfield. This is my lineage. These are the ones I am connected with. This is my identity. These are my people. I am one of them. I rejoice in this. Because it is by the grace of God that we will be partakers of faith as Abraham was and we will inherit the promises. Let us not come short. Let us not so identify with the past that we say, 'I'm a Calvinist and five-pointer—full, not just 4.573.' There is more to the Scriptures than Calvin. We thank God for those battles Calvin fought and won.[16] But there are many battles he has not engaged in; therefore, he never fought and never won. It remains for us to continue and complete that work. I thank God for Van Til. He has contributed to personal godliness. He fought in his day and we are to continue and complete that work. Yes, I thank God for Bahnsen. He fought, but the work has to continue and be completed.

Our identity needs to be traced spiritually, not physically, because it is through faith that we inherit the promises. You might ask, 'Who are your favorite people in the Bible? Who do you identify with most? Who do you feel closest to?' Of course, a lot of them, but who do you feel like, 'Yes, this is my model.' There are three such persons for me, and maybe we will talk about it another time. There are three such persons I identify with. I feel that I am in their position. Their lives speak to me a lot because they are lives of faith. So our identity, who we are, is one of faith.

CENTRAL THEME:
The Superiority of the Son

This letter is written to the Hebrews, saying, **"In the past God spoke to our forefathers through the prophets."** It was through the Hebrews that God spoke. **"Our forefathers"** is written by someone who is Jewish, who shares that word, **"our forefathers."** God spoke to them. It says, **"In the past God spoke to our forefathers through the prophets at many times and in various ways"** (v. 1). The prophets are particularly mentioned, and it is the ways in which God spoke through the prophets that comes through. The contrast is made: **"but in these last**

---

16. Surrendra Gangadean, *History of Philosophy: A Critical Analysis of Unresolved Disputes* (Phoenix: Public Philosophy Press, 2022), 127–130.

days he has spoken to us by his Son" (v. 2a). Of course, this must be seen as a contrast between the past and the present: the last days. What are the last days? The last days are from the coming of Christ. But in a particular way, in this letter, the last days are the last days of the old dispensation. The last days before that dispensation expires, which would be consummated with the destruction of the temple. In these last days, God has spoken to us in His Son, and it has a particular urgency in connection with the last days of the old order and the last days of the temple.

A contrast will be made between the Son and the angels. There is one sense (an absolute sense) in which the Son is so much greater than the angels. There simply is no comparison. He is absolutely greater. No creature can ever be compared with Him. This is important to note. This is part of it. It is also the case in terms of the law and the dispensation of the law, that the law was given by God and was mediated through angels. Stephen, at the end of his discourse in Acts 7:53, says, "you who have received the law that was put into effect through angels but have not obeyed it." This was part of the glory of the law.

When we look at Christ, particularly His humanity and His humiliation, it does not appear that His glory is as great as the angels. It is important to see who Christ is and what His glory is, so that when a comparison is made, it does not appear that the old dispensation was gloriously dispensed to us through the angels. No, Christ is superior *in every way*, and He is certainly superior to the angels. This is the theme that continues on in the rest of this book. Why? Because the angels have mediated the law, and Christ Himself came and spoke: **"but in these last days he has spoken to us by his Son"** (v. 2a). There is an absoluteness of the Son, **"whom he appointed heir of all things"** (v. 2); everything is given to the Son. There is an absoluteness about it, and we will see that we must keep this in mind, that we are complete in Him, **"through whom he made the universe"** (v. 2b). "Through him all things were made; without him nothing was made that has been made" (Jn. 1:3). Who can be so glorious as the One who made the universe and who is the heir of all things?

Further, He is the Son of God, and the Son is like the Father. **"The Son is the radiance of God's glory and the exact representation of his being"** (v. 3a). He is the likeness of God, the *exact* likeness. He is the radiance of God's glory, the eternal Son of God, who is God. Who can possibly be greater than the Son? He is **"sustaining all things by his powerful word"** (v. 3). He is not a creator at a distance, as someone said, but He is the One who sustains all things. "Are not two sparrows sold for a penny? Yet not one of them will fall to the ground apart from the will of your Father" (Matt. 10:29). Many people have gotten into worshiping the spirits because 'if God is there, his spirits are who we have to deal with more.' No. He is the One who sustains all things. He is the One who is the heir of all things, in whom we inherit anything we have. Any good we have is going to come through Him, and He is the One who will bring it to pass because He sustains. He creates and sustains, and more than that, He purifies us from our sins, because with sin, we will never be pure and we will never inherit. He purifies us from our sins and **"sat down at the right hand of the Majesty in heaven."**

The focus of the comparison to follow is going to be on the Son as **"he sat down at the right hand of the Majesty in heaven"** (v. 3b). **"You are my Son; today I have become your Father"** (v. 5). What is this referring to? All of what is to come speaks about the throne on which He sits. The significance of His throne, and how it shows His glory, is not the absolute sense but the relative sense in which the Son is greater than all the angels. It says, **"he sat down at the right hand of the Majesty in heaven,"** and then Paul introduces the comparison with the angels: **"So he became as much superior to the angels as the name he has inherited is superior to theirs"** (v. 4). As a Son, He is all glorious, equal in glory with the Father, but He has been given a name that is above every name—*given.* In connection with His death on the cross, His resurrection, and His ascension, He has been given a name that is above every name.[17] This is the point of His glory that is not always seen. Christ is seen in His humiliation, but here He is in His glory, ascended into heaven, sitting at the right hand of God, and it is in this way that He is so much more glorious than all the angels. This administration of the grace of God is dispensed by Christ Himself, who is the mediator of the better covenant because He is seated at the right hand of God. Moses is not there. No angel is there. No one else is there. As the Hebrews come to see and understand this One who is administering the dispensation of the grace of God—how glorious He is and how superior He is—they will know that this dispensation

---

17. *Philippians 2:9–11.*

is superior. They will not be so zealous for the law mixed in with tradition in a way that will cause them to stumble, fall, apostatize, and be disconsolate. They will gladly go out of the city, bearing the reproach of Christ with them.

"For to which of the angels did God ever say, 'You are my Son; today I have become your Father'" (v. 5a). All kinds of discussions are raised about this: 'Does He become the Son? Is He the eternal Son?' We believe that what Paul is speaking of here is what was said in Romans 1:2–4:

> The gospel he promised beforehand through his prophets in the Holy Scriptures regarding his Son, who as to his human nature was a descendant of David, and who through the Spirit of holiness was *declared* with power to be the Son of God by his resurrection from the dead: Jesus Christ our Lord.[18]

He was *declared* to be the Son—He is the eternal Son of God—in connection with the resurrection, He is declared to be the Son of God by the Spirit of holiness. In connection with this declaration, His resurrection, ascension, and sitting on the throne in that respect are much better than the angels. **"I will be his Father, and he will be my Son"** (v. 5b).

Second Samuel speaks about the Son that is to build a temple. Not just Solomon, but the One who will build the temple that will last, in which God will dwell forever. The One who ascended on high; He is the One who will build the temple of God. **"And again, when God brings his firstborn into the world, he says, 'Let all God's angels worship him'"** (v. 6). Questions have been raised: 'When? What is this referring to?' Again, we believe this is the ascension of Christ into heaven, and all the angels will worship. This is in reference to Deuteronomy. It is not in the NIV, but it is in the Masoretic text,[19] that all the angels of God will worship Him. Christ is better than the angels. The angels administered and mediated the old covenant; Christ brings the new. **"In speaking of the angels he says, 'He makes his angels winds, his servants flames of fire'"** (v. 7). They are powerful. They have great glory. But about the Son, he says that He sits on the throne. This is the focus again. **"Your throne, O God, will last for ever and ever, and righteousness will be**

---

18. Emphasis added.
19. *Deuteronomy 32:43*; See: Dead Sea Scrolls and Septuagint.

the scepter of your kingdom" (v. 8b). Why will His throne last? Because it is righteous. It will be just. "**Your throne, O God, will last for ever and ever, and righteousness will be the scepter of your kingdom. You have loved righteousness and hated wickedness**" (vv. 8–9a). This is the heart of the King. He loves righteousness and He hates wickedness, "**therefore God, your God, has set you above your companions**" (v. 9). No one can compare to Him and His love for righteousness and hate for wickedness. It says, "**by anointing you with the oil of joy**" (v. 9b). This is joy connected with loving righteousness and hating wickedness because it is in this way we come into the fullness that there is in God.

So the angels are servants and the Son is reigning on the throne. "**He also says, 'In the beginning, O Lord,** [in terms of the lasting nature and the glory of that throne] **you laid the foundations of the earth, and the heavens are the work of your hands. They will perish, but you remain; they will all wear out like a garment. You will roll them up like a robe; like a garment they will be changed. But you remain the same, and your years will never end'**" (vv. 10–12). Christ has a throne that will last forever. He is seated on that throne. He is reigning. He has inaugurated the new dispensation. He is so superior to the angels, and so is the covenant, that we have to give heed. "**To which of the angels did God ever say, 'Sit at my right hand until I make your enemies a footstool for your feet?'**" (v. 13). Again, this is the ascension and Christ is seated at the right hand of God with authority. At this point, He administers the new covenant. It is at this point that He sends the Spirit, the glorious Spirit, to lead the Church. The Spirit that comes into our hearts and into our minds. It illuminates our minds and helps us to understand what the types and shadows mean and brings us into the reality. "**Are not all angels ministering spirits sent to serve those who will inherit salvation?**" (v. 14). Angels are servants, Christ is the Son.

Paul says at the beginning of chapter 2, "We must pay more careful attention, therefore, to what we have heard, so that we do not drift away" (Heb. 2:1). Christ is superior to the angels. The covenant that He brings is superior, and we are not to hold onto the old, as the new is superior. Paul, the one who was zealous for God, says, "But whatever was to my profit I now consider loss for the sake of Christ. What is more, I consider everything a loss compared to the surpassing greatness of knowing Christ Jesus my Lord, for whose sake I have lost all things. I consider them rubbish, that I may gain Christ" (Phil. 3:7). This is the way that God calls us to walk.

2

JESUS: THE MERCIFUL AND FAITHFUL HIGH PRIEST

Hebrews 2

[1]We must pay more careful attention, therefore, to what we have heard, so that we do not drift away. [2]For if the message spoken by angels was binding, and every violation and disobedience received its just punishment, [3]how shall we escape if we ignore such a great salvation? This salvation, which was first announced by the Lord, was confirmed to us by those who heard him. [4]God also testified to it by signs, wonders and various miracles, and gifts of the Holy Spirit distributed according to his will.

[5]It is not to angels that he has subjected the world to come, about which we are speaking. [6]But there is a place where someone has testified:

"What is man that you are mindful of him,
the son of man that you care for him?
[7]You made him a little lower than the angels;
you crowned him with glory and honor
[8]and put everything under his feet."

In putting everything under him, God left nothing that is not subject to him. Yet at present we do not see everything subject to him. [9]But we see Jesus, who was made a little lower than the angels, now crowned with glory and honor because he suffered death, so that by the grace of God he might taste death for everyone.

[10]In bringing many sons to glory, it was fitting that God, for whom and through whom everything exists, should make the author of their salvation perfect through suffering. [11]Both the one who makes men holy and those who are made holy are of the same family. So Jesus is not ashamed to call them brothers. [12]He says,

> "I will declare your name to my brothers;
>   in the presence of the congregation I will sing your praises."

[13]And again,
> "I will put my trust in him."

And again he says,
> "Here am I, and the children God has given me."

[14]Since the children have flesh and blood, he too shared in their humanity so that by his death he might destroy him who holds the power of death—that is, the devil—[15]and free those who all their lives were held in slavery by their fear of death. [16]For surely it is not angels he helps, but Abraham's descendants. [17]For this reason he had to be made like his brothers in every way, in order that he might become a merciful and faithful high priest in service to God, and that he might make atonement for the sins of the people. [18]Because he himself suffered when he was tempted, he is able to help those who are being tempted.

INHERITANCE IN CHRIST:
Pay More Careful Attention

"WE MUST PAY MORE CAREFUL ATTENTION, therefore, to what we have heard, so that we do not drift away" (v. 1). "What we have heard" refers to what was summed up in Hebrews 1, and what was summed up in Hebrews 1 has been spoken of all throughout the Scriptures of the Old Testament and the New Testament. What have we heard? In Hebrews 1, we heard that "in these last days he has spoken to us by his Son, whom he appointed heir of all things" (Heb. 1:2a). This One who is heir is the One who has made the world. "The Son is the radiance of God's glory and the exact representation of his being, sustaining all things by his powerful word. After he had provided purification for sins, he sat down at the right hand of the Majesty in heaven. So he became as much superior to the angels" (Heb. 1:3–4a)—the name that is above *all* names.

The theme of the inheritance of Christ and our inheritance in Him is before us. This is the promise that **"we have heard"** (v. 1). This is to what **"we must pay more careful attention"** (v. 1a), and what we must do **"so that we do not drift away"** (v. 1b). We should think of what it is to drift away. Notice in the next verse: **"how shall we escape if we ignore such a great salvation?"** (v. 3a). There is a greater salvation that is ours in Christ in this age. If we ignore this, it will be neglected. It will slip away if we do not pay careful attention to it. The promise has slipped away from the Church by and large. The Church is still looking for an escape from this world in the world that is to come (heaven) and we have neglected the promise that God has given us, that Christ is the "heir of all things" (Heb. 1:2a) and will accomplish His purpose through His people. The Church has let this slip away. **"We must pay more careful attention"** (v. 1a).

Those who have heard and embraced the promise, who have entered into the kingdom with the anticipation that Christ will be the "heir of all things" (Heb. 1:2a) and that we will inherit alongside Him, often find themselves letting that assurance slip away. We do not hold onto this assurance. We deliberately let these things slip. We get taken up with other things. The self-life that remains in us responds to the circumstances that come into our lives in such a way that, instead of turning to God, we struggle with our circumstances. We get absorbed in our circumstances, and the thing that God has promised us slips away.

The purpose of the curse in our lives is not understood. We get taken up with getting through the suffering without seeing God's purpose and coming to know what we should. We neglect the Word because of sin remaining in us. So, **"We must pay more careful attention, therefore, to what we have heard, so that we do not drift away"** (v. 1). Think of a ship that is just sitting in the waters. There is a movement in the waters, the currents in the waters, and the ship drifts away. This picture of drifting away, or not holding fast to what we have, is a theme that is there throughout this entire book.

Later, it says, "We have this hope as an anchor for the soul, firm and secure" (Heb. 6:19a). This anchor keeps us from drifting. If we stay focused on the goal, the inheritance that is in Christ, the promise that God has given to man, the promise of salvation that is in Christ, and we keep this before us constantly, we will not drift away. We will make progress toward this great salvation. This is what the ancients kept in mind. This is how they endured. This is how they persevered. They kept the hope before them.

A NEW ECONOMY:
A Greater Salvation

Now, it is possible, in the context of this letter written to the Hebrews, that they were holding on to something less than the hope embodied in the new economy. They were zealous for the law, the promises, and coming to the Promised Land. We will see that the promise was much more than the Promised Land. "For if Joshua had given them rest, God would not have spoken later about another day" (Heb. 4:8). There is more to come. The Israelites entering into Canaan was pointing forward to a much *larger* and *greater* salvation.

The Word says, **"For if the message spoken by angels was binding, and every violation and disobedience received its just punishment, how shall we escape if we ignore such a great salvation?"** (vv. 2–3a). The point here is this: In order to enter into the Promised Land, they had to live according to the laws of God—the promise is then limited to the extent to which it was given. We have the promise, in reality, coming to us by the end of the age, no longer the type and shadow. If they were to obey to enter that Promised Land, how much more must we obey if we are to enter into the fullness that God has promised— into **"such a great salvation"** (v. 3) that is before us?

A Greater Salvation Requires Greater Obedience

When the Israelites did not continue in obedience, sin built up, and they were taken out of the land. They could not enter into the land because they did not continue in obedience. Sin was permitted at one point in Achan at Ai when he took a piece of gold, silver, and a garment and hid them in his tent. Because of this, the whole camp suffered.[1] **"For if the message spoken by angels was binding, and every violation and disobedience received its just punishment, how shall we escape if we ignore such a great salvation?"** (vv. 2–3a). This is an *a fortiori* argument. All the more, we must be obedient, because there is a connection between obedience and possessing the land. We cannot possess the land without being obedient, and we are made obedient by Christ. We are to obey in the way we order our prayers, the way parents instruct children, the way we keep our membership vows, and

---

1. *Joshua 7.*

the diligence with which we read the Bible. Do you think that you can enter into the promises and the blessing and rest in God apart from reading the Scripture diligently and seeking God diligently? Apart from prayer? Apart from the communion with the saints, fellowship with God's people, being knit together, and learning how to love and serve one another? If we neglect this Word and the way in which we are to have it, we will come short, and this will be a loss for us and a punishment. So, **"We must pay more careful attention"** (v. 1a); we must be more diligent, we are to enter into the fullness that God has for us in Christ.

We cannot escape this because there is a necessary connection between inheriting the promise and obedience: "Therefore go and make disciples of all nations . . . teaching them to obey everything I have commanded you" (Matt. 28:19a–20a). Do you believe that you can come into this inheritance, this promise, without obeying all that God has commanded? Our educational system must be renewed, our economics must be reconsidered, and our social justice must be recovered according to the Word of God. We must not profess a semblance of justice where sincerity takes the place of integrity. We must truly know what is just and speak it. We cannot enter in and possess the promise divided as we are.[2] Every turning aside, every point on which the Church is divided, becomes a point of disobedience. If, in the old covenant, **"every violation and disobedience received its just punishment, how shall we escape if we ignore such a great salvation?"** (vv. 2–3a). Christ is the heir of all things, and we are heirs with Christ. In order to possess the earth, we must live as our Lord Jesus Christ did.

A Greater Salvation Requires a Greater Priest

Here is a great problem. We have a fuller, richer salvation given to us, not in type and shadow, but in reality—but we are sinners, just the same as our fathers were from the days of Adam. With the greater promise before us in this new age, how do we come into it given our sinful condition? We need something more, and we have that in Christ Jesus our Lord. Not only do we have a greater promise, but we have someone who is able to bring us into that promise: Christ Jesus our

---

2. Surrendra Gangadean, *The Unity of the Church: That They May Be One That the World May Believe* (Phoenix: Logos Papers Press, 2024).

Lord. This is the point of speaking about the priesthood of Christ and why it is that He was made a priest in the way in which He was: He is able to bring us into this salvation. The promise is ours in Christ Jesus.

A Greater Revelation Requires a Greater Confirmation

This salvation was first announced by the Lord, not in an absolute sense, but in the final sense. In a clearer sense it was announced by the Lord and confirmed by those who heard Him, that is, the Apostles and others whom He taught. God showed that He confirmed this Word with signs, wonders, various miracles, and gifts of the Holy Spirit distributed according to His will. In the early Church, gifts of the Holy Spirit were supernaturally bestowed and supernaturally operating. Today, the gifts of the Church are operating through more natural means: supernaturally given but working through natural means. In the early Church, there were supernatural gifts, working supernaturally. Prophecy, interpretation, healings, words of knowledge, and along with those gifts, there were miracles that were done by the Apostles that were signs and wonders before the people. Clearly, God was with the people. The point of the signs, miracles, wonders, and gifts of the Spirit was to confirm the Word. The Word had to be spoken, and the gifts were given in confirmation of the Word. Once the Word is confirmed, one is not to continue to look for signs, miracles, and wonders.

We believe in the cessation of the *charismata*, the cessation of the gifts, because it served a particular purpose.[3] It is not to be abstracted from the context where it was to minister mercy. The gifts were signs of the great goodness that God would bring about. It was not just the removal of natural evil but the removal of moral evil. The healing of the physically blind is a sign to us that Christ removes spiritual blindness. The healing of the leper speaks to us of Christ removing the leprosy of sin that is in our lives, i.e., pride. They are signs that we are to understand, and we should receive them as such and affirm the salvation that there is in Christ. That Word was confirmed. Certainly, the Word spoken by Moses, through Moses, was confirmed. There were signs and manifestations on the mountain.[4] This Word continues with

---

3. Gangadean, *The Westminster Confession,* 14–18; Gangadean, "Paper No. 122: Contra Charismatic Distinctive," in *The Logos Papers,* 651–653.

4. *Exodus 19–20.*

us, but this Word was confirmed in greater fullness in the signs and wonders that were done. In the days of Moses, we did not have the signs we had in the New Testament period. We have this Word of a greater salvation spoken of, accompanied by greater signs, so we should not neglect the Word. We are not to allow ourselves to drift away. It is like water running off and dissipating, seeking its own level; this is the idea of drifting away. It happens so naturally, and we have to watch; we have to be careful.

A NEW ECONOMY:
Co-Heirs with Christ

That this salvation is so great is spoken to us in verse 5, and that this salvation comes to us through Christ, is spoken to us here: **"It is not to angels that he has subjected the world to come, about which we are speaking. But there is a place where someone has testified: 'What is man that you are mindful of him'"** (vv. 5–6a). We know exactly where this reference is, it is Psalm 8. It is spoken by the Psalmist. The contrast is made between the Old Testament, where the Word of God was administered through angels, and the superiority of Christ, that He is superior to the angels. Here it says, **"It is not to angels that he has subjected the world to come"** (v. 5a). The world to come is the age to come or the economy to come. *Oikonomia* means the management of a house, and the order of things to come.

There is an order that is to come, a new order that Christ is bringing about, and He did not subject the new order of things to angels; rather, He subjected it to man. Christ is the second man after Adam, and this whole order is subjected to Him and to us in Him, not to angels. It would not be surprising at all to think that the enmity that man has with fallen angels is due to God's honoring man in this way and that the angels would be made ministering servants to man. The angels are not given the position of privilege and glory and honor. Rather, it was given to man. It was given to Christ as the second man and given to us in Him. For the Scripture says, **"What is man that you are mindful of him, the son of man that you care for him? You made him a little lower than the angels; you crowned him with glory and honor and put everything under his feet"** (vv. 6b–8a). This is a reminder of the Word that was spoken in Genesis 1:26, "Let us make man in our image, in our likeness, and let them rule over the fish of the sea and the birds of the air, over the livestock, over all the earth, and over all the creatures that move along the ground." In this new order of things, this new economy speaks of the management of the affairs of a community with reference to the source of income and expenditure and development of its natural resources. This is the subjection that God has given; this is the economy that God has established; this is the order of things that God has established.

We can speak about the economical Trinity and the ontological Trinity—the Trinity of God as Father, Son, and Holy Spirit and the work of each, the economy, the dispensation, the ordering of it. There is a new world, a new order to come after sin has entered, but it will be even greater than before. God has subjected this order to man, not only in the beginning but in redemption, too. We are to manage the affairs of the world and order it right with respect to the benefits, how we expend our energies, and to the development of its natural resources. Consider the resources that are in this room, the talents and abilities given to each one, and how glorious that can be. These are to be developed in Christ. As we have the vision of the good, we grow up to be mature sons and daughters of God and serve Him with the gifts and abilities that He has given us: gifts of the Holy Spirit.

This new order of things will come about. God has given to the Church pastor-teachers to prepare the saints for works of service[5] by which God will be glorified. Psalm 8:1 begins, "O LORD, our Lord, how majestic is your name in all the earth!" and it ends with, "O LORD, our Lord, how majestic is your name in all the earth!" (Ps. 8:9). The purpose of this economy, this management, this subjection of faith, is that the glory of God that is revealed in all of creation may be made known, that "the earth will be full of the knowledge of the LORD as the waters cover the sea" (Is. 11:9b). This will be done by Christ, the second Adam, who came to *undo* what Adam did and *do* what Adam failed to do. We are in Christ by the grace of God. **"You made him a little lower than the angels; you crowned him with glory and honor and put everything under his feet"** (vv. 7–8a). Not one thing is exempt from being put under His feet. In this new order of things, in the

---

5. *Ephesians 4:11–12.*

economy, in the management of the work of developing the creation that God has given, not one thing is exempt.

One of the things I have particularly rejoiced in is that there will be poetry in this new order of things. The poets are given the ability to see and to express realities that we do not often see and that we need to see. All of us should feast on this. Not all poetry is all that it should be, but there is life in everything that is poetry, and we need to come to this richness; some of us have not even begun to get a taste of it. We have an inclination of something there but we are in the shadows. Poetry is just one of so many, in this new order of things; it declares the glory of God. It helps us to see and to celebrate it all the more. This is part of the fullness that is in Christ, it is one of so many, many things. There is nothing that is exempt. **"In putting everything under him, God left nothing that is not subject to him"** (v. 8). Dance is also His. Shiva is not the lord of the dance; Christ is. Those of you who know something of Hinduism know how that is celebrated. The true reality is to be found in Christ. There is not anything under the whole creation that is not subjected to Christ—*every* form of art, *every* creature. I have been sitting and looking out my window and seeing the sparrows there, and I say, 'We are heirs with Christ. This is the gift of God to us, and what will it be when it is completed? How glorious it is. Heirs with Christ. Nothing is exempt.'

I looked at the ground and saw how cursed and barren it is and how we have to struggle now, and I thought of the mist that went up from the face of the ground and watered the plants in the Garden. Then I thought of the new order of things and the economy in the world that is to come; these things will all be subjected to Christ, and there will be *life!* There will be abundance, fruitfulness, and joy that is unspeakable because the riches of God will be made known. We will not anymore serve and worship the creature and get attached to the gifts, but we will see through the gifts to the glory of the giver and the love of God for us. We will see how God gives Himself to us in the way He manifests His glory to us. We will rejoice before God, and we will love Him more. It is through the death of Christ Jesus our Lord that we are brought back to God instead of being put into the darkest of dungeons, in that pit forever, that bottomless pit, that pit of horror, too dreadful to think about. But we are not left there; rather, we are raised to such glory in Christ, and we will sing of His love and praise His name. In every trial of our lives, day by day, week by week, in all of them, we see how God sustains us, keeps us, provides for us, and blesses us, and we sing of His faithful love in *every* circumstance.

Oikonomia has a special reference to economy and business—doing *His* business. Those who are in the world of business have an important point of contact with how to manage the affairs of things and develop the resources that there are. There is no aspect of business that is not subject to Christ, and there is no aspect of technology that is not subject to Christ; His name is above every name. There is nothing in the quantum world or in the macro-world of the galaxies that is not subject to Him to reveal the glory of God. The whole creation is His: "Whom he appointed heir of all things, and through whom he made the universe" (Heb. 1:2b). This is the glory of God to be revealed—this is the world to come. We cannot neglect so great a salvation. We must be obedient. If we are to come into this, we must learn to relate one with another in the order that God has established. We sang in Psalm 119Q, "Judgment I have done and justice . . . love I Thy commandments more than gold, the finest gold,"[6] because we see that it is by these precepts that we come into what God has for us.

Some of us are learning the precepts about male and female and we are rethinking the *worldly* view. These aspects of our being are created by God, they are named by Christ, His name is above all else, and His glory is revealed in all of these. We are to learn His precepts in our relations one with another, truly, not a semblance of it. If we learn the precepts of God and how we are to come together, we begin to rediscover something of God's order[7] in headship, in giving in marriage, and how this is to be done. As we meditate on this, we see the wisdom of God. How gracious God is in this. How protecting God is, how we can thrive the way we ought to as we follow God's precepts. We cannot neglect *any* precept or command of God if we are to come into the fullness that there is in God. Everything is made subject to Christ. "God exalted him to the highest place and gave him the name that is above every name" (Phil. 2:9).

---

6. *Psalm 119:121a, 127, The Book of Psalms for Singing* (Pittsburgh: The Board of Education and Publication, Reformed Presbyterian Church of North America, 1998).

7. Gangadean, *Philosophical Foundation*, 245–254.

> Yet at present we do not see everything subject to him. But we see Jesus, who was made a little lower than the angels, now crowned with glory and honor because he suffered death, so that by the grace of God he might taste death for everyone (vv. 8b–9).

This is not merely "taste," like a small taste, this is to *experience* it, to eat it. He experienced death for everyone by the grace of God. It was because He "became obedient to death—even death on a cross!" (Phil. 2:8b). He suffered the ignominy of death on the cross—the worst possible humiliation in death. People sometimes die quietly with dignity with loved ones around them in hospitals or in their own bed. Christ is nailed to a cross, naked, with a crown of thorns.

CHRIST:
A Faithful High Priest

"He humbled himself and became obedient to death—even death on a cross! Therefore God exalted him" (Phil. 2:8b–9a) and "**crowned him with glory and honor**" (v. 7b). He was made a little lower than the angels for the suffering of death but raised now and seated at the right hand of God and given the name that is above every name in this age and in the age to come. He is to fill the universe in every way—in every need, in every aspect of our life—because every aspect of our being is created by Him and governed by Him for the purpose of revealing the glory of God. So, in everything, He is to be honored. In everything, He needs to be obeyed. In everything, He needs to be sought diligently. We are not to be conformed to this world that is passing away. Christ is ruling now at the right hand of God and will continue to rule "until he has put all his enemies under his feet. The last enemy to be destroyed is death" (1 Cor. 15:25b–26). We do not see now all things subject to Him, but it will be, by His grace, through His suffering and death and all the benefits that come as a result. It is fitting that it is so.

"**In bringing many sons to glory.**" We are to see the glory that is revealed and rejoice in it. "**In bringing many sons to glory,**" the glory is of being conformed to the image of Christ—"**In bringing many sons to glory, it was fitting that God, for whom and through whom everything exists, should make the author of their salvation perfect through suffering**" (v. 10). We are now brought from the depths of sin, and the degradation of sin and death. We are not simply where we were initially in Adam. We are being brought from the depths; we are being brought by Christ our Savior from the depths and into this glory. We are not merely being brought out of sin and death into the glory that was in the economy of the Old Testament. We are being brought into a much greater, fuller salvation. We are not coming to the tabernacle made with hands. We are coming to the tabernacle in heaven, the true tabernacle, made by God and not by man, in the new order of things. This order comes out of the very character of God as just and merciful, wise and gracious. We are coming to this. We are not coming through the blood of bulls and goats; we are coming through the blood of Christ, which is much greater than the blood of bulls and goats. They could not take away sin; only Christ's blood could. We are coming through the gift of the Holy Spirit, poured out upon us abundantly, to enable us to do this work. We have a greater work to do, a greater salvation, a greater blessing, a greater glory that is ours. Christ, who is our head, will lead us into this. He has gone before us, has gone through death, and then He has been raised to glory. **"It was fitting that God, for whom and through whom everything exists, should make the author of their salvation perfect through suffering"** (v. 10b). One of the things that people were particularly zealous for in the Old Testament was the continuation of the tabernacle, the laws, and the regulations connected with the priesthood. Here, we speak about the priesthood of Christ and how, by what He experienced, He is able to be a greater priest, greater than the high priest in the Old Testament, and able to bring us into this great salvation, which is ours in Him.

In saving us from sin and death, Christ bore in Himself, in His own body on the cross, our sin. "God made him who had no sin to be sin for us, so that in him we might become the righteousness of God" (2 Cor. 5:21). Our sin was put upon Him, pressed down upon Him. He bore the weight of our sin; He knows what it is to be under sin. He knows what it is like for us to be under sin. If He was going to save us from sin, it was right, and it was fitting that He bore it and that He knew what it was to be cut off from God. He cried out, "My God, my God, why have you forsaken me?" (Ps. 22:1a). He knows what it is to suffer the agony of death in the worst possible way. Jesus knows this. The author of our salvation is made perfect through suffering. When we talk to each other, sometimes we may think, 'They sort of understand,' or we may think, 'They don't get it.' Christ knows. The author of our salvation, is made perfect through suffering. **"Both the one who makes men holy and those who are made holy are of the same family"** (v. 11a). He is *close* to us. The priest represents man to God. He especially deals with those in sin. The priesthood is ordained because of sin, to bring man back to holiness. We are created to be holy, and as our Savior, He needs to be holy. It becomes us to have someone who is like us, tempted in every point as we are, yet without sin, and only Christ could be without sin. Yet He knows what it is like to have the weight of sin upon Him—the weight of the sin of humanity upon Him. Only Christ could do so. It is fitting that we be of the same family, and being of the same family, we are brothers, children of the same Father. We are children by adoption. Christ is the Son of God eternally and by the Spirit of holiness by the resurrection of the dead. "You are my Son; today I have become your Father" (Heb. 5:5). Christ is the Son of God in a unique way, and we are really truly sons of God through Christ. We are brothers with Christ. As a Son, He is heir of all things, and being brothers with Him, He does not take the whole inheritance for Himself and let us go our way; rather, we are blessed with all of the inheritance in Christ Jesus our Lord. We are His brothers.

"So Jesus is not ashamed to call them brothers" (v. 11b). Some people are ashamed to recognize their family. Some may say, 'I do not belong to that family,' because of sin and the bad things done. We say we do not belong there. But, "While we were still sinners, Christ died for us" (Rom. 5:8b). **"Jesus is not ashamed to call them brothers."** He knows it does not end there for us. He is going to bring us to glory. This is why He is not ashamed to call us brothers. Yes, we are sinners, but we have a glorious future before us. He is the One who will bring it to pass because He knows sin, and He knows how to help us even through our sin to bring us into this great salvation. He says, **"I will declare your name to my brothers; in the presence of the congregation I will sing your praises"** (v. 12). After He suffered on the cross, He declared this in Psalm 22:22. In Isaiah, it says, **"And again, 'I will put my trust in him'"** (v. 13a).

Regarding the salvation that God is bringing and the elect that remain who will be preserved by God from the nation of Israel, He says, **"Here am I, and the children God has given me"** (v. 13b). The children are those whom He redeemed, those whom He kept by His name for Himself. We are brothers with Christ; we are of the same family. He took part in flesh and blood. In this, it seems that He is lower than the angels. He was the Son of God eternally; He became less than the angels, **"a little lower than the angels"** (v. 7), especially more in suffering death, and God has exalted Him higher, giving Him a name that is above every name. Since the children have flesh and blood and He is to be near to those whom He will save, He, too, took part in their humanity. In doing so, He brought about salvation.

Jesus is not only near in that He knows what it is to have flesh and blood, but He knows what it is for that flesh and blood to undergo suffering and death. Jesus Himself underwent death, and by His death, He destroyed him who holds the power of death, that is, the devil. Christ freed those who all their lives were held in slavery by their fear of death. Behind the curse that we try to escape, in every form, is death. All of our resistance to the curse is reflecting the fear of death. Toil, famine, and hunger lead to death. Strife and war lead to death. Sickness and old age lead to death. We are so bound up all of our lives with the curse, the fear of it, and the struggle against it. All our lives, we are held in slavery by that fear, and Christ has come and has tasted death for every man. He has taken the sting out of death. He was raised from the dead, and He delivers us from the fear of death that has been ours all our lives.

Christ is able to save us. Christ who bears our humanity—fully. He is fully man and fully God. He is seated at the right hand of God in the position of authority, not by virtue of His eternal sonship, but by virtue of His perfect obedience. He is exalted to a position to rule on the earth, to bring about His purpose, and to deliver us from fear that we might truly serve God. We do not have to be occupied by what we will eat or what we will drink. We do not have to have fear of any sort in any way. We can trust in Christ, that **"He might destroy him who holds the power of death—that is, the devil—and free those who all their lives were held in slavery by their fear of death"** (vv. 14b–15). It is not the angels He helps. Angels are not heirs of salvation. Rather they are made ministers to the heirs of salvation. These heirs are Abraham's descendants.

Last time, we spoke about the natural seed of Abraham and those who are the seed of Abraham by faith—**"For surely it is not angels he helps, but Abraham's descendants"** (v. 16). They are the heirs of salvation. It goes beyond saying that it was fitting that He should take part in our flesh and blood, to be near to us and that in doing so He overcame the fear of death that we have. **"For this reason he had to be made like his brothers in every way."** More than fitting, it was *necessary* for Christ to become one of us. **"For this reason he had to be made like his brothers in every way, in order that he might become a merciful and faithful high priest in service to God, and that he might make atonement for the sins of the people"** (v. 17). In addition to delivering us from the fear of death, He became a merciful and faithful high priest, and part of the work of the high priest is to offer the sacrifice for sin. Here, He does not offer a sacrifice that cannot take away sin, but He offers a sacrifice that does take away sin, which is the true sacrifice. This is why those who were very zealous for the law continued to offer the sacrifices without seeing the reality of sin that the signs were pointing to, that only Christ can take sin away.

Jesus made atonement for the sins of the people by His own blood—what could never be done in the tabernacle by the blood of bulls and goats. It was *necessary* for Him, not just fitting, to take part in our humanity, to be made a little lower than the angels, and yet rise above them. We may see Christ in His humanity only, and not think of Him being exalted. We may think He is exalted 'as if the angels were higher.' No, His name is higher than all the angels. The covenant He mediates is a greater covenant, a fuller covenant, a richer covenant. We are to let go of the old to possess this greater fullness that is in Christ. We are not to hesitate at all.

Christ frees us from the fear of death. He makes atonement for the sin of the people and He is a merciful and faithful high priest in service to God. There is not anything that we suffer, nothing that we suffered this past week, this past year, for all the past of our lives, nothing—there is no point of suffering that Christ is not fully acquainted with. So, when we cry out to Him, He knows how we feel. He cares. He has not only died for us (showing His care) but He knows how we feel in our struggle against sin. He knows our weaknesses, not only in our humanity, but in our sinful humanity. Because He struggled with sin on the cross. He knows what it is to sweat great drops of blood in His struggle against sin. He knows what it is to pray: "If it is possible, may this cup be taken from me. Yet not as I will, but as you will" (Matt. 26:39b). He knows our struggle with sin. He is touched with our feelings, He is merciful, He is full of mercy. He is faithful to His promise, and He will perform according to His promise.

We can come to Christ: **"Because he himself suffered when he was tempted"** (v. 18a). We cannot go through temptation without suffering. He went through temptation without sin, but not without suffering. He Himself suffered when He was tempted, and so **"he is able to help those who are being tempted"** (v. 18b), in many ways. He is able to help in those times when we feel nothing, those times when we are depressed, those times when we are so slothful, tempted to sloth, and not engaged in the discipline needed to do what we should. We struggle with this and we cry to the Lord: 'Lord help me!' He knows our temptations, He is faithful and He is merciful. So we must give more careful attention to the Word that is spoken, lest we drift. There is a great salvation. Christ is the heir of all things; all things have been subjected to Christ. And we must be careful to obey all that God has said, that we may come into the fullness of the promise that is ours in Christ Jesus our Lord. Amen.

3

Fix Your Thoughts on Jesus

Hebrews 3

¹Therefore, holy brothers, who share in the heavenly calling, fix your thoughts on Jesus, the apostle and high priest whom we confess. ²He was faithful to the one who appointed him, just as Moses was faithful in all God's house. ³Jesus has been found worthy of greater honor than Moses, just as the builder of a house has greater honor than the house itself. ⁴For every house is built by someone, but God is the builder of everything. ⁵Moses was faithful as a servant in all God's house, testifying to what would be said in the future. ⁶But Christ is faithful as a son over God's house. And we are his house, if we hold on to our courage and the hope of which we boast.

⁷So, as the Holy Spirit says:
  "Today, if you hear his voice,
⁸do not harden your hearts
  as you did in the rebellion,
    during the time of testing in the desert,
⁹where your fathers tested and tried me
    and for forty years saw what I did.
¹⁰That is why I was angry with that generation,
    and I said, 'Their hearts are always going astray,
    and they have not known my ways.'
¹¹So I declared on oath in my anger,
    'They shall never enter my rest.'"

¹²See to it, brothers, that none of you has a sinful, unbelieving heart that turns away from the living God. ¹³But encourage one another daily, as long as it is called Today, so that none of you may be hardened by sin's

deceitfulness. [14]We have come to share in Christ if we hold firmly till the end the confidence we had at first. [15]As has just been said:

"Today, if you hear his voice,
    do not harden your hearts
  as you did in the rebellion."

[16]Who were they who heard and rebelled? Were they not all those Moses led out of Egypt? [17]And with whom was he angry for forty years? Was it not with those who sinned, whose bodies fell in the desert? [18]And to whom did God swear that they would never enter his rest if not to those who disobeyed? [19]So we see that they were not able to enter, because of their unbelief.

"**H**OLY BROTHERS, WHO SHARE in the heavenly calling, fix your thoughts on Jesus**" (v. 1a). Get your thoughts off of yourself, get your thoughts off of the world, get your thoughts off of others, and fix your thoughts on Jesus. To fix your thoughts on Jesus means to get your thoughts on Jesus and keep them there. This is necessary if we are to be like Jesus, if we as brothers are to be like Him, if we are to become holy, if we are to **"share in the heavenly calling."** We have seen how glorious this calling is. It is our calling that is in Christ Jesus, who is the apostle, the One sent by God, the Messiah, who has been crowned with glory and honor, having suffered death in atonement for all, to fulfill God's purpose and to destroy the works of the devil.

Jesus has been raised, He has been seated at the right hand of God, and He is fulfilling the purpose of God because all authority in heaven and on earth has been given to Him.[1] **"Fix your thoughts on Jesus"** (v. 1). He is our apostle and He is our high priest. He is the One who took upon Himself our flesh, that He might suffer death to atone for our sins, that He might be in every way like His brothers, that He may be touched with the feelings of our infirmity,[2] and that He may be able to help us to the uttermost. **"Fix your thoughts on Jesus"** and keep them there. Jesus was faithful in the calling that He received. We have received the calling in Him, and we are to be faithful. He was faithful to the One who appointed Him.

---

1. *Matthew 28:18.*
2. *Hebrews 4:15* KJV.

CREATOR-CREATURE DISTINCTION:
The Builder of the House and the House Itself

Moses was also appointed by God, and Moses was faithful. Though Moses failed at one point, struggled and came short, he is considered faithful, and he has been highly regarded by the Jews. His way has been affirmed, particularly in the day that the Apostles wrote and by those to whom the Apostles were writing. They highly regarded Moses and would consider it contrary to God's Word if in any way they slighted the law that was given by Moses. Moses was indeed faithful, and he is to be honored, yet Christ has been found worthy of greater honor than Moses. How much greater? Much greater. Greater in a way that cannot be compared; it is a difference between the honor due to the one who builds the house and the honor due to the house—the Creator and creature distinction.

Christ is the One. He is the Son of God by whom all things were made, in whom all things consist. He is the One for whom the house was made. He is the heir of all things.[3] He is the **"son over God's house"** (v. 6a). He is the One who builds the house of God where God will dwell. We heard in the Call to Worship: "For this is what the high and lofty One says—he who lives forever, whose name is holy: 'I live in a high and holy place, but also with him who is contrite and lowly in spirit, to revive the spirit of the lowly and to revive the heart of the contrite'" (Is. 57:15). Christ our Lord is that One. He says, "I am gentle and humble in heart" (Matt. 11:29). "He humbled himself and became obedient to death—even death on a cross!" (Phil. 2:8b). More humble than this, one cannot become. He was exalted to the right hand of God, and He rules over everything in the universe. "We do not see everything subject to him" (Heb. 2:8b), but we see Jesus at the right hand of God who will bring everything into subjection. Christ, the Son of God incarnate, our Creator and our redeemer, has more honor than Moses. Therefore, though we honor Moses and thank God for Moses, we worship Christ. To Him, honor must be paid, and to the Word spoken through Him; for "in these last days," God the

---

3. *Hebrews 1:2.*

Father "has spoken to us by his Son" (Heb. 1:2a). The words spoken through His Son must be given the greater attention.[4]

The salvation that comes through the Son is greater than the salvation that came through Moses—rather, we say Moses spoke of what was to come. He testified to what would be said in the future, and we must consider how Moses testified. We must consider all the revelation that was given to Moses: from Genesis 1–3 (and the summary of the message of redemption there),[5] the call of Abraham, Isaac, and Jacob (the Patriarchs), the law that was given over 400 years later to the people of Israel (the tabernacle, the priesthood, and the sacrifices); all of this spoke of what was to come. All of this spoke of Jesus. Jesus said,

> You diligently study the Scriptures because you think that by them you possess eternal life. These are the Scriptures that testify about me . . . Your accuser is Moses, on whom your hopes are set. If you believed Moses, you would believe me, for he wrote about me (Jn. 5:39, 45b–46).

Christ: The Reality of Whom Moses Spoke

Moses spoke of the things that were to come. He spoke, through all the law (the ceremonial law, the civil law, and the moral law), of Christ as redeemer and Christ as king. The very work that God gave Moses to do to bring the people out of Egypt and into Canaan spoke of what Christ was to do: To bring the people *out* of sin and *into* the fullness of eternal life. Moses was faithful, but Christ is the Son over the house, and He *is* the Word of God, the full Word of God, the final Word of God. Let us not hold on to the law of Moses in such a way that we do not see how it points to Christ and in such a way that we are kept from coming to Christ in all that He said. Let us not hold on to the types, shadows, and ordinances and not see that these are passing away as Christ has brought in a new covenant. Christ has ushered in the kingdom. It was Christ Himself, by His presence on earth, who ushered in the kingdom of God spoken of in the Old Testament. In the Old Testament, salvation was there in reality, but administered in type

---

4. *Hebrews 3:1–6.*

5. Surrendra Gangadean, *The Biblical Worldview: Creation, Fall, Redemption. Genesis 1–3: Scripture in Organic Seed Form* (Phoenix: Logos Papers Press, 2024).

and shadow—people really were saved, regenerated, and had eternal life—but what they had in the old economy was pointing forward to what was to come. If we honor Moses, we would look at what Moses said and give ourselves to what will come.

What occurred with the people of God in the Old Testament is something that occurs in all of us. We spoke about our spiritual fore-bearers and our natural ancestors, and we have a great tendency to look at the outward and the natural rather than the spiritual. We have a tendency to go back to tradition. Tradition is a thing that has been highly exalted among the Jews. It was also highly exalted in the medie-val church. Each one of us walks with our own particular background, our own particular tradition, our own baggage, and our own comfort level. We are inclined to go back, rest in tradition, be satisfied, and not press on to the fullness that there is in Christ. This Word is spoken to the people, the Jewish believers in that day. Believers they were, but still holding on to tradition. Because of coming short in understand-ing (not understanding), we too have the temptation to hold on to our tradition, our own particular background, and our own comfort level. Every one of us has this temptation.

We have a tendency to hold on to tradition, settle in, and not press on for the fullness that there is in Christ Jesus. Moses spoke of what would be said in the future. Christ is the Son over God's house. Let us give heed to Christ. He is the reality of whom Moses spoke, and we are the house of Christ. The people of God is where Christ dwells, where God dwells. The Father and the Son and the Holy Spirit come and make their abode, their dwelling place, in us as His people.[6] He has built this creation. No building we can build is sufficient for God, but God dwells in a living temple in the people of God, in the body of Christ. By God's grace, *we* are the house of God in which He dwells. We are that house if we hold on to our courage and the hope that is set before us. We may not hold on to it, we may let it go, we may come short of it.

When the people came out of Egypt, they were not simply coming out of Egypt; they were coming out with a promise of going into the Promised Land. They were leaving one for the other—that was their hope. God had promised this to Abraham and yet the generation that

6. *John 14:23* KJV.

came out of Egypt did not enter the Promised Land. They did not hold on to the hope. They did not hold on to their confidence. Christ is a faithful high priest. We are called to be faithful, to hold on to our confidence. The word *confidence* here is the word *parrhesia* (παῤῥησία)—meaning outspokenness. It has to do with boldness in speaking out. It is a boldness because of confidence, because of understanding, and because of faith. We are to hold on to our confidence and the hope of which we boast—the hope in which we rejoice. People were looking forward to coming into the Promised Land. Those who come into the kingdom of God are coming into a kingdom that is joy and peace in the Holy Spirit. We come into righteousness in the world and joy and peace in the Holy Spirit. When we came to Christ, we came for life, and we came for the fullness of it. Sometimes, we settle down because we are comfortable according to our tradition, and we do not press on to come into the fullness that there is in Christ. We do not become the house of God in which God dwells.

God's fullness cannot dwell within us unless we reach for fullness. Unless we are stretched that we might be filled with all the fullness of God. Our hope is in Christ. He was sent by God to accomplish this. He is our "**apostle**," the Messiah, and He is our "**high priest**" (v. 1b). There is a particular job that the priesthood has and that the high priest is responsible for, that is, to make us holy, to make us godly, to remove from us *all* that is of self (creaturely-self that we put in the place of God), that we might be fully devoted to God in every way. Every word of our mouth and every thought of our heart is to be pleasing to God. Because Christ is our "**apostle**," the One sent by God to this end, and because He is our "**high priest**," abundantly able to accomplish this, tempted in all ways as we are, able to uphold us, encourage us, and strengthen us, let us keep coming to Him. Let us hold to the confidence that Christ was sent to accomplish this, and let us express our confidence by continuing to come to Him, trusting that He will enable us to overcome sin and will equip us to do the work God has called us to do. Let us fix our thoughts on Jesus. Later on, he is going to say, let us fix our eyes on Jesus. He is the One sent for this purpose. He is "**the apostle and high priest**" (v. 1b) of our profession.

Christ Will Complete the Work

What we have boasted in, what we have joyed in, what we have rejoiced in, is that the earth will be filled with the knowledge of God[7] and all nations of the earth will be discipled.[8] We will accomplish the work of redemption and we rejoice in that on the Sabbath day. This work will be done—we will know God. The glory of God fills the earth— we rejoice in this, we boast in this. And this rejoicing is our strength. Let us hold on to it. We are continually called throughout this book to "**hold on**" (v. 6). In Hebrews 2 it says, "pay more careful attention, therefore, to what we have heard, so that we do not drift away" (Heb. 2:1). Here it says to "**hold on**." Later on it states: "We have this hope as an anchor for the soul, firm and secure" (Heb. 6:19a)—steadfast. It reaches beyond the veil into the heavenlies. We have this fullness; we have this blessing in Christ. He will accomplish it.

We keep coming to Christ Jesus our Lord so that we might find grace to help in the time of need. This is why we are to "**fix** [our] **thoughts on Jesus**" (v. 1). Get our thoughts off of everything else—off of ourselves, our own worries, our own fears, or everyone else—and get our eyes on Jesus and *keep* our eyes there. Let us not keep glancing up at Him and down, back up, and down, as Peter did while walking on water. He was sinking. We are to get our eyes on Jesus, not on anything else, and keep them there. We have a warning from God. We are not to be careless about this. We have seen how failure has occurred in a major way in the history of the Church: In Moses' day, after Moses' day, in the history of the Church, and in our day, failure has occurred. Let us not presume that we are not going to be troubled and tempted by this and come short. Let us heed this warning of Scripture. "**As the Holy Spirit says: 'Today, if you hear his voice, do not harden your hearts'**" (vv. 7–8a). When you hear this word concerning who Christ is and what He has come to do and the fullness of the blessing, "**do not harden your hearts as you did in the rebellion**" (v. 8a).

The rebellion is spoken of as that entire 40-year period. But there is one point which is especially spoken of in this section. It is called *the rebellion*. The rebellion was at Kadesh Barnea. Kadesh Barnea was where the Israelites came to the border of the land. They sent spies in and they

---

7. *Isaiah 11:9.*

8. *Matthew 28:18–20.*

came back with a report. Instead of remembering what God had done for them, how great God is, instead of meditating on, understanding, and seeing how God began the work, sustained them, and delivered them in such a great way from Egypt and continued to uphold them and care for them, they lightly regarded it. They disesteemed it and, in doing so, showed contempt for God, thinking that God could not do this, that they could not trust in God to bring this about, and they turned back. When we hear the word of promise, that God has called us to make disciples of all nations,[9] to take every thought captive,[10] to fill the earth with the knowledge of God,[11] let us not say as they did, 'There are giants in the land, we cannot do this, it cannot be done.'[12]

CHRIST'S PURPOSE:
Filling the Earth With the Knowledge of God

We should not justify ourselves by concocting stories for ourselves, saying that 'this is not God's purpose, God's purpose is that we will die and we will go to heaven and then receive the blessing.' Or that 'Jesus will come back and Jesus will do it.' We appear to exalt God, but we do not know His ways and we do not know God when we speak in this way, and we do not honor Him. **"Today, if you hear his voice, do not harden your hearts"** (vv. 7b–8a). Do not lightly and thoughtlessly regard His Word and let it slip. When we have trials, we are not to fail to understand how these trials are preparing us and calling us to trust in God, to learn to walk with Him, and to put aside remaining sin. Do not lightly esteem the trials of God, the ways of God, but trust in Him, knowing that He is preparing us for the work that is ahead, that we might give ourselves for the work, not lose heart, and keep our confidence. Christ, who has died for our sins and sent the Holy Spirit to regenerate us, to bring us out of sin and death, is the One who can continue to work in us and enable us to overcome sin. He sent the Holy Spirit to illumine our minds. Let us not lightly esteem this.

---

9. *Matthew 28:18–20.*

10. *2 Corinthians 10:4–5.*

11. *Isaiah 11:9.*

12. *Numbers 13:26–33.*

Christ, through the Holy Spirit, can enable us to understand His truth and give us grace to persevere in understanding. God works His trials into our lives, the trials of faith pressing us to call upon Him, to understand more, to seek Him diligently, to know Him and to give ourselves to this work and to order our whole lives for this, that we might seek first the kingdom of God and His righteousness.[13] Let us regard God in this and not harden our hearts, let it pass, and settle back to our comfort level. Yes, we will go through trials where the heat will be on, we will be melted, and the pressure will build so much we will feel we are going to shatter into a thousand pieces. All we can do then is fall on our face before God and trust that Christ our Lord will save us. He brought this into our lives for our good, and we should wait upon Him and trust, honor, and obey Him.

> **Do not harden your hearts as you did in the rebellion, during the time of testing in the desert, where your fathers tested and tried me and for forty years saw what I did. That is why I was angry with that generation, and I said, "Their hearts are always going astray" (vv. 8–10a).**

Warning: Do Not Harden Your Hearts under Trials

Remember they, too, had the promise of entering into the land. We have the promise of seeing all the nations discipled,[14] and we are not doing well. We are not doing any better than Israel did. You might say by comparison we are doing worse than Israel did because we have more light. We have their example, and we have more teaching, but we are not regarding it. Let us **"not harden [our] hearts"** (v. 8a). We have a false view of God's blessing, a false view of good and evil. Original sin remains with us, and we have concocted for ourselves some other account of what the blessing is, as we spoke of earlier in Psalm 1.[15] We settle back because we are comfortable with our tradition. Oh, how Reb Tevye reveled in tradition in *Fiddler on the Roof.* He sang it with gusto: 'Tradition!' We must give heed to the Word of Christ, the apostle and high priest whom we confess. We must give more careful heed

---

13. *Matthew 6:33.*

14. *Matthew 28:18–20.*

15. This reference is to the psalm meditation presented during this particular service.

that we do not let these things slip.[16] It is easy, easy, all too easy to let these things slip. Many hear, but many do not persevere.

We must know God's way. We must know what God's purpose is, why these trials come into our lives, and we must call upon Christ in the midst of trials. If we persist in not hearing, if we, through the trials, keep turning aside and not calling upon God or trusting in God, there can come a time, as there did come a time, when what God did to the people then, He will do to us. He will declare in His anger that we, this particular generation, if we persist in our unbelief, He will swear on oath: 'That's it! No more.' And we will perish in the wilderness. Let us not put the Lord to the test as we come into trials. Let us fall on our faces before Christ our Lord, who is our high priest. Let us come before Him to find grace to help in the time of need. **"Today, if you hear his voice, do not harden your hearts"** (vv. 7b–8a). We are warned against having a sinful, unbelieving heart that turns away from the living God. This sinful heart is a self-centered heart, where sin can take any virtue, any precept, any law of God, and turn it towards self and try to make it serve the purpose of self. Even a precept such as 'husbands love your wives, wives submit to your husbands'[17] is a precept that we, in our sin, can turn in a selfish way. There is a virtue in this law, but if it is turned improperly, it could be a vice.

We have sin remaining in us, and this sin can manifest in the appearance of obedience where we think we are obeying but we are really serving ourselves. Be careful. He says, **"See to it, brothers,** [and each one of us must examine ourselves to "see to it"] **that none of you has a sinful, unbelieving heart that turns away from the living God"** (v. 12). It is sin and sin alone that turns us away from God. It is our own self-life and the many ways in which it comes about. We turn from finding our satisfaction in God to finding it in temporal blessings that God may give. Over and against the curse, we have these blessings, and our tradition has encouraged us in this.

We can fight for freedom and democracy without fighting for the honor of God. You know why? Because there is blessing in them, there

---

16. *Hebrews 2:1.*

17. *Colossians 3:18–25.*

is some blessing. At the end of the movie *Braveheart*,[18] William Wallace cries out with the shout: "Freedom!" Freedom is a virtue. It is not the good. Freedom can become a vice, and it is precisely this freedom, coupled with self-centeredness, which has become self-indulgent, that has stirred the wrath of many peoples against us. Be careful **"that none of you has a sinful, unbelieving heart that turns away from the living God"** (v. 12b). Adam turned away from the living God. He turned away from the good as God has determined it. Adam determined the good as something other than what God determined for him, putting himself in the place of God to please himself. We have to examine ourselves so that does not happen. We are rather to **"encourage one another daily, as long as it is called Today, so that none of you may be hardened by sin's deceitfulness"** (v. 13). Jeremiah 17:9 says, "The heart is deceitful above all things, and desperately wicked: who can know it?"[19] In that same chapter, he speaks about the one who does obey God as being like a tree planted by the waters, whose leaves do not fade, who brings forth its fruit in season[20]—all the blessedness of the man who knows God and knows the way of God and honors God. All he does shall prosper. The wicked are not so.[21] Our hearts are desperately wicked.

Encouragement: Seek Diligently

We must come to diligently, even desperately, seek the Lord. As when Jesus asked, "'You do not want to leave too, do you?' And Simon Peter answered him, 'Lord, to whom shall we go? You have the words of eternal life.'" (Jn. 6:67–68). Paul said, "I consider everything a loss compared to the surpassing greatness of knowing Christ Jesus my Lord" (Phil. 3:8a). There is a vehemence, a violence, doing violence to the flesh and anything that would come in the way of knowing God that is required. I fear when I preach these words. I fear for myself. Lest having preached this, I stumble and become a stumbling block to others. May God give me grace.

---

18. *Braveheart*, Randall Wallace and Mel Gibson (Icon Productions and The Ladd Company, 1995).

19. KJV.

20. *Jeremiah 17:7–8.*

21. *Psalm 1.*

We are not to be hardened by sin's deceitfulness. It is there in our hearts. It is present. It is lurking. The trials bring sin to light. This is what is going on in our lives. The thoughts of our hearts are being manifested through all of the trials. They come up, and we fall on our faces before the Lord Jesus, confess our sins, and ask Him for mercy. We are to encourage one another in this. We are not to commiserate with others in their self-indulgence. Watch it. The Israelites were, in modern terms, 'whiners and slackers.' They were complaining about their feelings. 'I have feelings.' But what do they have feelings for? Some would say, 'I do not *feel* anything. Eating this manna, I do not *feel* anything. It doesn't stir me. We have feelings for the leeks and the garlic and the onion.' You know, a good garlic toast with salmon is really great. You can't beat that. Leeks, garlic, and onions beat granola any day. 'I got feelings. We got feelings.' We may commiserate with others in our self-indulgence. He said, **"But encourage one another"** (v. 13a).

We are to encourage one another, not to enable one another in our self-life. We are slackers. I discovered this morning what a slacker is. A slacker is one who allows someone else to pick up the slack that is in their life. A slacker is one who expects someone else to come seeking them to help them in their walk with God rather than seeking God diligently. I have been guilty of enabling slackers. I have commiserated with whiners and complainers, and I have not encouraged others daily in terms of what is good: to seek Him diligently. I have listened to complaints on the phone. What I should say when someone says, 'I do not have feelings,' is what the Lord said, "He is the rewarder of those who diligently seek Him."[22] Are you diligently seeking Him? This is where life is. If they say, 'I've sought God, and I do not *feel* anything still,' then I should say: Let God be true and every man, every woman, every child, be a liar because that is the truth of God's Word. God is the rewarder of those who diligently seek Him. If you are not finding the reward, it is a *necessary truth* that you are not diligently seeking Him, just as it is a necessary truth that because it is clear we are inexcusable. We are to encourage one another, not enable one another in our sin-life.

Scripture speaks about hardening by sin's deceitfulness. After a while, we start deceiving ourselves about our seeking. We think, 'We're okay. This is all right. I'm doing all that I should do.' Remember Job. Then,

---

22. *Hebrews 11:6.*

we may avoid the company of other believers in order to avoid being accountable, and we find some reason or other to not be with others and interact. Sometimes, we blame others and justify ourselves. Be careful, that you not be hardened by sin's deceitfulness. **"Today, if you hear his voice, do not harden your hearts"** (v. 15). **"We have come to share in Christ if we hold firmly till the end the confidence we had at first"** (v. 14). There is that phrase again, to **"hold firmly"** to the confidence, the assurance, the essence, the substance, the assurance of what we had, the support of what we had at first. Many have come into this congregation, they have heard about this wonderful promise of the earth being filled with the knowledge of God, they have been thrilled, they have been excited, and then weeks, months later, one drops off here, one settles back there. We are not pursuing the promise and we are not holding firmly till the end to the confidence we had at first. We go out to witness and encounter problems. We let things slip because we cannot make headway. In our day, we face multiculturalism, pluralism, diversity, and the 'appropriate response' in all of this political correctness and its view of tolerance. If we allow this to stand in our thinking, in our way, we are already defeated because all that comes out of the worldview that says, 'it is not clear, and truth is not exclusive of error.' It comes out of a major distortion of what culture is. Culture is a system of beliefs and shared values that are institutionalized—put into practice in all of our institutions. We have been neutralized; we might even say we have been 'neutered' by this distortion. We have not kept on the belt of truth.[23] The first aspect of the belt of truth is the clarity of general revelation[24] and the concept of truth, which is not 'what is true for me and what is true for you' but *truth* about the world which excludes other views. We have not kept the concept of truth and the exclusiveness of it.

We have allowed a view of tolerance to come in where we cannot discuss ideas, and rather, we 'appreciate.' Even in our National Cathedral, we have the manifestation of a desire to be inclusive. We have clerics of many faiths pray, who do not acknowledge Christ as Lord and Savior. We think that those who have rejected Christ—*fundamentally*

---

23. *Ephesians 6:10–18.*

24. Gangadean, "Paper No. 102: The Clarity of General Revelation," 527–529; "Paper No. 41: What Is Clear About God," 225–229; "Paper No. 112: Why General Revelation Is Basic in the Christian Worldview," in *The Logos Papers,* 583–585.

rejected Christ, and the whole faith is built on that—can be heard by God. We may wince, we may feel a bit uncomfortable with it, but we encounter this daily.

'It is all right to have your faith as long as you keep it private,' which is to say, 'your values cannot be brought into the institutions,' which are by nature, public, and 'keep your culture private,' which is a denial of the essence of culture. There is a war to be fought. It is a good war. It is a holy war. It is a war in which we demolish arguments and every pretension that sets itself up against the knowledge of God, and take them captive to become obedient to Christ,[25] who fills everything in every way.[26] He is Lord of lords and King of kings.[27] We cannot be apologetic about this. We have to find ways to break through these implications of skepticism, that 'nothing is clear, no one really knows, we cannot say, and therefore we must make room for many cultures.' We have been neutralized, neuterized, by failure to see that the vitality of culture is the expression of these laws and values institutionally in our public life. Where are they? When we fight, we must wear the belt of truth.

We must hold firmly till the end the confidence we had at first.[28] When we come up against these oppositions, these things opposing the knowledge of God, we do not say as the Israelites did, 'What can I say? I had nothing to say. I didn't know what to say. I just had to back down. I just hit a stone wall.'[29] Instead of demolishing what was raised up against God, our view was smashed against a wall and was demolished. **"Hold firmly till the end the confidence we had at first"** (v. 14b) and grow and increase it, as God brings us through all kinds of trials, that we might know Him better.

This is very relevant for us, because it was at Kadesh Barnea that they turned back when they were going in to possess the land. We are warned. It is exactly what we face. **"Who were they who heard and rebelled? Were they not all those Moses led out of Egypt? And with**

---

25. *2 Corinthians 10:4–5.*

26. *Ephesians 1:22–23.*

27. *Revelation 17:14, 19:16.*

28. *Hebrews 3:14.*

29. An analogy to the rebellion at Kadesh Barnea in their inability to see a way forward faithful with God's truth.

whom was he angry for forty years?" (vv. 16–17a), or 1,600 years? "Was it not with those who sinned, whose bodies fell in the desert? And to whom did God swear that they would never enter his rest if not to those who disobeyed?" (vv. 17b–18). Please notice this because in the next chapter, we will go into this: Entering into rest is entering into the Promised Land.

When they say there is a rest remaining for the people of God, we must understand that it is parallel to entering into the Promised Land. There is a rest remaining for us. There is a Promised Land for us to enter. We are warned here. See to it that we do not have a sinful heart, an unbelieving heart: "So we see that they were not able to enter, because of their unbelief" (v. 19). There are many ways in which unbelief is connected with the self-life, and at the core, expresses itself.

We need to take heed. We need to keep our eyes on Jesus. Later in this book, Paul will say that in the midst of all of our struggles, all of our trials, we are to fix our eyes on Jesus, that we do not grow weary and lose heart.[30] There is a great goal that is set before us—a great promise. To turn back from this is rebellion. To turn back is not to trust in God, not to honor God as able, not to persevere and be prepared and give ourselves to the preparation to be discipled. It is to rebel against God. It is to express a heart of unbelief. Brothers, holy brothers, who share the heavenly calling, fix your thoughts on Jesus.

---

30. *Hebrews 12:2–3.*

4

Dividing Soul and Spirit

Hebrews 4

¹Therefore, since the promise of entering his rest still stands, let us be careful that none of you be found to have fallen short of it. ²For we also have had the gospel preached to us, just as they did; but the message they heard was of no value to them, because those who heard did not combine it with faith. ³Now we who have believed enter that rest, just as God has said,

"So I declared on oath in my anger,
'They shall never enter my rest.'"

⁴And yet his work has been finished since the creation of the world. For somewhere he has spoken about the seventh day in these words: "And on the seventh day God rested from all his work." ⁵And again in the passage above he says, "They shall never enter my rest."

⁶It still remains that some will enter that rest, and those who formerly had the gospel preached to them did not go in, because of their disobedience. ⁷Therefore God again set a certain day, calling it Today, when a long time later he spoke through David, as was said before:

"Today, if you hear his voice,
do not harden your hearts."

⁸For if Joshua had given them rest, God would not have spoken later about another day. ⁹There remains, then, a Sabbath-rest for the people of God; ¹⁰for anyone who enters God's rest also rests from his own work, just as God did from his. ¹¹Let us, therefore, make every effort to enter that rest, so that no one will fall by following their example of disobedience.

¹²For the word of God is living and active. Sharper than any double-edged sword, it penetrates even to dividing soul and spirit, joints and marrow; it judges the thoughts and attitudes of the heart. ¹³Nothing in all creation

is hidden from God's sight. Everything is uncovered and laid bare before the eyes of him to whom we must give account.

[14]Therefore, since we have a great high priest who has gone through the heavens, Jesus the Son of God, let us hold firmly to the faith we profess. [15]For we do not have a high priest who is unable to sympathize with our weaknesses, but we have one who has been tempted in every way, just as we are—yet was without sin. [16]Let us then approach the throne of grace with confidence, so that we may receive mercy and find grace to help us in our time of need.

THE PROMISE OF ENTRY STILL STANDS

WE HAVE THE WORD THAT GOD HAS SPOKEN, which is **"sharper than any double-edged sword"** (v. 12). We have Christ Himself, who has spoken this Word, who has embodied this Word, who is our Great High Priest, who is there to help us in our time of need. Christ is exalted higher than the angels.[1] He is seated at the right hand of God.[2] He has become the heir of all things; He has been given a name that is above every name.[3] We are not to be so taken up with what we have had so as not to see Jesus. We should not hold on to the past order of things in the old covenant, as doing so will prevent us from fully seeing Jesus' glory, the future glory He is meant to bring us to, and the glory He is destined to bring to God.

The writer—we believe, the apostle Paul—speaks of this rest. Those who came out of Egypt were not able to enter. They let it slip. Their hearts wandered. They were hardened by sin's deceitfulness. They did not enter. They turned back at Kadesh Barnea[4] when they were called to enter. Though they had seen the works of God, they did not give heed. They lightly and thoughtlessly regarded it. They took the name of God in vain.[5] They did not give heed to the Word spoken. We have a Word spoken that is *fuller* and *clearer,* in that what came before was a type and shadow. We have the reality that is in Christ, and we must give heed to this.

1. *Hebrews 1:4.*
2. *Hebrews 1:13.*
3. *Philippians 2:9.*
4. *Numbers 13–14.*
5. *Exodus 20:7.*

In several ways, Paul speaks about the rest that still remains. You must understand that some people have thought that the rest was given when Joshua entered and conquered the Promised Land. That was the rest under the old covenant—in type and shadow. It was pointing forward to something greater: that all the families of the earth would be blessed in Christ Jesus. The Jewish believers did not see this greater fullness and were struggling to understand how it would come about. They thought that those who came into the covenant must come in under the order that was given through Moses, and they were zealous for the law. Thus, they were not seeing something of this fullness. They were not understanding something that needed to be understood, just as the Israelites coming out of Egypt did not understand what they ought to have understood. The gospel they heard was not mixed with faith (with understanding). It is the same with the people Paul is writing to now, who are in a position where they may not understand and they may come short. They may not see that there remains a rest. We, too, may, like the people coming out of Egypt, not see the hope, not hold on to it firmly, not think that we can possess it, and not think that we have the help that is needed to go in. We fail to see that Christ Jesus, our Lord, is with us.

We are being warned in this book that we should not come short, that we should give heed and come to the fullness that is in Jesus Christ. He is the Creator of all things, the upholder of all things, the redeemer of all things. He is the heir of all things.[6] He has a name that is above every name,[7] and He is able to bring to pass what He has promised. As we read the Book of Hebrews, we are to understand that this book focuses on the fullness that is in Jesus Christ. Christ is *greater* than the angels, He is *greater* than Moses, His priesthood is *greater* than the Aaronic priesthood, and He has entered into the true tabernacle, not made with hands—into the heavenlies itself. We are going to be reminded of all those in the past, from Abel on, who looked for this promise, who were waiting, and who worked for it.[8]

This book is *full* of eschatology. In the past, I have thought about trying to select verses on eschatology out of the New Testament and

---

6. *Hebrews 1:2.*

7. *Philippians 2:9.*

8. *Hebrews 11.*

the Old Testament here and there, but we should say that the whole Bible is an eschatological book. It speaks about the hope that is before us, and we must learn to think in this way and to understand all those things that we raise up in our minds, which hinder us. We must see the things in our thinking and practice that hinder us, that the hope, theoretically and practically, will be ours, and we will be steadfast in what God has called us to, that we will not come short of it. This is the great fear that we should have. Sin and coming short of the glory of God and not seeing the fullness of the glory that is for *all* the families on the earth. The great fear that we should have is that we will not give ourselves to this, that we will not prepare ourselves, and that we will not sacrifice ourselves for this. We should give up things that are important to us *for* this. This is a sacrifice. We should guide our whole lives, our decisions, and what we are going to be doing with our lives *by* this, that we will keep on pressing when we come short. In this fourth chapter, the writer of the Book of Hebrews is continuing in what he had said. This is in contrast to those who rebelled and did not enter because of their unbelief. He says, **"the promise of entering his rest still stands"** (v. 1a).

The Rest, Hope, and the Good

Paul speaks about the Israelites who did not enter into the rest—clearly, this rest is coming out of Egypt to come into Canaan. This is a model we must keep in mind. When we speak about the rest and the Sabbath rest throughout, we must keep this in mind. We must also remember that coming out of Egypt and into Canaan was type and shadow. It was real, and it was symbolical. It was not the fullness. Immediately after the statement, **"They shall never enter my rest"** (v. 5b), he says, **"It still remains that some will enter that rest"** (v. 6a). Obviously, the rest for us is not that we will go into Canaan. I trust it is obvious; there is no discussion needed on this. The rest is that we will come into what God has truly promised, that all the families of the earth will be blessed. That rest remains for us. We must be careful that none of us be found to have fallen short of it. Some have already fallen short of it. Some have bypassed it altogether. Many think that when we die, we go to heaven. 'We enter into the rest.' That is not the rest spoken of here. Many think that Jesus Himself will bring this about supernaturally after His second coming. Some people see the events that are going on in the world today as a precursor to Jesus' second return. They have missed it and they have misspoken.

"Let us be careful that none of you be found to have fallen short of it" (v. 1b). Even when we confess with our mouths, we may not be pressing on. We will see that he calls us to press on in a way that involves speed, urgency, diligence, fervency, and not casualness. We may hold to this hope in a way that we may be casual and say, 'It won't happen in my lifetime. It will take another 3,000 years to happen,' and we will come short of it. There are many ways in which we can come short of it. I have heard of some who think, 'The way in which it will come about is through my children, so I'm going to have many children, I'm going to raise them, and then they will raise their children, and then that is how we will multiply this thing into existence—we will outpopulate them.' No, the gospel is to go into all the earth, and we are to make disciples of all nations. There are many ways in which we can come short of this. That is why it says, "let us be careful that none of you be found to have fallen short of it" (v. 1b).

Some may say, 'What can I do?' In this war that is being fought against terrorism, many of us say, 'What can I do?' There is a war to be fought against terrorism.[9] That was a criminal act of war. It is not just an act of war; it is a criminal act, because civilians were targeted, and it must be dealt with as such. But that crime comes out of sin, and we have sin, and our war is against sin. First in us, in *our* unbelief, in *our* coming short of the glory of God, not acknowledging Him in His fullness and not ascribing *all* glory to God that belongs to Him. We must deal with sin in us, and in that war, we can say, 'But what can I do?' There is a great deal that each one of us can do in the war against sin.

We have to see this conflict is occurring on two levels: (1) In terms of a political act, there is a physical response in war. Terrorism must be stopped. It must be rooted out, but it will not be rooted out apart from the root of terrorism, which is sin. It is one thing to stop those acts; it is another thing to root it out. It can recur if it has not been rooted out. (2) In terms of the spiritual war, we are all able to engage, and engage a great deal more than what we are doing. We must prepare ourselves, become disciples, discipline our lives for godliness to grow

---

9. This sermon series was given within a year of the September 11, 2001 attacks.

in the knowledge of God, learn what has been taught already in the Church (the pastor-teachers), build on that teaching, engage with the issues of our day and of the last few centuries, and learn to take thoughts captive. We must give ourselves to this and not scratch our "innocent behinds" as that horse did on the tree in Wystan Hugh Auden's poem reflecting on Pieter Brueghel's *The Fall of Icarus*.[10] It is a painting by one of the masters, and this is a poem about it. Great events are occurring. Tragedies are occurring. Let us not be like the horse or the mule that does not understand. Let us give ourselves to understanding.

Hearing the Promise with Understanding

"For we also have had the gospel preached to us, just as they did; but the message they heard was of no value to them, because those who heard did not combine it with faith" (v. 2). It is possible to hear and not understand. It is possible to hear the message of the gospel and not understand—twice in this passage, it speaks about the gospel. The word *gospel* comes from a combination of two words, *eu* and *ángelos,* and a derivation of that. It is not just the messenger but the message. It is the good message, the good news. We can put it in our terms: It is news about the good, that the earth will be filled with the knowledge of God, and all the families of the earth will be blessed. What else is it that is the good but that? This is the message. We have spoken from time to time about the good, and we need to see the good as being at the heart of the gospel. The word *eu* like *eu*genics, good genes; or *eu*thanasia, a good death; or *eu*phoria, a good feeling. *Euángelos*: good news, good message. The message about the good. It cannot get any better than this, can it? You cannot get any message better than this: The earth will be filled with the knowledge of God as the waters cover the sea.[11]

This is the good, the knowledge of God, and the fullness of this is the earth will be filled—and this was the message: "Go in and take possession of the land" (Deut. 1:8a). And what they were doing in the conquest will be done fully in the future—the whole earth will be made disciples of Christ. We will be taught to observe all that God has

---

10. "Auden, Musée Des Beaux Arts." n.d. https://english.emory.edu/classes/paintings&poems/auden.html.

11. *Isaiah 11:9.*

commanded,[12] and all the nations will come singing. I want to hear those songs, those peculiar songs, and see the dances of the nations. I want to see that singing and dancing done to the Lord. The nations chanting their praises in Chinese, in Swahili, in Portuguese, and the Eskimos—all the shouts and ways that we might express our joy and praise before the Lord. "The nations will walk by its light, and the kings of the earth will bring their splendor into it" (Rev. 21:24).

God calls us to live for this. "Man's chief end is to glorify God, and to enjoy him forever" (SCQ. 1). Do not come short of it. Be careful. People are continually coming short of it, one way or another. We see sin in ourselves, we see sin in the Church, we see sin in the nation, and we say, 'Oy vey, how can we do it? We can't do that.' We have the gospel preached to us and we must mix it with faith. Christ is able to bring it about. He is the Word of God. He has spoken the Word of God to us. He is the Word of God incarnate, and He has lived out the Word. This is why we were told in the last chapter: "fix your thoughts on Jesus" (Heb. 3:1).

Get your thoughts off anyone else and put them on Jesus and keep them there. When you feel that your thoughts are going off, bring them back—watch and pray.[13] Through the week, we are going to be tried and tried and tried again; sin, in many forms, is going to come up, surprise us, and it is going to take all we have to get through it and overcome it. Sin will come up, I assure you it will. It will happen every week and throughout the week in many ways and become pointed, and we will become discouraged, and we will fall short. Be careful. Keep your eyes on Jesus. He is able to do it. Be steadfast and be firm so that 20 years from now you will be burning in your zeal with knowledge.

Build yourselves up in the most holy faith[14] so that we will not be pulled aside, that we will abide day by day, and take it to heart. Be careful that none of us be found to have fallen short of it. Be careful that we do not respond as they did then. We have that same sin in us. We have that same desire for the natural things of life as they did. We have that same spirit of complaining, murmuring, and whining. We think, 'I don't deserve this. I deserve better.' Of course we do; we deserve

---

12. *Matthew 28:18–20.*

13. *Matthew 26:41.*

14. *Jude 1:20.*

much better than we think; that is why God is bringing us through these trials. Did not God say that "he is a rewarder of them that diligently seek him" (Heb. 11:6b KJV)? Are we lacking a reward? Then we must conclude the necessary implication—we need to seek Him more diligently. We need to come before Jesus. We need to see Jesus more carefully. It is not, 'What would Jesus do' but 'What did Jesus do' in a situation relevant to mine. If we do not get to what He *did*, we will sentimentalize the *would* because we do not have an anchor. That was part of the difficulty a lot of people had with 'WWJD'—it should be 'What did Jesus do?' What He did is obey God in general and He was in our situation; He was tempted in all points as we are—all points—we have to find that point. By fixing our eyes on Jesus and keeping our eyes there, we learn to discern that point, and we will find hope. We will say, 'Jesus, Lord, you know where I am. I come to you to help me.' The promise stands: We must have faith/understanding in order that we might rest.

It says, **"Now we who have believed enter that rest, just as God has said, 'So I declared on oath in my anger, "They shall never enter my rest"'"** (v. 3a). This is written here in the past tense, but in the Greek, it is a present continuing: the ones *believing* enter the rest, and the context supports that reading. Sometimes it is said, 'I believe in Christ, I have entered the rest, I'm justified by faith and I'm going to heaven, and I don't have to be involved with my works of justification', as if the essence of salvation is justification. This is the context that is often used to read this passage about works and rest. This is the way we often hear it, rather than seeing that just as God completed His work, our work will be ended, and this is the work of dominion and the fullness of salvation. This is salvation; this is what God has come to bring us into. We must not think about this rest as just the rest of justification (as many have been inclined to read this passage), but we must think of it in the context of the rest that is comparable to what the Israelites entered into, which was not the final rest.

The Meaning of "My Rest"

Paul speaks of entering into that rest **"just as God has said"** (v. 3), in contrast to **"They shall never enter my rest"** (v. 3). This expression **"my rest"** introduces a question that the writer is going to answer, and he is going to explain a possible misunderstanding. It is not that God has some rest to enter into—Paul says here, **"And yet his work has been finished since the creation of the world. For somewhere he has spoken about the seventh day in these words: 'And on the seventh day God rested from all his work'"** (vv. 3b–4). So when it says, **"my rest,"** it is not a rest for God in the future. God has rested. He has done His work and rested. Yes, He does the work of providence, including the work of redemption, but we have to understand how He speaks about **"my rest"** so that we do not misunderstand this rest. What is meant by **"They shall never enter my rest"** (v. 3)? As I said, some have taken this rest to mean justification by faith and not the works of the law by which we would be justified, as against seeing that it is the works of *obedience* by which we come into this rest. We see in the passage later on where it says: **"Let us, therefore, make every effort to enter that rest"** (v. 11a). It is not the rest of justification that is being spoken of here.

God has entered into His rest, and Paul repeats again, **"They shall never enter my rest"** (v. 5b). This time, the emphasis is not on **"my rest"** understood as something future for God, but **"they"** in contrast to others, **"they"** shall not enter into my rest. *Some* will enter, but *they* will not because of their unbelief—that is the clarification in the next section. **"It still remains that some will enter that rest, and those who formerly had the gospel preached to them did not go in, because of their disobedience"** (v. 6). So Paul takes this passage and works through the nuances, implications, and emphases, that it may take captive misunderstandings. He is clarifying the meaning of **"They shall never enter my rest"** (v. 5b). Since they will not, does that mean that it is all over? No, *some* will enter. Does it mean a rest in the future for God because it says **"my rest"** as against *their* rest? No, God calls it **"my rest"** (v. 5b), as we see, because God is going to work to bring this about. He did not say that they shall not enter into *their* rest; He says **"my rest."**

Then Paul clarifies the meaning of **"today."** Therefore, he says, **"It still remains that some will enter that rest"** (v. 6a). Paul emphasizes, **"It still remains"** (v. 6a), and **"Therefore God again set a certain day, calling it Today, when a long time later he spoke through David"** (v. 7a). David came *after* Joshua—obviously. So, when he says, **"They shall never enter my rest"** (v. 5b) and **"some will enter"** (v. 6a), it means there is a *future* rest. He is establishing the point that there remains a rest for the people of God—it is future. It is not Joshua: **"For if Joshua** had given them rest, God would not have spoken later about another day" (v. 8). So, Paul sums it all up again: "There remains, then, a Sabbath-rest for the people of God" (v. 9). He takes it all the way back to the very beginning: God's Sabbath, and man, *in* God, entering into that Sabbath.

Christ has come and has obeyed the covenant of works made with Adam, and He is seated at the right hand of God. He secured that rest, so now our work, the work that Adam would have done in history, can be done from a position of security and rest. Christ has come, Christ has suffered, He has been raised from the dead, and He has secured the work—this is the Sabbath rest. We are now working under that condition. They did not work, and if we do not, it remains, and God will bring it about through others. Let us not be like them. Let us strive to enter in. It says, "for anyone who enters God's rest also rests from his own work, just as God did from his" (v. 10). Does this mean we do not work? Some have used this to say we do not work. But when we enter into His rest, we enter in the same way He did: He worked and completed His work.

Paul says, "anyone who enters God's rest also rests from his own work" (v. 10). There are two possible ways in which resting from one's own work can be taken, and in any case, they will both be true. (1) We cease from dead works—our own work that is apart from God, independent from God, for our own end—when we understand God's work and enter into God's rest. Dead works is certainly one of the things that we cease from. (2) Then, we cease from our own labor in and of ourselves when we come to understand that it is God who works in us "to will and to act according to his good purpose" (Phil. 2:13b). It is not *we* who are going to take the land. It will be God through His people. It is God who brought us out—apart from anything we do— and it is God who will bring us in. In bringing us in, He will work *in* us and *through* us, but it will be God. It is equally God. It is God in the creation without *any* act on our part, and it is God in providence (upholding, directing, disposing, and governing all of His creatures).[15] We cease from our own work in either and both of these senses when we enter into God's rest, the rest that comes to us in Christ.

---

15. *WCF* 5.1.

Make Every Effort

In case you think that, 'We cease from our own work means we don't work at all,' the next verse says, **"Let us, therefore, make every effort to enter that rest"** (v. 11a). This is the word for labor—*spoudasō*. It has the sense of speeding, making an effort, being diligent and prompt as against drifting and not holding firm; we have to labor, make an effort, exert effort. Sometimes, we find ourselves speeding, listening to a song on the radio, going on the freeway and singing along, and we find ourselves at 85 mph before we know it. That is not what is meant by speeding here. Speeding is like when you have to get to a place fast and you are driving very deliberately, not unconsciously, and pressing it to make it. 'You must get back to Arizona by 6:00 p.m. in order to return the car on time.' And you are trying your best to keep it right below 10 mph above the speed limit and giving it all your attention—that sense of urgency. It is a deliberateness; it is not a careless, out-of-control speeding. Let us speed it, make an effort, and be diligent. There is no casualness, no lackadaisicalness. Let us labor to enter that rest. That means that we have to exert ourselves. The kingdom of God is being preached, and the violent take it by violence.[16] It is like a concert that you are going to, and you want to get a good seat or standing place; you want to get into the heart of a U2 concert, and you will press to get in there. You have to do it, right? That is the diligence with which we must seek the kingdom of God. It is much more than that, but I hope you can relate; initially, start with that and go from there.

We must press in. Let us be diligent, let us labor, and **"make every effort to enter that rest, so that no one will fall by following their example of disobedience"** (v. 11b). It requires steady, earnest pressure, like running a race. That is the kind of pressure; think about a marathon. You have to pace yourself, but you give it all you have, all the way. That is the kind of effort that God is calling us to make to enter His rest. It is not paddling a canoe in a park. It is like salmon swimming up the current; that is a beautiful sight. If salmon can do it, we can do it, right? That is the idea. The Christian life involves effort. **"Let us, therefore, make every effort to enter that rest, so that no one will fall by following their example of disobedience"** (v. 11). We want every salmon to make it all the way up. No one is to fall short. I do not

---

16. *Matthew 11:12* KJV.

know if salmon encourage each other; as far as I can tell, each one is on their own doing their thing. But we are to encourage one another daily. Part of it is that we have to make it together, being careful that no one comes short.

Warning: From Massah to Meribah

We are warned here, "**so that no one will fall by following their example of disobedience**" (v. 11b). We have an example of disobedience in God's deliverance of the Israelites from Egypt. God appeared to the people in ten miraculous judgments in Egypt, God brought them through the Red Sea, God gave them the covenant, God was with them, and He provided for them many times until they came to Kadesh Barnea. And yet they disobeyed. Do you think that if you were there, that would not have happened to you? 'I know better.' No, be careful; we can have God working in our lives in so many ways, and every time we might have this surge of thankfulness and obedience—they rejoiced after coming across the Red Sea. You would think that would really clinch it forever, wouldn't it? Three days later they were without water and complained. Remember, *from Massah to Meribah,* that should be part of our thinking. That is a great image. Massah is where they tested God regarding water. Moses struck the rock, and water came out. And that murmuring and complaining continued all the way through the wilderness until nearly the end of the journey at Meribah, where Moses struck the rock again.

THE WORD OF GOD IS ALIVE AND POWERFUL

From Massah to Meribah. You have to watch the attitude about yourself. That is why it says, "**the word of God . . . judges the thoughts and attitudes of the heart**" (v. 12). Let this Word speak to you and discern. Be careful to deal with it as it shows up, "**so that no one will fall by following their example of disobedience**" (v. 11b)—from Massah to Meribah. We have to search our hearts to see that we do not have this in us. The Word of God is given that we may search our hearts. "**For the word of God is living and active. Sharper than any double-edged sword**" (v. 12a). I need an accurate metaphor for this (since we do not use swords). I do not know about weapons, but we do not use swords anymore. The idea being that it is alive and powerful. Perhaps you might think of the sword of the Jedi warrior, or the sword used in *Crouching Tiger, Hidden Dragon*[17] to stop the bullets. The use of the sword stops them all. We should learn how to stop everything that comes. I warn you, the fiery darts[18] are going to come, and we have to be able to stop them all. We have to go after them, take them out, and conquer.

"**The word of God is living and active**" (v. 12a). The Word of God comes to bring us light and life, and it has power to demolish. The Word penetrates in the darkness, eliminates the darkness once and for all, and it will transform us. It will change us. It is able to be focused directly on what needs attention. It is like a laser going after cancer; I do not think that we have perfected this yet. It is powerful; it is able to destroy. I use the reference to cancerous cells because sin in us is like cancer, and the Word of God is going to cut it out. The cancer is the self-life. "**Sharper than any double-edged sword, it penetrates even to dividing soul and spirit**" (v. 12a). The Word divides what is natural and what is spiritual. When 1 Corinthians 2:14 says, "The man without the Spirit," this is not what it says in Greek; it says the *psuchikos anthropos,* that which is of self and that which is of spirit—that is what is being divided asunder. The Word of God is so sharp that it can do this. We look to Jesus, the Word of God incarnate, and see how it is embodied in Him and in how He lived. The Word will separate between that which is natural and soul-ish in us, of the self, and that which is spiritual of the spirit. These two are interwoven, like a cancer is interwoven. The Word of God is sharp and powerful, and it can discern. It knows how to cut reality at the joints. Sometimes we cut meat right through the bone instead of cutting at the joint. We need to cut reality at the joint and not bludgeon it. We need to discern it properly, and more than that, we need to penetrate. It is not just going between the joints; we are going to go into the bone, and we are going to go into the marrow. You cannot get any further than the marrow.

The Word of God is penetrating the marrow. It gets to the *root* of things, it gets to *root* sin. The marrow is where life comes from; that is where the blood cells are manufactured and protected—in the very marrow of the bone. The Word of God will penetrate there. This is the

---

17. Schamus, James, ed. 2000. *Crouching Tiger, Hidden Dragon.* Directed by Ang Lee.

18. *Ephesians 6:16* KJV.

Word we have to give heed to, lest we have a heart of unbelief in us, lest we have that self-life in us. **"It judges the thoughts and attitudes of the heart"** (v. 12b). Now, to help you see this concretely, think about Saul of Tarsus, who was zealous for God. He was a *natural* man. Think of Nicodemus, a teacher in Israel; he was a natural man. Think of the nation of Israel; how many religious clerics do not have a conviction of the need for Jesus Christ as their Savior because they do not have a conviction of sin and death? Faults and mistakes are not regarded by some as sin, and some regard what should be sin as faults and mistakes. This is a *natural* way of looking at it.

We have to ask if we have a conviction of sin against God. Not just a conviction of fruit sin but a conviction of root sin. Have we confessed this sin and are we ready to root it out? The Word of God will bring us to this. **"It judges the thoughts and attitudes of the heart"** (v. 12b). Our attitude toward dealing with root sin in our lives will be made manifest; the Word will show where our hearts really are. The Word of God is able to do this; it requires this kind of work in order that there be no unbelieving heart in us and no coming short of the promise. We must be cleansed. **"Nothing in all creation is hidden from God's sight. Everything is uncovered and laid bare before the eyes of him to whom we must give account"** (v. 13). God has created us in this way. God knows us thoroughly. The Word of God will search our hearts, and we sing of this searching of God[19] and we thank God for it. God searches our hearts in our trials. He puts the heat on, and then we see what comes to the surface.

I have worked with metal in smelters, and when I smelted, I saw the dross come to the top. You scrape that off, and it is bright and shining. You can see your face reflected in it. But then you let it sit, heat it up again, and more dross emerges. The Word of God is like silver tried in an earthen vessel, purified seven times,[20] and the Word of God will purify us in the same way. It is going to take seven times to do it. A complete number, through many trials, many days, and many ways. What do we do in our trials? As God is preparing us to go and take the Promised Land, we are falling apart left and right, thinking we are not going to make it. What are we going to do? What we tend to do

---

19. *Psalm 139A, The Book of Psalms for Singing.*
20. *Psalm 12:6.*

is get discouraged and say, 'That's it, stop it! I can't take it anymore. Don't talk to me about doctrine; I'm so hurt by all the divisions that it has brought in. Don't talk to me about it anymore!' We reach our limit and we stop. Do we do that? Hasn't the Church done that? 'It hurts so bad.' We miss it; we feel judged, condemned, and so hurt. 'Stop it. I can't take it anymore.' The Word of God will search us. God wants us to be clean, to be pure, and to be holy, so that we might acknowledge His glory and fullness. Only those who are holy can see His glory and fullness, so He makes us holy. It is here that the encouragement comes in about Jesus again.

JESUS, OUR GREAT HIGH PRIEST

When the Word of God searches us and discerns the thoughts and intents of our hearts, we have Jesus, our Great High Priest. Who has suffered in every way as we have, yet without sin. He is able to help us to the uttermost. We come to him to find grace to help in our time of need. Jesus, our Lord, is our priest; He is like the doctor of our soul, and you go back to your doctor to get this cancer taken care of. Jesus is wise, He knows what He is doing, and He has the cure. He is not like earthly doctors who are trying to get a cure and make it work; He has it. We keep coming to Jesus to be cured of our self-life: the spiritual cancer of self-life that is in us.

Jesus does it because He is near to us. He is like us, yet without sin. He *feels* our pain; He is the only one who really does. We are not coming to someone distant and far away, that we have to come fearfully, wondering and with uncertainty. We can come with confidence to Jesus and find grace to help in the time of need, that we might be holy, that we might be a people for His praise. Amen.

5

———

PERFECT THROUGH SUFFERING

Hebrews 5

¹Every high priest is selected from among men and is appointed to represent them in matters related to God, to offer gifts and sacrifices for sins.

²He is able to deal gently with those who are ignorant and are going astray, since he himself is subject to weakness. ³This is why he has to offer sacrifices for his own sins, as well as for the sins of the people.

⁴No one takes this honor upon himself; he must be called by God, just as Aaron was. ⁵So Christ also did not take upon himself the glory of becoming a high priest. But God said to him,

"You are my Son;
today I have become your Father."

⁶And he says in another place,

"You are a priest forever,
in the order of Melchizedek."

⁷During the days of Jesus' life on earth, he offered up prayers and petitions with loud cries and tears to the one who could save him from death, and he was heard because of his reverent submission. ⁸Although he was a son, he learned obedience from what he suffered ⁹and, once made perfect, he became the source of eternal salvation for all who obey him ¹⁰and was designated by God to be high priest in the order of Melchizedek.

¹¹We have much to say about this, but it is hard to explain because you are slow to learn. ¹²In fact, though by this time you ought to be teachers, you need someone to teach you the elementary truths of God's word all over again. You need milk, not solid food! ¹³Anyone who lives on milk, being still an infant, is not acquainted with the teaching about righteousness.

¹⁴But solid food is for the mature, who by constant use have trained themselves to distinguish good from evil.

W E HAVE A GREAT HIGH PRIEST, JESUS, who entered the holiest place of all through His own blood on our behalf for our sin. We have a Great High Priest who is touched by the feelings of our infirmity;[1] He is able to uphold us and bring us close to God. Concerning this high priest, the writer of Hebrews now speaks in terms of the office itself and the one who is in that office. Paul speaks about the office of the high priest: what it is, and that Jesus is the one who is suited, the only one suited, for that office.

THE ORIGIN OF THE OFFICE OF HIGH PRIEST

"**Every high priest is selected from among men**" (v. 1a). The high priest must be a man, for if he is going to represent men, he must be a man. Jesus is man—very man. He is God, and very God, but He came down, He became incarnate, He took upon Himself human nature (and is of the seed of David), and He was, therefore, qualified to be in this office.[2] "**Every high priest is selected from among men and is appointed to represent them**" (v. 1a). There are two aspects here: (1) he is a man, and (2) he is appointed. He is appointed to represent man and to represent us in a particular way. He represents man "**in matters related to God**" (v. 1) in a particular way. The office is representing man, in his sin, to God in His holiness. It is a different office from that of a prophet, who represents God to man. Jesus, who is our high priest, must represent us in our sin to God. In doing so, this priest must "**offer gifts and sacrifices for sins**" (v. 1b). We see a whole theology connected with offering gifts and sacrifices.[3] There is a whole way in which this works for those who have sinned and are being represented in this way. Further, He is able to deal gently with those who are ignorant and going astray. This must be one of the characteristics of the priest: "**He is able to deal gently with those who are ignorant and are**

---

1. *Hebrews 4:15* KJV.

2. Gangadean, *The Westminster Confession,* 121–135; Gangadean, *The Westminster Catechisms,* 159–163

3. Gangadean, *The Westminster Confession,* 111–120.

going astray" (v. 2a). We have to look at both of these concepts. What does 'ignorance' consist of? How does it lead us astray? How must the priest deal with those who are ignorant and going astray? And how is Jesus able to do so?

Appointed from Among Men to Represent Men

The priest is appointed from among men and can deal gently because **"he himself is subject to weakness"** (v. 2b). He feels what they feel; He knows their weakness. **"This is why he has to offer sacrifices for his own sins, as well as for the sins of the people"** (v. 3). There is a difference between the earthly priest and Christ on this point. Christ is without sin. He knows our weakness and what it is to be tempted, but He is without sin. He does not offer sacrifice for Himself, but He offers sacrifice for the sins of the people. Here are the characteristics of the priest again: (1) He must be a human being, not an angel. If He is to represent man, He must be man. (2) He is ordained for man, as against being for God. It is a different direction to bring man to God as opposed to bringing the will of God to man—it is a very different direction. There is a very different reality between changing and growing. Sometimes, we do not recognize this difference sufficiently. He must be ordained, (3) He must offer sacrifices for sin, and (4) He must be able to deal gently. How is it that our Lord Jesus qualifies, and how is it that *only He* qualifies as a high priest? Paul reiterates, **"No one takes this honor upon himself; he must be called by God, just as Aaron was"** (v. 4). If He is going to represent man to God, God has a say in this. (5) God will decide *who* will represent men to Him. He is very much the other party in this. It is not just men choosing this One, but God choosing Him. It says, **"he must be called by God"** (v. 4) so that He is able to do this work and is enabled by God to do it.

Aaron was an example. He was chosen by God to represent men before God. Aaron had weaknesses like other men. In the matter of the golden calf,[4] he was leaning too much to one side. He was too sympathetic, perhaps too gentle with the people, and he accommodated them. He himself was sinful; he did not have a mind clearly set on the holiness of God to represent men in this way. But Aaron was called by

---

4. *Exodus 32.*

God. When his being called by God was questioned and there was an uprising, many notable persons objected.[5] There was Korah, Dathan, Abiram, and many other elders. They said, "The whole community is holy, every one of them, and the LORD is with them" (Num. 16:3). God brought judgment on all of those who dared to come before Him this way and failed to recognize the one He had appointed. God is the one who will select. When the murmuring and fear persisted, God resolved the situation by instructing that the staffs of leaders from each tribe of Israel, each bearing their names, be collected and placed before Him. The next morning, the staffs were brought out. There was one staff, the one with Aaron's name on it, that "budded, blossomed and produced almonds" (Num. 17:8b). A dead stick in the presence of God became alive; not just any dead stick, because there were 12 dead sticks. There was one dead stick, in particular, that God chose and made quite manifest. The one whom God will give this life to, this *resurrection life*—he is the one who is appointed. We see how this points to Jesus Christ our Lord. He was appointed. He was appointed by the fact that He was raised from the dead—to represent men to God. Aaron was called in this way. It says, **"So Christ also did not take upon himself the glory of becoming a high priest"** (v. 5a). He is One who can stand between and mediate. He is One who is holy and can come to God. Yet, He can be with men without being so defiled by men that He cannot come before God. He must be holy.

Very often, when we are around others, we pick up their worries, we accommodate, we do not see, and we get befuddled. We make allowances. We do not know what it is to be merciful and compassionate. We give a little bit here, we give a little bit there, and it adds up. Then, pretty soon, we are not able to represent men to God. We are not holy and cannot come close to God. When Aaron came, he came according to the type and shadow. Only once a year on the Day of Atonement could he come in to the Holy Place (and not without blood) for himself and the people. Christ also did not take upon Himself the glory of becoming a high priest. **"But God said to him, 'You are my Son; today I have become your Father'"** (v. 5b). Again, it says, **"You are a priest forever, in the order of Melchizedek"** (v. 6b).

---

5. *Numbers 16;* Gangadean, "Paper No. 64: Aaron's Rod," in *The Logos Papers*, 341–352.

Christ Was Declared the Son by the Resurrection

The first reference, **"You are my Son; today I have become your Father"** (v. 5b) is from Psalm 2:7 and is explained in Romans 1:4. We are told that Christ was declared to be the Son of God with power by the resurrection from the dead: "who through the Spirit of holiness was declared with power to be the Son of God by his resurrection from the dead: Jesus Christ our Lord." When it says, **"today I have become your Father"** (v. 5b), it is understood to mean that today, God made manifest that Christ is His Son. This was made manifest when God raised Christ from the dead and seated Him at His right hand in the position of authority. This is not to be confused with the eternal sonship of Christ, but it is the *manifestation* of the eternal sonship by the fact that He was raised from the dead, was appointed, and is seated at the right hand of God to carry out the will of God on the earth.

Psalm 110 speaks about both the sonship of Christ and the priesthood of Christ, and these two come together in the Psalm. When David speaks of the sonship, we know from the words of our Lord Jesus that David was speaking of Him: "Sit at my right hand until I make your enemies a footstool for your feet" (Ps. 110:1b). Notice how this connects to the sonship of God: "Sit at my right hand." It is at this point that He is declared to be the Son of God, *manifested* to be the Son of God, by the Spirit of holiness that raised Him from the dead. The Psalm says, "The LORD says to my Lord: 'Sit at my right hand until I make your enemies a footstool for your feet.'" In addition, in Matthew, the Lord Jesus asks:

> "What do you think about the Christ? Whose son is he?" "The son of David," they replied. He said to them, "How is it then that David, speaking by the Spirit, calls him 'Lord'? For he says, 'The Lord said to my Lord: "Sit at my right hand until I put your enemies under your feet."' If then David calls him 'Lord,' how can he be his son?" (Matt. 22:42–45).

There is a brilliance in our Lord Jesus Christ, taking the Scriptures as they are really spoken, drawing the right inferences, and asking: How can it be? David would not call him "my Lord," if he was merely his son. Rather, a father has a place of honor over his son. When he calls him "my Lord," it shows that this One is exalted above him and that

He is more than his son. Therefore, he is not just the son of David; He is also the Son of God.

In this passage that speaks about the priesthood of Melchizedek, we read the words of David, "The LORD says to my Lord" (Ps. 110:1a), and then the exaltation to the right hand:

> The LORD will extend your mighty scepter from Zion; you will rule in the midst of your enemies. Your troops will be willing on your day of battle. Arrayed in holy majesty, from the womb of the dawn you will receive the dew of your youth. The LORD has sworn and will not change his mind [This is a double assurance]: "You are a priest forever, in the order of Melchizedek" (Ps. 110:2–4).

YOU ARE A PRIEST FOREVER, IN THE ORDER OF MELCHIZEDEK

The priesthood of Aaron is not forever in that the priests died, and the very Aaronic priesthood *itself* is not forever; it was ministered in type and shadow. Christ was a Great High Priest, greater than the priesthood of Aaron, but many of those to whom this letter was written were holding on to Aaron's priesthood instead of exalting Christ. When the Lord speaks, we know that it is true forever. The Word of the Lord endures forever.[6] We do not have to say that He "will not change his mind." That should be obvious, but in case you missed it, He is drawing out the inference: "The LORD has sworn and will not change his mind" (Ps. 110:4a). For God, to merely speak is enough. We know by inference that He will not change His mind. God not only spoke, but He *swore*. There is nothing more solemn that men can do than to give their word in an oath. God wanted to make this promise clear without any doubt whatsoever—He swore.

God has sworn a number of times in history. He swore that they would not enter His rest.[7] This was spoken about the generation that came out of Egypt, that would not give heed, that did not understand, that did not set their heart to seek God and turned aside. He swore that they would not have rest. He swore to David that of his seed, one

---

6. *1 Peter 1:25.*

7. *Hebrews 4:3b, 5b.*

would be raised up to sit on his throne forever.[8] He gave the promise to Abraham.[9] God swore a number of times regarding the priesthood. We should see the significance of this, that God *will* bring this about. Adam failed. He was to be prophet, priest, and king. The One that comes in the place of Adam will be prophet, priest, and king. Adam was to live forever, but because of his sin, he could not remain forever. Christ, because of His righteousness, abides forever, and He will be the priest forever after the order of Melchizedek. In connection with this priesthood, notice the overcoming of evil: "The Lord is at your right hand; he will crush kings on the day of his wrath. He will judge the nations, heaping up the dead and crushing the rulers of the whole earth" (Ps. 110:5–6). This priesthood not only delivers the people of God from sin but enables them (by being delivered from sin) to do the work of dominion and put everything into subjection to Christ. This priesthood has both the *removal of sin* and the *enabling people* to do the work God has called them to do. So Christ became a high priest, being a man, and was appointed by God.

Christ Is Able to Deal Gently with Those Who Are Ignorant

"He is able to deal gently with those who are ignorant and are going astray" (v. 2a). We need to understand what it is to be 'ignorant and going astray' and to understand how this gentleness and the ability of Christ to deal with us comes about. We need an analysis of ignorance, an exploration, an anatomy of ignorance, if you will. We will look at this and provide abundant examples; we have no shortage of examples of ignorance. On the other side, there may be a shortage.[10]

We should note that **"He is able to deal gently with those who are ignorant and are going astray"** (v. 2a). He is dealing with them. There are those who are ignorant and going astray with whom He is not dealing. We have to see that those with whom He is dealing gently are the ignorant who have come in repentance to the priest and not

---

8. *Psalm 132:11–12.*

9. *Genesis 15.*

10. This is a reference to the position of voluntarism and the claim that one knowingly does evil or that one can know the truth and and not do it, or rebel against what one knows. For further discussion on the subject, see: Gangadean, "Paper No. 120: Contra Voluntarism," in *The Logos Papers*, 611–647; Gangadean, *Philosophical Foundation*, 32–33.

the ignorant *in general*. What shall we say? 'The ignorant, in general, get treated harshly, but the ignorant who are repentant are dealt with properly?' Certainly we want to know that when we come back to God, God will deal with us gently; He understands. But we have to deal with the ignorant *in general* because there is a sense in which the work of Christ, through His Spirit, extends to those who are His but who are unregenerate and going astray, who have not come to Him yet. This is the whole area of prevenient grace; the grace is now working to bring us back out of sin and death. We do make a distinction between those who are ignorant, repenting, and coming to the Lord, and those who are ignorant and going astray. We nevertheless have to see how this dealing with the ignorant occurs. There is a lot of difficulty here. And because we are ignorant, we do not see how God is dealing with us. We do not understand it, and we might react improperly.

The Source of Ignorance

We are ignorant, fundamentally, because we have not been seeking God. "For he that cometh to God must believe that he is, and that he is a rewarder of them that diligently seek him" (Heb. 11:6b KJV). Both of these must be true. Sometimes, we may say, 'I believe that God exists,' and we may even say (but not with understanding), 'I believe He is the rewarder of those who diligently seek Him.' Yet the way we speak and act often indicates that we do not really believe that He is the rewarder of those who diligently seek Him. We say we do not find much satisfaction in our walk with God. 'I don't feel close to God. Is it going to be like this all the time? A dull, dreary, numb existence.' How does that square with the idea that "he is a rewarder of them that diligently seek him" (Heb. 11:6b KJV)? They cannot both be true. In reference to this, we have recently said, "Let God be true, and every man a liar" (Rom. 3:4a). If we have no joy, it is because we are not diligently seeking Him. There *is* a reward for those who diligently seek Him. We must pay attention to what it is to diligently seek. Transformation and renewal occurs in us because we are seeing God clearer and clearer every day. If we look back over the last 5 or 10 years, and we do not see much change or growth, we need to ask ourselves: Where is the joy of the Christian life? Where is the reward that comes from diligently seeking Him? The Lord says, "You will seek me and find me when you seek me with all your heart" (Jer. 29:13). He speaks about those who seek wisdom as for hidden treasure.[11] Like those whose hand "assaults the flinty rock and lays bare the roots of the mountains. He tunnels through the rock; his eyes see all its treasures. He searches the sources of the rivers and brings hidden things to light" (Job 28:9–11). He says, "You will seek me and find me when you seek me with all your heart."[12] It is not something casual. We might say that if you are going to be casual about it, perhaps you should reconsider whether you should even go this way. It is better to be hot or cold, not lukewarm. We are deceiving ourselves by this.

We are ignorant because we have not sought God, and there are indications in the lack of reward in knowing God. This is not to say we will not have trials, but through *all* trials, we should come out with a greater knowledge of God. We should be able to say with Paul, "I consider that our present sufferings are not worth comparing with the glory that will be revealed in us" (Rom. 8:18). "For our light and momentary troubles are achieving for us an eternal glory that far outweighs them all" (2 Cor. 4:17). Job went through much suffering, but he came to a greater knowledge of God. Then, all of his complaining ceased. We have to continue to seek the Lord. "Jehovah hear thee in the day when trouble He doth send."[13] The Lord sends troubles to see whether we are going to break and go away, turn and become discouraged, or whether we will call upon Him. Call upon Him, seek Him diligently, and learn.

Recently, I spoke about 'slackers' and 'whiners.' Slackers are those who do not pull their weight and let others carry the weight for them. They are those who do not seek God and expect others to come and seek them out for God. We have to take responsibility for this. I ask, is this what it is to deal 'gently'? To bring this out? We look at the priestly ministry. How are we to deal with the ignorant? What kind of ignorance is there, and why is there this ignorance? We need to see this so that we might know how we are to deal with it. We say that ignorance (or the lack of understanding) comes from not seeking God diligently. There is a certain amount of 'seeking after' or 'going after' others who are 'straggling.' You go after stragglers a few times, and if

---

11. *Proverbs 2:4.*

12. *Jeremiah 29:13.*

13. *Psalm 20:1, 20A, The Book of Psalms for Singing.*

they do not begin to seek God diligently, what do you do? We have to say, 'This person is not diligently seeking God.' "For he that cometh to God must believe that he is, and that he is a rewarder of them that diligently seek him" (Heb. 11:6b KJV). It is like saying, 'I don't believe the second part of that. I can believe the first part only, that He is, but not that He is the rewarder of those who diligently seek Him.' These two go together. They cannot be separated.

Culpable Ignorance

We have to go back and say: Where are you in relation to seeking God? When you hear the Word of God preached, how much do you take it to heart? How much do you lightly and thoughtlessly regard it? Ignorance, lack of understanding, are due to not seeking. We see examples of this in Nicodemus and Saul of Tarsus. I have pointed these examples out before, but these are notable because they *lacked knowledge*. Paul, Saul of Tarsus, was persecuting the church. He said he did it *ignorantly* and in unbelief: "Even though I was once a blasphemer and a persecutor and a violent man, I was shown mercy because I acted in ignorance and unbelief" (1 Tim. 1:13). The high priest must deal with those who are ignorant. Jesus dealt with Saul. He said, "Saul, Saul, why do you persecute me?" (Acts 9:4b). Saul was in a rage against our Lord. He was faultless regarding the law.[14] He attended church every Lord's Day. Yet, Paul had not been seeking to understand some basic things. He did not seek—he did not see the meaning of what he practiced. He saw the need for atonement; he probably observed the Day of Atonement (Passover) and all the ordinances, but he did not see how all these pointed to Christ.[15] He did not see the need for Christ. Was he ignorant? Yes. Was he diligent? Yes. Was he diligent in everything that he believed? Yes, he was diligent. But he was not diligently seeking God. It was ignorance—that should cause us to fear. You would not think that Saul of Tarsus was a 'slacker,' but with regard to the knowledge of God, he was. He had not seen what he should have seen.

---

14. *Philippians 3:6.*
15. *Galatians 3:24.*

Nicodemus was a seminary professor. He did not see some important things. He did not understand what he was teaching.[16] He was ignorant. Those who crucified the Lord were ignorant.[17] There is a dimension of ignorance that is called rebellion and treachery. Those are two interesting pieces that go together in Isaiah. Rebellion would be with respect to the outward act, what we may call *fruit sin*, which is acting autonomously in unbelief. Treachery has the added element of explaining the revelation of God away. When God shows that He is God, not only in creation but in history, whether by imposing the curse, the Flood, or the Exodus, in treachery we explain away these providential events in natural ways and do not turn to God. Those who crucified the Lord should have known; they were ignorant. The priest has to deal with this ignorance. When the Israelites went into captivity in Babylon, there was, as we said, rebellion and treachery, fruit sin and root sin. The Lord pronounced judgment would come in that generation. In A.D. 70, it came. "Woe to you, teachers of the law and Pharisees, you hypocrites! . . . You blind guides! You strain out a gnat but swallow a camel" (Matt. 23:23a–24). This is ignorance. The Pharisees had disciples, and yet they did not understand the first truths. They were ignorant, and they made their disciples twice the children of hell.[18] We need to learn to think about ignorance in this way. We are not to think of it in some easy-going, 'Oh, you didn't realize that; let me explain.' It is ignorance because we are not seeking God, and it is deep-seated and widespread. It comes down to this: There is no sense of sin and death. In all of Judaism today, if there were a conviction of sin and death, they would be coming to Christ. In Islam today, there is talk about God and sin and God's justice and mercy, but if there were a conviction of sin, they would have seen a need for Christ. How widespread is this? In all of liberal Christianity and much of traditional Christianity, there is not a conviction of sin and death and the need for Christ. In a lot of popular Christianity, ignorance is present because we are not seeking. The first truth is that of *sin and death,* and with this, the need for Christ and the Church.

---

16. *John 3:10; Acts 3:17.*
17. *Luke 23:34.*
18. *Matthew 23:15.*

God can bring about conviction within us, and we might say that life is empty without God. But if we do not see that emptiness is death and ask ourselves, '*Why* is our life without God?', if we do not see that we have not regarded God and that we have turned our backs on Him, if we do not see sin and we only see death and say that life without God is empty, that is not enough. We must see that we are without God *and* that we are responsible for being without God. We must see what we deserve according to our deeds. We turn our backs on God; we deserve to have God turn His back on us. We deserve for Him to leave us in this state to go on without Him forever. Someone may come to speak about death in this sense, 'Life is empty without God,' and still not come to Christ for forgiveness of sins. They may try to live on that level, 'At least God exists; He has given the moral law, there is order in the world, that makes sense, and that is meaningful.' Look at other things that are meaningful: Why is there physical death? Why is the curse there? Who is this God we should come to? To disregard the curse is ignorance of God. No one who thinks about the curse as the curse can fail to see the need for God. Some persons will turn the curse of death into part of the payment for sin. If we understand what sin is and what death is, we would never view the curse as payment for sin.

We have the witness of the curse all around us. We are being called back, but we are not heeding it. We are not seeking. One of the reasons that this ignorance is so persistent, how we can be in this condition of death and not in some sense be aware of the emptiness of our lives without God, is because to get to sin from death, we have to go through a certain process. We have to see that we have been justifying and explaining away a lot of conditions that would prevent us from seeing. We are justifying ourselves. We think death is natural. 'That's just the way it is. That's the way God made it.' Or we find some other way to say, 'We're okay. We haven't done wrong.' On top of this self-justification, there is self-deception about seeking. Some people are so vehement in speaking about truth, as if they are really concerned about truth. If they are so concerned about truth, how is it that they do not see what is clear? There is self-deception. Sometimes, there is a need to bring correction into someone's life. They get upset if they do not see the need for correction and sin and death remaining in their lives. They will think that they are being personally attacked. The response will be a counter-attack. That is where a lot of *ad hominem* comes from.

There is a popular way in which classes in philosophy and logic speak about *ad hominem:* speaking against the person rather than what the person is saying. Much of *ad hominem* comes about because when correction comes into someone's life, and they do not see the sin and death and the need for correction, they take it personally as if one is speaking against the person, as if it is a personal attack, and then they counter-attack. This is ignorance. This is ignorance of sin and death as it was for Saul of Tarsus, as it was for Nicodemus, as it was for the people of Israel, as for the others we have mentioned—multitudes of people.

The priest must be able to deal gently with those who are ignorant. Jesus prayed, "Father, forgive them, for they know not what they are doing" (Lk. 23:34a). He recognized their ignorance. At one level they knew. They wanted to kill Him; they intended it. But at another level, if they had known the truth, which they should have known, they would not have done it. Even His own disciples failed to know the things that they should have known. Christ reproved them for this after the Resurrection. He rebuked them before His death and resurrection; He strongly rebuked them. Jesus said to Peter, "Get behind me, Satan! You are a stumbling block to me; you do not have in mind the things of God, but the things of men" (Matt. 16:23). The priest must deal gently. This is an example of dealing gently.

Slow to Learn: Obedience Is Learned Through Suffering

There are other times that Jesus had to face ignorance. We look at His example of how He deals with men. One of the ways in which we know that He is able to deal gently is that He learned obedience by the things He suffered. **"Although he was a son, he learned obedience from what he suffered"** (v. 8). That should give us an indication of how the ignorant will learn. If Christ, being so perfect, learned obedience by the things He suffered, we, too, will have to learn by what we suffer. Dealing 'gently' in a casual way with those who are ignorant is not going to allow learning through suffering. Rather, the priest has to point out that this is deep-seated, and we have to suffer to learn. We need to go through this. When more unbelief arises, we come to the priest, confess it, and take responsibility for it. 'I didn't see it, and I should have seen it.' We must acknowledge this sin at the root level and be cleansed of it. And when more comes up, we must go through it. The priest will go over this with a person again and again and again through their lives. He is able to deal gently with those who are ignorant.

We have seen the extent of ignorance, suffering, and its causes. Now, we look at Jesus as the One who is able to do this. **"During the days of Jesus' life on earth, he offered up prayers and petitions with loud cries and tears to the one who could save him"** (v. 7a). Prayers with tears and petitions with loud cries—wouldn't you like to look in on Jesus praying? Do you wonder what the sound of His praying was like and what His loud cries were? Maybe this is one of the reasons why He went off by Himself alone to pray. When was the last time you prayed with a loud cry? When was the last time you prayed with tears? Jesus went through this. He understands what it is to cry out in prayer and to pour out His heart in tears before God. No one can say, 'He didn't suffer; He doesn't know my suffering.' There is only one person who can say, 'I feel your pain,' truly. I know we have rough ideas, but Jesus knows intimately. The suffering Jesus had was a certain exasperation with sin, both before His death and after His death. This is what comes up now, when it says, **"We have much to say about this, but it is hard to explain because you are slow to learn"** (v. 11).

Jesus had to deal with slow learners. How slow? Extremely slow: **"In fact, though by this time you ought to be teachers, you need someone to teach you the elementary truths of God's word all over again"** (v. 12a). Is that slow? When you should be like an adult and a teacher, you have to be taught the milk. Is that slow? When you should be 25, you are acting like a five-year-old. Is that slow? I do not mean a cutesy five-year-old; I mean a dull five-year-old. It is not like 20 going on five; it is like five going on five. Will we get beyond that? *We are slow.* We, all of us in this room, are slow, and Jesus had to put up with that. We cry out when we are under the curse, 'How long, Lord, how long?' He cries out, "how long shall I stay with you? How long shall I put up with you?" (Matt. 17:17); this perverse and wicked generation. Jesus came down from the Mount of Transfiguration and there was a boy frothing at the mouth and his father said, "Lord, have mercy on my son" (Matt. 17:15a). "Jesus replied, 'how long shall I stay with you? How long shall I put up with you?'" (Matt. 17:17).

We get exasperated. Sometimes putting up with sin and dealing with sin is very difficult. After His resurrection from the dead, He spoke to His disciples; these were the guys who went through seminary, a three-year program, and He revoked their degree. "He said to them, 'How foolish you are, and how slow of heart to believe all that the prophets have spoken! Did not the Christ have to suffer these things and then enter his glory?'" (Lk. 24:25–26). Is Jesus able to deal with the ignorant? Does it mean that you do not suffer to learn? Does it mean that He will not rebuke us? Does it mean that He will put the curse on us, drive us out of the Garden to live under the curse, and then intensify the curse through the centuries? Is that not dealing gently? The curse is strong medicine; the priest is not to compromise. If this sin is more than skin-deep, the priest is to say, 'This is a deep uncleanness,' and deal with it. He is not to compromise the way Aaron did. But the priest is to be faithful; you come again, he will deal with it again, you come again, he will deal with it again. You should expect that you have to come many times before this is dealt with. We tend to think we only need to come once. We are to be prepared in our minds that we are slow and we have to come again and again; we have to come numerous times, and the fundamental principle will be coming continually through our lives. We will be crucifying the self-life all of our lives.

Christ learned obedience by what He suffered. He was made perfect through suffering, and therefore, is able to deal gently with those who are ignorant and going astray and with those who come to Him. The fact of our ignorance is seen in this statement: "**though by this time you ought to be teachers, you need someone to teach you the elementary truths of God's word all over again. You need milk, not solid food!**" (v. 12). We are like infants: "**solid food is for the mature, who by constant use have trained themselves to distinguish good from evil**" (v. 14). The original problem is with understanding good and evil as God has defined it and not putting any idolatrous thing in the place of God. Jesus, then, is a man appointed to represent man to God with gifts and sacrifices, and He is able to deal with the ignorant, and we are the ignorant. Thank God for His great mercy to us in Jesus Christ our Lord.

6

HOPE:
AN ANCHOR FOR THE SOUL

Hebrews 6

¹Therefore let us leave the elementary teachings about Christ and go on to maturity, not laying again the foundation of repentance from acts that lead to death, and of faith in God,

²instruction about baptisms, the laying on of hands, the resurrection of the dead, and eternal judgment. ³And God permitting, we will do so.

⁴It is impossible for those who have once been enlightened, who have tasted the heavenly gift, who have shared in the Holy Spirit, ⁵who have tasted the goodness of the word of God and the powers of the coming age, ⁶if they fall away, to be brought back to repentance, because to their loss they are crucifying the Son of God all over again and subjecting him to public disgrace.

⁷Land that drinks in the rain often falling on it and that produces a crop useful to those for whom it is farmed receives the blessing of God. ⁸But land that produces thorns and thistles is worthless and is in danger of being cursed. In the end it will be burned.

⁹Even though we speak like this, dear friends, we are confident of better things in your case—things that accompany salvation. ¹⁰God is not unjust; he will not forget your work and the love you have shown him as you have helped his people and continue to help them. ¹¹We want each of you to show this same diligence to the very end, in order to make your hope sure. ¹²We do not want you to become lazy, but to imitate those who through faith and patience inherit what has been promised.

¹³When God made his promise to Abraham, since there was no one greater for him to swear by, he swore by himself, ¹⁴saying, "I will surely bless

you and give you many descendants." [15]And so after waiting patiently, Abraham received what was promised.

[16]Men swear by someone greater than themselves, and the oath confirms what is said and puts an end to all argument. [17]Because God wanted to make the unchanging nature of his purpose very clear to the heirs of what was promised, he confirmed it with an oath. [18]God did this so that, by two unchangeable things in which it is impossible for God to lie, we who have fled to take hold of the hope offered to us may be greatly encouraged. [19]We have this hope as an anchor for the soul, firm and secure. It enters the inner sanctuary behind the curtain, [20]where Jesus, who went before us, has entered on our behalf. He has become a high priest forever, in the order of Melchizedek.

INTRODUCTION:
Jesus Is Qualified to Be Our High Priest

LET US REMEMBER FROM THE STUDY of Hebrews 5 that Jesus is fitted for being high priest. He is qualified: He is a man, ordained, represents us, and offers sacrifice. He is able to feel in measure with the ignorant and those who are going astray. He was made perfect through suffering. The priest is the one who sanctifies the people of God by teaching the Word of God. The prophet brings the Word of God, but the priest repeatedly applies the Word. It is an intensely personal act. Jesus represents man on behalf of God. He is able to deal with their ignorance. We are taught that we are sanctified through the truth. The Word of God is the truth.[1] God enables the priest to bring this truth again and again and work it in detail into a person's life. "He is able to deal gently with those who are ignorant" (Heb. 5:2a). This does not mean to deal casually but gently. By dealing gently we mean step-by-step and not running ahead. Jesus is able to do so; He knows how to apply the truth subjectively.

Step-by-step is equated with gentleness, not missing any steps, not taking too big a step, but knowing what step is to be taken. It usually involves us being able to go back and not miss a step. If the basic things are not in place, that is what we have to address. The ignorant are so because some *basic* things are not in place. At the end of Hebrews 5, we read, "In fact, though by this time you ought to be teachers, you

---

1. *John 17:17.*

need someone to teach you the elementary truths of God's word all over again" (Heb. 5:12a). We are like those who live on milk, being an *infant* instead of being mature. The one who is mature is the one who is able to take in the deeper truths of God. The elementary truths are not the deeper truths. It may appear to us as 'deeper' relative to where we are. Perhaps this is so. But these elementary truths that are mentioned here, the foundational truths, should be in the life of every Christian.

The Nature of Our Ignorance

Paul is able to take in the deeper truths concerning the priesthood of Christ, Melchizedek, and the Melchizedekian priesthood. This is in contrast to the Hebrews at the time, who were tempted to be zealous for the law, to keep to the law, to hold on to the practices that they have held, and not see this new and living way of the new covenant that is being opened up. They need greater maturity. If the elementary things were in place, they would be able to go on to the deeper truths. If they understood sin and death, they would see the need for Jesus Christ, for His death on the cross. The nation missed this. Those who came to Christ out of the nation of Israel came to see this. Remember, Nicodemus had not seen it. Paul had not seen it. The elementary things were not in place. But Paul did come to see it, and he was able to teach it—there is hope. Those who become mature become so by virtue of training, and this training is constant. It says, "But solid food is for the mature, who by constant use have trained themselves to distinguish good from evil" (Heb. 5:14). Training cannot be sporadic. Some of us try to go to the fitness center at least three times a week, and sometimes we go once a week. That is not the way to get trained. You cannot train for any team or athletic event in that way; it has to be *constant;* it has to be *training.* You have to do it again and again. What training is this? It is training in the fundamentals.[2] It is always that way. It is always the fundamentals.

---

2. Gangadean, "Paper No. 43: My Last Lecture," in *The Logos Papers,* 237–253.

THE BASICS:
Elementary Truths—*Stoicheia*

What are the fundamentals? Good and evil. This is pretty fundamental. It does not get any more fundamental than this. This is exactly what the Word of God says. They "have trained themselves to distinguish good from evil" (Heb. 5:1b). It involves understanding good and evil and avoiding misunderstanding. In all the conversations that we have with one another, all the circumstances, and all the trials that we have, we are being trained to distinguish good and evil. When we are upset, when we suffer loss, when we encounter trials of our faith, the Scripture says: Count the trying of our faith of greater worth than gold, which perishes even though refined by fire.[3] Sometimes, we particularly notice financial loss. Even here, we must train ourselves to rethink and say: 'These are the things the Lord has wanted me to learn.' We have to go into extended training if we are going to become mature in distinguishing good and evil. This is the area of ignorance that the priest must teach and he must guide people through this training process. He said, "We have much to say about this"—about the Melchizedekian priesthood, which is a lasting priesthood forever and therefore, better, than the Aaronic priesthood—"but it is hard to explain because you are slow to learn" (Heb. 5:11). We saw that Jesus rebuked His disciples after three years of full-time training. "He said to them, 'How foolish you are, and how slow of heart to believe all that the prophets have spoken! Did not the Christ have to suffer these things and then enter his glory?'" (Lk. 24:25–26). What were the things missing?

We have recently spent eight weeks going over foundation.[4] As we go through this, we will not go into all those details, but we will review it and try to understand it. The question is: What are these elementary things? Elsewhere it is called the *stoicheia*: the elements out of which everything else is made. This word is used to refer to elements, principles, or rudiments—the building blocks for everything. It is also called the foundation on which everything rests. Here, I will refer to them as *the basics*.

---

3. *1 Peter 1:7.*

4. A sermon series on "The Foundation (Hebrews 5:12–6:2)" was given at the founding of Westminster Fellowship Church (2001), which has been added as the second part of this book.

What are the basics? There is sin and death, repentance and faith, **"instruction about baptisms, the laying on of hands, the resurrection of the dead, and eternal judgment"** (v. 2). We believe this contains a whole system of theology.[5] Sometimes, we think, 'this might be too much' or 'this might be too little' for a whole system of theology. We see that many systems of theology do not have this much in place. If asked about these doctrines, we may say, 'Oh, yes, I believe in sin and death. I believe in these things.' Then we may ask a bit further, 'What does that mean? Can you elaborate? Can you tell me about sin and death?'

Sin and Death

Sin is a seven-layered cake. It is not just one thing; there are many levels.[6] I would like to identify some of the basic levels for us.

First, there is *autonomy* in sin. It says, **"not laying again the foundation of repentance from acts that lead to death"** (v. 1). Acts that lead to death arise from sin. These are the acts, or the fruit (not to speak of the root sin which is certainly there), that lead to death. We should understand God is constantly calling us away from sin in this deeper sense. The *self-life* is expressed in *autonomy*: We put ourselves in the place of God; we raise ourselves up to be like God. We are self-centered. We love ourselves more than God. It is autonomy in the self-life, in that we believe we are the determiners of good and evil. There is a form of idolatry here, the idolatry of self, a lack of the fear of God. This is one aspect.

Second, sin is understood as *root sin*: not seeking God, not understanding, and not doing what is right.[7] These three encompass the whole aspect of the heart. We need to see how our failing to understand is because we have not sought the Lord. We speak about it as root sin, as unbelief, and not simply an outward act.

Third, sin is *idolatry*. We say, 'there is no God,' or we may have a misconception of God and put this in the place of God. Right now, the struggle with Islam has come more to the fore, and Islam claims to

---

5. Surrendra Gangadean, *Theological Foundation: A Critical Analysis of Christian Belief* (Phoenix: Logos Papers Press, forthcoming).

6. Gangadean, *The Westminster Confession*, 99–110, 369–376; Gangadean, *The Biblical Worldview*, 37–54, 177–195.

7. *Romans 3:10–12.*

believe in God but does not believe in Christ.[8] Many have claimed to believe in God but do not believe in Christ. Deists have, and many who have been brought up in Christian homes say they believe in God, but they do not see the place for Christ. This is a misconception of God, and is root unbelief. What kind of God is it we believe in?

Fourth, sin is understood in an *ontological* sense. Sin is what is contrary to our nature, and specifically, it is contrary to reason. It is a shutting of our eyes to avoid what is clear. It is a *neglect* in not seeking. It is an *avoiding* when it is brought to one's attention. It is a *resistance* with objections of many kinds. Then, it is a *denial*—an outright, flat denial of reason, even to the point of mocking reason in various acute ways. It could be a postmodernist form of mocking or the deliberate statement of mystics who say, "Those caught in the meshes of intellect are said to be worse than dogs. They are like elephants stuck in deep mud."[9] It could be the Zen Buddhist who says we must have the death of the intellect in order to achieve ultimate enlightenment.[10] It could be those who are trichotomous and say there is a realm of our being (spirit) that can directly commune with God above and apart from our understanding. It could be the mystical, new age, experience-oriented, spiritual persons who do not understand the vitality of the physical creation. By spiritual, we mean it does not have to do with the body. There are many ways in which we neglect and deny reason.

Fifth, sin is *treachery;* I began to use this word recently. There is the complication of self-deception and self-justification in 'treacherousness.' We try to explain something, then someone tries to twist it, turn it, and make it work in some other way to avoid it. They think they are okay and try to influence others to justify themselves. This, too, is sin and must be repented of.

Sixth, sin is the outward act of *rebellion* against what God commands. God said to go in and take the land, and they said, 'No.' God says, 'Go to church, have personal devotions, teach your children in the way they should go, read your Bible diligently.' And we say, 'No!'

---

8. Gangadean, "Paper No. 91: Christianity and Islam," in *The Logos Papers*, 479–484; Gangadean, *The Westminster Confession*, 21–27, 37–41, 67–69, 129–130, 236–238.

9. Chandradhar Sharma, *A Critical Survey of Indian Philosophy* (Delhi: Motilal Banarsidass Publishers, 1962), 89.

10. Wing-Tsit Chan, *A Source Book in Chinese Philosophy* (Princeton: Princeton University Press, 1963), 425–449.

Rebellion, when it comes to an explicit level, is an explicit act. Treachery is at the more basic root level, and rebellion is at the fruit level. Then sin descends from there and spirals downward into gross immorality.

Seventh, sin is *gross immorality*. We tend to pick up on sin as gross immorality (sins of the flesh), but this is not at all the whole story behind sin. Many are not caught in gross immorality. Sometimes, for some of us, it has to come to this; it has to slap us in the face in order for us to see it. Sin, as we said, is a seven-layered cake. I resist that metaphor because a cake is something nice, but if we look at sin as something that is sweet in the mouth but really poisonous, perhaps we can get the metaphor to work. Sin is pleasurable for a season. In any case, the point is that there are many dimensions to sin. It is usually at the basic level that we come to a true conviction of sin. What is our notion of sin? Is this in place, or is this 'way too deep'? Is this deep, or is this basic? We need to go on to maturity. This is being said of the basics. We must have an understanding of sin. There are many people who do not have an understanding of sin and death. Everyone who is not a believer fails to understand sin and death. Many who are believers are still struggling to understand it. Let us get the foundational pieces laid.

We speak about death as the death of the soul, in the aspects of the soul (meaninglessness, boredom, and guilt), and death in relationships. What happens is that we experience death, but we do not identify it as death. We interpret it away, 'Tis but a scratch, just a flesh wound, not death, not quite dead.' We minimize, explain away, and often do it in acute, sophisticated, or ironic ways. We try to avoid death by speaking about it in ways that minimize it. As soon as we encounter death as death: 'This is serious, this is the big one, there is no escape, I'm not getting out of this alive,' and see that it is due to sin—understood in this way, *then* we see our need for Jesus Christ. *Then* we repent.

Repentance and Faith

The second part of this foundation is repentance and faith. We are no longer making excuses. We are no longer giving explanations. We acknowledge our attempt to blame others for what we have done. We acknowledge our attempt to say, 'We are okay; I am a good person. I have a few faults, but I am basically a good person, there are a lot of people like me.' We see that we have to go beyond this. We cannot make excuses. We acknowledge it and begin with an awareness of the fear of the Lord in understanding sin and death. We repent of our sin as an act against God, which is something very personal. Turning our backs to God to say 'I want my way' is like the saying, 'It's my way or the highway.' This is the motto of sinners. Remember Frank Sinatra singing, "I did it my way."[11] You know that old crooner, that old charmer, "My way." 'And if it's not my way, then it's the highway. Tell God, take a hike.' This is the true nature of sin. It is not the way of the cross. Jesus said, "yet not my will, but yours be done" (Lk. 22:42b).

In repentance and faith, there is a true repentance based on conviction of sin and death, and there is faith in God. We spoke about faith in God, and we spoke about this as involving evidence, support, understanding the visible as revealing the invisible, and the manifest as revealing the unmanifest. It involves understanding, and there is content to this faith: *He is*. There is further content in saying that "he rewards those who earnestly seek him" (Heb 11:6b).[12] Notice that in this matter of faith, all three aspects of philosophy are involved: epistemology (of seeing and understanding), metaphysics (what is understood is the nature of reality, that God is the Creator), and ethics (He is the rewarder of those who diligently seek Him—the good). Hebrews 11 is a summary for understanding faith and its content. Do we have this in place? If not, we cannot go on to maturity; we cannot become fruitful.

Baptism

Baptism signifies regeneration and union with Christ. Baptism assumes the *ordo salutis*[13] and that we are moved from Adam's representation to Christ's. Baptism further entails our union with the Holy Spirit, who has come to dwell in us and enables us to do the work Christ called us to do. He brings us to understanding; He illumines our minds. He brings us to understand the truths that are relevant for us to do our work and to take every thought captive.[14] All the background that we bring to our lives as Christians has to be unpacked. When we go out

---

11. Frank Sinatra, *My Way*. Edited by Paul Anka. 1969.

12. Gangadean, *The Biblical Worldview*, 3–20.

13. Gangadean, *The Westminster Confession*, 143–169; Gangadean, *The Westminster Catechisms*, 191–203.

14. *2 Corinthians 10:5*.

and witness to a new person or a group of persons, we come in contact with their historical values, worldviews, and whole systems of thought. The Holy Spirit has enabled the Church to take these captive through the centuries, and we benefit from this work.

In addition, every Christian should be prepared with this basic truth: there is a baptism by fire. We *must* suffer. We have been expelled from the Garden. We must live under the curse. We do have sin. We must go through fiery trials which are to try us.[15] This must be part of our thinking. It must be a daily taking up of the cross and following our Lord Jesus.[16]

The Scriptures speak of three baptisms. Union with Christ, union with the Holy Spirit, and the baptism by fire. These are basics that should be in place. These are not the deep truths. They are deep in that they are foundational, but they are not the deep truths. They should be where we start, not where we end.

Resurrection of the Dead

The teaching in Scripture about eschatology is that when all things have been subdued to Christ, then the resurrection of the dead takes place.[17] It also speaks about what the hope is. The hope is not the beatific vision (going to be with God in heaven apart from our body);[18] it is the resurrection of our bodies, living on the earth, which is filled with the knowledge of God as the waters cover the sea.[19] Eschatology has a *what* and a *when*, and the resurrection of the dead captures both of those. Are these in place? These are the basics needed to go on to maturity. The priest must do this work, and Christ, through His body, will do this work.

---

15. *1 Peter 4:12–14.*

16. *Matthew 16:24.*

17. *1 Corinthians 15:28–29.*

18. Gangadean, *On Natural and Revealed Theology*, 9–39; Gangadean, "Paper No. 106: The Good and Heaven," 547–556; "Paper No. 116: The Knowledge of God vs. The Hope of Heaven," in *The Logos Papers*, 597–598; Gangadean, *Philosophical Foundation*, 40–41, 71–73.

19. *Isaiah 11:9.*

Eternal Judgment

Eternal judgment speaks of the infinite justice and goodness of God. The eternal justice and goodness of God are manifest in the judgment. It is something inherent. Here, we see a full manifestation of sin and death, and the good and life, in contrast to the popular views of heaven and hell. Here, we speak about the works that we are to do, and being engaged in works that will last over and against what will be burned up. We are to build upon the foundation: "If any man builds on this foundation using gold, silver, costly stones, wood, hay or straw, his work will be shown for what it is, because the Day will bring it to light. It will be revealed with fire, and the fire will test the quality of each man's work" (1 Cor. 3:12–13). We will not be filled with our own ways or ideas; instead, we will subject ourselves to training to discern good and evil, to become mature and be faithful and fruitful servants in the kingdom of God.

The priest deals gently and does not allow any steps to be skipped. He knows how to speak objective truths, in order, and he knows how to bring those truths subjectively, in order, to a particular person. Christ does this. He is able to deal gently with those who are ignorant and those who are going astray. So we see something of the work that is to be done and where that work must begin.

Paul says, "**And God permitting, we will do so**" (v. 3). That is, we will leave, not in the sense of abandonment, but leave the elementary truths about Christ and go on, the way you leave a foundation and go on to build on it. You do not abandon it; you build on it. You are not forever digging the foundation and trying to get it in place. You get it set, and you go on. Yesterday, I was involved in pouring concrete. We examined the footing and foundation that was done earlier. It is a good footing, very solid, and all the rebar is in there. But I am anxious to go on from there. I admire the foundation; I like it. I could get up and go outside and look at it, just stand near it and get the feel of it. I like seeing that work done. But I am not satisfied with just the foundation. I want to see the building go up. I want to see the walls go up. I want to see the siding go on and the roofing go on. Then I want to see it finished and painted, and then have the leisurely time to sit around with others late into the night on a rocking chair and discuss theology. The foundation must be in place. We have to go on from the foundation.

WARNING:
Those Once Enlightened

Regarding those to whom Paul is speaking, he is asking, inquiring, and wondering whether they are in Christ, and yet he reaffirms that they are in Christ. He says:

> **It is impossible for those who have once been enlightened, who have tasted the heavenly gift, who have shared in the Holy Spirit, who have tasted the goodness of the word of God and the powers of the coming age, if they fall away, to be brought back to repentance** (vv. 4–6a).

To whom does this apply? A lot of people get very shaky at this point and say, 'That's me, isn't it? I know it's me. He's speaking to me. I've fallen away. It's impossible for me to be renewed. I'm dead. It's over, might as well forget it.' Some people fear and tremble in this way.

The context could help us to understand. It says, **"if they fall away, to be brought back to repentance, because to their loss they are crucifying the Son of God all over again and subjecting him to public disgrace"** (v. 6). This involves a profession of faith that is public and then a turning back from it which involves disgrace for our Lord as in the case of a divorce. When one person divorces, they give the impression that 'this person was inadequate, I didn't care for them, I didn't like them, it wasn't a happy situation at all.' You disgrace publicly the person from whom you turn away because you took the public mark on you, in this case, of being a Christian. In addition to that, you are crucifying Christ all over in this rejection.

Concerning Christ, it is crucifying Him, rejecting Him from one's life; instead of rejecting sin, we reject Christ. As far as a witness is concerned, it is subjecting Him to public disgrace. You professed to be a Christian and you rejected Christ. When Christians, or those who profess faith, those who had some connection to the covenant, turn away, it is impossible to renew them. This is being stated here as a warning. Let us not take it for granted. Let us fear the Lord, watch, and see whether we are honoring God and desiring Him. It is intended here as a warning that people can be outwardly connected but are not inwardly connected because they do not diligently seek God. When the test comes, they turn away. He explains that it is impossible for people who turn away to be renewed because they have gone to a deeper level of denying the truth. This is particularly about those who have the truth of the new covenant; they have tasted the goodness of the Word of God and the powers of the coming age to renew them. They think they know, and they have only known it outwardly. These are the hardest people to reach. If this has really happened, it says it is impossible to renew them.

CONFIDENT OF BETTER THINGS

This is a warning, and we are to take heed. Paul does speak encouraging words. He speaks in terms of bearing fruit: "**Land that drinks in the rain often falling on it and that produces a crop useful to those for whom it is farmed receives the blessing of God**" (v. 7). There is fruit in a person's life, and it is manifest in deeds. On the other hand, "**land that produces thorns and thistles is worthless and is in danger of being cursed. In the end it will be burned**" (v. 8). Has there been fruit in your life? Or has your Christian experience been one painful experience for you and others and not profitable? Paul immediately goes on to distinguish between blessing and the curse. He says, "**Even though we speak like this, dear friends, we are confident of better things in your case—things that accompany salvation**" (v. 9). Why is he thinking that there are better things? Why is he confident of better things in their case, things that accompany salvation? For those who believe and are shaken in trials, the work of God is there; it is not just thorns and thistles. There has been fruit in some, and there are others where there is no fruit; by their fruit you shall know them.[20]

It says, "**God is not unjust; he will not forget your work and the love you have shown him as you have helped his people and continue to help them**" (v. 10). This involves being in fellowship with the people of God, serving them, and encouraging them. This is one of the vows we take: "Do you recognize your responsibility to work with others in the Church and do you promise to support and encourage them in their service to the Lord?"[21] We can support and encourage in many ways, sometimes by giving labor, sometimes giving money, sometimes giving

20. *Matthew 7:16.*

21. Gangadean, *The Westminster Catechisms*, 355–356.

comfort, encouragement, hospitality, and giving to others in various ways. There is fruit when this is the case, and we should be encouraged in God. God is not unjust to forget your work and the love you have shown. You may not receive back certain things that you would like to. Sometimes, we like to get as we give. We like to get love the way we give love. But there are a number of ways in which this comes back to us. Ultimately, God gives to us in the way that we need. We have to learn to submit to God and learn of His ways. God is not unjust to forget that, but He wants believers to be diligent about this matter.

There is a hope that is sure. He says, **"We want each of you to show this same diligence to the very end, in order to make your hope sure"** (v. 11). What does "diligence to the very end" mean? In other words, you help the people of God, you continue to help them, do not give up now, keep going. It has been 20 years, it has been 30 years. You know what? You have about 10, 15, 20 more years to go. Keep going, as you have gone, *to the very end,* until you cross the finish line. Do not collapse 500 yards from the end of the line—continue. If your leg is out of joint, limp, crawl, whatever you can do, continue to the very end. Continue your faithfulness in the worship of God. Continue your faithfulness in prayer. Continue your faithfulness in service. This is land that produces fruit. Continue your hospitality. Continue caring for people. Do not give up; be diligent. When you encounter sin in your own life and in the world, it is a temptation for your love to grow cold. Overcome it by looking to God and keeping your eyes on Jesus.[22] Your love may grow wiser, but it is not to grow colder. You may not do some of the things that were not based on wisdom, but you are to keep going on to the very end. I think of *Lawrence of Arabia*[23] and his feat; they thought it could not be done. He crossed the desert with a band of people. Sometimes it is like that. Paul says, as he came near to the end of his life, "I have fought the good fight, I have finished the race, I have kept the faith" (2 Tim. 4:7). He did not turn aside. Sometimes, you might think it would be doing a great deal just to keep the faith, to not renounce it, and to finish what God has given. Be diligent, and by doing so, your hope will be sure. If you do not continue in the service of God, your hope will be shaken. *Your* hope will

---

22. *Hebrews 12:2.*

23. Robert Bolt, ed. *Lawrence of Arabia.* Directed by David Lean. 1962.

be shaken, subjectively, as far as you know, not the certainty of hope objectively; that hope is certain. To this, Paul speaks next. Not only does he want people to be certain subjectively, he wants them to know objectively. There are two aspects of the truth: the objective aspect and the subjective aspect.

THE HOPE TO ABRAHAM IS THE SAME OBJECTIVELY FOR ALL BELIEVERS

Paul now addresses the objective aspect: "**When God made his promise to Abraham, since there was no one greater for him to swear by, he swore by himself, saying, 'I will surely bless you and give you many descendants'**" (vv. 13–14). God swore. This is right after Abraham offered up his son Isaac. Think about how long Abraham waited for Isaac. After Isaac was born and became something of a young man, Abraham was asked to take Isaac and offer him as the sacrifice.[24] The spot that is supposed to be the Temple Mount, the spot that is so disputed, the spot where the Muslims built The Dome of the Rock, one of the greatest mosques in the world—there Abraham offered up his son. There God met with Abraham. On the mount of God, it will be seen. God said, "I swear by myself, declares the LORD, that because you have done this and have not withheld your son, your only son, I will surely bless you and make your descendants as numerous as the stars in the sky and as the sand on the seashore" (Gen. 22:16–17a). This is more than his physical descendants. These were spiritual descendants that Abraham would have. Hopefully, all the physical descendants will be spiritual descendants as well. This has not always been the case, but He said there will surely be descendants like the stars in the sky. God swore on oath; He swore by Himself; there was nothing higher to swear by. "I will surely bless you and make your descendants as numerous as the stars in the sky and as the sand on the seashore" (Gen. 22:17a). These descendants will possess the gates of their enemies. They will be victorious.

Paul goes further and explains how the hope is made sure: As we give diligence in continuing to obey and serve the Lord, the same objective hope is made sure for us. He explains how this is so on the level of human

---

24. *Genesis 22:1–2.*

relations: "**Men swear by someone greater than themselves, and the oath confirms what is said and puts an end to all argument**" (v. 16). That is it; the oath settles it. Swearing an oath settles the matter. There is no longer a place to argue about anything. In that sense, it is clear. Because God wanted to make the unchanging nature of His purpose very clear. Think about these words together: "**the *unchanging nature of His purpose very clear.***"[25] If some things are clear, some things are very clear. The unchanging nature of His purpose is *very clear* because an oath is added to it. "**Because God wanted to make the unchanging nature of his purpose very clear to the heirs of what was promised, he confirmed it with an oath**" (v. 17). That is the difference between clear and very clear. Is that very clear to you? God did this so that it is clear by two unchangeable things: the nature of His purpose and His oath. The very nature of the purpose of God is unchangeable. It is grounded in His nature. He will glorify Himself. When He permits evil, He will purpose to order it to His own glory,[26] and good will overcome evil. The good will be not just the manifestation of the glory of God but the knowledge of the glory of God. This is His purpose; we can know this purpose. Then God gave it with an oath. He will give Abraham many descendants. He said there are two unchangeable things: the nature of the promise itself in God and what God said. "**God did this so that, by two unchangeable things in which it is impossible for God to lie, we who have fled to take hold of the hope offered to us may be greatly encouraged**" (v. 18). It cannot be any clearer or truer than this.

THE HOPE IS AN ANCHOR FOR THE SOUL

The matter is settled. It is fixed; whatever you do with the 'intermediate state,' it is settled. If we see that it is settled, then we will persevere. "**We have this hope as an anchor for the soul, firm and secure. It enters the inner sanctuary behind the curtain**" (v. 19). An anchor is sometimes used as a symbol of hope. In this, we see the whole emphasis on 'take hold of the hope, don't let it go, hold on to it, don't drift, hold steadfast, persevere, it will happen, it is sure.' You give the diligence so that it may be sure to you subjectively, so that you persevere to the

---

25. Emphasis added.
26. *WCF* 6.1.

end. "**We have this hope as an anchor for the soul, firm and secure. It enters the inner sanctuary behind the curtain, where Jesus, who went before us, has entered on our behalf**" (vv. 19–20a). Jesus is the guarantee of this hope. He will accomplish it. "**He has become a high priest forever, in the order of Melchizedek**" (v. 20b). Jesus is the One who will make us holy. He is the One who will sanctify through the truth by sending His Holy Spirit to accomplish this purpose. He is the One who will be the heir of all things, by whom God will be glorified. He is the Son of God, the Word of God, Christ Jesus, God of very God, man of very man, our Savior. Amen.

7

CHRIST:
A PRIEST FOREVER

Hebrews 7

¹This Melchizedek was king of Salem and priest of God Most High. He met Abraham returning from the defeat of the kings and blessed him, ²and Abraham gave him a tenth of everything. First, his name means "king of righteousness"; then also, "king of Salem" means "king of peace." ³Without father or mother, without genealogy, without beginning of days or end of life, like the Son of God he remains a priest forever.

⁴Just think how great he was: Even the patriarch Abraham gave him a tenth of the plunder! ⁵Now the law requires the descendants of Levi who become priests to collect a tenth from the people—that is, their brothers—even though their brothers are descended from Abraham. ⁶This man, however, did not trace his descent from Levi, yet he collected a tenth from Abraham and blessed him who had the promises. ⁷And without doubt the lesser person is blessed by the greater. ⁸In the one case, the tenth is collected by men who die; but in the other case, by him who is declared to be living. ⁹One might even say that Levi, who collects the tenth, paid the tenth through Abraham, ¹⁰because when Melchizedek met Abraham, Levi was still in the body of his ancestor.

¹¹If perfection could have been attained through the Levitical priesthood (for on the basis of it the law was given to the people), why was there still need for another priest to come—one in the order of Melchizedek, not in the order of Aaron? ¹²For when there is a change of the priesthood, there must also be a change of the law. ¹³He of whom these things are said belonged to a different tribe, and no one from that tribe has ever served at the altar. ¹⁴For it is clear that our Lord descended from Judah, and in regard to that tribe Moses said nothing about priests. ¹⁵And what we have

said is even more clear if another priest like Melchizedek appears, [16]one who has become a priest not on the basis of a regulation as to his ancestry but on the basis of the power of an indestructible life. [17]For it is declared:

"You are a priest forever,
   in the order of Melchizedek."

[18]The former regulation is set aside because it was weak and useless [19](for the law made nothing perfect), and a better hope is introduced, by which we draw near to God.

[20]And it was not without an oath! Others became priests without any oath, [21]but he became a priest with an oath when God said to him:

"The Lord has sworn
   and will not change his mind:
'You are a priest forever.'"

[22]Because of this oath, Jesus has become the guarantee of a better covenant.

[23]Now there have been many of those priests, since death prevented them from continuing in office; [24]but because Jesus lives forever, he has a permanent priesthood. [25]Therefore he is able to save completely those who come to God through him, because he always lives to intercede for them.

[26]Such a high priest meets our need—one who is holy, blameless, pure, set apart from sinners, exalted above the heavens. [27]Unlike the other high priests, he does not need to offer sacrifices day after day, first for his own sins, and then for the sins of the people. He sacrificed for their sins once for all when he offered himself. [28]For the law appoints as high priests men who are weak; but the oath, which came after the law, appointed the Son, who has been made perfect forever.

INTRODUCTION:
Tradition versus Fullness in Christ

B Y WAY OF INTRODUCTION TO THIS SECTION of the book of Hebrews, there is an ongoing conflict that all of us as human beings have in the way in which we look for comfort. Some of us look to our tradition for comfort; we look to our past and what has been attained. Some look to the future for comfort, not the past, and to the fullness that there is in Christ Jesus our Lord. There is a very striking difference between the two. It is true, is it not, that we seek comfort in our tradition? There is a certain peace; things are settled, we know our way around, and we can be satisfied with our tradition.

We can be thankful for the good things that have been in our tradition by the grace of God, but that has not yet gotten us to the fullness that is in Christ. Think about what we have been seeing throughout this entire book about the fullness in Jesus Christ: He is the heir of all things, He is higher than all, all things are made subject to Him, and the hope that is ours in Him is that we are reaching for this fullness. Can we have comfort in this hope? It is very truncated, ultimately stifling, to have simply the past, the tradition, to look to and fall back on. Many of us go so far, and then we settle back. This is an ongoing, underlying theme in this book: the past or the future, and our comfort. Are we looking to what we have attained or to what there is ahead of us? Our true comfort is in the fullness in Jesus Christ our Lord, and there is more to come.

This book and its theme are addressed to the Hebrews, who had the very revelation of God. That is, it is addressed to the Christians of Jewish descent. They had God's very revelation, which was rich and real. If we use the word *tradition* in the very best sense of the term, that would be a tradition worth holding to. The main purpose of this book is *to exhort those believers to continue in Christ and to reach for the fullness that there is in Christ.* The Hebrews were very zealous for the law and the traditions and festivals handed down. Even today, many Hebrew Christians maintain a certain zealousness for that way. We wonder to what extent they see the fullness in Christ and that this is a blessing for all peoples and all the nations of the earth are to be gathered. It is not in terms of the old covenant that we are to be gathered. The very holding on to the old covenant reflects a deficiency in their understanding of the hope.

Paul had it right when he spoke in the Book of Ephesians about the fullness that is in Jesus Christ; he says Jesus is to fill the whole universe[1]—He is to fill everything in every way.[2] He spoke about no division remaining and being one body.[3] Paul spoke about the unity of the Spirit, coming to the unity of the faith, and attaining the whole measure of the stature of Christ.[4] The whole measure, and not something

---

1. *Ephesians 4:10.*

2. *Ephesians 1:23.*

3. *Ephesians 4:1–6.*

4. *Ephesians 4:11–13* KJV.

coming short of it. This book is written in the context of the particulars that they were holding on to, specifically the priesthood and what goes with it. Here, it says, **"for on the basis of it the law was given to the people"** (v. 11). This is not just the Ten Commandments (which is permanent), but the ceremonial law and the civil law.[5] Particularly, the ceremonial law was given on this basis, by which they were to deal with sin and then come into the fullness in Christ. Now, Paul is speaking about the priesthood and that there is a change intended in the priesthood, which is to go further. This is a big matter for the Hebrew Christians who, for centuries and centuries, were living by this Word of God that spoke about the priesthood and they expected that the temple would last forever. Paul is instructing them to go further in Christ and to strive for what is better.

CHRIST'S PRIESTHOOD IS BETTER THAN THE LEVITICAL PRIESTHOOD

The basic theme is that in Christ is fullness, and Christ is better than all else that has come before. We are to fix our thoughts on Jesus and continue in Him. Paul particularly applies this to the priesthood after the order of Melchizedek. In all the Scripture, there are just two passages that speak of Melchizedek prior to Paul. It appears so quickly that if you blink, you miss it. Yet so much is made of it. This is reasoning from Scripture *par excellence.* It is remarkable the way Paul draws all sorts of inferences from just these two mentions and also what is not mentioned in every detail. It says in Hebrews 4:3, "So I declared on oath in my anger, 'They shall never enter my rest.'" Similar reasoning is going on here. It will do you well to try to take notes on this and notice carefully how he reasons to move us from our place of comfort in tradition—looking to the past—to the hope that there is in the future. Paul reasons to move us to the comfort that is in hope rather than the comfort that is in tradition; the comfort that there is in the future rather than the comfort that there is in the past.

The two passages that speak of Melchizedek are in Genesis 14 and Psalm 110. Abraham had just returned from the slaughter of the kings

---

5. Gangadean, *The Westminster Confession,* 207–221; Gangadean, *The Westminster Catechisms,* 215–267.

that had come in to raid that area and had taken off with a lot of the people in Sodom, including Lot. Abraham had gone out with some others he was associated with, and they had defeated these kings and brought back those who had been taken captive. It is at this time that Melchizedek came out to meet Abraham. It is interesting to note that he came out to meet Abraham.

> After Abram returned from defeating Kedorlaomer and the kings allied with him, the king of Sodom came out to meet him in the Valley of Shaveh (that is, the King's Valley). Then Melchizedek king of Salem brought out bread and wine. He was priest of God Most High, and he blessed Abram, saying, "Blessed be Abram by God Most High, Creator of heaven and earth. And blessed be God Most High, who delivered your enemies into your hand." Then Abram gave him a tenth of everything. The king of Sodom said to Abram, "Give me the people and keep the goods for yourself." But Abram said to the king of Sodom, "I have raised my hand to the LORD, God Most High, Creator of heaven and earth, and have taken an oath that I will accept nothing belonging to you, not even a thread or the thong of a sandal, so that you will never be able to say, 'I made Abram rich.' I will accept nothing but what my men have eaten and the share that belongs to the men who went with me—to Aner, Eshcol and Mamre. Let them have their share" (Gen. 14:17–24).

In this event, when Abraham brings back the captives of Sodom including Lot, the king of Sodom and Melchizedek come out to meet Abraham. Abraham paid the tithe to Melchizedek, a tithe of the plunder, and Melchizedek blessed him. Then, the king of Sodom came and told Abraham to keep everything and give it to the people. He would give, but Abraham does not receive; he will not take anything from the king of Sodom. This is a striking contrast. Immediately after this, God appears to Abraham: "After this, the word of the LORD came to Abram in a vision: 'Do not be afraid, Abram. I am your shield, your very great reward'" (Gen. 15:1). God Himself visits. This is the context in which it happened, and you would miss it if you were not paying attention.

Melchizedek: The First Priest

There is no reference to Melchizedek before or after. This is the only reference, next to Psalm 110. He comes here as a priest. He was a priest of God Most High. This is the first mention of a priest in the Bible. Nothing was mentioned before the days of Noah, through the Flood, Babel, and up to the time of Abraham. Sacrifices were being offered, but it is Melchizedek who is called *priest* for the very first time in the Bible. While it is mentioned just twice, the first mention requires it to be given significance. He brought out bread and wine after the battle, there was food and celebration, he blessed Abraham, and Abraham gave him a tenth of everything. It is also significant that it is Abraham who gives Melchizedek a tenth of everything. Abraham, who is the father of the faithful. When we put together these various factors, we begin to see how significant this is. We want to see how Paul reasons from this, draws so many implications, and establishes the doctrine of a change that was to come.

This was told before the law was given. Melchizedek made his presence known to Abraham before the law was given, and tithing was made before the law was given. After the law was given, it speaks of one who is to come. Who is this one that is to come who will be priest? Specifically, the Messiah. In Psalm 110:1–4, God speaks:

> The LORD said to my Lord: [God the Father, speaking of Christ] "Sit at my right hand until I make your enemies a footstool for your feet." The LORD will extend your mighty scepter from Zion; you will rule in the midst of your enemies. Your troops will be willing on your day of battle. Arrayed in holy majesty, from the womb of the dawn you will receive the dew of your youth. The LORD has sworn and will not change his mind: "You are a priest forever, in the order of Melchizedek."

This becomes the basis of all teaching and is what we should expect. What are its implications for us, particularly with respect to our hope in the future? Remember throughout this book, the fullness that is in Christ, the hope that is ours, the anchor of our soul is before us, and this is going to be brought about by Christ Himself. We will see how this ties into something better yet to come. There is a better rest to come. Otherwise, He would not have spoken of a rest after the days of Joshua. There is a better priesthood, a new covenant, a new order of things. There is a new law in terms of the way we are to come to God, in terms of the fulfillment of the ceremonial law, because it is a new priesthood. The law is given on the basis of the priesthood.

Melchizedek: Priest and King

Psalm 110 is the second mention of Melchizedek. Look at the circumstances. It speaks of one who is to come as king, who is to rule over his enemies, and who will conquer them. Remember the blessing that came to Abraham as he came back in conquest. This *One* who is to rule as king is also a priest. The Messiah, the promised One, is not only a king but a priest. "The LORD has sworn and will not change his mind" (Ps. 110:4a). Notice the double affirmation that He has sworn and certainly will not change. There is an oath that is being made here by God. It says, "You are a priest forever" (Ps. 110:4b), and it goes back to the priesthood of Melchizedek; He said, "in the order of Melchizedek." Notice the statement "forever" and "in the order of Melchizedek," you are a priest. You who are king will be a priest forever after the order of Melchizedek. These are the only two mentions.

Melchizedek is also a king. Where did we get that? It is spoken of here in Genesis 14:18: "Then Melchizedek king of Salem brought out bread and wine. He was a priest of God Most High." Melchizedek is a king and a priest, as the Messiah is to be king and priest. Christ combines these offices as Melchizedek does.[6] Also, **"his name means 'king of righteousness'; then also, 'king of Salem' means 'king of peace'"** (v. 2b). This Melchizedek, his name meaning "king of righteousness," is also king of Salem. He is the king of righteousness, and he is the king of peace. Both of these go together in Scripture. It is right and fitting that from the very beginning, these two are present in this one person, Melchizedek. Psalm 85:10 says, "righteousness and peace kiss each other." The kingdom of God is righteousness and peace and joy in the Holy Ghost.[7] Righteousness and peace are continually linked, and we find them here in Melchizedek. Christ is a priest after the order of Melchizedek, who will bring about righteousness and peace.

---

6. Gangadean, *The Westminster Catechisms*, 165–168.

7. *Romans 14:17.*

Melchizedek: A Priesthood Forever

Melchizedek met Abraham, returning from the defeat of the kings, and blessed him. Abraham gave him a tenth of everything. These few things are brought out, and then the significance of his name is given. Then it says in Hebrews 7:3, **"Without father or mother, without genealogy, without beginning of days or end of life, like the Son of God he remains a priest forever."** The Scripture explicitly says, "You are a priest forever, in the order of Melchizedek" (Ps. 110:4b). Please notice the word *forever.* It is a lasting priesthood. Unlike the priesthood of Aaron, His priesthood will go on forever. There has been a lot of puzzling over this remark about, **"Without father or mother, without genealogy, without beginning of days or end of life"** (v. 3a). We know that Melchizedek is introduced without any reference to who his father is or when he was born or when he died. Of the kings of Judah, it is always recorded who the father is, born of so and so, and he died and is gathered to his fathers at the time of his death. The priests are often spoken of in this way. As a matter of fact, the priests are required to have this genealogy. You cannot enter the priesthood if you do not have your genealogy and order recorded. There were people in the days of Ezra who were not listed in the genealogy, and they had to step back from the office of priesthood.[8]

The priesthood established through Aaron had a genealogy, and you would think that all priesthoods would have genealogies, but Melchizedek did not, not in the absolute sense. Melchizedek was human; priests must be human in the sense of keeping record of it. There has been a lot of discussion, a lot of treatises written about this, and speculation about who this person might be.[9] Especially picking up with the state-

---

8. *Ezra 2:62.*

9. Dr. Gangadean held the view that there is good reason to infer that Shem is Melchizedek, given the following: (1) This view is commonly held in the Hebrew tradition. (2) Melchizedek was a human vs. non-human (divine, theophany). He was the king of Salem, an office which had a history and an enduring presence on earth. (3) One would expect Shem (and only Shem) to fill all the roles and offices that Melchizedek does. (3a) There is good reason that the description of Melchizedek being "without father or mother, without genealogy, without beginning of days or end of life" (without birth or death) is to be taken in the relative vs. absolute sense. Given that Shem outlived at least 8 generations after the Flood, and overlapped Abraham's life by minimally 150 years, he would have this appearance to those generations, resembling the Son of God. No one else at that time would. (3b) Shem, being the oldest living male in the line of the promise (head of the clan), would be priest of God

ment, "Without father or mother, without genealogy, without beginning of days or end of life" (v. 3a). There is no record of his death and no record of his birth. We are not saying there is not a birth or there is not a death; we are saying there is no record. And to come into the priesthood, a record was essential, at least the Aaronic priesthood. But this one came into the office of the priesthood in a much greater way than by genealogy. He came by way of oath. The oath is much greater than the genealogy.

Melchizedek: The Lesser Is Blessed by the Greater

We can and should have expected from the beginning, long before this, that there would be another priesthood. There would be a change in the priesthood and the law because there is more to come in connection with the fullness that was given to Abraham. Remember, Abraham had the promises in Genesis 12, and having the promises put him in a prominent position. Abraham is such a great person, and yet he is blessed by Melchizedek. The argument is, without doubt, that the lesser is blessed by the greater. Think about how prominent Melchizedek is, and yet he has no genealogy. But priests must be appointed. He must be appointed; the way in which He is appointed is with an oath.

Abraham had the blessing, and part of the blessing is that "all peoples on earth will be blessed through you" (Gen. 12:3b). There is a land, a great nation, but the fullness was that "all peoples on earth will be blessed through you." There was fullness to be had, and the priest of God enabled Abraham to fulfill the promise in blessing him.

Abraham was able to say, "I have raised my hand to the LORD, God Most High, Creator of heaven and earth, and have taken an oath that I will accept nothing belonging to you" (Gen. 14:22–23a). This came

---

Most High over all who descended from him, including Abraham. (3c) Shem's concern for holiness, in connection with the knowledge (the promise) preserved by and passed down to and through Noah, was revealed in his righteous actions. One would expect him to oppose the unbelief and apostasy of his day (Babel—Nimrod) as a righteous leader (king), and that he would anticipate and pass on the knowledge of the promise (going back to Gen. 1–3) to another in his line (Abraham) as a holy priest. (3d) There is good reason to think that given his worldview (man's origin and destiny, God's purpose in world history, sin and death, the curse and the promise), and the heightened revelation of the Flood and the apostasy at Babel, Shem would understand the land of Mesopotamia was doomed to destruction and, therefore, as the forerunner to Abraham, would leave that land for a city with foundations (the promise).

about in the circumstance of Melchizedek blessing Abraham. Then the Word of God came to Abraham again, "Do not be afraid, Abram. I am your shield, your very great reward" (Gen. 15:1b). This is the fullness that there is for all of us. God is our exceeding great reward, as we increasingly come to see and behold Him, who has created heaven and earth and rules in all things that come to pass. The hope was there for Abraham. It was confirmed through the ministry of Melchizedek.

Abraham responds to the king of Sodom: 'I will not take any of this, not one thing; God is the one who will make me rich.' He wanted to make that very clear, and he wanted no compromise with the world. Abraham would rather stay out of all the worldly ways and blessings that Lot went after, knowing that his inheritance is in God. He left Ur of the Chaldees, knowing that the city was doomed to destruction. "For he was looking forward to the city with foundations, whose architect and builder is God" (Heb. 11:10). Abraham had his eye on the hope, the fullness, the future, what it will be. Without a doubt, it will come about. For that reason, he endured. And believers through the centuries have endured in the same way. We, too, are called to have our eyes on the future and to have our eyes on the Lord Jesus so that we might come into this fullness.

Melchizedek Blessed Abraham and Abraham Tithed

Melchizedek has no record of genealogy, yet he becomes a priest. This is a contrast, but he is going to be a priest forever, unlike the priests on earth who do not continue forever, and he became a priest by oath, which is stronger than the natural descent of genealogy. **"Just think how great he was: Even the patriarch Abraham gave him a tenth of the plunder!"** (v. 4). This was the tithing which confirmed his office as priest. Priests are called to collect and receive tithe from those to whom they minister. Melchizedek received that tithe. The Aaronic priesthood did, too, but if Abraham is great and paid tithe to Melchizedek, how much greater is Melchizedek in terms of his office as a priest? **"Now the law requires the descendants of Levi who become priests to collect a tenth from the people—that is, their brothers—even though their brothers are descended from Abraham"** (v. 5), they have the privilege and status of being descended from Abraham. How much more is Abraham great, yet tithes are collected from him?

The priesthood, with respect to the descendants of Abraham, shows a relative position of greatness. Just think how great Abraham was. The Aaronic priests collect tithes from their brothers, who are Abraham's descendants, putting them in a higher position—not a higher person, but a higher position. How much more so that Abraham, the father of all of them, would pay tithe to Melchizedek? **"Just think how great he was: Even the patriarch Abraham gave him a tenth of the plunder!"** (v. 4). **"This man, however, did not trace his descent from Levi, yet he collected a tenth from Abraham and blessed him who had the promises"** (v. 6). Notice how the greatness of Abraham is emphasized. He had the promises, it is no small thing, and that made all the difference. Esau abandoned it and Lot abandoned it. Many have turned away, but the blessing is in the promise to be the heir of the whole world.[10] The one who has the promises is blessed by Melchizedek. It says, **"And without doubt the lesser person is blessed by the greater"** (v. 7). If blessing is a kind of bestowing, then the one who bestows must have more than the one on whom it is bestowed. Notice Melchizedek receives a tenth, and the priest receives a tenth, but that is not the blessing; that is honoring the person in the office of priest. So Abraham gave the tithe, and Melchizedek gave the blessing. The greater thing is the blessing by which the promises are brought about. The promise itself is a blessing, but there is a need for grace by which the promises will be realized. The one who can bestow grace, the giver of grace, in God, is greater.

Paul is drawing out all of these inferences. Melchizedek has no genealogy but he is a priest and he is a king of righteousness and peace. He was king of Salem, the king of Jerusalem, the city chosen by God. The place where Abraham would later offer up his son, Isaac, at Mount Moriah, which later became the Temple Mount.[11] Melchizedek was also the priest of Salem in Jerusalem, he received the tithes and blessed Abraham. All of these things are emphasized in contrast to the Aaronic priesthood.

Paul goes on to say that even the priests, who will die, receive a tenth, and yet being in that office puts them in a greater position. **"In the one case, the tenth is collected by men who die; but in the other case, by**

---

10. *Genesis 12:1–3.*

11. *2 Chronicles 3:1.*

him who is declared to be living" (v. 8). In the case of Melchizedek, he continues forever and receives the tithe. Again we see how, by way of contrast, Melchizedek is greater. Paul goes on to confirm it even further by saying, **"One might even say that Levi, who collects the tenth, paid the tenth through Abraham, because when Melchizedek met Abraham, Levi was still in the body of his ancestor"** (vv. 9–10). We are not inclined to think in the way of corporate unity, but the Scripture does. Abraham, as the father of Levi, is greater than Levi, and in Abraham, Levi pays a tenth. You can see in every way that you might cut it that the priesthood of Melchizedek is a greater priesthood than that of the priesthood of Levi.

Melchizedek: Appointed by an Oath

Paul goes on to point out the need for a greater priesthood. First, we are to consider how great Melchizedek was and then consider the need for something greater than the Aaronic priesthood. **"If perfection could have been attained through the Levitical priesthood (for on the basis of it the law was given to the people), why was there still need for another priest to come—one in the order of Melchizedek, not in the order of Aaron?"** (v. 11). Please note that the priesthood is more basic than the law that the priest carries out. It says, **"If perfection could have been attained through the Levitical priesthood . . . why was there still need for another priest to come—one in the order of Melchizedek, not in the order of Aaron?"** (v. 11). While the Aaronic priesthood speaks to what Christ will accomplish, the priesthood after the order of Melchizedek speaks more fully. If the Aaronic priesthood was sufficient, why would the Scriptures say of the Messiah, **"You are a priest forever, in the order of Melchizedek?"** (v. 17). **"The Lord has sworn and will not change his mind"** (v. 21). When God speaks, we must listen, and when God swears an oath, we must bow down and hear. "The LORD hath sworn, and will not repent, Thou art a priest for ever after the order of Melchizedek" (Ps. 110:4 KJV). So, another priesthood was to come after the Aaronic priesthood was established. In the second mention, Paul infers, *if* perfection were by the Levitical priesthood, why should we have another? But we *do* have another by an oath, so clearly, there is something not less but greater to come. It is not doing away with the priesthood office; it is another priest to come.

We need priests; we definitely need priests. We need to be made holy, and the priest is the one who will bring about in us that devotion. Some of us find our priests in the world. It could be the teachers in the university. It could be those who sing songs to us (popular music). They are the ones who will maintain our devotion to some ideal, so we come to them and listen to them again and again. What priest are you listening to? Where are you going to get your devotions kindled, kept alive, and burning? The Aaronic priesthood? Some worldly priest? Or Christ? Who is our priest? Or is it that we are not ready to put away the world? We still love the world and what the world has to offer; that is our good, our view of the fullness of the riches. Are you saying it does not get any better than this? Have you considered Christ the Creator, upholder, redeemer, and heir of all things? The very brightness of the glory of God through whom all excellence comes? What are you holding on to? How long will you hold on to it, listen to other priests, and have your devotions kindled? What songs do you listen to? What teachings and authors do you read with delight to have your affections and devotions kindled? Do you find more delight in these than in the Word of God? Do you find that is when it really comes alive for you? In that case, you do not know God very well; you know Him from afar, and you have not beheld the beauty of the Lord that you would go for these others. We need a priest. One in the order of Melchizedek, not in the order of Aaron. One who will continue.

Melchizedek: Change of Priesthood Requires a Change of Law

There is no record of the genealogy of Melchizedek, but there is an expected need for another priesthood, and when that One comes, there will be a change. When there is a change of the priesthood, there must also be a change of the law—the law understood as a covenant. We have a new covenant now; something has changed. We are going to see that in the next chapter. What is it that will change? We should anticipate it. Jeremiah 31:31–33 says:

> "The time is coming," declares the LORD, "when I will make a new covenant with the house of Israel and with the house of Judah. It will not be like the covenant I made with their forefathers when I took them by the hand to lead them out of Egypt, because they broke my covenant, though I was a husband to them," declares

the LORD. "This is the covenant I will make with the house of Israel after that time," declares the LORD. "I will put my law in their minds and write it on their hearts. I will be their God, and they will be my people."

It is no longer an external connection with the law, the way children are taught by rules and regulations: 'Do this and do that.' It is no longer that one has to hold someone by the hand and lead them through it because they do not understand and are immature. On the contrary, the person described in this passage is someone who has come to maturity of understanding, and the law has been internalized and has become a delight. The law is in the heart; they are no longer being held by the hand. This is the new order that will come as a result of Christ's priesthood.

Paul said, **"For when there is a change of the priesthood,** [because there is One promised to come] **there must also be a change of the law"** (v. 12). Furthermore, the One who is to come, the Messiah, who will be this priest—He is not of the house of Levi, He is not of that tribe at all, He is of the tribe of Judah. Yet the Messiah is spoken of in Psalm 110 when it says, "You are a priest forever, [you who are of the house of David, the king, will be a priest forever] in the order of Melchizedek" (Ps. 110:4b). So there will be a change, we can know this, we should expect this because there is greater fullness to be attained.

"And what we have said is even more clear if another priest like Melchizedek appears, one who has become a priest not on the basis of a regulation as to his ancestry but on the basis of the power of an indestructible life" (v 15–16). This is another factor about this priesthood because it says, **"You are a priest forever"** (v. 20b). We can draw from that word *"forever"* that there is another priesthood, a better priesthood, coming. Part of the greatness of this priesthood that is coming is that it is directed toward a better hope. Hope has two aspects. One is what we are to get, and the other is how we are to get it. These two go together.

When we are children, we do not have the fullness of our inheritance; there is a trustee. The regulation says, 'Give this person so much money as they are growing up. But when they are 21, give them a quarter of their inheritance; when they are 33, give them everything.' We will not reach for that fullness until we come of age. There is a question of what we are to get and how we are to get it. "**The former regulation is set aside because it was weak and useless**" (v. 18). It could not bring us into the fullness that there is in God.

Christ: Such a Priest Meets Our Needs

Think about the baptism of the Holy Spirit and all that comes with it—teaching and leading us into all truth as we go out and engage to be witnesses in all the world. It is the difference between a child and an adult, between the young and the mature. What is so sad is that in this age, when we should be teachers, we are like infants needing milk with respect to basic truths.[12] The former regulation was weak; it could not bring us into fullness, and therefore, since it could not bring us into fullness, ultimately, it failed and was useless. These are strong words. It was *weak* and *useless*. It was fitting for the time, but what good is it if you get a person halfway across and not all the way there? 'We will bring you a quarter of the way there, and then we will get you lost, and you will be lost forever. We will get you three-quarters of the way there, and then you will be almost there. We will bring you nine-tenths of the way there, but not quite, and you will be lost after all that effort.' If it cannot get us all the way there, then in that sense it is weak and useless. "**(For the law made nothing perfect), and a better hope is introduced, by which we draw near to God**" (v. 17). This is the hope that is in Christ Jesus.

Furthermore, the perfection and greatness, and that this is a better priesthood, is affirmed by an oath. This priesthood of Melchizedek was not without an oath. Others became priests without an oath, but he became a priest with an oath when God said to him, "**The Lord has sworn and will not change his mind**" (v. 21b). Notice every particular piece is being drawn out to show the need for this change to come in connection with the future and the fullness that there is for us. "**The Lord has sworn.**" With this oath, we have a surety that it will be accomplished. It says of Jesus, "**Because of this oath, Jesus has become the guarantee of a better covenant**" (v. 22).

This last expression is drawn out more: "**You are a priest forever**" (v. 21b).

---

12. *Hebrews 5:12.*

Now there have been many of those priests, since death prevented them from continuing in office; but because Jesus lives forever, he has a permanent priesthood. Therefore he is able to save completely those who come to God through him, because he always lives to intercede for them (vv. 23–25).

Prayer is one of the works of the priest. He carried the breastplate attached to the ephod and on it were the 12 precious stones with the names of each tribe written.

Christ continues to pray for us all the days of our lives from before we are born. In that, we are born, and in that, we are brought all the way through. Christ is a priest forever, and therefore, He is able to save us completely, **"Such a high priest meets our need"** (v. 26a). We have this need. His characteristics are given: **"one who is holy, blameless, pure, set apart from sinners, exalted above the heavens. Unlike the other high priests, he does not need to offer sacrifices day after day"** (vv. 26b–27a). Christ is sinless, He is pure, He is set apart, He is blameless, and He is holy.

We had priests that had their own sin. Christ was touched with the feelings of our infirmities.[13] He suffered, and He was made perfect through suffering without sin. And because He is sinless, He can see clearly and bring us to God. Others sacrificed for their own sin; He sacrificed, too, not for Himself, but for the sins of others: **"He sacrificed for their sins once for all when he offered himself"** (v. 27b). Christ does not have that weakness. By an oath, He is a priest forever. Because of this, we can hope in Him. He can save us to the uttermost as we keep coming to God through Him and are delivered from all of our sin; that we might come into the fullness that is ours in God. Jesus Christ, a priest forever. Our priest. Amen.

---

13. *Hebrews 4:15.*

THE NEW COVENANT

Hebrews 8

¹The point of what we are saying is this: We do have such a high priest, who sat down at the right hand of the throne of the Majesty in heaven, ²and who serves in the sanctuary, the true tabernacle set up by the Lord, not by man.

³Every high priest is appointed to offer both gifts and sacrifices, and so it was necessary for this one also to have something to offer. ⁴If he were on earth, he would not be a priest, for there are already men who offer the gifts prescribed by the law. ⁵They serve at a sanctuary that is a copy and shadow of what is in heaven. This is why Moses was warned when he was about to build the tabernacle: "See to it that you make everything according to the pattern shown you on the mountain." ⁶But the ministry Jesus has received is as superior to theirs as the covenant of which he is mediator is superior to the old one, and it is founded on better promises.

⁷For if there had been nothing wrong with that first covenant, no place would have been sought for another. ⁸But God found fault with the people and said:
    "The time is coming, declares the Lord,
        when I will make a new covenant
    with the house of Israel
        and with the house of Judah.

⁹It will not be like the covenant
        I made with their forefathers
    when I took them by the hand
        to lead them out of Egypt,
    because they did not remain faithful to my covenant,
        and I turned away from them, declares the Lord.

¹⁰This is the covenant I will make with the house of Israel
  after that time, declares the Lord.
I will put my laws in their minds
  and write them on their hearts.
I will be their God,
  and they will be my people.

¹¹No longer will a man teach his neighbor,
  or a man his brother, saying, 'Know the Lord,'
because they will all know me,
  from the least of them to the greatest.

¹²For I will forgive their wickedness
  and will remember their sins no more."

¹³By calling this covenant "new," he has made the first one obsolete; and what is obsolete and aging will soon disappear.

WE HAVE SUCH A HIGH PRIEST

"SUCH A HIGH PRIEST MEETS OUR NEED—one who is holy, blameless, pure, set apart from sinners, exalted above the heavens" (Heb. 7:26). We have a high priest who meets our needs. This is a summary of what Paul is saying. Focusing now on the beginning of Hebrews 8, this high priest we have, whose priesthood is forever, has sat down at the right hand of the throne of the majesty in heaven. He has been raised from the dead, ascended into heaven, and given position and authority above every name. This is what is signified when it says, **"We do have such a high priest, who sat down at the right hand of the throne of the Majesty in heaven"** (v. 1). Jesus was incarnated. He had to be human. He came having a body not merely to do the work of the prophet but to do the work of the priest, to offer Himself up as the Lamb of God—once and for all. He was incarnated, crucified, raised from the dead, and ascended into heaven. This One is our high priest, and this priesthood of Jesus is set in contrast to the priesthood in the Old Testament—a priesthood still held by the Jewish people, a priesthood still longed for. They did not understand the nature of sin, the nature of the fullness that is in God; they held on to the old covenant and failed to recognize and receive Jesus as the Messiah.

We do have such a high priest who is in the heavens, One **"who serves in the sanctuary, the true tabernacle set up by the Lord, not by** man" (v. 2). Christ is serving, and it is necessary that He serves. He is not a priest merely in name; He is a priest in act and deed. Paul says, **"Every high priest is appointed to offer both gifts and sacrifices, and so it was necessary for this one also to have something to offer"** (v. 3). Christ must have, and does have, something to offer as high priest. It is not an idle office, nor an office that is a mere position of honor; it is an office with *real* work to accomplish.

JESUS:
A Superior Ministry

If Christ is the high priest and the old priesthood is being set aside, the question naturally arises, 'If every high priest must offer gifts and sacrifices, where is He offering gifts and sacrifices, and what gifts and sacrifices is He offering?' The answer is that He offers gifts and sacrifice in the *true* tabernacle. We have a distinction between the tabernacle here on earth, and that which is in heaven; the earthly tabernacle is a copy, a shadow, of this true tabernacle. We see the greatness of Christ's priesthood in that He is serving in the true tabernacle. He entered into the sacred space that symbolized the very presence of God on earth—the Most Holy Place. This presence was represented by the Shekinah glory, a radiant light positioned above the Ark of the Covenant, and the mercy seat. Christ, however, did not enter into a representation of God's presence; instead, He entered directly into the very presence of God, the Most Holy Place. It was in this sacred space that He present-ed His offering. Christ did not merely enter there but had to offer a sacrifice. He offered the sacrifice of Himself, His own blood that was shed. There, on the basis of the blood that was shed, His own blood, He pleads for the forgiveness and the cleansing of His people as high priest.

Christ is doing the work as high priest; He has offered gifts and sacrifices, He has offered Himself, His own sacrifice, He continues to work, and He ever lives to make intercession for us. It is not only that the sacrifice is offered once—it is certainly offered once and only once—but the benefits of that sacrifice are pleaded again and again and again on behalf of everyone who comes to Christ, who comes to God in His name. As we come with sin, we do not deserve to be heard; we deserve to be left to ourselves and forsaken. We always come with sin; even when we confess our sins, we still come short. Nevertheless, Christ graciously extends forgiveness for the sins we confess, and this forgiveness is grounded in the atoning power of His shed blood, affirming that His sacrifice was made on our behalf. He pleads for our prayers to be heard on the basis of *His* perfect righteousness, put down to our account, and we are received not on the basis of our own righteousness.

Think of how many prayers are being offered, how many times a day you have prayed, and how many times you have prayed in Christ's name. All those prayers must be taken by Christ, our high priest, and presented before God so that they may be accepted and God may hear and answer. Christ's office as high priest is an office that is full of service. The accuser of the brethren, Satan, perpetually seeks to condemn and discredit, saying, 'Look at this one. How could you possibly listen to this one? Consider what he has just done, and observe what is happening in his life right now!' He is the accuser of the brothers, the one who hurls dung, 'the dung hurler.'

Satan throws that on us and says, 'This dirty so and so has no right to come before you.' And Christ pleads His blood as high priest. This is why we come to Him. This is why we need a high priest who has entered into the very heavens with His own blood, one who will be there always and plead the benefits of His shed blood for us. Such a high priest meets our needs, and we do have such a high priest.

The priests on earth were still, at that time, offering gifts. When Jesus died on the cross, the veil in the temple was rent from top to bottom supernaturally by God. It was a very thick veil, separating the presence of God from the rest of the tabernacle. God Himself split the veil, tore it, and rent it asunder, signifying that the way into the Most Holy Place was made fully open now through the death of Christ so that we could draw near to God through Him and find grace to help in the time of need. It also signified the end of that order, because Jesus had done on the cross what was signified in all the sacrifices that were offered. He had completed it; He had said, "It is finished,"[1] and it was finished.

The priests on earth continued to serve in the tabernacle. They sewed the veil back together. They did not understand; they did not believe that the rending of the veil signified the finished work of Jesus Christ. It must have been quite a challenge to think of how they would continue, trying to understand what had happened and why this was

---

1. *John 19:30.*

done. It was no event that any human being did, and yet they had not understood the point. Though God had, in this signal way, made it clear that the old order had been accomplished, God permitted and gave time to those who had served in the tabernacle to hear the word of preaching and turn in repentance. They persisted for almost 40 years in not hearing and still opposing, then the Lord destroyed everything in the temple. He did not merely rend the veil, but He took it away. Through His Son, God established the new covenant in His blood. The priests on earth were offering gifts as prescribed by the law, and if Christ were on earth, we would expect Him to be offering gifts visibly, but He is not on earth; He ascended into heaven. It is there that He offered the gift and sacrifice of Himself for us.

Our inclination is to pay attention to and believe what is visible. When priests engage in rituals following a highly visible order, we are captivated by that tangible expression, and it becomes a tangible reality for us. Later on, we are going to speak about how faith is that by which we grasp and understand the invisible.[2] It is more than that we were simply attached to the visible; God Himself had given this, but we took the visible and did not go beyond it, we did not see what the visible signified. Here, it says that the priests **"serve at a sanctuary that is a copy and shadow of what is in heaven. This is why Moses was warned when he was about to build the tabernacle: 'See to it that you make everything according to the pattern shown you on the mountain'"** (v. 5). This was not a positive command, the pattern that was given to Moses was a pattern of a reality in heaven. It was a visible pattern on earth of an invisible reality in heaven. In this sense, what was on earth *signified*. It was a sign pointing to something else, but this sign was not understood as pointing to something else. There was a holding on to this old order as if it were the reality. Many, even of those who had come to Christ, still had not seen the need for the old order to be done away with. They were zealous for the law, and they observed the law. It was a gradual process by which they came to understand the significance of Christ's work. Remember, even after Christ was raised from the dead and He spoke to them for 40 days, the disciples still had to be called away from their old work to the work that Christ had called them to. This was the account of Peter deciding to go fishing and others

---

2. *Hebrews 11:3.*

going with him. The Lord outdoes them and shows them that He is fully able to provide for their needs. They are to leave that altogether and come to serve Him as He has called them.[3]

The disciples asked, "Lord, are you at this time going to restore the kingdom to Israel?" (Acts 1:6). There was surprise in seeing the Gentiles come in, and not come in the way they had previously. The way Cornelius had come in was by receiving the full blessing of the Spirit without observing the ceremonial law. The tabernacle was **"a copy and shadow of what is in heaven"** (v. 5a). A copy is not the real thing, and a shadow is not; there is a resemblance between the two, but the real thing is in heaven. What was on earth spoke to this, but the people had not understood it. If they had, they would not have turned aside, turned away, and they would not have rejected the Lord Jesus. Those who did accept Him would not have continued to hold onto the law the way they did.

The command concerning the tabernacle was not a positive command. It was pointing to a reality and had to be made in a certain way, and Moses was to observe the details of it. **"See to it that you make everything according to the pattern shown you on the mountain"** (v. 5b). It is a spiritual reality, and the visible reveals the invisible. Even in our own bodies, the visible sight reveals something about the spiritual sight. The visible act reveals something about the spiritual act. The visible walk reveals something about the invisible walk. The whole creation is a visible revelation of the invisible God.[4] If we had understood this, we would not have stumbled. We would have seen the difference between sign and reality and not taken the sign as if it were the reality.

JESUS:
A Superior Covenant

Jesus received a ministry superior to the one on earth, the way the reality is superior to the sign. In connection with this superior ministry in which He entered into heaven itself, there is a superior covenant; there is a change in the covenant. **"For if there had been nothing wrong with that first covenant, no place would have been sought for**

---

3. *John 21:1–14.*

4. Gangadean, *The Biblical Worldview,* 21–36, 91–108.

another" (v. 7). This line of reasoning is what we have encountered before in Hebrews 4:8: "For if Joshua had given them rest, God would not have spoken later about another day." Hebrews 7:11 says, "If perfection could have been attained through the Levitical priesthood (for on the basis of it the law was given to the people), why was there still need for another priest to come—one in the order of Melchizedek, not in the order of Aaron?"

These references in Scripture anticipated that which was to come. David said, "Today, if you hear his voice, do not harden your hearts as you did in the rebellion" (Ps. 95:7b–8a). And in Hebrews 4:3b: "They shall never enter my rest." Hebrews 4:9: "There remains, then, a Sabbath-rest for the people of God," more than the rest that was given in the days of Joshua. Likewise, we should have realized and anticipated that another priesthood would come, another priest would come after the order of Melchizedek. Notice the parallel: another rest (a promise), another priest (who will bring about this greater promise), and another covenant (law) by which this will be effected.

This is drawn from the quote in Jeremiah 31:31, "The time is coming," declares the LORD, "when I will make a new covenant with the house of Israel and with the house of Judah." The Jewish people, in reading this, should have understood and anticipated there will be a new covenant. The new covenant is specifically contrasted with a covenant that they were observing at that time. It continues in Jeremiah, "It will not be like the covenant I made with their forefathers when I took them by the hand to lead them out of Egypt" (Jer. 31:32a). That was the covenant made on Sinai. Not only were the Ten Commandments given, this is the moral law that is perpetual,[5] but there was a civil and ceremonial law; there were various laws of sacrifices and teachings connected with the priesthood, laws of cleansing and purification, and the festivals to be observed speaking about God's promise. The Passover, First Fruits, the Feast of Harvest—which speaks about the ingathering of all—and the Day of Atonement were the ways in which the covenant was administered in the days of Moses.

The new covenant was set in contrast to the covenant made with Moses in a particular way. The challenges arose in discerning the nature of the contrast that would emerge in this context for those who

---

5. Gangadean, *The Westminster Confession*, 207–221.

failed to see and understand the contrast. **"It will not be like the covenant I made with their forefathers when I took them by the hand to lead them out of Egypt"** (v. 9a). This expression, **"I took them by the hand,"** is significant. If we understand this expression, what it is to be led by the hand, we can understand the difference between the old and the new covenant. It says this is going to change **"because they did not remain faithful to my covenant, and I turned away from them, declares the Lord"** (v. 9b). Not only had they not remained faithful then and there while Moses was still on the mount, but even afterward, repeatedly, they did not remain faithful to that covenant. In Jeremiah's day, Jeremiah spoke this word, after he declared that the Babylonians would come in, destroy the city, and take the people captive. This is perhaps the most horrible thing that could happen to the people. It showed their full rejection, the judgment of God coming upon them to the uttermost, in connection with their not heeding the covenant.

JESUS:
Better Promises

In the section where Jeremiah speaks, he says that God will do this: Through Babylon, the people will be taken away, but God will restore the people. Jeremiah spoke about the coming restoration.[6] Right after this word, he is told to go and buy a field.[7] When a nation has come upon you and has destroyed everything, and you remain a solitary city that is soon about to fall apart, and everybody will be taken out, you do not have much interest in real estate. You are not going to invest at that point. Yet, Jeremiah, to be a sign to the people, was told to buy a field, have it recorded, testified to, seal the contract, and bury it for safekeeping. Jeremiah is looking forward to a time when they will be restored. In this connection, one may have thought that the new covenant, the time that is coming, would be at the time of the restoration from Babylon, about 70 years later, because this is the historical context in which he spoke about the new covenant. It is not specified just when it will come about. It might have been reasonable to think that when God restored the people from Babylon, that would be the time that

---

6. *Jeremiah 31.*

7. *Jeremiah 32.*

this new covenant would be given, but it was not. The people were to expect a new covenant, unlike the one that was made, and this word was given by Jeremiah in the midst of the near captivity of all the people.

We know that the new covenant did not come about until Christ came and fulfilled the sacrifices given under the Mosaic economy. This had to be fulfilled when He entered into heaven with His own blood and sent the Spirit to bring about the promise that was made. As far as the time is concerned, with the expression, "The time is coming, declares the Lord, when I will make a new covenant" (Jer. 31:31a), one may have thought that it would have been at the time of the restoration.

There is another puzzle here, too; it is said that it will be made "with the house of Israel and with the house of Judah" (Jer. 31:31b). If, in A.D. 70, the house of Israel and Judah, by and large, turned away from the Word of the Lord, in what sense is this covenant made with the house of Israel and the house of Judah? I think the way we are to understand this is to see something more of the terms of this covenant. In Galatians 3:15–16, we can see how this is explained:

> Brothers, let me take an example from everyday life. Just as no one can set aside or add to a human covenant that has been duly established, so it is in this case. The promises were spoken to Abraham and to his seed. The Scripture does not say "and to seeds," meaning many people, but "and to your seed," meaning one person, who is Christ.

You can imagine that the Israelites may have missed this point, but it should not have been missed; it should have been seen, and Paul is drawing attention to it. The promise was spoken to Abraham before the law was given. It was given to Abraham and to his seed, and it is made explicit that it is Christ. This is according to Scripture. It does not say *seeds*, meaning many people, plural, but *to your seed*, meaning one person, who is Christ. Galatians 3:17 says, "What I mean is this: The law, introduced 430 years later, does not set aside the covenant previously established by God and thus do away with the promise." This promise was made 430 years before the giving of the law at Sinai.[8] Remember, it said, **"It will not be like the covenant I made with their forefathers when I took them by the hand to lead them out of**

---

8. *Exodus 20.*

Egypt" (v. 9a). We have to go back beyond the covenant with Moses to the covenant made with Abraham.

The point in Galatians is this, that the covenant is made by way of promise through Christ, through the seed of Abraham, and not by way of the law. "For if the inheritance depends on the law, then it no longer depends on a promise; but God in his grace gave it to Abraham through a promise. What, then, was the purpose of the law?" (Gal. 3:18–19a). You might ask, what was the point of the covenant made through Moses? He continues:

> It was added because of transgressions until the Seed to whom the promise referred had come. The law was put into effect through angels by a mediator. A mediator, however, does not represent just one party; but God is one. Is the law, therefore, opposed to the promises of God? Absolutely not! (Gal. 3:19b–21a).

This is important because many today have stumbled just at this point, making the covenant with Moses a covenant of law, a legal covenant to be saved by, and they set aside the Old Testament by saying, 'We are not under the law, we are under grace.' Here, we see that this is not the point of the law. "Is the law, therefore, opposed to the promises of God?" No, they are not opposed, *emphatically* not. Paul says, "Absolutely not!"[9] How could it be stated any stronger than that? Yet, people today have not seen this—they have not seen the continuity between the Old and the New Testament. They have made a radical discontinuity. He continues in Galatians 3:21–23:

> For if a law had been given that could impart life, then righteousness would certainly have come by the law. But the Scripture declares that the whole world is a prisoner of sin, so that what was promised, being given through faith in Jesus Christ, might be given to those who believe. Before this faith came, we were held prisoners by the law, locked up until faith should be revealed. So the law was put in charge to lead us to Christ that we might be justified by faith.

The whole point of the Mosaic economy was to lead us to Christ. Notice, it is to lead us to Christ; it is not to be done apart from Christ; there

---

9. *Galatians 3:21.*

is a continuity. Galatians 3:24–25 says, "So the law was put in charge to lead us to Christ that we might be justified by faith. Now that faith has come, we are no longer under the supervision of the law." The law was supervising in a certain way to lead us to Christ and, in this case, to take us by the hand. Now, you do not teach an adult by taking them by the hand; you teach a child that way. This is part of the difference, but they will also come to Christ. It says in Galatians 3:26–29:

> You are all sons of God through faith in Christ Jesus, for all of you who were baptized into Christ have clothed yourselves with Christ. There is neither Jew nor Greek, slave nor free, male nor female, for you are all one in Christ Jesus. If you belong to Christ, then you are Abraham's seed, and heirs according to the promise.

It is in this sense that the covenant is made in the New Testament with the house of Israel and the house of Judah. We are in Christ, the One with whom God has made this promise, to Abraham and to his seed, and being in Christ, we become heirs of the promise. We are seen as continuing the promise made to Israel and Judah.

To explain more specifically what it is to be led by the hand, Galatians 4:1 says, "What I am saying is that as long as the heir is a child, he is no different from a slave, although he owns the whole estate." The son, who is underage, is a child, and the child is heir of all the promises, but he does not receive it in its fullness at that time. He is under supervision to be led to Christ, in whom he will have the promise in its fullness. Judah and Israel were to have the promise in Christ. Those who have it in Christ are the seed of Abraham and stand in the place of Judah and Israel. There are not two bodies, there is one.

The Book of Romans says that the natural branches were broken off, and we were grafted into that same root.[10] We should not be high-minded or boastful because we stand by faith. We can fall. God is able to graft the natural branches in again, and according to Scripture, it will be so. There will come a time when all of Israel will be saved. What will that be like? That will be like rising from the dead. In this context, it speaks about the consummation of all things. Before the

---

10. *Romans 11:17–24.*

consummation of all things, the nation of Israel will be saved. They will be grafted into the one tree, which is Christ.

This is why we can say, while Hebrews speaks about the promise, quoting from Jeremiah, "**I will make a new covenant with the house of Israel and with the house of Judah**" (v. 8b), it is in this sense, that all those who are in Christ are the seed of Abraham and are considered the house of Israel and the house of Judah—not two bodies, but one, neither Jew nor Greek. Outside of Christ, there are distinctions among the nations, but in Christ, these distinctions fall away. When the time comes, He will make a new covenant, which is contrasted in a particular way with the covenant God made with the people coming out of Egypt, which they had not continued in.

What is the content of the new covenant? It is stated here in three ways:

First, "**The time is coming, declares the Lord, when I will make a new covenant with the house of Israel and with the house of Judah**" (v. 8). "**This is the covenant I will make with the house of Israel after that time, declares the Lord. I will put my laws in their minds and write them on their hearts**" (v. 10a).

Second, "**I will be their God, and they will be my people**" (v. 10b). The third, cumulative way,

No longer will a man teach his neighbor, or a man his brother, saying, "Know the Lord," because they will all know me, from the least of them to the greatest. For I will forgive their wickedness and will remember their sins no more (v. 11–12).

Let us think about what it means to say, "**I will put my laws in their minds and write them on their hearts.**" This is to be understood in contrast to the laws that were given by which they were led by the hand. In many of the external practices that were supervising them to lead them to Christ, the content was focused on Christ, but the way in which it focused on Christ was by external operation. This is fitting for the Church in its earliest stages, and the Church was to be instructed in this way, but there will come a time when there is to be a greater fullness. When that time comes, God will write His laws in their minds and on their hearts.

PROBLEM IN UNDERSTANDING THE CHANGE FROM THE OLD TO THE NEW

We have to distinguish between the ceremonial laws, that were signs pointing to reality, and the reality. The content is not different in the sense of substance. The reality that was being pointed to in those times is no different than the reality now. What was different is that it was given to them in sign, outward, and ceremonial. Putting one's hand on the sacrifice and confessing one's sin pointed to Christ. The substance was the same, the reality was the same, but it was taught differently. The reality of what had been taught—the same reality—now becomes *internalized*. It is not a difference in content as far as the reality is concerned. There is a difference in content as far as the sign is concerned. We do not have those signs anymore; those signs have been fulfilled. We dare not bring an animal sacrifice to the Lord, but we must bring the sacrifice when we come to the Lord, the sacrifice of the Lord Jesus Christ. We dare not come before the Lord without that sacrifice. We dare not try to stand before God in our own righteousness. This reality has become internalized, especially with the coming of the Spirit, preparing us for the work of making disciples of all the nations,[11] being led into all truth,[12] and taking every thought captive.[13]

Internalization of the reality is not in regard to the moral law *per se* because the moral law is written in the hearts of all men, according to Romans 2.[14] This is the way in which God has created us. The internalization is particularly regarding the Mosaic economy and the context we are speaking about, the priesthood and the laws connected with the priests, and the ceremonial laws. These become internalized, written on the heart. The point of it was always the same, one and the same. **"I will be their God, and they will be my people"** (v. 10b). The point is to establish us in a personal relationship with God where there is no other god before us. He is the only one, the one God over all; He is the only one we acknowledge in all of life—we are not divided.

---

11. *Matthew 28:19.*

12. *John 16:13.*

13. *2 Corinthians 10:5.*

14. *Romans 2:15.*

Remember, our great tendency is to be divided, regarding the remaining self-life, in splitting the worship of Jehovah and service to Baal. We have a strong tendency to be split in this way, but this is to be overcome. It was taught then, **"I will be their God"** (v. 10a). They are to have no other gods before Him. We will be His people; we belong to the Lord; we are the Lord's people. It is possible to be raised in the covenant and to have the covenant privileges as a child in the Church today. But God is not the God of the covenant child, in that the reality has not been effected; the child may grow up, not acknowledge the Lord as their God, and not be part of His people. This must be internalized.

Under the Old Testament, for those with faith, this was a reality. They not only had the sign, but they also had the reality. In the New Testament, we have the reality without the sign. In both cases, the reality must be appropriated by faith, and in both cases, the reality may not be appropriated when there is a lack of faith. There is no change in the reality. There is a greater fullness in this reality in terms of the Spirit being poured out through Christ.

Further, the content of this covenant is summed up in this way: **"No longer will a man teach his neighbor, or a man his brother, saying, 'Know the Lord,' because they will all know me, from the least of them to the greatest"** (v. 11). Some have puzzled over this, and have said, 'This will only happen in the final state in heaven.' We say, this is to be understood not in an absolute sense, that no one will teach as if in the New Testament the ordinances of Christ do not include pastor-teachers; that is simply not true. There is a way in which the teachings and instructions were put into effect in the Old Testament, compared to the way it is administered now. The Spirit of God will work to bring us to this knowledge of God apart from some of those teachings and instructions, the pedagogical devices: the fringes on one's garment, the phylacteries, the words on the doorposts, and the ceremonies—those things will be done away with. The teaching purpose of those things will be done away with, and how we were taught through those ordinances will be done away with. We will not be taught any longer through the signs. It does not mean we will not be taught any longer in any way. Rather, we will not be taught in that way. We will all know the Lord from the least to the greatest.

"For I will forgive their wickedness and will remember their sins no more" (v. 12). It was always in Christ that sin was forgiven, in the

Old Testament and in the New. Here it is, fully realized, as the way to the Most Holy Place is opened, and we now have access into the Most Holy Place that we did not have before. Everyone in Christ can come to God, before the presence of God, and minister as a priest in a way that we could not before. Because sin is fully taken away, we have come of age, the Spirit has been sent upon us, and we no longer have to be taught in those concrete ways. God has acknowledged us in giving us a greater fullness in Christ.

When exactly is this covenant being fulfilled? It was fulfilled at the coming of Christ, and it is being fulfilled. The writer says, **"By calling this covenant 'new,' he has made the first one obsolete; and what is obsolete and aging will soon disappear"** (v. 13). The last remnants of the old economy, while the temple is still standing, the priesthood, will disappear. Remember, it was changed by the tearing of the veil at the death of Christ, but it remained standing and was growing old and obsolete. God gave it a time of transition, and that will soon disappear. It will disappear in terms of God judging those who will not hear and understand what is being taught.

There is a dual problem before us here. Some take the Scripture literally in every part and do not see where it is a sign pointing to reality because they take the sign to be the reality—there is a lack of understanding. Others say it is a symbol, not the reality, but they themselves have held on to the sign without the reality. They say the sign is not the reality, but this is a sign without the reality. The meaning of the sign becomes subjective. Some are legalists and some spiritualize, and both miss the reality. Let us give heed that we do not miss the reality. Let us not empty the ordinance of God of meaning or let our talk become meaningless. Let us see that there is a continuity of the reality, not of the sign. Let us not reject the sign and the reality. Let us hold to the reality now that it has come.

9

THE CONTRAST BETWEEN THE OLD AND THE NEW

Hebrews 9

¹Now the first covenant had regulations for worship and also an earthly sanctuary. ²A tabernacle was set up. In its first room were the lampstand, the table and the consecrated bread; this was called the Holy Place. ³Behind the second curtain was a room called the Most Holy Place, ⁴which had the golden altar of incense and the gold-covered ark of the covenant. This ark contained the gold jar of manna, Aaron's staff that had budded, and the stone tablets of the covenant. ⁵Above the ark were the cherubim of the Glory, overshadowing the atonement cover. But we cannot discuss these things in detail now.

⁶When everything had been arranged like this, the priests entered regularly into the outer room to carry on their ministry. ⁷But only the high priest entered the inner room, and that only once a year, and never without blood, which he offered for himself and for the sins the people had committed in ignorance. ⁸The Holy Spirit was showing by this that the way into the Most Holy Place had not yet been disclosed as long as the first tabernacle was still standing. ⁹This is an illustration for the present time, indicating that the gifts and sacrifices being offered were not able to clear the conscience of the worshiper. ¹⁰They are only a matter of food and drink and various ceremonial washings—external regulations applying until the time of the new order.

¹¹When Christ came as high priest of the good things that are already here, he went through the greater and more perfect tabernacle that is not man-made, that is to say, not a part of this creation. ¹²He did not enter by means of the blood of goats and calves; but he entered the Most Holy Place once for all by his own blood, having obtained eternal redemption.

¹³The blood of goats and bulls and the ashes of a heifer sprinkled on those who are ceremonially unclean sanctify them so that they are outwardly clean. ¹⁴How much more, then, will the blood of Christ, who through the eternal Spirit offered himself unblemished to God, cleanse our consciences from acts that lead to death, so that we may serve the living God!

¹⁵For this reason Christ is the mediator of a new covenant, that those who are called may receive the promised eternal inheritance—now that he has died as a ransom to set them free from the sins committed under the first covenant.

¹⁶In the case of a will, it is necessary to prove the death of the one who made it, ¹⁷because a will is in force only when somebody has died; it never takes effect while the one who made it is living. ¹⁸This is why even the first covenant was not put into effect without blood. ¹⁹When Moses had proclaimed every commandment of the law to all the people, he took the blood of calves, together with water, scarlet wool and branches of hyssop, and sprinkled the scroll and all the people. ²⁰He said, "This is the blood of the covenant, which God has commanded you to keep." ²¹In the same way, he sprinkled with the blood both the tabernacle and everything used in its ceremonies. ²²In fact, the law requires that nearly everything be cleansed with blood, and without the shedding of blood there is no forgiveness.

²³It was necessary, then, for the copies of the heavenly things to be purified with these sacrifices, but the heavenly things themselves with better sacrifices than these. ²⁴For Christ did not enter a man-made sanctuary that was only a copy of the true one; he entered heaven itself, now to appear for us in God's presence. ²⁵Nor did he enter heaven to offer himself again and again, the way the high priest enters the Most Holy Place every year with blood that is not his own. ²⁶Then Christ would have had to suffer many times since the creation of the world. But now he has appeared once for all at the end of the ages to do away with sin by the sacrifice of himself. ²⁷Just as man is destined to die once, and after that to face judgment, ²⁸so Christ was sacrificed once to take away the sins of many people; and he will appear a second time, not to bear sin, but to bring salvation to those who are waiting for him.

INTRODUCTORY REVIEW:
Greater Fullness, Hope, and Comfort

AS WE COME TO HEBREWS 9, WE HAVE SEEN throughout the Book of Hebrews the call to something better, something more, something greater, a greater fullness, a hope that cannot fade away, intended for our comfort and establishment in that hope. This hope is an anchor for our soul. This hope is connected with the coming of Christ, who brings in all that was promised and spoken to us in type and shadow in the Old Testament. The reality is in Christ, and the greater fullness of the blessings are in Christ. We say it is greater because there was the blessing of Christ in the Old Testament, but not in its fullness. People in the Old Testament were saved by looking to Christ even as they are in the New. They looked forward to Christ coming. As they confessed their sins in sacrifices and went through these ordinances, they were being taught the way of God and the worship of God. They were being taught as it is taught to a child, outwardly in type and shadow, but now, with the coming of Christ and the sending of the Spirit of God, we have the *reality* of it, and we have a greater fullness. We should keep in mind that while this greater fullness has come with Christ, it is a fullness that is increasing in history, and in the history of the Church.

In the Book of Ephesians, we are told of the fullness that is in Christ; He is to fill everything in every way.[1] He is to fill the entire universe. This is why He has been given a name that is above every name.[2] We are not to be tossed back and forth,[3] but we are to listen to the work of the Holy Spirit through the pastor-teachers, through the history of the Church, until we reach maturity in Christ and until we attain to the fullness that is in Christ Jesus our Lord.[4] Even now, in the history of the Church, while we have made some progress, there is progress yet to be made.

The Church is uneven with respect to its adherence to Historic Christianity. Throughout history, God and the Holy Spirit have worked through the pastor-teachers as they wrestle with unbelief in the Church and the unbelief of new converts from diverse backgrounds. Christ said, "when he, the Spirit of truth, comes, he will guide you into all truth."[5] This is one of the principal ways in which He does so. As people come with their backgrounds, these thoughts are taken captive, and they are

---

1. *Ephesians 1:23.*

2. *Philippians 2:9.*

3. *Ephesians 4:14.*

4. *Ephesians 4:13.*

5. *John 16:13.*

summed up in the creeds of the Church.[6] As we attain and hold on to this understanding, we can go further and attain fullness. Even those who have held on to all that has been attained in the history of the Church have yet further to go. Even the Westminster Confession of Faith, for example, which we believe is the high-water mark of Historic Christianity, has further to go.[7] There have been a lot of challenges in the last 350+ years (from 1650 to the present), a lot of challenges that the Church has yet to respond to, and it is quite divided on many things.

We have hope before us. The fullness is in Christ Jesus. We do not yet see all things subject to our Lord Jesus Christ, but we have the promise that, through the Church, this will come about. This letter is written to the Hebrews who are being told that there is fullness in Christ and they are not to simply go back and hold on to the old ways. We know that there are Jewish believers who have a predilection, a tendency, to go back to some of the practices of the Old Testament and hold on to them. This letter was written to those Jewish believers who were very zealous for the law, as we saw in the Book of Acts. They did not see all the fullness that exists in Christ Jesus. There was an admixture of the old—what they were accustomed to, what they knew about—and the new. They did not see how the Old Testament pointed to Jesus Christ in every way. We are warned not to settle back into our traditions, be comfortable there and have our hope and comfort in them, but we are to be continually pressing on in Christ Jesus our Lord.

We see in this book that it is anticipated that there will be another rest. Joshua had not given them the rest.[8] There was a rest yet to come, a fullness, a completion in Christ. There was to be another priest after the order of Melchizedek.[9] Scripture spoke about Melchizedek so that we could have anticipated another priest to come. There was going to be another covenant. Hebrews 8:8 says, "The time is coming, declares the Lord, when I will make a new covenant with the house of Israel and with the house of Judah." The Old Testament was anticipating the New by its very structure, words, and teaching. There is no need

---

6. Gangadean, *The Westminster Confession, xvii–xxix, 349–351.*

7. Surrendra Gangadean, *The Westminster Confession of Faith: A Doxological Understanding* (Phoenix: Logos Papers Press, 2024); Surrendra Gangadean, *The Westminster Shorter and Larger Catechisms: A Doxological Understanding* (Phoenix: Logos Papers Press, 2023).

8. *Hebrews 4:8.*

9. *Hebrews 7.*

to hold on to the old. We should understand the goal and keep pressing on toward it, even as Paul said, "but I press on to take hold of that for which Christ Jesus took hold of me . . . Forgetting what is behind and straining toward what is ahead."[10] This is our true comfort, our true hope, our anchor, and our blessing. This is our life, the life that is in Christ Jesus. We do not need to be disconsolate, discouraged, or hopeless. However it may seem around us, we have meaningful work in Christ Jesus our Lord to do, and God will bless our work to the advancement of His kingdom. We have every reason to be cheerful, joyful, encouraged, strong in the Lord, and give ourselves faithfully and diligently to this work, regardless of how it may seem around us. This is the context of the Book of Hebrews, and we will see this continuing to build in the remaining chapters. We will hopefully become more established in God through this.

STRUCTURE OF OLD TESTAMENT WORSHIP

In this chapter, we have a further contrast between the old covenant and the new. There is a further contrast between the worship and regulation for worship in the old covenant and in the new. Hebrews 8 established that there was going to be a new covenant. Hebrews 9 speaks more about the details of this covenant, comparing and contrasting the two, so that we can see more clearly how we are to hold on to the new covenant in Christ Jesus. The first covenant had regulations for worship referred to in Hebrews 9, which speaks about the tabernacle that was set up, the Holy Place, the Most Holy Place, and the content of each. **"Now the first covenant had regulations for worship and also an earthly sanctuary. A tabernacle was set up. In its first room were the lampstand, the table and the consecrated bread; this was called the Holy Place"** (vv. 1–2). The people were instructed in types and shadows as to how they were to approach God.

The Table of Showbread

The people were to feed on the Word of God from the table of showbread in the Holy Place. The priest represented the people eating from

---

10. *Philippians 3:12–13.*

that bread, the Word of God. In our devotions and reading of the Word, we are to live by the Word of God, and we are to take in the Word of God daily. Some of you like fasting; you can go for days without reading the Word. Try going without food for days; you will soon realize it is needed. "Man does not live on bread alone, but on every word that comes from the mouth of God" (Matt. 4:4). How can we possibly starve ourselves in this way? 'I'm on a spiritual fast,' you say. No, we are to take in this food daily. The table of showbread was something that the priest ate daily. The priest represented the people to show that we must have the Word of God daily. We have set it as our goal to seek God diligently, to read the Bible diligently, and we believe that diligence will involve about half an hour a day reading, which is the low end of diligence. If we read—not study, but if we read—we can read through the entire Word of God in one year. We remind you and we encourage you to do this and think about doing it year after year after year with attention and how you can grow in grace in the knowledge of God—the table of showbread. We see the difference between the activity that the priest represented and our activity.

The Candelabra

Besides the table of showbread, there was the seven-stick candelabra. This picture represents the Church, the people of God as a witness in the world. It is our witness individually and together. Seven candles accumulate and intensify the light; it is a complete witness. We are to be witnesses of God. One of the questions asked on the Novitiate[11] is about how we are doing with our witness. Are we discouraged before we even start? Do we say, 'There are a lot of people who don't want to hear.' That's the big news, isn't it? People don't want to hear. No, that is so old, that is not news. The Scripture says, "There is no one righteous, not even one; there is no one who understands, no one who seeks God" (Rom. 3:10–11). But you find yourself discouraged when you talk to people and they are not interested—as if this is news to you. It is as if these times are worse than before. No one seeks God. Do we simply go home discouraged, or do we learn to witness in this condition? Has God witnessed in this? We have to reckon with the self-deception

---

11. Gangadean, *The Westminster Confession*, 389–390.

and self-justification that is covering our not seeking God. God has brought the curse and the promise together from the very beginning in the Garden. We have to learn to speak the Word of God to people. This was part of the priest's life in representing the people.

The Golden Altar of Incense

There was the showbread and the lampstand in the Holy Place. "**Behind the second curtain was a room called the Most Holy Place, which had the golden altar of incense and the gold-covered ark of the covenant**" (v. 3–4a). Interestingly, the golden altar of incense is mentioned in connection with the second room. It was set up right in front of the Most Holy Place. It was directed to God, whose presence was in the Most Holy Place. Perhaps this connection is mentioned because it pertains to the Most Holy Place, even when physically situated in the first room. The emphasis might be on the direction of prayer, which is oriented towards the Most Holy Place. It speaks about the prayers of the people of God, especially the priest, who represents the people and prays daily for the people of God. We know that this was the need. Jesus taught us to pray. We have the example of the Old Testament, where the priest had the breastplate with the 12 precious stones and the names of the 12 tribes of the people of Israel on it. The priest bore it on his breast before God to carry others in prayer in this way. He was to pray for all the people of God. This is why we are taught to pray, "Our Father which art in heaven . . . Give us this day our daily bread" (Matt. 6:9, 11) in the order that the Lord has taught us. Prayer is part of the worship of God, not only corporately on the Lord's Day, but daily in our own lives and in our families. The priest did this in representing the people.

The Most Holy Place

In the Most Holy Place was the gold-covered Ark of the Covenant. "**This ark contained the gold jar of manna, Aaron's staff that had budded, and the stone tablets of the covenant**" (v. 4b). Notice the focus is on the covenant. It is a divinely imposed agreement where God commits to something and calls the people to commit to it. It is called the Ark of the Covenant. It is how God stands in relation to His people in history. In this ark was the gold jar of manna, which shows how God had provided for His people, speaking about the true bread of God. Aaron's rod that budded, speaking about the priesthood and the resurrection of life, which is a sign of the priesthood that was given to Christ. There were also the stone tablets of the covenant. Above this was the very presence of God. **"Above the ark were the cherubim of the Glory, overshadowing the atonement cover"** (v. 5a). This is where God met with His people, above the Ark of the Covenant. The lid of the Ark was called the mercy seat. It is represented as God's throne, as if He is seated there on the mercy seat, ruling in the affairs of man. Above the Ark of the Covenant and the mercy seat was a light, the Shekinah glory, signifying the very presence of God with His people. The cherubim of glory, with their wings overshadowing God, serve as symbols that cry out and proclaim God's holiness and glory. The whole earth is full of His glory[12] because God is holy. He has a zeal for His covenant and for His name. Everything that comes to pass, from the greatest to the least, reveals the glory of God. Angelic beings, the cherubim, sing the song of the glory and the holiness of God. This was given to us in a visible picture in the tabernacle.

This was how it was structured—**"When everything had been arranged like this, the priests entered regularly into the outer room to carry on their ministry"** (v. 6)—the reading of the Word, the witness in the world, and prayer. **"But only the high priest entered the inner room, and that only once a year, and never without blood, which he offered for himself and for the sins the people had committed in ignorance"** (v. 7). A clear distinction is being made between the Holy Place and the Most Holy Place. There is a distinction between the priest in the regular ministry and the high priest in his ministry who, only once a year, would enter the Most Holy Place and never without blood. This spoke about God's holiness, man's sin, how we come short of the glory of God, and how that brings death into our lives. As we turn away from God and, in our sin, disregard God, God turns away from us, leaves us to go our own way, and we go into corruption and spiritual death. Sin must be dealt with. In the Most Holy Place, the priest entered once a year with the blood of the slain animal and sprinkled it on the mercy seat.

---

12. *Isaiah 6:3.*

Paul introduces all of this to make the point: that was the old, how it was ordered, and there is a continuity between the old and the new, but there is a discontinuity. How is that? In verse 8, **"The Holy Spirit was showing by this that the way into the Most Holy Place had not yet been disclosed as long as the first tabernacle was still standing."** The priest entered in this way and the very existence of this order was type and shadow. It was continuing, and as long as it continued here on earth, it showed that the way into the Most Holy Place was not yet made manifest; it was not yet opened. As long as the first tabernacle was standing—the tabernacle made by the hands of men, set upon the earth, with this priestly ministry—as long as this was present, something else was not yet present.

The future arrival of the second is meant to displace what is present. As long as the first one persists, the arrival of the second is still pending. This regulation involves the high priest, the offering of blood, and the presence of the Ark of the Covenant. Today, we do not even give a second thought to the Ark of the Covenant. It is not something magical that we must somehow have and get special powers from, as some popular movies try to portray. There is nothing magical about it. It is gone. We are not to seek to try to recover it and restore it because the reality has come. As long as the first was standing, the way into the Most Holy Place had not yet been disclosed.

> This is an illustration for the present time, indicating that the gifts and sacrifices being offered were not able to clear the conscience of the worshiper. They are only a matter of food and drink and various ceremonial washings—external regulations applying until the time of the new order (vv. 9–10).

Why is it that the offerings could not clear or perfect the conscience of the worshiper? Because **"they are only a matter of food and drink and various ceremonial washings—external regulations applying until the time of the new order"** (v. 10). Think about those who seek to perpetuate worship with the Ark, expressing a concern to rebuild the temple in Jerusalem. The struggle revolves around this aspiration, with many anticipating the reconstruction of the temple. This sentiment is shared by numerous Christians, particularly those who adhere to premillennial beliefs. For them, the expectation is centered on Christ's return, the rebuilding of the temple, and the reestablishment of some of the old patterns of worship.

Those who would try to approach God apart from the reality that is in Christ show that they do not understand the reality of sin and death. They do not understand what sin is and how it produces death because there is not an understanding of the reality of sin; though that reality is present, there is a level at which the conscience has not yet been cleansed. It is a condition of self-deception, present from the beginning in Adam when he covered up. He deceived himself about the sin by which he departed from God in the Garden, by which he put himself in the place of God to determine good and evil, and ate from the tree.[13] Surely, Adam did not know God as he ought. He had not been seeking God as the goal of his life. God had said, "for when you eat of it you will surely die" (Gen. 1:17b). We may not recognize death, the emptiness of life, and the many ways we try to fill the emptiness without God. This is not to say death is not present or sin is not present, but one has not yet come to acknowledge this and has not seen the need for forgiveness of sins in Christ so that the conscience is not yet cleared.

Those who participated in the old order only had the external regulations applied to them until the time of the new order. Those who did not see that this was pointing forward to Christ to come had a deficient view of sin. Consider Saul of Tarsus, how zealous he was for the law, yet what was his understanding of sin? Later on, when he confessed his sin, he said, "Even though I was once a blasphemer and a persecutor and a violent man, I was shown mercy because I acted in ignorance and unbelief" (1 Tim. 1:13). He went about trying to find his own righteousness, not the righteousness that comes from God. Saul had a defective view of sin and death. Think of Saul of Tarsus, the best that those who approached the covenant outwardly were able to achieve. However, we say that those who approached it with understanding, by the grace of God, saw it pointing to Christ and received grace from Him. Hebrews 9:8–10 explains how as long as the old order was standing, the way into the Most Holy Place was not yet made manifest, and it could not clear the worshiper's conscience. It was a matter of external regulations.

---

13. Gangadean, *The Biblical Worldview,* 37–54, 177–195.

NEW TESTAMENT WORSHIP:
In Spirit and in Truth

The Greater Tabernacle

The contrast is now with Christ's coming. There are a number of points in the contrast between the old and the new covenants in connection with the coming of Christ. **"When Christ came as high priest of the good things that are already here, he went through the greater and more perfect tabernacle that is not man-made, that is to say, not a part of this creation"** (v. 11). The copy of the thing is not the real thing. It is not as great as the reality. We have the word, **"he went through the greater and more perfect tabernacle."** This is the sense in which there is more to come, and it is not man-made. The tabernacle on earth was a copy of that which was to come. Christ did not enter into the Most Holy Place. If anyone could and should have entered the Most Holy Place on earth, it would have been Christ, but He bypassed that entirely. He was often at the temple, preaching and teaching. Christ never entered into the Holy Place, let alone the Most Holy Place, though He had the right to do so because of His holiness. Does that mean He never enters the Holy Place, He who is the high priest after the order of Melchizedek, a priest forever? The answer is that Christ certainly did enter the Most Holy Place, heaven itself, into the presence of God. That is one of the first contrasts. This is a copy, a shadow of the reality. Christ, as the mediator of the new testament, enters into the Most Holy Place, the **"more perfect tabernacle that is not man-made"** (v. 11b).

Remember, the Most Holy Place represented God's rule over the mercy seat, the presence of God. We might be impressed in wanting to see the Shekinah glory and the cherubim. That would impress us, I think. We are impressed by the visible, not with the amount of understanding of the invisible. We have to gear our minds to think about what it is to be in the presence of God because of Jesus Christ, because of His righteousness that is imputed to us, and the way that cleanses us from our sin.

The very presence of God is open to us in Jesus Christ, though it was so far from us under the old covenant. People did not enter the Holy Place and all the more they did not enter the Most Holy Place. In the Old Testament, they could come as far as the altar. In the New Testament, we are able to enter with Christ into the heavenlies itself.

This is why the Scripture says He has seated us with Him in the heavenly realms in Christ Jesus.[14] God is present with us. He dwells with us and in us. Closer than this, we cannot come. Jesus said, "If anyone loves me, he will obey my teaching. My Father will love him, and we will come to him and make our home with him" (Jn. 14:23). Now, that does not seem very impressive to us. We go through life not being aware of the presence of God in many ways. All we have to do is think back to the time before we came to Christ and what life was like without Christ, without God.

Think about the billion or so Muslims in the world who profess faith in God but not through Christ. They do not come to see the need for the sacrifice.[15] Think about their understanding of sin and the holiness of God, how deficient their understanding is, how their consciences can never be cleansed apart from coming through Christ in His blood. Think of how zealous some of them are for the *sharia* law. But without Christ, there is no remission of sin. God is holy; we have sin, we have come short of the glory of God, and *only* through Christ is it dealt with. Think of how absolutely empty our lives were as God worked conviction in our lives. We forget. Remember the Jews were called to observe the Passover and to remember their coming out of Egypt. Next week at the Lord's Supper we will do this. We will remember what we were like before we were in Christ. At that time, we will be able to appreciate what it is to have the presence of God in our lives, the Word of God in us. Those of you who have not had the conviction of sin and death without God, the emptiness of life without God, and who have not been convicted that we are without God because of our sin—seek God. Seek for His mercy so that you might have a true understanding because if you attempt to come to God apart from Christ, you will not be able to do so. There is one God and one mediator between God and man, the man Christ Jesus. "Whoever believes in the Son has eternal life, but whoever rejects the Son will not see life, for God's wrath remains on him" (Jn. 3:36). You may not be aware of this. It does not mean it is not there.

---

14. *Ephesians 2:6.*

15. Gangadean, *Philosophical Foundation*, 191–192; Gangadean, *The Westminster Confession*, 21–27, 37–41, 67–69, 129–130, 236–238; Gangadean, "Paper No. 91: Christianity and Islam," in *The Logos Papers*, 479–484.

Think of how many profess belief in God but not in Christ. What they have made for themselves is an idol. As zealous as the Muslims are to avoid idolatry, they have only avoided idolatry in the gross, outward, external form. The god they hold to is not the God of justice and love and mercy. They may believe in hell, they may believe in the resurrection of the dead, but they do not believe in the forgiveness of sins through Christ. They do not see God's unalterable holiness and justice. What they have is not the true God, it is an idol that has been manufactured. Their consciences cannot be cleansed apart from the acknowledgment of sin and death and forgiveness in Christ. If we have any doubts about the holiness of God and being in the very presence of God, think of what it was like before we were converted. If that does not help you, then think about others who are now dead in their trespasses and sins. Look around you, how many people you know, how many people close to you that you know who are dead in their trespasses and sins. Let that stir you up to thankfulness in God. Not just the utterly bad cases, but people whose lives are *decent* but *empty* and how desperate they are. Think, 'There but for the grace of God, go I.' We need to open our eyes and think, see, remember, and know what it is to have the presence of God in our lives through Jesus Christ our Lord. Do not take it for granted that Jesus entered into the Most Holy Place. We entered with Him. We are in Him.

Christ Entered by His Own Blood

First, Christ entered the true tabernacle, the great and more perfect tabernacle. Second, **"He did not enter by means of the blood of goats and calves; but he entered the Most Holy Place once for all by his own blood, having obtained eternal redemption"** (v. 12). Jesus is the high priest. As the high priest entered into the Most Holy Place, Jesus entered into the Most Holy Place, not on earth, but the true Most Holy Place. As the priest on earth entered with the blood of animals, so Jesus also entered with His own blood. Think of it: Jesus is our high priest. He enters the Most Holy Place once and for all by His own blood. Jesus could do so because His life was perfect and His death was perfect. Jesus perfectly obeyed God. He was righteous, and He had to undo the result of our sin. He had to undergo the forsaking of God on the cross (what we deserve) and all the things that accompany that, all the forms of the curse, including death. "Christ redeemed us from the curse of the law by becoming a curse for us, for it is written: 'Cursed is everyone who is hung on a tree'" (Gal. 3:13). Christ had a crown of thorns that were pressed into His head. He suffered the most ignominious death, naked, nailed to a cross because of sin—man's sin. In this, we see what our sins deserve. The reality of *our* sin is seen most clearly in the death of Christ on the cross. God would not have sent His Son, His only Son, to die if there was some other way around this. If we could have suffered for 10,000 years and be on our way, God would not have sent His Son. Hell is forever; it is only through Christ that we are forgiven and by no other way.

> **He entered the Most Holy Place once for all by his own blood, having obtained eternal redemption. The blood of goats and bulls and the ashes of a heifer sprinkled on those who are ceremonially unclean sanctify them so that they are outwardly clean. How much more, then, will the blood of Christ, who through the eternal Spirit offered himself unblemished to God, cleanse our consciences from acts that lead to death, so that we may serve the living God!** (vv. 12–14).

He is the spotless Lamb of God, without sin, tested in every way and yet without sin. His blood will **"cleanse our consciences from acts that lead to death, so that we may serve the living God!"** Before this, we served ourselves. We were self-centered; we were not God-centered. We may even be religiously self-centered. We may come with all of these offerings and outward things, but not with a broken spirit and contrite heart before God,[16] not broken because of our sin, and we think we are serving God as Saul of Tarsus thought he was.[17] But we are not serving the living God; we are serving the god of our creation, an idol that we have made, and through this, we serve ourselves.

When we look at Christ and Him crucified, we see the reality of our sin. He is the one who died, was buried, was raised again, and is seated at the right hand of God. These are the fundamental realities of Christ: His incarnation, that He came to earth in a body, that He suffered under Pontius Pilate, was crucified, dead, buried, and He

---

16. *Psalm 51:17.*

17. *1 Timothy 1:13.*

rose again the third day, the resurrection of the dead. The incarnation, crucifixion, resurrection, and ascension collectively convey the work of Jesus Christ as a high priest. These events highlight the necessity for Christ to overcome the dominion of sin and death that prevails in the world outside of Christ. We have forgiveness in Christ. Because of His perfect righteousness that we receive by faith, our consciences are cleansed from sin and the self-life, that we may serve the living God. The blood of bulls and goats cannot accomplish this. They are not of that stature. Christ entered the Most Holy Place and entered with His own blood. This, unlike the first covenant, cleanses our conscience from sin and acts that lead to death so that we might serve the living God.

The Promised Eternal Inheritance in Christ

"For this reason Christ is the mediator of a new covenant" (v. 15a). God wanted us to have this; He wanted us to serve Him fully all the days of our lives. We are called to serve Him, be witnesses on the earth, and make disciples of all nations. The people of Israel were not given this task in the Old Testament. They served God in another way. They served God by maintaining a corporate witness *in* the land, and nations were to come and see this. That was the service operative then. But now the people of God are to go into *all* the world, take *every* thought captive,[18] and bring *all* the nations to the obedience of Jesus Christ.[19] God always had it in mind that we would serve Him in this way. Christ has made this possible. This is why He is the mediator of the new covenant. There had to be a new covenant; we had to have this kind of service; this was part of the promise. It says, **"that those who are called may receive the promised eternal inheritance—now that he has died as a ransom to set them free from the sins committed under the first covenant"** (v. 15). In connection with the death of Christ, there is a new covenant, and in connection with the death of Christ, there is an inheritance.

Christ has established a *new* testament, a *new* will. In connection with His death, there is a will; in connection with the will, there is an inheritance. What is the inheritance? The Scripture speaks about it this

---

18. *2 Corinthians 10:4–5.*
19. *Matthew 28:18–20.*

way: "take your inheritance, the kingdom prepared for you since the creation of the world" (Matt. 25:34). This is the very kingdom that we are involved in seeking daily. Christ said, "But seek first his kingdom and his righteousness, and all these things will be given to you as well. Therefore do not worry about tomorrow, for tomorrow will worry about itself. Each day has enough trouble of its own" (Matt. 6:33–34). Do not worry; give yourself to the work of the kingdom. We seek the kingdom in this way. As the Israelites sought to conquer Canaan, so we seek to take every thought captive. This is a truer and fuller inheritance that is ours in Christ. For this to come about, Christ had to become the mediator of the new covenant so that we might receive the promised eternal inheritance, which will last forever. Abraham was looking for a city with foundations,[20] which was not Jerusalem. It is a heavenly Jerusalem. It is a Jerusalem from above coming down from God, that diamond city, that consummation of all the efforts of everything good done by human beings throughout history. This city is represented as a perfect cube, 1,400 miles long and wide and high, shining with the glory of God coming down out of heaven. This is the city that Abraham looked for. This is the eternal inheritance that we will dwell in forever. Christ entered into the true Most Holy Place with His own blood. According to the new covenant, the New Testament, the new will in which we have the eternal inheritance.

COPIES PURIFIED THROUGH THE SACRIFICE

In the case of a will, it is necessary to prove the death of the one who made it, because a will is in force only when somebody has died; it never takes effect while the one who made it is living. This is why even the first covenant was not put into effect without blood (vv. 16–18).

The will is not in effect until the person dies and it can be shown that the person has died. So, too, Christ died in the shedding of His blood. It was this way in the Old Testament when Moses took the animal's blood and sprinkled it on the people and the scroll.

---

20. *Hebrews 11:10.*

> When Moses had proclaimed every commandment of the law to all the people, he took the blood of calves, together with water, scarlet wool and branches of hyssop, and sprinkled the scroll and all the people. He said, "This is the blood of the covenant, which God has commanded you to keep." In the same way, he sprinkled with the blood both the tabernacle and everything used in its ceremonies (vv. 19–21).

The Old Testament and the old covenant were sealed with blood, and the New Testament was sealed with blood—the blood of Christ Jesus Himself. It says here, "**In fact, the law requires that nearly everything be cleansed with blood, and without the shedding of blood there is no forgiveness**" (v. 22). Christ has died in shedding His blood. The New Testament has been established through which we will receive the fullness of the blessing of God, the eternal inheritance. This is the *greater*, the *more* that we are to be looking forward to. We are not to be looking forward to Christ returning to Jerusalem and somehow establishing this kingdom apart from His people, but He is to do this work *through* His people. He says, "Therefore go and make disciples of all nations, baptizing them in the name of the Father and of the Son and of the Holy Spirit, and teaching them to obey everything I have commanded you. And surely I am with you always, to the very end of the age" (Matt. 28:19–20). This is how Christ will accomplish His purpose, He and those united to Him. This is our hope. We hold to this steadfastly. This is what we rejoice in on this Sabbath Day, which speaks about the rest to come. This work that God has given us in Christ will be accomplished. "**It was necessary, then, for the copies of the heavenly things to be purified with these sacrifices, but the heavenly things themselves with better sacrifices than these**" (v. 23). It was only with the blood of Christ. This contrast is also made:

> For Christ did not enter a man-made sanctuary that was only a copy of the true one; he entered heaven itself, now to appear for us in God's presence. Nor did he enter heaven to offer himself again and again, the way the high priest enters the Most Holy Place every year with blood that is not his own (vv. 24–25).

The *perfection* of the sacrifice, the *completion* of the sacrifice, is seen in that Christ did it once and for all. It was sufficient to satisfy the divine justice and purchase redemption for the whole world. It will come to pass in all those for whom God intends it. All those who are elect in Christ will be brought in due time to Him:

> **Then Christ would have had to suffer many times since the creation of the world. But now he has appeared once for all at the end of the ages to do away with sin by the sacrifice of himself. Just as man is destined to die once, and after that to face judgment, so Christ was sacrificed once to take away the sins of many people; and he will appear a second time, not to bear sin, but to bring salvation to those who are waiting for him (vv. 26–28).**

Christ will appear a second time. It will not be to bear sin again when He appears because He has completed that work. It does not have to be done again because it was perfect. It is perfect because He was perfect. He was the sinless, spotless Lamb of God. Christ obeyed God in every respect, and we are called to do so in Him. When He comes a second time, He will not come to bear sin but to bring salvation for those waiting for Him. This is why our focus is on the Lord Jesus. We are to fix our thoughts on Him. We are to have our eyes on Christ Jesus crucified, raised from the dead, and seated at the right hand of God. He is ruling now, and when He comes, He will bring in the final removal of the last vestiges of sin. He will bring about the resurrection from the dead. When Christ comes a second time with a shout, with a voice, He will raise the dead, and the last remnants of sin and physical death will be removed. He will bring in the fullness of salvation, and we, in our incorruptible bodies, no longer subject to decay, will inherit the kingdom of God, promised from before the foundation of the world, our eternal inheritance.

These are the blessings of the new covenant, administered with less outward glory but in a much, much, much greater richness and fullness held forth to us. So let us keep our eyes on Jesus, look to Him, and find our hope in Him. Amen.

10

CHRIST:
THE LASTING SACRIFICE

Hebrews 10

¹The law is only a shadow of the good things that are coming—not the realities themselves. For this reason it can never, by the same sacrifices repeated endlessly year after year, make perfect those who draw near to worship. ²If it could, would they not have stopped being offered? For the worshipers would have been cleansed once for all, and would no longer have felt guilty for their sins. ³But those sacrifices are an annual reminder of sins, ⁴because it is impossible for the blood of bulls and goats to take away sins.

⁵Therefore, when Christ came into the world, he said:
  "Sacrifice and offering you did not desire,
    but a body you prepared for me;

⁶with burnt offerings and sin offerings
    you were not pleased.

⁷Then I said, 'Here I am—it is written about me in the scroll—
    I have come to do your will, O God.'"

⁸First he said, "Sacrifices and offerings, burnt offerings and sin offerings you did not desire, nor were you pleased with them" (although the law required them to be made). ⁹Then he said, "Here I am, I have come to do your will." He sets aside the first to establish the second. ¹⁰And by that will, we have been made holy through the sacrifice of the body of Jesus Christ once for all.

¹¹Day after day every priest stands and performs his religious duties; again and again he offers the same sacrifices, which can never take away sins. ¹²But when this priest had offered for all time one sacrifice for sins, he sat down at the right hand of God. ¹³Since that time he waits for his enemies

to be made his footstool, [14]because by one sacrifice he has made perfect forever those who are being made holy.

[15]The Holy Spirit also testifies to us about this. First he says:

[16]"This is the covenant I will make with them
  after that time, says the Lord.
 I will put my laws in their hearts,
  and I will write them on their minds."

[17]Then he adds:
 "Their sins and lawless acts
  I will remember no more."

[18]And where these have been forgiven, there is no longer any sacrifice for sin. [19]Therefore, brothers, since we have confidence to enter the Most Holy Place by the blood of Jesus, [20]by a new and living way opened for us through the curtain, that is, his body, [21]and since we have a great priest over the house of God, [22]let us draw near to God with a sincere heart in full assurance of faith, having our hearts sprinkled to cleanse us from a guilty conscience and having our bodies washed with pure water. [23]Let us hold unswervingly to the hope we profess, for he who promised is faithful. [24]And let us consider how we may spur one another on toward love and good deeds. [25]Let us not give up meeting together, as some are in the habit of doing, but let us encourage one another—and all the more as you see the Day approaching.

[26]If we deliberately keep on sinning after we have received the knowledge of the truth, no sacrifice for sins is left, [27]but only a fearful expectation of judgment and of raging fire that will consume the enemies of God. [28]Anyone who rejected the law of Moses died without mercy on the testimony of two or three witnesses. [29]How much more severely do you think a man deserves to be punished who has trampled the Son of God under foot, who has treated as an unholy thing the blood of the covenant that sanctified him, and who has insulted the Spirit of grace? [30]For we know him who said, "It is mine to avenge; I will repay," and again, "The Lord will judge his people." [31]It is a dreadful thing to fall into the hands of the living God.

[32]Remember those earlier days after you had received the light, when you stood your ground in a great contest in the face of suffering. [33]Sometimes you were publicly exposed to insult and persecution; at other times you stood side by side with those who were so treated. [34]You sympathized with those in prison and joyfully accepted the confiscation of your property, because you knew that you yourselves had better and lasting possessions.

³⁵So do not throw away your confidence; it will be richly rewarded. ³⁶You need to persevere so that when you have done the will of God, you will receive what he has promised. ³⁷For in just a very little while,

"He who is coming will come and will not delay.
   ³⁸But my righteous one will live by faith.
And if he shrinks back,
   I will not be pleased with him."

³⁹But we are not of those who shrink back and are destroyed, but of those who believe and are saved.

INTRODUCTION AND REVIEW

THERE IS NO TURNING BACK. The people to whom this letter was written were tempted to turn back. They encountered difficulty, and they were wavering. The letter is written to remind them of the hope that is ours, the greater fullness that there is in the new covenant, and that our comfort is in looking forward to this hope. Paul shows them that it is scriptural to expect change. According to the Scripture, many things were to change: the mediator of the Old Testament and the mediator of the New, the Sabbath rest, the priesthood, the covenant, the tabernacle, and the sacrifice.

On the basis of this change and the temptation that we face to fall back into our tradition (what we are comfortable with), the exhortation comes in a number of ways. The first part of this is reminding us of the change in the sacrifice. Notice how the whole system is changing. Paul is concerned with showing how there is change, continuity, and justification for the particular form of the change. This book, of all books, helps us to see the relation between the Old and the New Testament.

THE CEREMONIAL LAW BEING
REPLACED IN CHRIST

The Law: A Shadow versus Reality

There is a change in the sacrifice. There is not only a change in the tabernacle; of course, there must also be a change in the sacrifice, which is made explicit. We saw the change in the tabernacle accompanying the change in the covenant and the priesthood. The whole ceremonial law, as spoken of here, is being fulfilled. This is how the change occurs. **"The law is only a shadow of the good things that are coming—not the realities themselves"** (v. 1). This verse refers to the things that are coming. In the past, we have spoken of the law in three parts: (1) The moral law, which is perpetual since it is written on the hearts of all people.[1] (2) The civil law, which expired with the nation of Israel. We are bound only by the general equity of the law. It was an application of the Ten Commandments under those conditions. (3) The ceremonial law speaking about Christ coming.[2] In the Epistle to the Hebrews, we speak about the law, specifically the aspects of ceremonial law and worship. It says, **"That was a shadow of the good things that are coming, not the realities themselves"** (v. 1a). The contrast here is between the shadow and the reality. It is a shadow of good things that are coming. We should expect better things with the reality, which is exactly what we hear throughout the Book of Hebrews. It is affirmed in this epistle that the sacrificial system is to be done away with. Being a shadow and not the reality, it can never do what the reality will do. There was a difference from the very beginning, and that difference is manifested in a particular way.

"For this reason it can never, by the same sacrifices repeated endlessly year after year, make perfect those who draw near to worship" (v. 1b). This specifically was something the sacrifice could not do. And yet, the Roman Catholic Church has somehow managed to turn the sacrifice of Christ, which was once and for all, into a sacrifice that is repeated every time the mass is celebrated. The mass is viewed as an actual sacrifice of Christ anew. It is a distortion of this truth. Those who participate in the mass recognize that their consciences cannot be made perfect. As long as one gets into this repeated pattern, grace takes away sin, but sin removes grace. It is not a once-and-for-all sacrifice that brings peace. Martin Luther was not at peace; he did not have peace of conscience under the sacramental system. So whether it is the Old Testament or the New, where the sacrifice is repeated, as long as it is repeated, the conscience cannot be cleansed and be made perfect. How remarkable is it that somehow we manage to take a good thing

---

1. Gangadean, *Philosophical Foundation*, 171–284; Gangadean, *History of Philosophy*, 61–69; Gangadean, *The Westminster Catechisms*, 227–267; Gangadean, *On Natural and Revealed Theology*, 127–139, 166–178.

2. Gangadean, *The Westminster Confession*, 207–221.

and make it bad when it should be a good thing from the old, being made better? However, Roman Catholics have taken the good thing of the New Testament and made it bad by turning back to the Old. It shows that we did not understand the once-and-for-all sacrifice of the Lord Jesus Christ.

Millions and millions of people in the Roman Catholic faith, who observe the mass as a sacrifice, cannot have peace. It is one of the reasons why there is such a thing as extreme unction. At the end of one's life, the work of the priest can eliminate whatever sin remains. The sacrifice of Christ was misunderstood after the pattern of the Old, rather than seeing it as a shadow of good things to come. We should not take it for granted that we will hold onto this truth. Think about how many times the sacrifices were made year after year, particularly the atoning sacrifice done annually. The emphasis comes in the endless repetition. Year after year for about 1,400 years the sacrificial system went on since the time Moses instituted it. That is a long time, is it not? But it could not take away sin. Being the shadow, it could not, and being repeated, it could not. Think about the dynamics of the sacrifices being repeated. 'Well, it took away last year's sin, so is there no sin this year, or is there more sin to be repeated and taken away again? Why is there more sin of that sort this year? What sins are they? New sins or old sins still remaining there?' The sacrifice is repeated, but the shadow could not take sin away.

The repetition itself is an indication that they were not able to take it away. **"If it could, would they not have stopped being offered? For the worshipers would have been cleansed once for all, and would no longer have felt guilty for their sins"** (v. 2). In the case of Jesus Christ, there is one sacrifice, one and only one—the everlasting sacrifice. Christ's sacrifice was done once because it was perfect and could take away sin, unlike the sacrifice of the Old Testament. The sacrifice of Christ cleanses once for all. Let me be careful because this doctrine has been distorted. Some people speak about being wholly sanctified and think they are, therefore, without sin. There is a teaching about the sacrifice of Christ being sufficient for all of our sin once and for all even though we continue to have sin. We speak about justification as once and for all, and we speak about sanctification as a process.[3] Sometimes, the word is used in the sense that we are set apart once and for all for Christ. The work of regeneration will never be undone. Those who truly come to Christ will never fall away. In that sense, we are sanctified and set apart once for Christ. Even though we continue to sin, we are in a new position in Christ. In this sense, it says, **"For the worshipers would have been cleansed once for all,"** in Christ.

"Those sacrifices are an annual reminder of sins" (v. 3), but in the case of Christ, He purchased our salvation once and for all; it needs to be done once and only once. In those sacrifices, there was a reminder of sins, a reminder to the people. Interestingly, they were not just remembering their sins, but God was reminding the people that their sins were being remembered until Christ came to remove them completely. God accepted them on the basis of Christ, but they had to look forward to Christ's coming. The annual offering for sin was a reminder to the people that this was not the sacrifice by which their sins would be forgiven. God is reminding them that there is One to come, through whom their sins will be forgiven. It is a reminder to them, subjectively, **"because it is impossible for the blood of bulls and goats to take away sins"** (v. 4). It indicates that God remembers their sin until the One who comes will remove it completely. We see this explicitly in the Scriptures when it says, **"Their sins and lawless acts I will remember no more"** (v. 17).

Impossibility of Atonement Through Animals (Psalm 40:6–8)

There is to be a change in the sacrifice, tabernacle, priesthood, covenant, and mediator, and we should have expected this. This passage is from Psalm 40, which we spoke of last time; it is quoted here in a similar way that other passages have been quoted, showing that we should have expected this change to come. How so? Not only could the sacrifice never take away sin, but he adds, **"because it is impossible for the blood of bulls and goats to take away sins"** (v. 4). Notice this strong word: **"impossible."** If we understood the nature of sin and how costly our redemption is, we would know that no animal sacrifice could take it away. We should also know that we cannot sacrifice the fruit of our

---

3. Gangadean, *The Westminster Confession,* 143–206; Gangadean, *The Westminster Catechisms,* 191–207.

body, our children, for the sin of our soul. They are not without sin, they cannot be sacrificed, and they are not of the stature of Jesus Christ, the Son of God incarnate, to pay the penalty for our sin.

In history, many things have been tried in an attempt to take away sin, and they never have and never will succeed. We would have known this if we had understood the nature of sin. We should have understood that Christ's lasting sacrifice was coming, as seen in the Scriptures. In verse 5, it says, **"Therefore, when Christ came into the world, he said: 'Sacrifice and offering you did not desire, but a body you prepared for me.'"** And in verse 8, **"First he said, 'Sacrifices and offerings, burnt offerings and sin offerings you did not desire, nor were you pleased with them' (although the law required them to be made)."** How could this be? God does not desire sacrifice and offering, and yet He required it. The way it is to be understood is this: He required what it *signified*, not the sacrifice in and of itself—the sacrifice was a *reminder* of what was required. Immediately, He says, **"but a body you prepared for me"** (v. 5b); this is the Messiah, the One to come, the seed of the woman, the seed of Abraham, the seed of the line of Judah, the seed of David. He comes now and says, **"a body you prepared for me"** (v. 5b). In contrast, we see when we have these two juxtaposed, that God requires a sacrifice, yet He did not desire the sacrifices offered in the old economy. What God desired through the sacrifices and what it signified was to come through the Messiah who became incarnate: **"a body you prepared for me"** (v. 5b). He is incarnated for this one reason: to make atonement. He is incarnated for this one reason: to be the Lamb of God that takes away the sin of the world.[4]

The Contrast: Repeated Animal Sacrifices versus Christ's Once for All

"Then I said, 'Here I am—it is written about me in the scroll—I have come to do your will, O God'" (v. 7). He comes now, in the body, to be this sacrifice, and in place of this sacrifice, the old sacrifice is done away with. Paul is saying that the old is being set aside for the new, and we should have anticipated that the new is better. Paul says it a number of times throughout this book, and it becomes cumulative

---

4. *John 1:29.*

and more intense as it accumulates. The new is richer and fuller, and it accomplishes what the old could not because it was only a shadow and a reminder.

"Then he said, 'Here I am, I have come to do your will.' He sets aside the first to establish the second. And by that will, we have been made holy through the sacrifice of the body of Jesus Christ once for all" (v. 9). We have been made holy once for all. As a result of regeneration, justification, and adoption into the body of Christ, we are made holy as the children of God in Jesus Christ—once and for all—based on the one sacrifice of Jesus Christ.

Again, Paul repeats and emphasizes the point, **"Day after day every priest stands and performs his religious duties; again and again he offers the same sacrifices, which can never take away sins"** (v. 11). Notice the repetition: **"again and again"** the priest offers the same sacrifices, and in contrast, it can never take away sin. **"But when this priest had offered for all time one sacrifice for sins, he sat down at the right hand of God"** (v. 12). The sufficiency of Christ's sacrifice is that it is done once, and He is seated at the right hand of God. What has He accomplished through this? It is spoken of as redemption accomplished; Jesus Christ, by one sacrifice, accomplished redemption. It is in the process of being applied—to us individually and through the history of the Church. What do we expect this redemption to bring about? **"Since that time he waits for his enemies to be made his footstool"** (v. 13). Christ conquered sin and death by purchasing forgiveness for all those given to Him. This is being worked out by all His enemies being made His footstool. This is worked out by the nations being discipled and everyone coming to bow before our Lord Jesus Christ.[5] Jesus has accomplished redemption by His death. He is seated and ruling through His Church, waiting for this to be accomplished. He is waiting. What is He waiting on? Jesus is waiting in the sense that He is accomplishing the work of discipling the nations through His body. Just as the woman was given as a helpmeet to the man, so the Church is the bride of Christ (the helpmeet), and they together are to accomplish the work of being fruitful, multiplying, filling the earth, and subduing it.[6] Christ, through the Church, will accomplish what Adam failed to accomplish.

---

5. *Matthew 28:18–20.*

6. *Genesis 1:28.*

What a salvation in God! Who would have possibly thought that God would use this, that Christ may be exalted in every way? The Son of God would have this honor and glory.

Jesus Christ is seated until all his enemies are made his footstool. It says next, **"because by one sacrifice he has made perfect forever those who are being made holy"** (v. 14). There are two senses of sanctification, not to be confused; once and for all redemption is accomplished in being set apart, and now it is being applied in our lives by making us holy.

Scriptural Confirmation: The New Covenant

Scripture confirms elsewhere how holiness is to be attained. **"The Holy Spirit also testifies to us about this. First he says: 'This is the covenant I will make with them after that time, says the Lord. I will put my laws in their hearts, and I will write them on their minds'"** (v. 15–16). Jesus said, "Therefore go and make disciples of all nations, baptizing them in the name of the Father and of the Son and of the Holy Spirit, and teaching them to obey everything I have commanded you" (Matt. 28:19–20b). He said, "But when he, the Spirit of truth, comes, he will guide you into all truth" (Jn. 16:13a). This includes understanding the law. The process of growth in understanding and taking thoughts captive is happening in the history of the Church. The Church has responded and needs to continue responding to misunderstandings of the law. Post-biblical Judaism has been 'law-focused,' and so have theonomists. In the Roman Catholic Church, appeal has been made to canon law. Furthermore, there has been the development of a whole civil code that seeks to spell out by law how we are to live. In Islam, great emphasis has been placed on *sharia* law.[7] Yet, over and against all these misunderstandings, the law of God will prevail. The law that will prevail in the earth is the law of Jesus Christ—the law that is focused on the knowledge of God as the good,[8] the law that is focused on life in every detail.

---

7. Gangadean, "Paper No. 91: Christianity and Islam," in *The Logos Papers*, 479–484.

8. Gangadean, *Philosophical Foundation*, 171–177, 208–211; Gangadean, *The Westminster Catechisms*, 109–111, 321–325; Gangadean, *On Natural and Revealed Theology*, 33–39, 127–139; Gangadean, "Paper No. 115: Doxological Christianity," in *The Logos Papers*, 595–596;

We have talked about the moral law from general revelation.[9] Many of you have heard its exposition. You have seen the comprehensiveness of the law, the clarity of this law, and the critical nature of this law. This law will be written on our hearts, not only in its objective, formal sense, but it will be internalized and put into practice. An outworking is going on through history where the Church will indeed learn the law of God and all of its marvelous, wonderful blessings that will come in obedience to the law of God.

> On that day HOLY TO THE LORD will be inscribed on the bells of the horses, and the cooking pots in the LORD's house will be like the sacred bowls in front of the altar. Every pot in Jerusalem and Judah will be holy to the LORD Almighty, and all who come to sacrifice will take some of the pots and cook in them (Zech. 14:20–21a).

All this comprehensiveness, down to the pots and pans, all the details and applications of life. We will eat to the glory of God. We will do all that we do to the glory of God. Next time you get in your car, ask yourself, 'Is this car that I'm driving and the life that is involved in this car that I'm driving an acknowledgment of God's grace and is it all done to his glory?' The whole of our life bound up in these blessings that God has given us will be to the glory of God. He will write His laws in our hearts and on our minds.[10] We will meditate on the law day and night.[11] We will learn the law. This is the purpose of the Church in making disciples, teaching them to observe all that He has commanded. In the weeks, months, and years ahead, you can expect this to be operating and present in your life.[12] I will try to speak of it in such a way that you will see that I am coming at this from the

---

"Paper No. 116: The Knowledge of God vs. The Hope of Heaven," 597–598; "Paper No. 117: Knowing and Making God Known," in *The Logos Papers*, 599–601.

9. Gangadean, *Philosophical Foundation*, 171–284; Gangadean, *History of Philosophy*, 61–69; Gangadean, *On Natural and Revealed Theology*, 127–139, 166–178; Gangadean, "Paper No. 9: The Moral Law: Derived from Human Nature," 43–46; "Paper No. 10: The Moral Law (ONLAC)," in *The Logos Papers*, 47–68.

10. *Jeremiah 31:31–34.*

11. *Joshua 1:8; Psalm 1:2.*

12. This is referring to the progression from doctrine to life. As noted in the Series Preface, Pastor Gangadean took a recognizable shift in emphasis towards sanctification in the life of the church. See: Series Preface for a larger context.

law of God, from the Word of God understood comprehensively, and learning to live by that law.

The law includes *thinking is presuppositional* and *meaning is more basic than truth*. That is a good one, isn't it? That reaches down, doesn't it? That gets us beyond skepticism and fideism. It surely does, and it gets us beyond rationalism and empiricism and every admixture of the two. This could solve a lot of problems.[13] We will speak about how, when we are blocked in one place, the law of God speaks about things even more basic: the curse and the promise, the nature of sin, and going deeper to understand sin so that we will not be blocked and we do not become discouraged. The latter part of this is specifically warning against discouragement. As I have spoken with many of you through the weeks and months, I know many of you have encountered discouragement in your witness. The law of God is within your heart; we learn to overcome, we learn to live by this law, think by this law, and sleep by this law. This is a good thing to do, to sleep by the law. Sometimes, you have to get up at 4:30 in the morning. It happened that I got up at 4:30 this morning, and I am learning, as Elisabeth Elliot has learned, that old people get up early. You know, no one has called me at 4:30 in the morning, and don't you dare! I have time to do some good writing at that time. I learned to live by this law. It is a great thing. God has ordered everything right.

Then he adds: **"Their sins and lawless acts I will remember no more"** (v. 17). There has been forgiveness in Christ. Some of you struggle with conscience before God and your acceptance before God. You should know the law of God. You should know that once-and-for-all sacrifice. You should look upon Jesus and not doubt the love of God towards you. If there is anything you can doubt, it is whether we have received Christ as Savior. I do not want to say that because I know if I give you a little something to doubt, you are going to grab all of it and use that as a wedge to doubt as much as you can—your own salvation. Some of you are given to this. I would instead emphasize obedience to the Lord. Take knowledge of His Word, receive it, and have a clearness of conscience. Remember, this is a big thing for us. We now have, by the Word of God, cleansing of conscience, once-and-for-all acceptance, and a peace with God that we are a child of God. In the midst of our

---

13. Gangadean, *Philosophical Foundation*; Gangadean, *History of Philosophy*.

afflictions and trials, God has not abandoned us. He is working for our good. You can say categorically: "And we know that in all things God works for the good of those who love him, who have been called according to his purpose" (Rom. 8:28). I spoke with someone who is struggling with the reality of his wife having been raped and having to bring the Word that God will work this together for good and believing that God will. He did it for Job, and He can do it for each one of us.

EXHORTATION TO PERSEVERE AND OVERCOME

There are multiple reasons for the exhortation, multiple things being exhorted, and multiple ways the exhortation comes, not only in terms of promise but also in terms of warning and reminder. In the first part, we have the promise of God. The second part is the warning for not heeding it. The third part is the reminder of what we have done before.

The Promise of God: Draw Near to God

Here, then, is the exhortation based on the Scripture. There is a sense in which this exhortation is building on, not just what immediately goes before in Hebrews, but the entire Scripture. This new covenant is richer and fuller, for all the reasons that have been given. Paul proceeds, **"Therefore, brothers, since we have confidence to enter the Most Holy Place by the blood of Jesus, by a new and living way opened for us through the curtain, that is, his body"** (vv. 19–20). Christ has entered there and we, in Him, have entered through His sacrifice. **"Since we have a great priest over the house of God"** (v. 21). These are premises Paul has laid down. He says **"let us"** four times; notice these and how they interact. **"Let us draw near to God with a sincere heart in full assurance of faith, having our hearts sprinkled to cleanse us from a guilty conscience and having our bodies washed with pure water"** (v. 22a). The next chapter is going to speak about faith connected with hope. Remember, "And now these three remain: faith, hope and love. But the greatest of these is love" (1 Cor. 13:13). Love is the greatest in the sense that it is the most complete. We should have full assurance of faith. For those who are wavering in the move from the old to the new covenant, you should see clearly how the Scriptures anticipated this in so many ways, again and again. Remember all those Scriptures about Melchizedek's priesthood, the rest that was to come (not through Joshua), the new covenant, and Christ the priest, the sacrifice once and for all—these are strong arguments to support this. We should have full assurance of faith and not waiver. **"Having our hearts sprinkled to cleanse us from a guilty conscience and having our bodies washed with pure water"** (v. 22b). We should not be troubled by guilt. We should recognize that we are accepted in the beloved. Yes, we have sinned, but let us not diminish the work of Christ. We are accepted in the beloved. And when accepted, we are accepted with our root sin and all of the other sins that go with this—actual sins, instances of all the fruit sins, and future sins that will come. We are accepted in the beloved; we are accepted in Jesus Christ. This is the sense in which our consciences have been cleansed. We do not have to have guilt and all that goes with it. We have to learn to recognize the many forms that guilt takes. We are not to be tripped up by this: **"Having our hearts sprinkled to cleanse us from a guilty conscience and having our bodies washed with pure water"** (v. 22b). Our whole being belongs to God. We are made holy, and we are to serve God with our whole bodies and live holy lives.

Let Us Hold On Unswervingly

"Let us hold unswervingly to the hope we profess, for he who promised is faithful" (v. 23). A number of times in the Scriptures, it speaks about the *hope*.[14] **"Let us hold unswervingly to the hope we profess."** Hebrews 11:1 says, "Now faith is being sure of what we hope for and certain of what we do not see." Let me help you to anticipate something that is coming. There are different kinds of postmillennialism.[15] There are also premillennialists and amillennialists, but we are not even talking about those. There are different kinds of postmillennialism, and we hope you are the right kind of postmillennialist.[16] We will identify these types.

---

14. *Hebrews 3:6, 14, 4:14, 6:8, 10:23.*

15. The three waves of postmillennialism will be explained in the introduction to *The Book of Revelation: What Must Soon Take Place—Doxological Postmillennialism.*

16. Gangadean, "Paper No. 104: Eschatology (Twelve Points)," 539–544; "Paper No. 118: Eschatology (Seven Points)," 603–607; "Paper No. 119: Pauline Eschatology," in *The Logos Papers,* 609–610; Gangadean, *On Natural and Revealed Theology,* 41–57, 229–238; Surrendra Gangadean, *The Unity of the Church: That They May Be One That the World May Believe* (Phoenix: Logos Papers Press, 2024).

Spur One Another to Love and Good Deeds

Part of doxological postmillennialism is, **"Let us hold unswervingly to the hope we profess, for he who promised is faithful"** (v. 23). What hope? The hope that all of Christ's enemies will be made His footstool. Let us hold *unswervingly*, let us draw near, **"And let us consider how we may spur one another on toward love and good deeds"** (v. 24). It says, **"And let us consider one another to provoke unto love and to good works"** (v. 24 KJV). We can provoke one another and merely provoke them, 'You annoy me, you are just annoying!' That is not what we are talking about. We are to provoke one another to good deeds and love. We are to help and encourage one another in the body of Christ. Have you ever provoked, encouraged, or spurred one another on? You know, spurring as you ride a horse? When you spur a horse, you say "yah!" and spur the side of the horse, and you get the horse moving. Have you ever spurred someone on to good deeds or do you merely annoy others? Or do we exempt ourselves by saying, 'Since I'm an annoying person, I just won't do anything.' No, put off the old and put on the new. Spur others on to good deeds.

Let Us Not Give Up Meeting

Here is one of the first ways in which we can encourage one another: **"Let us not give up meeting together, as some are in the habit of doing"** (v. 25a). Some people have fallen into a bad habit of not attending church regularly. This is a bad habit. You know what? When you do not come, that is a discouragement to others. When you are here, your mere presence, the fact that you hauled your body out, dragged it in, and plunked it down, and you are here is an encouragement. As generally said, 95% of life is just showing up. Be here, whatever it takes. Your attendance should be closest to 100% unless you are sick with a contagious disease.

Notice, do not give up meeting together; there is discouragement when people do not show, **"as some are in the habit of doing, but let us encourage one another—and all the more as you see the Day approaching"** (v. 25b). The day is approaching; the Day of the Lord, the day of the kingdom of God, the day of light flooding the earth over and against the night of the kingdom of darkness. The day of the kingdom of God is approaching and dawning. It is going through history as we disciple the nations. We should have more and more reason for coming to church; somehow, people find less and less reason to attend church and usually give up. Usually, as you get older, many people just give up on using the ordinary means. Have you noticed? They become discouraged. Reflect: what will happen to you? Will you become somewhat discouraged as you get older, or will you be burning more and more with zeal? How many burnt-out idealists are there by 30? Your lamp should be burning brighter and brighter. The older we get, the surer our hope should be. We should see the day approaching; we should have perspective. We should be able to look back on history, our lives, and understand the progress that has taken place. **"Let us not give up meeting together, as some are in the habit of doing, but let us encourage one another—and all the more as you see the Day approaching"** (v. 25).

If We Keep Serving: Fearful Expectation

The alternative is that the people who did not continue died in the wilderness. Some may go so far back as to deny the Lord—both of these are under the category of those who turn back. Some may turn back not to ultimate perdition but to perishing in the wilderness. We are not saying they are not saved. Some may turn back further than that, so we have a warning against turning back—a double-edged sword for both. **"If we deliberately keep on sinning after we have received the knowledge of the truth, no sacrifice for sins is left"** (v. 26). Giving up meeting together? Let us not do that; let us persevere. If we give up, turn our backs, what is left **"but only a fearful expectation of judgment and of raging fire that will consume the enemies of God"** (v. 27). This is true particularly for those who turn back all the way. It is spoken of here because these persons have rejected the truth more fully. **"Anyone who rejected the law of Moses died without mercy on the testimony of two or three witnesses"** (v. 28). These are not those who died in the wilderness, as they did not die on the testimony of two or more witnesses, but some of those in the Church died because they rejected more fully the law of God. They were cut off with witnesses. **"How much more severely do you think a man deserves to be punished who has trampled the Son of God under foot"** (v. 29a). They had more light, more grace, more glory, and more honor owed to Christ.

If we turn our backs on Christ, we are trampling the Son of God underfoot. **"Who has treated as an unholy thing the blood of the covenant that sanctified him, and who has insulted the Spirit of grace?"** (v. 29b). If we turn back, we are treating as unholy the blood of the covenant that sanctified us. Once and for all, treating it as unholy, the most holy thing in the universe, the blood of Christ. By treating it as unholy, we have insulted the Spirit of grace. We say that God's grace, God's Spirit that gives us grace, cannot enable us to overcome if we turn back. Let us not turn back in this way. Those who turn back and turn away from Christ in this way will put themselves under God's judgment, and God will judge them. **"It is a dreadful thing to fall into the hands of the living God"** (v. 31). Many in the Church do not acknowledge Christ as Lord and Savior; those who have more light turn away by rejecting this redemptive Word.

Remember the Earlier Days and the Great Contest

In many ways, the Church at large does not acknowledge Christ as Lord and Savior; they have explained Him away; they have made Him unholy. It will be a dreadful thing for those who have done this to the light of God. Paul says, **"Remember those earlier days after you had received the light, when you stood your ground in a great contest in the face of suffering"** (v. 32). Remember the church at Ephesus, Christ said, "You have forsaken your first love" (Rev. 2:4b). We should be going from that first love to higher and higher, but we often go from that to lower and lower.

> **Remember those earlier days after you had received the light, when you stood your ground in a great contest in the face of suffering. Sometimes you were publicly exposed to insult and persecution; at other times you stood side by side with those who were so treated. You sympathized with those in prison and joyfully accepted the confiscation of your property, because you knew that you yourselves had better and lasting possessions (vv. 32–34).**

We may see this go on 20, 30, 40 years and the Church does not prosper. We may say, 'This is getting old. I want to see some results.' What we need to do is focus on obedience and leave results in the hands of God. I have had to struggle with this, and I am learning that I must leave the results in the hands of God. I must be concerned about obedience. You might say, 'This is getting old; we don't want to do it anymore. It's not fun anymore.' Remember those times when you first came into being a postmillennialist, and you were so fired up? You were saying, 'Yes, this is going to happen,' and you expected six years later, a few nations to be converted. What happened after six years is that you have not had one person who has responded positively, and you are discouraged. What are you going to do? Paul says, **"So do not throw away your confidence; it will be richly rewarded"** (v. 35). God will see to it that it will bear fruit in the future, perhaps after you die, but you must be faithful. God will bring the fruit. We ordinarily expect it to come in this life, but even so, we believe it will be richly rewarded if we do not give up. **"You need to persevere so that when you have done the will of God, you will receive what he has promised"** (v. 36).

You might say, 'God is supposed to be coming, but He is delaying so long.' God is truly bringing about what is good. He is bringing you to the knowledge of God with a deeper understanding of Himself. With regard to this blessing, He is near at hand. He says, **"For in just a very little while, 'He who is coming will come and will not delay'"** (v. 37). You would be surprised. Usually, within the week, He comes. In every trial that goes by, within a week of that trial, the understanding, another level, another precept here or there breaks through. You know what? This is how it builds. This is how the treasure is built—little by little. **"He who is coming will come and will not delay"** (v. 37). God will reveal Himself. He will make Himself known to us. He will give us another truth. And we should hold on to it. Save it. Make it part of our lives. Be transformed. Know God in your way. Be renewed. He will not take long. Do not tread back, but do what is pleasing to the Lord.

I mentioned three kinds of postmillennialists. (1) The *pessimistic* postmillennialists are those who are postmillennialists; they are not like amillennialists or premillennialists—they are postmillennialists. They believe the kingdom of God will prevail in all the earth, but say, 'Alas, not in my lifetime. Perhaps something will happen 1,000 or 2,000 years from now, and surely God will bring it about.' They are postmillennialists, but they say it will take a long, long time, and they say, 'Let's just pace ourselves for this 2,000 year marathon, and we'll take it easy.' They pretty much say, 'Oh well, we're not going to break a sweat on this one.' (2) Then there are the *impatient* postmillennialists. They are those who want to find it quickly and do not see that the establishment of the kingdom requires a certain kind of work and that God is working in history, God is revealing His glory, and all things come to pass for the manifestation of His glory. They do not understand how God's program is working and they do not see that the earth is full of His glory.[17] They want to see certain results quickly. We need to get a historical perspective on the growth of the kingdom and the spiritual war. Often, an impatient postmillennialist turns into a pessimistic postmillennialist; they are kind of antinomies. They are very fired up quickly, and then they really settle down for the long haul, and it is not going anywhere soon. Then suddenly, there is neither an impatient postmillennialist nor a pessimistic postmillennialist, but there is a (3) *persevering* postmillennialist.

Persevering is not just settling back for the long haul. It is persevering as in a race. It is still a race, and the time factor is still a factor, so they are giving it all they can, yet they are pacing themselves to finish the work God has given them. Let us sort through this a bit and consider: What kind of postmillennialist are you? Here, the Word of God says, **"You need to persevere"** (v. 36a). You need to be a persevering postmillennialist—not a pessimistic, not an impatient postmillennialist, but a persevering postmillennialist. You need to do the will of God so that after doing His will, you will receive what He has promised.

God's Word is good. God is faithful. He has given us all His blessing in Christ Jesus our Lord—it is ours. As we come to the Table of the Lord, let us remember Him. We will be told to remember how He endured the contradiction of sinners against Himself, that you should not be wearied and faint in your minds. He says that we need to persevere. Time and again, we will have more summaries of this book so that you can get this book in perspective. How often is something stated better? Hold on, hold steady, and keep going. God's Word is true, and to that Word, we say, "Amen."

---

17. *Isaiah 6:3.*

11

THE COMMENDATION OF FAITH
PART I

Hebrews 11:1–19

¹Now faith is being sure of what we hope for and certain of what we do not see. ²This is what the ancients were commended for.

³By faith we understand that the universe was formed at God's command, so that what is seen was not made out of what was visible. ⁴By faith Abel offered God a better sacrifice than Cain did. By faith he was commended as a righteous man, when God spoke well of his offerings. And by faith he still speaks, even though he is dead.

⁵By faith Enoch was taken from this life, so that he did not experience death; he could not be found, because God had taken him away. For before he was taken, he was commended as one who pleased God. ⁶And without faith it is impossible to please God, because anyone who comes to him must believe that he exists and that he rewards those who earnestly seek him.

⁷By faith Noah, when warned about things not yet seen, in holy fear built an ark to save his family. By his faith he condemned the world and became heir of the righteousness that comes by faith.

⁸By faith Abraham, when called to go to a place he would later receive as his inheritance, obeyed and went, even though he did not know where he was going. ⁹By faith he made his home in the promised land like a stranger in a foreign country; he lived in tents, as did Isaac and Jacob, who were heirs with him of the same promise. ¹⁰For he was looking forward to the city with foundations, whose architect and builder is God.

¹¹By faith Abraham, even though he was past age—and Sarah herself was barren—was enabled to become a father because he considered him faithful who had made the promise. ¹²And so from this one man, and he as

good as dead, came descendants as numerous as the stars in the sky and as countless as the sand on the seashore.

13All these people were still living by faith when they died. They did not receive the things promised; they only saw them and welcomed them from a distance. And they admitted that they were aliens and strangers on earth. 14People who say such things show that they are looking for a country of their own. 15If they had been thinking of the country they had left, they would have had opportunity to return. 16Instead, they were longing for a better country—a heavenly one. Therefore God is not ashamed to be called their God, for he has prepared a city for them.

17By faith Abraham, when God tested him, offered Isaac as a sacrifice. He who had received the promises was about to sacrifice his one and only son, 18even though God had said to him, "It is through Isaac that your offspring will be reckoned." 19Abraham reasoned that God could raise the dead, and figuratively speaking, he did receive Isaac back from death.

WHAT FAITH IS BY PRECEPT AND EXAMPLE

THE ANCIENTS WERE COMMENDED for their faith. Hebrews 11 defines what faith is and the understanding of faith. The expression, *the understanding of faith,* may be taken in a couple of senses.[1] Faith involves understanding. In contrast to the more popular view,[2] faith involves understanding and a particular content that is understood. Both of these are to be kept in mind: (1) the process by which we have faith (the process of understanding), and (2) the content of this faith (or the worldview of faith). We are called to hold onto our hope and to persevere. This hope grows out of faith. "And now these three remain: faith, hope and love. But the greatest of these is love" (1 Cor. 13:13). Love is a complete expression of these three. It begins in faith and continues in hope. Hope continues in an understanding of the purpose of God for our lives, what He holds for us in the future, the fullness that there is in Christ, and the obedience in love by which we come to possess the promise.

---

1. Faith is understanding; faith is pleasing to God; faith is that by which we come to God; and faith is by diligently seeking God.

2. Fideism holds a belief without proof; proof is seen as either not relevant or not possible or may not actually be present; belief may either be theistic or non-theistic; fideism assumes basic things are not clear; belief without proof based on understanding loses all meaning.

You should expect, out of this message, to be stretched in your understanding of what faith involves. We are to anticipate that faith will be defined by precepts, principles, and by example. It will be defined negatively and positively.

WHAT FAITH IS NOT

One of the biggest things we have to be concerned about is what faith is not. There is a popular understanding of faith that is antithetical, or contrary, to what biblical faith is. We are not saying that those who have the popular understanding of faith do not have faith. It is possible to have some *measure* of faith; it is a different thing to give an *account* of faith. I remember my Master's thesis in the epistemology of religion, which gave an account of faith in contrast to other views, Wittgenstein, Kierkegaard, and others. It is one thing to have faith because of God's grace; it is another to give an account of faith. Just as it is one thing to have salvation, to be regenerated, and another to give an account of regeneration. Some people believe in decisional regeneration: One believes, and then one is born again.[3] As against, one is born again of God, and out of that comes a new awareness, conviction of sin and death, and repentance and faith.[4] Just as it is possible to be born again and not be able to give an account of it, so it is possible to have some measure of faith—and I say some measure—without giving an appropriate account of it. Hopefully, we will see more clearly and carefully what it is to have faith biblically.

---

3. Arminianism is a theological response to Reformed Theology. Jacobus Arminius formulated its main views in his Remonstrance (1610). The core beliefs are contrasted with TULIP, which was formulated in the Synod of Dort (1618–1619). Arminianism affirms the belief in Conditional Election (foreknowledge of faith and acceptance of Christ), General Atonement (Christ's atonement was intended for all who choose to believe), Partial Depravity (man is sick or weakened in sin and holds some degree of ability to do good), Resistible Grace (fallen man can by his free will accept or reject the grace of God), and Possibility of Falling Away from Grace (salvation is contingent upon the will of the person to remain in the faith).

4. Gangadean, *The Westminster Confession*, 143–206; Gangadean, *The Westminster Catechisms*, 191–207.

FAITH IS UNDERSTANDING

The first and most basic thing to be said about faith is given in the first verse; this is a summary precept, a definition: **"Now faith is being sure of what we hope for and certain of what we do not see"** (v. 1). Then, we have a list of the ancients, and we will go through some of these examples to get a clear sense of them. **"Being sure of what we hope for"**—notice the connection between faith and hope: **"and certain of what we do not see."** Notice the contrast between what is seen and what is not seen. The future is certainly not seen. We *hope* in regard to the future. Here, faith gives us what we call its substance, or reality. The word for *being sure* is *hupostasis* (ὑπόστασις), the underlying substance that supports the things that appear. For example, you can see the color of this cupboard, and it is light green, isn't it? We are just seeing the color; we are not seeing the substance, the matter itself in which this color exists. Matter is the substance; the color is not the substance, the substance is that in which properties inhere.[5]

Faith goes beyond sight to get to the underlying reality; faith grasps the reality, the substance, the underlying support of the thing that is visible. It goes beyond sight to get to the reality, not just in a metaphysical sense, **"the substance of things hoped for"** (v. 1 KJV), but more in the epistemological sense. That is, in a sense, in terms of knowledge and certainty. Faith supports our thinking about what we hope for. Faith grasps that which is a support for what we hope for. It is a certainty, the substance of things hoped for. By faith, we get hold of the substance, grasp it, and possess it.

Biblical Faith Contrasted with Fideism

To add to the exposition by parallelism and to strengthen it further, it says, **"faith is being sure of what we hope for and certain of what we do not see."** Faith has to do with *certainty.* The word in the King James is *evidence,* or *proof,* which is the proof of what we do not see. There is a strange juxtaposition between these two things. Some say that seeing is believing, but here, we do not see, and yet we believe. Some have said, 'Well then, your faith is blind.' Faith is anything but blind. Faith does not rely on sight, which gives only the surface appearance of

---

5. Gangadean, *History of Philosophy,* 38–39.

things. Faith goes much deeper; it involves understanding and having proof of what is invisible.

If we were to ask most people for the proof of God's existence, the proof regarding the future hope (eschatology), or the proof regarding the existence of the soul, we would receive unsatisfactory answers. The belief in these things without understanding is the position we call fideism,[6] faith-ism. It is almost like having faith in faith. It comes from the Latin term *fide,* which means having to do with faith or belief. Fideism is believing without having understanding or providing proof. As Christians, we are not fideists. Fideism is set in contrast to skepticism. It is what we call an antinomy—a polar opposite.[7] The contemporary worldview of our culture is skepticism:[8] 'We cannot know basic truths; no one really knows for sure.' They are skeptical, and what they have said is, 'Keep your faith personal and private and do not bring it into the public realm.' Though they are acting as though seeing is believing[9] and that since we can see the physical world, therefore we know it is there, what these persons are not telling you, is this kind of belief (that the physical is all that there is), is a kind of fideism also.[10] It is mere belief without proof. They rely on their senses because their reason is turned off. The reason by which they understand is turned off.

Interestingly, the great conflicts of today can be understood in terms of the conflict between fideism and skepticism.[11] The skeptics would have us keep our faith personal, or private, and have the public realm operate by way of secularism, naturalism, and science. The Islamic challenge says, 'No, we will not keep faith in the private realm; it should

---

6. Gangadean, *On Natural and Revealed Theology,* 152–153; Gangadean, *History of Philosophy,* 161–167.

7. Gangadean, *Philosophical Foundation,* 32–45.

8. Gangadean, *History of Philosophy,* 9–12; Gangadean, *Philosophical Foundation,* 17–31; Gangadean, *On Natural and Revealed Theology,* 150–152.

9. Gangadean, *History of Philosophy,* 139–149; Empiricism is the epistemological position that all knowledge arises from sense experience, affirmed by John Locke, David Hume, and in some claims made in the name of science; radical empiricism includes inner as well as sense experience.

10. Gangadean, *Philosophical Foundation,* 26–27; Common sense realism takes appearance for reality: the sun rises in the east; the earth is flat; the color of the ocean is blue; there is an external world; based on what is common to sense perception, rather than common sense as practical wisdom; it takes the condition/position of the perceiver for granted.

11. Gangadean, *History of Philosophy,* 171–172, 181–191.

be public.' There are two competing visions for the public realm. The skeptic, who should withdraw from the public realm, and the fideist, who should also withdraw, but both nevertheless see the need to claim authority in controlling the public realm. Over and against both skepticism and fideism, there is a doctrine of faith and clarity.[12] It is objectively clear that God exists; on this basis, we are held inexcusable for our unbelief. We should have knowledge. Faith is not contrasted with knowledge; faith is contrasted with sight. Sight, interestingly, does not give us knowledge of reality; it gives us appearances, not knowledge.[13] Sight does not enable us to see the underlying reality of substance but gives mere appearances.

We must engage our minds to hold on to the distinction between underlying substance and appearances. The ancients had their minds engaged. They saw what was not visible, and they were commended for their faith. They attained it by diligently seeking, not apart from it. Hear this Word again, **"faith is the substance of things hoped for"** (v. 1a KJV); the *hupostasis* supports what we hope for, and the certainty, or proof, of what we do not see. **"This is what the ancients were commended for"** (v. 2). We have two contrasts: Clarity is set against skepticism (no faith) and against fideism (false faith). Skepticism and fideism are polar opposites, one against the other, because both of them share a common assumption. The assumption is that we do not and cannot know the underlying reality.[14] Interestingly, both of them share this uncritically held assumption, just as capitalism and communism are antinomies.[15] Both share a common assumption: In capitalism, man individually owns absolutely, and in communism, man collectively owns absolutely, with both sharing the assumption that man owns absolutely rather than God.[16] We have had long conflicts between these two. We have also had long conflicts between fideism versus fideism:

12. Gangadean, *Philosophical Foundation*, 3–5, 287–292; Gangadean, *The Westminster Confession*, 1–13; Gangadean, "Paper No. 53: Common Ground (Part IV)," in *The Logos Papers*, 283–286.

13. Gangadean, *History of Philosophy*, 139–149.

14. Gangadean, *Philosophical Foundation*, 199–205; Gangadean, *On Natural and Revealed Theology*, 127–132.

15. Gangadean, *History of Philosophy*, 184–185; Gangadean, *Philosophical Foundation*, 261–262.

16. *Psalm 24:1*.

Christianity versus Islam, Christianity versus Judaism.[17] We have had internal conflicts among fideists. We have had internal conflicts among skeptics, and now we have conflicts between both of them. These conflicts are the death that is in our culture and our lives, which is a result of sin: not seeking and not understanding.[18] This is not what the ancients were commended for. They were commended rather for their seeking, for their understanding, and for their faith. In this way, we come into the promises and inherit the promises that God has for us. We might say, by way of contrast with other positions that have been articulated, I do not believe in order that I may understand. It is not *credo ut intelligam* as some have said,[19] but *credo est intelligam*: faith *is* understanding; it is synonymous with understanding.

Verse 3 says, **"By faith we understand that the universe was formed at God's command, so that what is seen was not made out of what was visible."** Notice again, grasping the invisible and seeing the visible in relation to the invisible. It is understanding that brings this about. Clearly, everyone will grant that faith is intimately connected with understanding in this verse: **"By faith we understand."** Anyone who gives any credence to Scripture would have to say that faith is connected to understanding, but would they say that faith is inseparable from understanding, that faith grows as understanding grows, that faith is tested as understanding is tested, and faith can only go as far as understanding can go—I believe insofar as I understand—*credo inquantum intelligō*? If this is the case, faith is to be identified with understanding who God is, and we grow in our understanding as we grow in faith.

"By faith we understand that the universe was formed at God's command, so that what is seen was not made out of what was visible" (v. 3). We understand, not just believe. Do not substitute the word *believe* by simply saying, 'I believe, yes, God made the world.' We *understand*; the word *understand* has to do with putting things together, seeing things in relationship one to another, starting with the basic things— we understand by connecting things together. Understanding entails connections between ideas, making inferences, and connecting things. **"We understand that the universe was formed at God's command, so**

---

17. Gangadean, *Philosophical Foundation*, 191–194.

18. *Romans 3:10–11.*

19. Gangadean, *History of Philosophy,* 111–114.

that what is seen was not made out of what was visible" (v. 3). What does Paul say in Romans about what may be known of God?

> Since what may be known about God is plain to them, because God has made it plain to them. For since the creation of the world God's invisible qualities—his eternal power and divine nature—have been clearly seen, being understood from what has been made, so that men are without excuse (Rom. 1:19–20).

Human beings perish forever if they fail to have some understanding of the existence and nature of God. The Scripture teaches about the fallen condition of man: No one seeks, no one understands, no one is righteous, not even one.[20] We marvel at, or are frustrated, as we witness and find people not responding. We should be thankful when *any* respond because it is by the sovereign grace of God. Human beings, left to themselves, do not seek. We seek to do our own will, to determine for ourselves good and evil, and it is the way of death and disaster. In God's providence, they will be left to sink deeper and deeper into that pit. 'They will know that I am the Lord,' as the prophets say over and over again; they will know the Lord in judgment.

I wonder what kind of knowledge non-believers have? They know God in judgment, and you have to wonder what it is. Or they may *experience* God's judgment in their being. Israel as a nation has been left for 2,000 years. India as a nation has been left for 3,000 years. Israel had light; India once had light. Going back to the days of Noah, people turned away from the light and lived as people under the darkness of unbelief. God's judgment is there. They will know God in judgment but may experience His judgment and do not understand. In Psalm 90, Moses speaks about this: "Who knows the power of your anger?" (Ps. 90:11), and Solomon in Ecclesiastes: "Generations come and generations go, but the earth remains forever" (Ecc. 1:4). There are all these things that we get so upset about, including world wars, the sound and the fury. What came out of World War II? How did we advance toward the knowledge of God? As we go through the War on Terror now in the world, will it advance us toward the knowledge of God?[21] Will we be somewhat wiser, or will it be "Full of sound and

---

20. *Romans 3:10–11; Psalm 14:2–3, 53:1–3.*

21. This sermon series was given soon after the September 11th attacks.

fury, signifying nothing."[22] We are called to understand. Faith is understanding; it involves seeing the invisible through the use of reason and the exercise of our understanding.

The object of faith has to do, first of all, with creation. In verse 3, **"By faith, we understand that the universe was formed at God's command"** (v. 3a). Faith also has to do with redemption. In verse 4, **"By faith Abel offered God a better sacrifice than Cain did"** (v. 4a). Abel received and understood the teaching. By way of contrast, many do not understand that the world was formed at God's command. They may say, 'The world is God, all is one.' New Age says this. The dualists and the pluralists do not see what is clear, either. We should contrast those who have understanding that only God is eternal with those who try to say otherwise—whether monism or dualism. It is a big contrast, is it not? Those who believe come through the cross of Jesus Christ and understand the reality of sin, death, and the need for atonement—they can never atone for their own sins. Not by the post-biblical Jewish view of atonement by one's good deeds, the Roman Catholic view of the atonement in the mass, or the Islamic view that says there is no need for atonement, which is the view of Cain.[23] God said to Cain, "But if you do not do what is right, sin is crouching at your door; it desires to have you, but you must master it" (Gen. 4:7b).

There is always a contrast between the faith of Abel—the understanding of Abel—and the way of Cain. The way of Abel recognizes the reality of sin and death, and the need to come through the cross of Christ. Our sin leads us to reject the Word of God, pushing it away from us. When that Word of God comes to us incarnate in the form of Jesus Christ, we also push Him away. And if He stands in our path, we will even go so far as to crucify Him. This is what our sin does. Do you recognize that in you? When your flesh rises up against the Spirit and the Spirit against the flesh, and they are warring against each other,[24] do you say 'yes' to the flesh and 'no' to the Spirit, or do you say 'yes' to the Spirit and 'no' to the flesh? Are you willing to take up your cross and follow Christ? If you have any integrity, if you seek God, if you have

---

22. William Shakespeare, *Macbeth*, (Chicago: Encyclopedia Britannica Inc, 1994), 5.5.27–28.

23. Gangadean, *Philosophical Foundation*, 191–192; Gangadean, *The Westminster Confession*, 21–27, 37–41, 67–69, 129–130, 236–238; Gangadean, "Paper No. 91: Christianity and Islam," in *The Logos Papers*, 479–484.

24. *Galatians 5:17.*

the first *iota* of truth and do not try to come off as one who has some integrity without knowing what is clear, you will come to Christ. You will acknowledge God, not merely some God out there, but God who is ruling in a world filled with old age, sickness, and death and who is calling us back through these from sin and death to acknowledge Him and to deal with our sin. Abel had faith, and he speaks to us to this day through that faith. **"By faith he was commended as a righteous man, when God spoke well of his offerings. And by faith he still speaks, even though he is dead"** (v. 4b).

ENOCH

Enoch was commended. **"By faith Enoch was taken from this life, so that he did not experience death; he could not be found, because God had taken him away. For before he was taken, he was commended as one who pleased God"** (v. 5). This is faith, particularly in regard to sanctification. Enoch continued to understand God and grow in such a way that he pleased God, and God was pleased to take him from the world without seeing death. Our goal is not to be taken the way Enoch was. I know a lot of us would say, 'Would it not be great to get out of death, just leave the world without dying.' The goal is not to avoid natural evil; the goal is to avoid moral evil. If it pleases God to take us out of this world, so be it. I do not want to hear from any of you, 'Wouldn't it be nice to be taken like Enoch?' This is not the point, so please do not get hung up on it. But Enoch grew, and it pleased God, sovereignly pleased God, to take Enoch away. Enoch is an example of faith growing; this is how we should be, not necessarily how he was taken, but how he grew in faith. Be like Enoch, not regarding how he was taken, but regarding his progress in sanctification.

FAITH IS PLEASING TO GOD

"Before he was taken, he was commended as one who pleased God" (v. 5b). Faith is pleasing to God. We want to please God, not ourselves; this is a contrast. **"And without faith it is impossible to please God, because anyone who comes to him must believe that he exists and that he rewards those who earnestly seek him"** (v. 6). We may do a lot of things without faith. We do these things perhaps as a result of our troubled conscience (which is not properly informed); we may do many good works, and a lot of it will be burnt up.[25] We can do these outward acts of obedience, ritual obedience, the way the Israelites were in Isaiah's day when they were bringing the sacrifices, and the Lord said:

> Stop bringing meaningless offerings! Your incense is detestable to me. New Moons, Sabbaths and convocations—I cannot bear your evil assemblies. Your New Moon festivals and your appointed feasts my soul hates. They have become a burden to me; I am weary of bearing them (Is. 1:13–14).

Look at St. Paul, Saul of Tarsus: "as for zeal, persecuting the church; as for righteousness based on the law, faultless" (Phil. 3:6). But it was not pleasing to God; he did not have faith, and he did not understand who God was until after his conversion. We tend to emphasize the action, but if it is not accompanied by faith, it is not what it should be. We can profess faith without action or have action without faith. Whichever way you cut it, neither is acceptable. If you want to please God, you must have faith. It is through faith that we come near to God. Here it is said, **"And without faith it is impossible to please God, because anyone who comes to him must believe that he exists and that he rewards those who earnestly seek him"** (v. 6). We must believe that He exists, with understanding.

Belief without understanding is empty. It gradually loses its meaning. We do not see how God is working in the world—that God is good, and the very creation speaks of God's goodness; that the original creation was very good and death is not part of the original creation.[26] These things are clear from the things that are made. We are not excused for not believing this. We must believe that He is (with understanding) and that He rewards those who earnestly seek Him. This is why it is pleasing to God, because we are understanding that our good is in Him. He is our reward.[27] Knowing Him, possessing God through knowing Him, and being in intimate fellowship with Him is our reward. We

---

25. *1 Corinthians 3:14–15.*

26. Gangadean, *The Westminster Confession*, 75–79; Gangadean, *The Biblical Worldview*, xvii–xlvi, 21–36, 91–108.

27. *Genesis 15:1; John 17:3.*

delight in God; we enjoy Him forever. This is why faith is pleasing to Him; faith seeks God and understands God.

FAITH IS BY DILIGENTLY SEEKING GOD

Faith is by diligently seeking God. It is not without seeking; it is not effortless. Faith involves seeking that we might understand. Because He is the rewarder of those who diligently seek Him, this is how we are pleasing to God. By seeking Him, understanding Him, seeing His glory, enjoying Him, rejoicing and resting in Him, and living our lives out of that overflow. This is what faith is. Our understanding by faith is cumulative. As we seek day after day, week after week, year after year, I hope that not a day goes by in your life when there is not some increase in understanding. In Isaiah, it says, "For precept must be upon precept, precept upon precept; line upon line, line upon line; here a little, and there a little" (Is. 28:10). In every trial, in every circumstance of life, we find our need, we learn to look to God and see Him in a new way, find Him, and find grace to help. We are to grow in the knowledge of God and come nearer to Him, and day in and day out, this accumulates. I think of every drop of rain that falls from the sky. Every snowflake that falls from the sky melts and flows together into a stream, becoming a river. I am thinking of Niagara Falls and how powerful it is. Our faith should be like Niagara Falls, the result of an accumulation, drop by drop, snowflake by snowflake, accumulating mightily.

We are to seek God diligently, year in and year out, in all the circumstances of life. Every circumstance is tailor-made for each one of us. As much as we complain that we would like to get out of our trials, God tailor-made these trials for us. This is the one where we are to seek Him; this is where we are to learn to call upon Him, find Him, grow in grace, grow in the knowledge of God, and overcome. This is what it is to seek the Lord diligently in reading the Word, understanding our circumstances of life in light of Him, and finding our reward in Him. So, faith has content; it is a process of understanding, coming from seeking, and there is a content in believing that He is and that He rewards those who diligently seek Him. We allow these words to go by too quickly, too lightly. Everything else will fade away, but the one who sets his hope in God finds his reward in God—come to Him and be established in God.

NOAH

Another example of faith is Noah. **"By faith Noah, when warned about things not yet seen, in holy fear built an ark to save his family. By his faith he condemned the world and became heir of the righteousness that comes by faith"** (v. 7). In Noah, we see the preserving of and the persevering in the Word of God. If Abel speaks about redemption, and Enoch speaks of sanctification, Noah speaks of perseverance. Notice the elements here: Noah is warned of things not yet seen, he was moved with fear, he understood the righteousness of God, and he understood the times. The world was full of corruption and violence, and Noah knew that God was righteous and would bring judgment. He understood the fall of man and the curse and the promise. He saw people apostatized. He was moved with holy fear; we should have that fear when we understand that sin is in the world. He understood that God would bring judgment when the wicked multiplied on the earth.

Noah built an ark to save his family with this understanding and the fear connected with it, holy fear and the fear of the Lord. Noah had to put great effort into building the ark and, through that, saved his family, preserving them through God's judgment and preserving all the work that was done by the grace of God. He preserved all the work that was done by redemptive grace, by common grace through the line of Cain and everyone else, and all the work of the cultural mandate that God had given Adam to do.[28] Noah preserved all of the dominion accomplished and brought that through the judgment so we would not have to repeat about two millennia of human history and start from scratch. Noah obeyed; he saw a future. It was not going to be a big judgment that was just thrown on the earth where he had to scramble for himself. God had a purpose. He was going to fulfill that purpose, and Noah was going to obey despite the failure of anyone to hear the witness. Do you think you had a bad day at the office? Do you think no one listens to your witness? Think about Noah and his persevering through all the ridicule.

Noah endured the ridicule that would have come for his witness and the building of the ark. He showed the contrast between those who understand and are saved and those who are not seeking, do not

---

28. *Genesis 1:26–28.*

understand, and with warning after warning after warning, perish. Judgment comes suddenly sometimes. A terrorist attack—we could have seen it coming. We had several years before this terrorist attack.[29] There was the attempt to bomb the World Trade Center, attempts to bomb embassies, bomb places where soldiers stay, bomb the USS Cole, and then it hit. The sight of those buildings coming down, the lives in those buildings perishing, and the sight of people jumping out of windows literally came crashing into our consciousness. We could not avoid it. Sometimes, judgment comes upon us like that—in a day, in an hour. All the warnings have been given, it continues not to be heeded, and judgment comes quickly. That is typically the pattern. Noah had faith and an understanding of who God was and why God would tell him to build the ark and expend the effort.

ABRAHAM

We have several verses devoted to Abraham as the example of faith.

By faith Abraham, when called to go to a place he would later receive as his inheritance, obeyed and went, even though he did not know where he was going. By faith he made his home in the promised land like a stranger in a foreign country; he lived in tents, as did Isaac and Jacob, who were heirs with him of the same promise. For he was looking forward to the city with foundations, whose architect and builder is God (v. 8–10).

Hebrews 11:8–10 speaks about the promise that was given to Abraham. He left to go to a place he would later receive, not knowing where he was going. You have to think about what it took for Abraham to leave. We have outlined this at other times in discussions about the faith of Abraham, the worldview of Abraham, his understanding of creation–fall–redemption, and his understanding of history.[30] What happened in the days of Noah? Abraham's life overlapped with Shem, who came through the Flood, for minimally 150 years. Look how much we have

---

29. Terrorist attack on September 11th, 2001.

30. Gangadean, *Philosophical Foundation*, 121–127; Gangadean, *History of Philosophy*, 163–167; Gangadean, "Paper No. 128: Abraham's Faith," 665–666; "Paper No. 129: Faith and Reason in the Life of Abraham" in *The Logos Papers*, 667–669.

learned in our short lives. Think how much Abraham could have learned during that time. His life overlapped with *Shem*.[31] Abraham had a worldview. This is the understanding of faith, the worldview of faith; he knew God's judgment in the past. He knew about Babel and the scattering of the nations. Abraham knew God reigned in history, and he knew that Ur was doomed to destruction; it was not the City of God. All those around him had apostatized; even his own father, Terah, had turned aside from God.[32] He was told to leave Ur of the Chaldees, the center of civilization in his day, to go elsewhere for a promise he would not see in his lifetime. It would take hundreds of generations for him to see it. How would he participate in this? What must Abraham have thought about the resurrection of the dead? This is not a promise where he dies and goes to heaven and gets the promise. It involves being in the land, on the earth.

Abraham would have known and believed and understood something about the resurrection of the dead from the beginning before he left Ur of the Chaldees. This was part of his worldview, the understanding of faith, he was drawing inferences. He was not living like an animal blindly through life, instinctually, and going into death, but he was thinking about these things and understanding them. He was understanding good and evil and understanding the promise, that the promise will be fulfilled. In him, all the families of the earth will be blessed.[33] We must understand that God is good, ruling in history, and that good will overcome evil. Abraham understood these things. Abraham was not a premillennialist; Abraham was a postmillennialist for sure,[34] or else he would not have done this. He was not waiting in Ur for things to get worse and worse and then for the rapture to take him out. He went out, obeyed, endured, and lived in tents. Sarah did not like it; she had to dust every day. Talk about an obedient wife; Sarah was an obedient wife. She was a woman who would leave to go out with a man who was hearing voices, leaving all the nice earthly goods behind. This is why Sarah is commended. She called him 'Lord.'[35] 'Yes my Lord,

---

31. For further information on Shem and Abraham, see footnote 9 on p. 106.

32. *Joshua 24:2.*

33. *Genesis 12:3.*

34. Gangadean, "Paper No. 104: Eschatology (Twelve Points)," in *The Logos Papers*, 539–544.

35. *1 Peter 3:6.*

ready to go? I'm with you. I'm on my camel, I'm there.' Abraham had probably talked with Sarah, they probably had pillow talk, not pillow fight, pillow talk. They lie in bed together and talk about the things of the Lord. What else was there to talk about? They didn't have TV in those days. Abraham had time to talk to Sarah and she understood. He would have explained further and loved his wife as Christ loved the Church. He would have made the effort to explain. So Sarah was able to go out with him; Abraham did not just say, 'Come on woman, let's go.' He talked to her, and she understood. What a pleasure it is to speak to your wife that way and for her to be thoughtful and receptive. Sarah heard the word and went out with him. That was quite an adventure for both of them.

Abraham had a worldview in which he understood that this was how the good was to come, and it would be for all the families of the earth. Abraham's worldview was connected with his obedience that this would come about. This is why I said Abraham was a postmillennialist—no question about it. Notice, **"By faith he made his home in the promised land like a stranger in a foreign country"** (v. 9a). He was expecting to possess this land. It was the Promised Land. It was not just Palestine, as some Zionists may make the focus; it was the whole world. In you, in your seed, all the families of the earth will be blessed.[36] There are two parts to this. First, the blessing, the reward in diligently seeking Him, is the knowledge of God. Second, all the families will be blessed—in connection with the earth and dominion over the earth. This is what the Jewish people were to lead the nations in doing. However, they did not have faith like their father, Abraham. They were covenant children who did not have this faith—intended for the whole world—and they lost it. But God is able to restore them and He will when it serves His purpose to bring glory to His name.

"For he was looking forward to the city with foundations, whose architect and builder is God" (v. 10). This is the diamond city. The city is 1,400 miles long, 1,400 miles wide, and 1,400 miles high, shining with the glory of God. It is completion, the perfection of beauty, the completion of culture, the uncovering of the glory of God—this is the city Abraham was looking for. He must have been thinking about this since he believed all the families of the earth would be blessed. The

---

36. *Genesis 12:1–3.*

blessing involves believing, knowing, understanding God, and finding Him as the reward. God had said to Abraham, "Do not be afraid, Abram. I am your shield, your exceedingly great reward" (Gen. 15:1). Abraham had an understanding of this and so he left Ur. It is this understanding that is called faith. It comes from diligently seeking the Lord and finding our good in Him.

> **By faith Abraham, even though he was past age—and Sarah herself was barren—was enabled to become a father because he considered him faithful who had made the promise. And so from this one man, and he as good as dead, came descendants as numerous as the stars in the sky and as countless as the sand on the seashore** (vv. 11–12).

When Abraham was past age, because he considered God faithful who had promised him, he was able to have a child. Abraham was 100 years old and Sarah was 90. They were as good as dead. Yet out of this one child, Isaac, came others; from Jacob (Esau turned aside), the 12 patriarchs. Then, in terms of the natural seed of Abraham, it is like the sand on the seashore, and in terms of the spiritual seed of Abraham, like the stars in the sky—numerous. Abraham was looking ahead. This is something that he saw at a distance. He saw it far off.

We have to make decisions and live now for 100, 500, 1,000 to 4,000 years in the future. We are now about 4,000 years since Abraham and 5,000 years since Noah. Part of faith involves us looking toward the future for the promise to be fulfilled. We are to act now in a way that would further the promise and in a way that is necessary for the fulfillment of the promise. We sometimes expect to see great things in our day, and there may or may not be. In any case, we must be faithful to the future, as the ancients were commended for their faith. We will have to leave it here for today and do this chapter in two parts. This is too much, too rich for one time. We will continue to think about faith.

12

THE COMMENDATION OF FAITH
PART II

Hebrews 11:17–40

¹⁷By faith Abraham, when God tested him, offered Isaac as a sacrifice. He who had received the promises was about to sacrifice his one and only son, ¹⁸even though God had said to him, "It is through Isaac that your offspring will be reckoned." ¹⁹Abraham reasoned that God could raise the dead, and figuratively speaking, he did receive Isaac back from death.

²⁰By faith Isaac blessed Jacob and Esau in regard to their future.

²¹By faith Jacob, when he was dying, blessed each of Joseph's sons, and worshiped as he leaned on the top of his staff.

²²By faith Joseph, when his end was near, spoke about the exodus of the Israelites from Egypt and gave instructions about his bones.

²³By faith Moses' parents hid him for three months after he was born, because they saw he was no ordinary child, and they were not afraid of the king's edict.

²⁴By faith Moses, when he had grown up, refused to be known as the son of Pharaoh's daughter. ²⁵He chose to be mistreated along with the people of God rather than to enjoy the pleasures of sin for a short time. ²⁶He regarded disgrace for the sake of Christ as of greater value than the treasures of Egypt, because he was looking ahead to his reward. ²⁷By faith he left Egypt, not fearing the king's anger; he persevered because he saw him who is invisible. ²⁸By faith he kept the Passover and the sprinkling of blood, so that the destroyer of the firstborn would not touch the firstborn of Israel.

²⁹By faith the people passed through the Red Sea as on dry land; but when the Egyptians tried to do so, they were drowned.

³⁰By faith the walls of Jericho fell, after the people had marched around them for seven days.

³¹By faith the prostitute Rahab, because she welcomed the spies, was not killed with those who were disobedient.

³²And what more shall I say? I do not have time to tell about Gideon, Barak, Samson, Jephthah, David, Samuel and the prophets, ³³who through faith conquered kingdoms, administered justice, and gained what was promised; who shut the mouths of lions, ³⁴quenched the fury of the flames, and escaped the edge of the sword; whose weakness was turned to strength; and who became powerful in battle and routed foreign armies. ³⁵Women received back their dead, raised to life again. Others were tortured and refused to be released, so that they might gain a better resurrection. ³⁶Some faced jeers and flogging, while still others were chained and put in prison. ³⁷They were stoned; they were sawed in two; they were put to death by the sword. They went about in sheepskins and goatskins, destitute, persecuted and mistreated—³⁸the world was not worthy of them. They wandered in deserts and mountains, and in caves and holes in the ground.

³⁹These were all commended for their faith, yet none of them received what had been promised. ⁴⁰God had planned something better for us so that only together with us would they be made perfect.

REVIEW OF THE MEANING OF FAITH

WE ARE CONTINUING IN HEBREWS 11 on the commendation of faith. Verse 2 says, **"This is what the ancients were commended for."** Then we proceed with a list of the ancients, what they did, and how they were commended. Through this, we see what faith is, and a twelvefold description of the nature of faith is illustrated in this chapter. In the context of the foregoing chapters, where the focus has been on the promise, the hope that is set before us is the greater fullness that there is in Christ, and the expectation that the greater fullness in Christ will come about.

Faith Is Necessary to Inherit the Promise of God

Scripture teaches: "now these three remain: faith, hope, and love" (1 Cor. 13:13a). These are three aspects of one reality, and there is an order within them; there is a unity. Faith involves our understanding of God's purpose and plan (His nature and existence), how that purpose and plan unfold, our expectation, our hope, and the obedience of love we are called to, by which we realize this hope. Faith is necessary to inherit the promise of God, both in one's lifetime and long term in history.

Faith Is Necessary to Please God

Verse 6 says, **"And without faith it is impossible to please God."** It is necessary—anything done without faith, whether it is obedience or devotion, without faith, is not pleasing to God. Whatever we do must be out of faith, out of understanding who God is and His purpose, and not done in some blind or ritual way without understanding. God is pleased with our faith.

Faith Is Having Certainty and Proof of What Is Not Seen

This chapter speaks generally about what is not seen, the invisible God. Faith is not blind because it is invisible; it has proof. This is what is said categorically of faith; the clearest statement about the nature of faith in all of the Bible is Hebrews 11:1, **"Now faith is being sure of what we hope for and certain of what we do not see."** In the King James Version, **"Now faith is the substance of things hoped for** [the *hupostasis,* the underlying reality of things hoped for], **the evidence** [the proof] **of things not seen."** This is not proof through the senses; this is proof through understanding.

Faith Is Having Understanding

Faith is necessary to inherit the promise of God. Faith is necessary to please God. Faith is having certainty and proof of what is not seen. Faith is based on understanding, or perhaps stronger, faith is having understanding. If there is no understanding and we believe something, we are believing it without meaning; it is a dead faith. It reflects our spiritual death, where we use words without meaning, and the words of God are emptied of meaning. If we say, 'Jesus forgives me of my sin,' and we have a very weak, superficial understanding of sin, then our faith is going to be weak and superficial. If we say, 'Christ came to give me life,' and we mistake life for an otherworldly heaven and the absence of the curse, this involves a misunderstanding. It is not true faith, it is not biblical faith. Somewhere in there, we may have some understanding, but we may have a lot of misunderstanding mixed in with it. Faith is based on understanding; it involves understanding. Faith brings us to God through its content.

Faith Has Content: That He Is and He Is the Rewarder of Those Who Diligently Seek Him

The primary content of faith is to believe, and we need to underscore this: believe with proof and understanding that (1) He is, and that (2) He rewards those who diligently seek Him. Both must be believed, not just one. Some may say, 'I believe that God exists.' I have heard many professing Christians say this, or they say, 'I believe in Christ.' But do you believe that He is the rewarder of those who diligently seek Him? Does that belief lead to seeking Him diligently? Is that seeking going on in your life? Are you getting the reward that comes from seeking Him? If we are not, there is a deficiency in our faith, and there will be a lack in our coming to God. He that comes to God must believe both: that He is (belief with understanding, which involves proof—evidence of things not seen), and that He is the rewarder of those who diligently seek Him. We must believe the reward is the knowledge of God and not substitute it for something else. In our autonomy, we are prone to want to determine good and evil for ourselves as our forefathers did in the Garden. Remember, from the Garden, Adam and Eve determined something else to be good, and they pursued lesser things,[1] and because it satisfied them for a while, they thought they could get away with it, but it will not satisfy.

It will inevitably fail, and it is failing even now. We are going into excess and transgressing the law of God to find satisfaction. Our reward is in Him, and He is the rewarder of those who *diligently* seek Him—not casually, not occasionally, not so-so, not half-heartedly, not now and again, but persistently, diligently, perseveringly seeking Him. We should be honest about it with ourselves and with one another. When we start speaking about how much comfort and reward we have in God, we must ask ourselves the prior question: are we diligently seeking Him? Do I have joy in God? Do we expect comfort and joy to come without diligently seeking Him? If you are not going to believe

---

1. Gangadean, *The Biblical Worldview,* 159–176.

that He is the rewarder of those who diligently seek Him and act on that, you might also give up the first point: that He is. Both of these go together. Let us be honest before God. Taking vows is not a substitute for keeping them. It does not do to take a vow promising to seek the Lord through the ordinary means and then not do it.[2] To vow that we will diligently read the Bible and not do it is taking God's name in vain. The Lord repeatedly warns us about saying and not doing or hearing and not doing. We may think of the preacher as one who sings pleasant songs. We like to listen to songs; we do it all the time, and we may treat the preaching as just another song. Our purpose here as a church is to worship and serve God. We come together on the Lord's Day to worship Him and to be prepared through the preaching to serve Him. As we go through the week, we confess that we will seek God diligently, that we are His disciples, and that we will take up our cross daily and follow Him, that we will deny ourselves and our self-love. We recognize the need to be discipled in many ways in our lives.

If we are not going to seek God diligently, let us be honest about it with ourselves and one another and say, 'I am not ready to pick up my cross and follow Jesus. I think that other things are important, and I'm not that interested right now in following Jesus in this way.' We should expect diligently seeking of each other and not deceive ourselves. We know that this is a problem: hearing and not doing. "Do not merely listen to the word, and so deceive yourselves. Do what it says" (Js. 1:22). We have the problem of self-deception. An added element is that we should not expect others to participate in our self-deception, to go along and act as if we are diligently seeking when we are not. We seek casually; we are not giving time and effort to this; we are unwilling to be His disciples. The Hall of Faith reveals to us the dedication of believers to God's work and the extent of their suffering for it, to which we are also connected. If we are not willing to dedicate ourselves in this way, let us accept the consequences and accept what is needed, namely, the chastening of God so that we might partake of His holiness.[3] Let us not harden ourselves to the chastening but say, 'I come short, and I

---

2. The fifth article of the Westminster Fellowship Church membership vow states: "To the end that you may grow in the Christian life, do you promise that you will diligently read the Bible, engage in private prayer, keep the Lord's Day, regularly attend the worship services, observe the appointed sacraments, and give to the Lord's work as He shall prosper you?"

3. *Hebrews 12:10.*

need a chastening trial of God in order to learn, to be exercised by it, hopefully, and to learn what I should learn.'

One of the things I am finding is that I have a false sense of love which wants to accommodate and not keep upfront, in all conversations, the question of diligently seeking God. Let that be the first question as we begin our discussion. By not beginning the discussion with the question of diligently seeking God, I allow a lot of things to occur. I allow the discussion to go on and find I am responding to a burden being expressed, and I am struggling through that burden with the person instead of coming back to the very first point of diligently seeking. **"Anyone who comes to him must believe that he exists and that he rewards those who earnestly seek him"** (v. 6). I am saying this so that you might expect it. I hope that by God's grace, I will do this, and that our conversations will begin with, 'How are you doing in terms of diligently seeking God?' The rest of the conversation will be understood in light of this. Is that a fair application? It is a little bit more pointed now, isn't it, now that I have put it that way? So, that will be at the beginning of our conversations. The absence of the question burdens the discussion.

Jesus set the standard. He did not set it high, but where it needs to be. "If anyone would come after me, he must deny himself and take up his cross and follow me" (Matt. 16:24). This church is about discipling. It is not about making converts and letting it end there. It is about making converts and discipling them, which involves "teaching them to obey everything I have commanded you" (Matt. 28:20a). We should expect discipleship. I am saying this, and I will repeat it from time to time, that this is what we should be expecting regarding this church. So if a question is raised to you, it should not take you by surprise or be seen as something unwelcome. Are you diligently seeking God? Do you have faith? Do you have this kind of understanding? Do you have the evidence of things not seen? If others ask, 'Where is this evidence of things not seen?' You should be able to give that evidence. It will not be just rattling off, 'If it's eternal, then it's self-maintaining; if it's not self-maintaining, then it's not eternal. That's it.'⁴ We want to see more than this. This is the minimum of the minimum. If this

---

4. This is in reference to the First Argument against Materialism in Gangadean, *Philosophical Foundation*, 73–80.

is all you have it is like the grade of "D-". We want understanding of showing the clarity of God's existence and the inexcusability of unbelief. I know people who can memorize words, and even Koko the gorilla can probably respond to that kind of training. Perhaps Koko could do sign language and show, 'If it's eternal then it's self-maintaining.' That would put us to shame. Let us not flatter ourselves about this sort of thing; let us have understanding. This is what is pleasing to God. Remember, "There is no one righteous, not even one; there is no one who understands, no one who seeks God" (Rom. 3:10–11). There is a connection between seeking and understanding and being righteous. This is what is pleasing to God.

Faith Involves a Worldview Held with Understanding

In the last sermon, we spoke about the creation: **"By faith we understand that the universe was formed at God's command, so that what is seen was not made out of what was visible"** (v. 3). What is seen is not as fundamental a reality as the unseen—the invisible. We see the connection between the creation and the Creator through faith, or understanding. Faith has to do with the invisible, the creation, and God as Creator. It has to do with sin and death and justification, as in the case of Abel offering the better sacrifice. It has to do with sanctification in the case of Enoch, who obtained a considerable degree of sanctification and was taken by God; he did not see death. It has to do with judgment, and understanding history, as in the case of Noah. He was warned, and for decades he built the ark to save himself and his house, preserve the work done in history, and continue the promise. These persons and their lives, in particular ways, show different aspects of this worldview.

In the case of Abraham, faith involved the foundation, goal, and plan of God. When he left Ur of the Chaldees, he was looking for a city with foundations; he knew the foundations were lacking in Ur. He wanted to see a city, a kingdom of God with foundations, and the goal was God's glory. He believed that God was going to bring this to pass over a period of time. Abraham understood the foundation and the goal and the plan of God and that is why he left Ur of the Chaldees. We put these together and what do we have? We have a worldview held with understanding—not something distorted, truncated, mixed in with a lot of external thought. It is not mixed with the dualism of the Greeks, nor New Age teaching that does not reckon with the resurrection and the reality of this world and the glory of God in this world. None of that is part of the Christian worldview; it is still part of the old world; it is part of the old system.

The Christian worldview is not mixed with naturalism, materialism, and empiricism, and being impressed by these persons who have four PhDs in science. We are way too easily impressed. When we look at the foundational beliefs of these persons who are stuck in empiricism, who believe that all knowledge is through the senses,[5] it becomes evident that they have yet to see some of the first and most fundamental truths. They do not even recognize that causality is not something knowable by experience, even though David Hume pointed that out centuries ago.[6] We understand the nature of reality through reason, and causality is part of the structure of God's world. Those who flirt with the current physics, quantum mechanics, uncaused events, being from non-being, and approaching things empirically, do not have some of the fundamental basics in place. We should not be impressed; we should not be taken up with the world in this way, enamored with the world. Those who hold certain epistemologists in high esteem, particularly those whose works are published in philosophy journals, often assert that engaging with these authors is essential for credibility. One such notable figure is Edmund Gettier, with 'the Gettier problem' being considered a significant focus in epistemology.[7] If being can come from non-being and if we cannot know, then the discussions surrounding justification, which Gettier grapples with, become irrelevant. Those in literature who seem to make a big deal about 'bio-confessionals' and seem to think that 'you do not become real until you talk about your body parts' do not have a clue about honesty. They are not even close to talking about clarity and dealing with fundamental truth. They will avoid it. Let us not be impressed with the world; let us leave it; let us go on in faith to the fundamental reality that is there.

"And without faith it is impossible to please God, because anyone who comes to him must believe that he exists and that he rewards

---

5. Gangadean, *History of Philosophy,* 21–22.

6. Gangadean, *History of Philosophy,* 144–145; Gangadean, *Philosophical Foundation,* 26–27.

7. Gangadean, *History of Philosophy,* 177–179.

those who earnestly seek him" (v. 6). These examples of faith show that faith involves a worldview. We should acknowledge this and be concerned that this is one of the things that is in place in our lives. Are you earnestly seeking God? How are you doing in terms of having the foundation in place, the worldview? Tell me your understanding of this worldview and how it impacts your thinking this week. How is it impacting the things that you are struggling with? Now, right now, in our conversation, let us put it into perspective. Are you concerned about having faith that pleases God? Do you take just one-quarter of one element and leave 90% of the Christian worldview out of the picture? Do you want to see change in the world? Do you want to see the change, the coming of the kingdom of God, which comes by being born again?[8] Are you impressed with those who speak in this way? Do you encourage and support those who speak about the necessity for regeneration to see change in the world? Have we bought into a secular view of change, the liberal gospel, the social gospel of the 19th century? If we want to change the world as Jesus wants us to, we are not going to be impressed by these secular views. We should have this worldview in place and call one another to account in our conversations to see whether we have faith that is pleasing to God. Faith understands the worldview and the elements of the worldview.

Faith Is Long-Term: It Sees the Distant Future and Works with Perseverance for It

"They did not receive the things promised; they only saw them and welcomed them from a distance" (v. 13). You know how long that distance is? Try this: From the beginning of creation with Abel, it has been 6,000 years; since Abraham, it has been about 4,000 years. Do we operate with this time frame, if necessary? We who call ourselves postmillennialists and want to see the kingdom of God come. I am guilty of this; I have wanted to see it come in my lifetime—yes, certainly, please Lord, let it be. But if it does not, am I ready to work long-term, looking to the next 100, 500, 1,000 years? What I do now by the grace of God is important. It is as important and necessary as Abraham leaving Ur of the Chaldees was for the kingdom of God. This

---

8. *John 3:3.*

work will stand. God has brought me into the kingdom, and brought you into the kingdom, and given gifts and abilities for such a time as this, to do this piece that is necessary and to say, 'It shall be,' even as the faithful waited and saw it from a distance and welcomed it.[9] There is a perception of faith which is able to see at a distance. Moses saw it at a distance. Isaiah saw it at a distance. Should we be discouraged if it does not happen in our lifetime? Or shall we work and plan for that? Let me tell you, it does not happen just by having children. Building the kingdom by having children is part of it. You may say, 'If I have seven children and disciple them, that's good.' Try 30! Do you want to have 30 children and disciple them? Go for it. How about 60? How about 100? That is the way the kingdom is built.[10] Do not tell me it is just by having lots of children. It is necessary, but it is not sufficient. I remember someone once told me, 'You're going to go with this and just have children, and their children will have children, and their children will have more children, and there it is.' That may have been true in the Old Testament, but not in the New Testament, where we are to go out and make disciples. We see it from a distance; we are working for it. This is what biblical faith is. There are not many faithful men and women who are operating with this understanding. We should not sit, moan, complain, gripe, or sing sad songs about it. Let us say, 'That's right, we have to do the work, and let us give ourselves to doing this work.' It is easy when we get together to say, 'Nobody is listening, nobody cares,' and sing the blues. But let us sing the Psalms, not the blues. If there are blues to be sung, they will be in the Psalms. We sang one this morning about our moaning, but we also sang about joy and hope in the precepts of God.

The ancients saw it from a distance; they could perceive, and we operate in that time frame, just as the ancients did, for which they were commended. Abraham left Ur of the Chaldees; he persevered, lived in tents, and did not settle down as Lot did in Sodom. He lived in tents—a stranger and pilgrim in the Promised Land. Abraham did not leave the Promised Land but went out and settled down. He did not return to Ur of the Chaldees or Haran. Abraham perceived, he planned, and he persevered. There is often a lot of perceiving at a distance and then

9. *Hebrews 11:10.*

10. *Matthew 13:8–9.*

settling down, as opposed to persevering and pushing forward. It is like a race, we have said. You set your maximum pace by which you can get to the end at maximum speed. It is a race, and we must press ourselves this way. Abraham did, the ancients did, and this is what they were commended for. They did not settle down, and they did not return. They were looking for a better country, a heavenly one. **"Instead, they were longing for a better country—a heavenly one"** (v. 16a).

Faith Reasons When Tested

Faith is tested as our understanding is tested. The way we overcome is the way Abraham did. When he received the supreme test of offering up Isaac, Abraham had to understand a number of things. He had to reason.

> **By faith Abraham, when God tested him, offered Isaac as a sacrifice. He who had received the promises was about to sacrifice his one and only son, even though God had said to him, "It is through Isaac that your offspring will be reckoned." Abraham reasoned that God could raise the dead, and figuratively speaking, he did receive Isaac back from death** (vv. 17–19).

The Scripture says explicitly here, **"Abraham reasoned."** The Greek term is from the word 'logos,' *logisamenos* ($\lambda o\gamma\iota\sigma\acute{\alpha}\mu\epsilon\nu o\varsigma$) is the word in the Greek. Abraham reasoned that God could raise the dead. So faith, when tested, reasons. It draws inferences, and goes deeper with these inferences to understand the nature and work of God, the plan of God, and it rests in this understanding. The content of Scripture is not only what is explicitly said, but it includes what by good and necessary consequence can be deduced from it. It seems some people think it is impious to draw inferences from Scripture, that it is pious to only take it at its surface value. 'It says what it says, and I believe it.' 'What does it say?' 'I don't know, but it says it. I believe it.' This is an example of spiritual death at work where words are being emptied of meaning. The Westminster Confession of Faith has it right: "The whole counsel of God concerning all things necessary for His own glory, man's salvation, faith and life, is either expressly set down in Scripture, or by good and necessary consequence may be deduced from Scripture" (WCF 1.6).[11]

---

11. Gangadean, *The Westminster Confession*, 28–32.

"Abraham reasoned that God could raise the dead, and figuratively speaking, he did receive Isaac back from death" (v. 19). Faith is long-term, faith is tested, and it reasons when tested.

Faith Passes on the Blessing, the Promise (Isaac, Jacob, Joseph)

We see faith in the passing on of the blessing in the life of Isaac and Jacob. "By faith Isaac blessed Jacob and Esau in regard to their future" (v. 20). Many things are said of Isaac and Jacob, but just these two things are brought out here by the Spirit of God for our attention. "By faith Jacob, when he was dying, blessed each of Joseph's sons, and worshiped as he leaned on the top of his staff" (v. 21). Being concerned with passing on the blessing to our children is involved in faith. We are to raise them in such a way, prepare them, and then impress them with the blessing by faith. People go to their parents at the time of marriage requesting their blessing. They go for the blessing of their parents at the time of death, and we should be able to bless in the name of the Lord according to the promise of God. The blessing given to Boaz and Ruth was, "May the LORD make the woman who is coming into your home like Rachel and Leah, who together built up the house of Israel" (Ruth 4:11). Faith is involved in looking forward to the blessing and blessing others in that way.

Likewise for Joseph, "By faith Joseph, when his end was near, spoke about the exodus of the Israelites from Egypt and gave instructions about his bones" (v. 22). When he was dying, he passed on this vision. "And Joseph made the sons of Israel swear an oath and said, 'God will surely come to your aid, and then you must carry my bones up from this place'" (Gen. 50:25). Faith was operating here. It would be another few hundred years before this happened. Do we even think in those terms? Let us confess it to one another; we do not think in those terms. We sometimes say, 'I've got so much trouble. If I can get through this day, I'm thankful. If I can get through the morning, I'm thankful.' This is true of faith, but this is not all of faith. Why do I want to get through the morning? Why do I want to get through this day? Why do I want to continue living? Because God has a purpose and a plan for me: to serve Him. I am not just getting through this day to get through this day. Who wants to just get through another day just for the sake of getting through another day? I want to get through this day and learn through the trials what God would have me learn and put it into practice so that tomorrow I will be further along. I do not want to walk around in circles, I want to climb out. I want to get to the top. I want to learn what God would have me to learn. For me, the picture is always of climbing out of a canyon, the Grand Canyon. All the way up, I want to do it well and I want to progress. So Joseph looked forward in this way and we are to look forward, too. Let us ask God for grace so that we might grow in faith and understanding and think in these terms, plan in these terms, work in these terms, and persevere in these terms. If you plan for little, you know what? You will get little. If you plan for nothing, that is exactly what you will get: nothing. If you plan to make it through this life, that is all you will get. You will make it through this life. But if you plan to do the work of the kingdom and you press ahead at the end of life, God blessing you, you will have fruit. It will last.

In the case of Abraham, it was one child and the promise. But he persevered, and he passed the promise on. He passed on a vision, a legacy, and a life that has come down to us in the Word of God and has remained with all of us through the centuries. He passed this on. Sometimes, this is what we pass on: a testimony, a life lived in faith. It may be that the truth and the clarity of general revelation will not catch on in this generation. I hope it will be said that at least one person, and by the grace of God, more than one, will confess the truth of clarity, which will be passed on in generations to come. If someone lived on the earth and said, 'the goal is to see the earth filled with the knowledge of God' and he said this in the face of the opposition and the opposing views of premillennialism and amillennialism—if it is only this, and it lives on as a testimony in the years and the centuries to come, so let it be. And let it bear fruit then. Maybe it is just that one person, by the grace of God, living through his life, holding on to this and not compromising. And that is so by the grace of God. If this is your testimony, so let it be. Abraham left a testimony, a witness that endured through the generations.

Faith Both Values and Evaluates Things

By faith Moses, when he had grown up, refused to be known as the son of Pharaoh's daughter. He chose to be mistreated along

with the people of God rather than to enjoy the pleasures of sin for a short time. He regarded disgrace for the sake of Christ as of greater value than the treasures of Egypt, because he was looking ahead to his reward (vv. 24–26).

Moses valued disgrace for Christ of much greater worth than the treasures of Egypt. This is all that the world had to offer, the best that the world had to offer. Egypt, in its day, was the pinnacle, the crown of world civilization. All the glory of Pharaoh and the wisdom of Egypt, the splendor, the art, the sensitivities, the subtleties, the niceties, and the delicacies of life were there in Egypt. Sometimes, we see these things, and then we look at the Christian, and we think, 'There is not much there, I don't like it. Christians are uncouth, they are not developed, they are not sophisticated, they can't appreciate certain fine things.' You know what? They appreciate sin enough to say, 'I have sinned, and I need the forgiveness of God.' And that is one of the finest things in the world. They may not appreciate art, but they can appreciate righteousness, which is something to be built on. When I speak that way, I do not speak against art.[12] But if you had to put these fundamentals of the faith, holiness, and righteousness over against reading Keats, Eliot, or some other contemporary poet and the subtleties of that, let us go with the disgrace for Christ. Because you know what? It is often the case that in the subtleties of the world, there is not a recognition of the reality of sin and death.

We are not advocating being uncouth. We are calling for the fullness of God, but we are calling for the fullness of God that has a real genuine beginning in holiness and righteousness. We are not sidestepping that beginning. We may have to suffer disgrace with the people of God. The people of God in Egypt were not an educated bunch; they did not have the opportunities for education. They were enslaved, and Moses, who had all the education and wisdom of Egypt, saw through this and saw the death—the odor of death there was in Egypt. With all these grubby, poor, uneducated, stinky, uncouth people who were despised by the Egyptians and the cultivated, Moses says, 'I'm there. I'm with you.' He **"regarded disgrace for the sake of Christ as of greater value than the treasures of Egypt"** (v. 26a). The least in Christ is greater than

---

12. Surrendra Gangadean, *The Contradictoriness of Sin: A Reading of Paradise Lost* (Phoenix: Logos Papers Press, 2024).

the best in the world. Let us not let our heads be turned by the false sophistication that the world has to offer. We are not advocating being uncouth, but sophistication without Christ is a sham.

Moses valued the things of God, and he valued the things of this world by faith, and he valued them correctly. He gave up the pleasures of sin for a short time, and he chose to be mistreated: suffering as against indulgence. This is what faith does; it endures and endures to the very end. Not merely enduring, not just enduring to the bitter end, but enduring in the strength and power of God. This is what biblical faith is. Moses persevered because he saw Him who is invisible. **"By faith he left Egypt, not fearing the king's anger; he persevered because he saw him who is invisible"** (v. 27). The one who is invisible manifested himself to Moses in the burning bush and said, "I AM has sent me to you . . . This is my name forever" (Ex. 14b–15b). Moses had the worldview; he had the understanding of the necessity for blood being sprinkled in sacrifice, the need for vicarious atonement: **"By faith he kept the Passover and the sprinkling of blood, so that the destroyer of the firstborn would not touch the firstborn of Israel"** (v. 28). He had trust in God by which God would deliver His people and bring them through the sea. **"By faith the people passed through the Red Sea as on dry land; but when the Egyptians tried to do so, they were drowned"** (v. 29).

Faith Fights the Good Fight

In the case of Jericho, when the fighting began, they marched around and shouted and knew the battle was the Lord's. **"By faith the walls of Jericho fell, after the people had marched around them for seven days"** (v. 30). The first of battles was done in a way fully acknowledging that the battle is the Lord's and God gives the victory. Of all people, Rahab, called here "the prostitute," had faith. Some have tried to say she was a kind of innkeeper to soften it, but prostitutes, too, may have faith. **"By faith the prostitute Rahab, because she welcomed the spies, was not killed with those who were disobedient"** (v. 31). Those guilty of gross fruit sins may be convicted of their sin, come to repentance, have faith, and they sometimes go into the kingdom of God before those who are self-righteous. Rahab, the prostitute, as translated here, saw the handwriting on the wall. Perhaps she had a deep sense of sin and recognized the judgment of God for sin, and perhaps she saw that this was coming because she had that conviction in her heart. She could leave that world and see that this is God's work and give herself to helping that work. This is one of the ways we fight and help in the fight. Faith fights the good fight. It is not passive; faith wars against unbelief in every form. Faith takes thoughts captive. There is an active side of obedience and a passive side of obedience. I have come to see that this passive obedience is of greater glory than the active. Here is listed the faithful that Paul did not get to explain:

> And what more shall I say? I do not have time to tell about Gideon, Barak, Samson, Jephthah, David, Samuel and the prophets, who through faith conquered kingdoms, administered justice, and gained what was promised; who shut the mouths of lions, quenched the fury of the flames, and escaped the edge of the sword (vv. 32–34a).

This is conquest, and there is a glory in it. This is the kind of glory we are looking for, the deliverance and conquest, but there is another glory; "**Others were tortured and refused to be released, so that they might gain a better resurrection**" (v. 35b). Perhaps to be released would compromise one's faith. They would not be released but held on to their faith. Persons who can suffer for their faith endure more than those who fight and conquer. There is a greater glory in suffering for one's faith. In this way, they give the ultimate. "**Some faced jeers and flogging, while still others were chained and put in prison. They were stoned; they were sawed in two**" (vv. 36–37a). They faced the contempt of others and their liberty was so curtailed. We have the report that Isaiah was sawn in two, the silver-tongued prophet who spoke such marvellous words. Was he not favored by God? Should we say when we suffer and die this way, that somehow God has abandoned us? No, Paul says, "No, in all these things we are more than conquerors through him who loved us" (Rom. 8:37). We have overcome; we are more than conquerors. Those in passive obedience who are willing to suffer and die for their faith are more than conquerors. There is a greater glory in this:

> They were put to death by the sword. They went about in sheepskins and goatskins, destitute, persecuted and mistreated—the

world was not worthy of them. They wandered in deserts and mountains, and in caves and holes in the ground (vv. 37b–38).

They were persecuted and hounded from place to place. We know this was true of David. Elijah was hiding in a cave, and many others were hounded in this way throughout history. The early Christians worshiped in the catacombs underground. They were willing to suffer.

Faith Wants the Consummation Beyond Death

The Scripture says, **"These were all commended for their faith, yet none of them received what had been promised. God had planned something better for us so that only together with us would they be made perfect"** (vv. 39–40). Let us face it: when we compare ourselves with them, we have a trial when we are not fully comfortable. We have not come close to their suffering. Remember, **"God had planned something better for us so that only together with us would they be made perfect"** (v. 40). We are building on and continuing their work. Let us live in the spirit in which they lived. If we have to suffer for the sake of the faith and lose everything, let us be willing to do so. This is what it is to truly honor the dead who have died in the faith: that we might live in this way as they have lived. Let us live in whatever way God calls us to live, that they would be made perfect in us. There are people yet to come, in generations to come, and we must pass on this Word of God in as clear a fullness as we possibly can so that this work might be completed. Faith has in regard the promise of God. Through this faith, as we persevere, we will inherit the promise of God, and together, we will be made perfect and complete.

13

DISCIPLINE FOR HOLINESS

Hebrews 12:1–13

[1]Therefore, since we are surrounded by such a great cloud of witnesses, let us throw off everything that hinders and the sin that so easily entangles, and let us run with perseverance the race marked out for us. [2]Let us fix our eyes on Jesus, the author and perfecter of our faith, who for the joy set before him endured the cross, scorning its shame, and sat down at the right hand of the throne of God. [3]Consider him who endured such opposition from sinful men, so that you will not grow weary and lose heart.

[4]In your struggle against sin, you have not yet resisted to the point of shedding your blood. [5]And you have forgotten that word of encouragement that addresses you as sons:

"My son, do not make light of the Lord's discipline,
    and do not lose heart when he rebukes you,
[6]because the Lord disciplines those he loves,
    and he punishes everyone he accepts as a son."

[7]Endure hardship as discipline; God is treating you as sons. For what son is not disciplined by his father? [8]If you are not disciplined (and everyone undergoes discipline), then you are illegitimate children and not true sons. [9]Moreover, we have all had human fathers who disciplined us and we respected them for it. How much more should we submit to the Father of our spirits and live! [10]Our fathers disciplined us for a little while as they thought best; but God disciplines us for our good, that we may share in his holiness. [11]No discipline seems pleasant at the time, but painful. Later on, however, it produces a harvest of righteousness and peace for those who have been trained by it.

[12]Therefore, strengthen your feeble arms and weak knees. [13]"Make level paths for your feet," so that the lame may not be disabled, but rather healed.

FORGIVENESS OF SIN AND CLEANSING
FROM IDOLATRY

WE COME TO HEBREWS 12, AND WE are being exhorted based on the teaching that has gone before. Most immediately, Hebrews 11, the *Hall of Faith,* provides examples of faith and what it is to have faith, how faith looks far into the future, and how faith perseveres in seeking the promise of God. We confess that we are sinners, and to sin is to come short of the glory of God. This is because we do not seek God as diligently as we should, we do not understand, and we do not do what is right.[1] God has brought salvation to us; He sent Christ, who has died for us, and through faith in Him, we are forgiven, and through faith in Him, we are cleansed from the sin that remains in us. This sin, for which we are forgiven, remains in us in some measure and brings death. This sin is our self-life. The self-life is bound up with the world and how much we are impressed, encouraged, and enticed by the world. This sin that Christ saves us from by cleansing us from sin is the sin of idolatry. Our sin is the sin of a false view of the good. In the Garden, Adam and Eve determined good and evil for themselves, according to what pleased them. This good that we hold up other than God, apart from God, and in the place of God, is idolatry, something put in the place of God.

Idolatry is something that we expect to find happiness and blessing in. We fantasize about it. We have a very rich fantasy life, and imagine vainly that this is the way to life, blessing, and happiness. If Christ is going to save us, He must remove this idolatry; He must remove this fantasy and these things to which we cling, which we have hope in but which turns out to be false hope. In the course of removing the idolatry, He must show us the emptiness of what we hope in, what we look to. When that which we long for, hope for, work for, and waited for is being taken from us, we are thrown into the midst of all kinds of trials, pains, hardships, and disappointments. It is impossible for us to be saved without going through disappointments. This is because, as sinners, we continue to have a false view of the good, we continue to have fantasies, we continue to have idols in our hearts, and they must be removed. We do not see clearly what truly is good. We have ways

---

1. *Romans 3:10–12.*

of mixing God's goodness with *our* goodness, and they must be disentangled and separated. All that we hold up as good must be brought to naught. We are not so inclined to let this go easily because, for one thing, we do not see it for what it is, and we hold on to it and long for it for months, for years, for a greater part of our life, but it must go. It is our love affair with the world. You might think, 'That sounds a little bit too strong.' It is our joy in the natural life, the things that we naturally and spontaneously hold to; those things are to be stripped from us—even relationships, spouse, children, parents, all things that we delight in, our natural affections. We must come to the point where we submit this to our Lord; Jesus is our example. In regard to His relations, "He replied, 'My mother and brothers are those who hear God's word and put it into practice'" (Lk. 8:21). Not just those who hear the Word of God, but those who hear the Word of God, do it, and obey it. Not those who hear the Word of God and think they are doing it, or those who hear and mix in certain things and who may be zealous, but it is not the Word of God. It is those who hear the Word of God and do it. Jesus is our example in this.

There is a natural joy that we have in our spouse; there is a natural joy that we have in children; it is the most natural thing. And yet, this, too, must be brought before God. We cling to this in a natural way, and we know that God gives these things, but because of our self-life, we take it for ourselves. It is given by God for God, but we take them for ourselves, and that must be untangled and there is pain in this and there is no way out. We are sinners, and Christ saves us from our sin and death, and He must use suffering, the curse, hardships, trials, and discipline to bring us to seek, understand, and do what is right. Given the reality of sin, these are the *ordinary means*, and there are hardships of every conceivable sort. Some seem so trivial that they are not worth being considered a hardship, but the effect of it is that it frustrates us. Sometimes it may be waiting in line, or just waiting for something ordinary, or your computer crashes, and you can lose it. This seems so mundane, and yet it is a trial. When you need all the time you can get to concentrate, this is just when the hardships come. At just those times, there are little piddling things that come, and it is death by a thousand cuts, and it just drains you away. They are not quite big enough to be called a trial, but when many of them come together, there is a trial, which is nevertheless a hardship. It comes in every size, color, shape, and wrapping, and no one here is exempt; every one of us has trials.

We should not only share our testimonies but also our trials in a way that does not magnify, 'Poor me, look at what I've had to go through. Can you top that?' 'I can do you one better than that!' We may boast and sling our trials around. But we should glory in God, who has upheld us through these trials. We should greet one another and say, 'How is the Lord helping you in your trials today?' and we get a story of it. Not, 'How are you?' I know how you are. You are having trials. We should say, 'How is God upholding you in your trials these days?' I did not say *if;* I said *how.* You may say, 'Well, God is not upholding me very well. God has just left me out here.' Oh, no, He has not left you out there; His eyes are on you, His eyes are very much on you, and He knows that you have to come to a breaking point. After hitting yourself against the wall so often, you will just have to stop it. How many times are we frustrated and come to the point of thinking and saying, 'Lord, what is going on here? This is not the kind of life you intend for me. What of peace and joy in the Holy Spirit? What is happening? What is going on in my life?' We learn to discover what is of the natural life and what is supernatural—what is of God. Remember, the Word of God divides between the soul and the spirit.[2] Many things quite naturally excite and naturally satisfy but leave us thirsty again. They are not the satisfaction that there is in God. They are not that secret spring of God's self-disclosure and self-revelation that satisfies us. God's self-revelation to us gives us a sense of nearness to God, the dearness of God to us, the sense that God is with us, God loves us, and we are His, and we want to give ourselves to Him. This is what God has for us.

There is a natural excitement that gives pleasure. I was talking to someone the other day, and he was referring to a Christian who likes listening to Christian rock. He pointed out that 'Christian rock is not so different from worldly rock. In this case, their rock is like our rock, or our rock is like their rock.' It has the effect of *exciting* but does not have the effect of *edifying.* There is a natural comfort, and then there is a comfort in God. The natural things will be shaken so that we might find our joy in God. Whatever blessing is given to us is given to us

---

2. *Hebrews 4:12.*

in a way in which we see that the Lord God is giving Himself to us through this blessing. It is not the blessing itself; it is not the person or the gift; it is the *giver* that is coming to us through the gift. The love of the giver is coming to us. Christmas time is coming, gift time, and present time, and you know how easy it is to get your eyes on the gift more than the giver. We would never want to do that, to have our eyes on the gift rather than the giver. This is to take the gift in place of the giver and not see the giver is giving himself or herself to us through the gift, that it is the person behind the gift. This natural way of living, of exalting the creature above the Creator, and exalting the blessings of God above God must be taken from us. We are to be saved from this kind of self-life where we take the blessing for ourselves and we do not see it in God.

TO PERSEVERE IN THE RACE, CONSIDER THE SUFFERING AND THE GLORY

In Hebrews 12 we are called to persevere in the race, a race that has been run by those who have gone before us, those who have handed on the witness and the work of the kingdom of God to us. We must persevere in this race. **"Therefore, since we are surrounded by such a great cloud of witnesses, let us throw off everything that hinders and the sin that so easily entangles, and let us run with perseverance the race marked out for us"** (v. 1). Secondly, we must **"Endure hardship as discipline"** (v. 7a). We are being warned in many ways why we must persevere and endure.

First of all, we are to persevere in the race. The word for race is *agon,* where we get our word *agony.* We must persevere in the agony. There is no question about it; it is an agony. You have heard the expression "the agony and the ecstasy." Which is first? The agony. Remember what our Lord, Jesus Christ, said after His resurrection, "Did not the Christ have to suffer these things and then enter his glory?" (Lk. 24:26). This is the pattern. There is a race that we must run here, and there is a time factor in every race. Sometimes, a race is spoken of in such a way that just finishing is great, but I think the sense in which we should understand this is that we finish the race, and the course is marked out for us. There are certain kinds of races where they mark out the course, and different people run different courses and so on, but there is a course marked out for each one of us. Christ Jesus has taken hold of us for a particular purpose, and we must fulfill that purpose. We want to get all the work given to us *done* before we die. This is the race. The night is coming, when no one can work. "As long as it is day, we must do the work of him who sent me. Night is coming, when no one can work" (Jn. 9:4). At death, our work ceases, and our individual work ceases.

In this work, there is a time and a season for everything.[3] If we do not do things in a timely way, in a seasonal way, guess what? We will fall behind, and then we will have to play catch-up, which is going to be difficult. We are in a race; we have to pace ourselves, take advantage of the downhill portions, but not too hard, or we may get hurt or lose the energy for later on, and there will be a number of uphills. You time yourself so you can run that race. However you run, it is going to be agony. Hopefully, you can run without injury, but even if you are in your best shape, you have to push yourself when you are running. If you run well and try to do all that God would have you to do, it will take *everything* you have.

The Cloud of Witnesses

Remember Abel, Enoch, Noah, Abraham, the Patriarchs, Moses, the Judges, David, and the Prophets; all of these have gone before us, and they have run the race. They pass it on to us, and we have to pass it on. There is a sense in which it is a relay race; we have been handed the baton. If the generation before us were slacking, we would be a bit behind, and we will have to make up for it. We have to finish the race, in the sense of finishing the work and finishing the course marked out for us. We have to finish the work that God has given to us and pass it on. In that sense, Paul says, "I have fought the good fight, I have finished the race, I have kept the faith. Now there is in store for me the crown of righteousness" (2 Tim. 4:7–8a).

Lay Aside Every Hindrance

To run this race, we must throw off, we must lay aside every hindrance, **"let us throw off everything that hinders and the sin that so easily entangles, and let us run with perseverance the race marked out for**

---

3. *Eccleciastes 3:1–8.*

us" (v. 1b). I have run a few 10Ks, and I know what it is to throw off. We run; our shoes must be just right, nothing extra. You are going to start out cold and want to bring a sweater, but you will have to haul it along with you; no, you want to strip. You want nothing that will hinder you; you have everything just right, and then you run. You do not pay attention to people behind you huffing, puffing, wheezing, and stomping along and passing you up. You run your race. You keep your eyes focused. You have to strip away every hindrance, every sin, every form of self-life, every desire that distracts us from the work of the kingdom; we have to let it go! This is part of the stripping, the throwing off. I see others there in such fine, splendid shape, and some are not in such good shape, but nevertheless, they run. There are some people there who've got it, and they have been doing all this training. Seeing someone in such fine shape and rejoicing to run the race is beautiful. They are going to come in about 15 minutes ahead of you, but they have also been training for that. You are going to run your race, the course is marked out for you, and you are going to finish the race like Paul told the Philippians, "I press on to take hold of that for which Christ Jesus took hold of me" (Phil. 3:12b).

Hopefully, we know this and have been working on it through the seasons of our lives. There is a time for everything. Let us be mindful of the seasonal aspect of life and make the most of it. There is a time to save, and there is a time to spend. The time to save, young people, is when you are young. Put that in savings and let it gain appropriate interest, compound it, and do not overlook this. There is a time to have children. There is a time to marry. Some of us have said, 'Yes, Lord, it's time. It's way past time. What's the deal?' You might be in difficulty, and marriage may not be coming, but God has a time, and we should be preparing our hearts to have a godly marriage—trust in God. There is a time to study as students; there is a time to learn. When you are younger than 12, you should have learned all the basics in grammar school.[4] You should know the three arguments against materialism. Do you? Those arguments you should just know, you do not have to understand, just know it. You should know the square of opposition, what an argument is, all the basic facts of history, this is grammar school.

---

4. The Logos Foundation, *Grammar Catechisms: Philosophical, Theological, and Historical Foundations* (Phoenix: The Logos Papers Press, 2023).

You should know all the fundamentals of philosophy, history, the sciences, and the periodic table of elements in chemistry. Lots of things! You should just memorize and store it up; this is the time for it. Dorothy Sayers[5] made a point of this, and there has been a long tradition of the Trivium. There is a time for memorizing Scripture and there is a time for using those Scriptures that you have memorized. Let us be aware of the season. We are in a race and we should use our time well.

There is a particular sin that hinders, what is called your 'most *besetting* sin.' Your *best* sin is what it is called, your specialty. This is what I specialize in; I specialize in despair and cynicism really easily because 'I wanted to change the world, and nobody else wants to change it anymore. I am left all by myself.' I want to change the world the way the world wants to change the world; everybody wants to change the world. But I have to learn to want to change the world the way Christ is going to change the world. I can get into despair very easily and discouragement. The three ways in which the devil defeats us are through *deception, discouragement,* and *distraction.* These are the three ways the devil defeats us. This you can remember. Discouragement is an easy way for the devil to defeat us. And cynicism: I am surprised at how much cynicism there is in Christians. Should they be called a Christian cynic? 'I belong to the church of Christian cynicism. The *third* church of Christian cynicism.' Let us watch out for our most besetting sin. It is the sin you have been wrestling with since you were 15, 16, and on. Do you remember those? Are they still around? They come back and hit you in ways that you were not expecting, but you should have expected. You say, 'This is the umpteenth time I am dealing with this thing. What's the deal? Am I ever making progress?' This is your besetting sin. The one you keep wrestling with over and over and over. When you throw off everything that hinders you, especially watch out for your best sin—the best one, the best sin, the most besetting sin. Watch for that, pray for that, trust God, and find ways to overcome it so you can run the race that is marked out for you with perseverance.

---

5. Dorothy Sayers, *The Lost Tools of Learning and the Mind of the Maker* (Waterford: Benediction Classics, 1947).

Fix Your Eyes on Jesus

When you run, fix your eyes on Jesus. **"Let us fix our eyes on Jesus, the author and perfecter of our faith"** (v. 2a), not on anyone else; you are not comparing yourself with someone else who is better than you; you are comparing yourself with perfection. You may follow another person as they follow the Lord, but it is always in the context of the Lord. Let us fix our eyes on Jesus in this race. There is a book by Malcolm Boyd, *Are You Running With Me, Jesus?*[6] The work should have been titled, *Am I Running With Jesus?* Jesus is not running with me, I am running with Him. I am keeping my eyes on Him; He is the leader; Jesus is the one who sets the example. I am not to be conformed in my life to some other person, I am to be conformed to Jesus Christ. Paul says, "Follow my example, as I follow the example of Christ" (1 Cor. 11:1). There is always a unique way in which each one of us must be conformed to Christ.

We are called to **"fix our eyes on Jesus, the author and perfecter of our faith"** (v. 2a). How did He run? He runs the way we are to run: **"who for the joy set before him endured the cross, scorning its shame, and sat down at the right hand of the throne of God"** (v. 2b). There comes a time when we must give up our love affair with the world, our praise of men, and what is highly esteemed among men, and we must get serious and give ourselves to do what the Lord would have us to do. Many of us have struggled for years, thinking, 'I'd like to go to this school or that school, this name school, you know, name brands.' That which is highly esteemed among men. We sometimes spend our time doing this and not giving ourselves to do what the Lord would have us to do. We are still enamored with the world and the honor that is given in the world, and we want the praise of men.

Jesus scorned the scorning of men. It was a scorn to die ignominiously on the cross, to give one's life in this way. Jesus knew it was contempt, utter contempt, that people had for someone who would live out their lives in this way and die on the cross. Jesus had to overcome that; He had to have His eyes on the goal and the joy that was set before Him. He had to bring many of these 'scorners' to true honor and the praise of God rather than men. To have the joy of having men set free from this bondage to sin, honoring themselves, and having honor

---

6. Malcolm Boyd, *Are You Running With Me, Jesus?* (New York: Cowley Publications, 1965).

from others. Jesus said, "If I glorify myself, my glory means nothing. My Father, whom you claim as your God, is the one who glorifies me" (Jn. 8:54). It is God who honors Christ; it was God who raised Christ from the dead—that is honor indeed! We are to seek the honor that comes from God, not from men. We have to watch out for being enamored and for our love affair with the world and looking at what men praise and seeking that more than the praise of God. Jesus had the joy set before Him, and He scorned the shame of the cross. We, too, must count the things that were gain to us, privileged positions, the way Paul did: "But whatever was to my profit I now consider loss for the sake of Christ . . . I consider them rubbish, that I may gain Christ" (Phil. 3:8). The King James Version says, "dung," there are more graphic words for it, but this is how Paul names it. "That I may win Christ, and be found in him, not having mine own righteousness . . . but that which is through the faith of Christ" (Phil. 3:8b–9a KJV). If we are going to run this race and not be distracted by the world, we must scorn its shame. We must have the true joy of God before us, and by comparison, then and only then, we can scorn the shame of the world as He scorned the scorning.

In *Shawshank Redemption,*[7] the main character had to go through the sewer, and then he came out free. Sometimes it is like that. We have to go through the sewer, or what the world considers a sewer. What is highly esteemed among men is not so with God; it is filthy, like filthy rags. Consider what the world did to our Lord. The songwriter Isaac Watts puts it this way, *"When I survey the wondrous cross, On which the Prince of glory died, My richest gain I count but loss, And pour contempt on all my pride."* The pride of this world. If the Prince of Glory died on the cross, then what things were gained to me I count as loss, that I may be there in Christ Jesus. Notice how it says, **"who for the joy set before him endured the cross, scorning its shame, and sat down at the right hand of the throne of God"** (v. 2b). To sit at the right hand of the throne of God was the joy set before Him. And in that, to bring many sons to glory, to send forth His Spirit into the hearts of men, to work conviction of sin and death through regeneration, and bring men and women to Himself. This is the joy Christ had before Him, to bring them out of the world. Remember how Moses left Egypt. Remember

---

7. King, Stephen, ed. 1994. *The Shawshank Redemption*. Directed by Frank Darabont.

how Abraham left Ur of the Chaldees. Remember how Daniel refused the pleasures and privileges of Babylon. Time and again, the people of God have turned from the world to identify with the despised people of God, knowing that it is in this that their true riches are found in life.

We Have Not Yet Resisted Unto Blood

If we are to run this race, our eyes must be on Jesus in this way. We are to think of such opposition from sinful men. When we read the Gospels, we see how they oppose Jesus and the things they said of Him: 'You are mad and demon-possessed.' Has anyone called you demon-possessed because you spoke the truth, and then took up stones to stone you? Consider Him, lest you grow weary and lose heart. There is a lot of sin; there is a reality of sin. When there is no place for the Word of God in our hearts, starting with the Word of God as reason and the concern for consistency—when there is no regard for this and for the truth of God that comes in this way, there will be no regard for the Word of God and redemption, special revelation, or the prophets who bring it. Just as they killed the prophets, they will kill the one who will bring the message, and they killed our Lord. The Word is this, 'I seek to glorify my Father. I don't seek to glorify myself.'[8] To seek to glorify self is what Satan did; this is the essence of satanism—self.[9] To seek honor for yourself and to please yourself rather than God. This is why there is no room in those who follow that way of life, the self-life, for the Word of God. They cannot hear it. Let us recognize it for what it is; let us not be enamored by all this hullabaloo that some make about evolution.[10] As some of you are going through studies now, you are seeing how empty it is, how lacking in support, how many arguments there are, and how there is a total lack in seriousness and concern for consistency in these people. They do not take truth seriously, and therefore, are not to be taken seriously. They should know this. Let us not be impressed by them. Let us not be impressed by the world, but let us overcome it. Let us not grow weary and lose heart when they object to the truth, but let us recognize it for what it is, call it for what it is,

---

8. *John 8:49–50.*

9. Gangadean, *The Contradictoriness of Sin.*

10. Gangadean, *Philosophical Foundation*, 86–100.

and treat it with the proper disregard that it requires. Sometimes, treating these things seriously is giving it much more regard than it should have. We are to see through it; we are not to be impressed by it; we are to call it what it is and go on and not lose heart.

Many of you have said, 'I've tried witnessing, and they're not interested.' That should not come as a surprise, and yet we stumble here. **"Consider him who endured such opposition from sinful men, so that you will not grow weary and lose heart"** (v. 3). Human beings, left to themselves, will resist God. We see it in our children, and we have them baptized, which speaks about their need for a new heart. We confess that they are sinners, and guess what? We are saying that God will do this, and if they grow up and God has not yet done it, we are surprised that our kids are sinners. Wretched sinners, miserable sinners, like anyone else, like Esau, who was a covenant child. Surprise, surprise. What do we confess when we baptize our kids? What do we confess about ourselves? That we are sinners, we still come short; we need the grace of God. Let us **"not grow weary and lose heart."**

GOD IS TREATING US AS SONS

The second reason to endure in this hardship is, **"God is treating you as sons"** (v. 7a). First of all, we could be suffering a whole lot more than we are. No one here has resisted to the point of blood. **"In your struggle against sin, you have not yet resisted to the point of shedding your blood"** (v. 4). No one here has; I know you. I know if you have resisted to the point of blood, I would have heard about it; it would have been loud and clear, 'Look! Look! Blood! Now, do you believe me?' No one here has resisted to the point of shedding blood. Wouldn't you like to have that? It could be worn as a scar, proudly, a battle scar, a veteran. No, there is a lot more that we might endure. God encourages us by saying not to treat discipline with contempt, do not make light of it: **"My son, do not make light of the Lord's discipline"** (v. 5b). Treat discipline as something precious. 'Thank you, Lord, I needed that. Thank you,' amid your tears. It is not, 'Who needs this? I don't deserve this. I deserve better.' You do not really want to know what you deserve, do you? You deserve something else a lot more. God is not so hard on us, "he will not let you be tempted beyond what you can bear" (1 Cor. 10:13). Paul says, **"do not make light of the Lord's discipline, and do** not lose heart when he rebukes you" (v. 5); we are not to joke about it or be casual about it. We are not to lose heart when He rebukes us. The circumstances of discipline can be different. Sometimes it comes in the way of a rebuke. A rebuke is stronger, very pointed, and has a sharp correction, and you know what? We need to be rebuked every once in a while. Actually, a lot more than once in a while. We need rebukes because we get pretty goofy, we get pretty casual about a lot of things, and we need a sharp word of correction, like a karate chop. Discipline and correction will come, and we are not to make light of it nor "lose heart" when He sharply corrects us.

"For whom the Lord loves He chastens, and scourges every son whom He receives" (v. 6 NKJV). The word is "scourges." Adoption is one of the blessings of salvation; it is one of the benefits that accompany justification. You are adopted into the family of God. Oh, yes, scourgings is the word. Scourgings are like whips on your back. Paul received scourgings many times, even 40 stripes minus one. Do not lose the richness, the color, the pain, the feeling of the word *scourging*. Things are deep within us, and the scourging opens our backs and causes some festering stuff to come out. God sometimes scourges us, He "scourges every son whom He receives." Scourging and sonship go together. I will say that once more—scourging and sonship go together. Do not disassociate these; associate them. Think of Paul and what he went through. Think of our Lord Jesus. Expect scourgings.

We like to expect that our fantasy life will be fulfilled, and in place of that, our fantasy life is shredded, and we complain and sing the blues. Our expectations are not what they should be. We are being treated as sons, and we are being exhorted and encouraged on this basis: "For what son is not disciplined by his father?" (v. 7b). Everyone undergoes discipline; believers and nonbelievers undergo discipline. Their fathers disciplined them, their parents. Everyone undergoes discipline. "If you are not disciplined (and everyone undergoes discipline), then you are illegitimate children and not true sons" (v. 8). It is a natural aspect of life. We need discipline and correction. Many of you were disciplined by non-believing parents, still, there was discipline, there is a universality to it. If you are a legitimate child and cared for by your parents, your parents would correct you. If you are not legitimate, they will not care about you; they will let you go. To be corrected is to have someone who cares enough to correct you. We can get angry, we can get really angry at times, and we can interpret correction as a lack of love, but here, scourging and sonship, discipline and sonship, go together. **"If you are not disciplined (and everyone undergoes discipline), then you are illegitimate children and not true sons"** (v. 8).

Secondly, **"Moreover, we have all had human fathers who disciplined us and we respected them for it"** (v. 9a). How is respect manifested? Submission. We submitted to it; we did not run away; we did not curse; we did not swear at our parents; we submitted to it. This is why it says, **"How much more should we submit to the Father of our spirits and live!"** (v. 9b). Part of acknowledging Jesus Christ as Lord is to recognize that He rules in all things, not just by His precepts, but by His sovereign rule in everything that comes to pass. Christ, the Lord, has designed all things to manifest His glory, sometimes in His justice (in the manifestation of sin and death), and sometimes to manifest His glory in His grace. He may leave us to our sins for a while, and we must learn to submit to His lordship and the wisdom of His lordship in all of this. We are not to complain and we are not to murmur. That is disregarding and not accepting the wisdom of it. **"How much more should we submit to the Father of our spirits and live!"** (v. 9b).

"Our fathers disciplined us for a little while as they thought best" (v. 10a), and it is not always the best, but as they thought best, **"but God disciplines us for our good, that we may share in his holiness"** (v. 10b). Sharing in God's holiness is to be devoted to God, not to our self-life, but to overcome our self-life; this is the sin of autonomy that He is cleansing us from. As we share in His holiness, we come to the place where we can see God—"without holiness no one will see the Lord" (Heb. 12:14b).

We will not have time for the warnings in verses 14–29 today; we will have to take them up next time. But there are warnings against the process of discipleship by which we learn holiness, by which we give up our self-life and learn to be devoted to the Lord and worship the Lord in the beauty of holiness. A truly holy person is a truly beautiful person. They do not have the self-life. Sometimes our spirituality reeks with self-life, 'I'm so spiritual.' We have false views of holiness and spirituality, and it is not lovely. The true holiness, where our self-life is gone, is a beautiful thing to see. God wants us to partake of this holiness without which no one will see the Lord, which is pleasing to Him.

A reason for submitting to enduring hardship as discipline is this: **"No discipline seems pleasant at the time, but painful"** (v. 11a). At the time, it is not pleasant; it does not seem pleasant, but painful, let us not kid ourselves, it is not pleasant. It is positively painful, but that is for now, at the present time, **"Later on, however, it produces a harvest of righteousness and peace for those who have been trained by it"** (v. 11b). We are to be trained to discern good and evil, as it said earlier in the Book of Hebrews. Under these conditions, **"Therefore, strengthen your feeble arms and weak knees. 'Make level paths for your feet,' so that the lame may not be disabled, but rather healed"** (vv. 12–13). We are not to allow things to hinder us, we are to put aside those things and not be weak, but be strong in the Lord. And let our lameness, and we are lame, spiritually lame, let it be healed rather than become a permanent disability. As we submit to God and learn what we should, these are the blessings that will come. We learn holiness; we learn to worship the Lord in the beauty of holiness.

God helping us, we will have to take up next time the warnings that support this exhortation to run with perseverance and endure hardship.

14

No Turning Back

Hebrews 12:14–29

¹⁴Make every effort to live in peace with all men and to be holy; without holiness no one will see the Lord. ¹⁵See to it that no one misses the grace of God and that no bitter root grows up to cause trouble and defile many. ¹⁶See that no one is sexually immoral, or is godless like Esau, who for a single meal sold his inheritance rights as the oldest son. ¹⁷Afterward, as you know, when he wanted to inherit this blessing, he was rejected. He could bring about no change of mind, though he sought the blessing with tears.

¹⁸You have not come to a mountain that can be touched and that is burning with fire; to darkness, gloom and storm; ¹⁹to a trumpet blast or to such a voice speaking words that those who heard it begged that no further word be spoken to them, ²⁰because they could not bear what was commanded: "If even an animal touches the mountain, it must be stoned." ²¹The sight was so terrifying that Moses said, "I am trembling with fear."

²²But you have come to Mount Zion, to the heavenly Jerusalem, the city of the living God. You have come to thousands upon thousands of angels in joyful assembly, ²³to the church of the firstborn, whose names are written in heaven. You have come to God, the judge of all men, to the spirits of righteous men made perfect, ²⁴to Jesus the mediator of a new covenant, and to the sprinkled blood that speaks a better word than the blood of Abel.

²⁵See to it that you do not refuse him who speaks. If they did not escape when they refused him who warned them on earth, how much less will we, if we turn away from him who warns us from heaven? ²⁶At that time his voice shook the earth, but now he has promised, "Once more I will shake not only the earth but also the heavens." ²⁷The words "once more" indicate the removing of what can be shaken—that is, created things—so that what cannot be shaken may remain.

²⁸Therefore, since we are receiving a kingdom that cannot be shaken, let us be thankful, and so worship God acceptably with reverence and awe, ²⁹for our "God is a consuming fire."

INTRODUCTION

The Goal: The Fullness in the Kingdom

IN THE BOOK OF HEBREWS, WE HAVE HAD the goal set before us, the fullness that is in God, the greater richness prepared in the Old Testament (which was looking forward to its fulfillment), and the richness which has begun with the expansion of the kingdom of God from Israel to the ends of the earth—this includes all the families of the earth as God promised Abraham, "in you all the families of the earth shall be blessed" (Gen 12:3b NKJV)—so that we do not settle down, we do not settle back, we do not settle for less. With all those who have gone before, we look forward to that city with foundations. Though we may see it from afar, we are nearer than they were. We live our lives waiting, working, watching, hoping, and praying for that city and seeing the advancement of God's work in the earth, as nation after nation, people after people, come under the sway of the preaching of the gospel, under the rule of Christ, and they come to submit themselves to the Lord. God allows these nations to prosper because there is greater richness under Christ. But if we do not continue to seek, and we turn back, we find that God's chastening is upon us. The blessings that are ours in Christ are removed, and we experience all the death that there is in sin. Our God is a consuming fire.[1] He is so, not as man, as in a finite, temporal, and changeable way; He is so in an infinite, eternal, and unchanging way.

God's Provision

As we read through this passage and think about it, we see a contrast between Mount Sinai and Mount Zion. This is not a contrast by way of opposition; this is a contrast by way of completion. It is a 'more so' argument. There is a contrast if we have 'more than.' In every way, Mount Sinai was grace, and Mount Zion is increased grace. As there

---

1. *Hebrews 12:29.*

was judgment then for those who neglected the grace of God, so there is greater judgment for those who neglect the Word of God, who do not press on, who do not keep on going; there is greater judgment for those who stop and who, in effect, turn back. There is no turning back in God; we either go forward or backward. There is no turning back from holiness. Let us recognize and set our hearts on this, that our God is holy, and He said, "Be ye holy; for I am holy" (1 Pet. 1:16 KJV) and **"without holiness no one will see the Lord"** (v. 14b). The Lord would have us come to Him, to know Him, to see Him. There is no turning back from holiness; there is no turning back from putting aside the self-life. The self-life in every form must go, and in place of the self-life must be devotion to God—holiness. There is no in-between, there is no compromise, there is no standing still; all of that is a turning back. When we come to the Lord, when we come to God who is holy, we must be holy. If we will stand before the presence of God, we cannot stand in our sin, in our self-life. Be prepared, people of God, be prepared, all of us, to reckon with the self-life in every form and worldliness in every form. There is no turning back. There is no standing still. We must press on. There is greater grace; God will bring us into that fullness; God is eternally gracious and just. Those who neglected the Word of God refused to hear. The chastening of the Lord works its way into our lives through the trials and circumstances that come into our lives; if we neglect the grace of God that is working in these trials and turn back, we will experience the death that is due to sin. We will experience the burning of fire in our very souls as what we seek is brought to naught; it is reduced to ashes before us. God is holy, and we must be holy and come in our holiness to see the Lord and have joy in seeing Him.

Peace and Holiness Through Chastening

God has made every provision for this greater fullness. He has given us a better covenant, a greater priesthood, and the promise of the Spirit coming upon us. Christ is, as the mediator of this new covenant, the high priest before God.[2] The One who sends the Spirit is able to bring us into this fullness. Jesus will accomplish what Adam failed to

---

2. Gangadean, *The Westminster Confession*, 111–135.

accomplish. He will accomplish what the prophets, the priests, and the kings of the Old Testament did not accomplish. He is the One who is seated at the right hand of God, ruling over nations and ruling in every one of our lives. In all the details of what we pray for, God is ruling. We must be able to say God is not only ruling, but He is Lord, and God has chosen to reveal Himself in this way in our lives. In some cases, He gives grace and brings us to see Him in a new way, and in some cases, He leaves us in our sin and causes sin and death to be manifest—God reveals Himself in this way, too.[3] Our concern is to be holy, to not have sin, to seek the Lord. We submit to Christ as Lord in all of this. We submit actively in obeying Him, but passively in submitting to the providences that He brings into our lives.

We are exhorted to consider this: "**Make every effort to live in peace with all men and to be holy; without holiness no one will see the Lord**" (v. 14). God chastens us that we might be partakers of His holiness. Holiness through knowledge is the reason why God chastens us. We must understand this in order to be submitted to Him. We have to acknowledge in an ever deeper way that we have sinned, come short of God's glory, and need to be transformed and renewed in every aspect of our lives. We have brought baggage from the past. We must look out, watch, be careful, and search diligently to see whether our own self-life, our own plans, and our own worldly ways of thinking are still dominating our lives. If so, watch out. God will bring trials into our lives, and when those trials come—not *if*, but *when*—watch that you do not let a bitter root spring up. God brings these trials so that we might learn holiness. Name your trials, the big ones, the little ones; take time to name them and ask, 'How have I responded to these trials?' Have I seen this as the grace of God coming into my life that I may learn holiness, or have I failed to see I need to learn holiness? Have I failed to learn what I should, and instead become bitter because I did not see the point of the trial? A root of bitterness springs up, and we harden ourselves before God; we dig in, settle back, settle down, and settle for less.

"**See to it that no one misses the grace of God and that no bitter root grows up to cause trouble and defile many**" (v. 15). Sometimes, we blame our problems on others, and we do not endure hardship as

3. Gangadean, *The Westminster Confession*, 204–206.

discipline, the scourging of God. We do not see that God is dealing with us as sons and let the scourging work against the self-life. This is what has to be 'scoured' out; it is very deeply stained in us. Have we used those categories when thinking about the trials and difficulties that have come into our lives? If not, then we are not thinking the way God would have us to think. We might blame others for our trials and not be at peace. God calls us to bless those who persecute us[4] and spitefully use us, bless and do not curse,[5] and He commands us to love our enemies.[6] Loving and seeking the good is certainly being at peace with all men,[7] over and against blaming others for the trials that come into our lives. Projecting our problems on others is part of our self-life, our self-deception, and self-justification. We are not at peace in this context, we are not at peace with others, and we will not learn holiness as long as we blame others and do not repent. In this case, we miss the grace of God. God is speaking from heaven. God is working in our lives. God rules. We are in the hands of God. God knows us and knows our every thought. Do not think that God is not concerned. God is concerned about you more than you are concerned about you. Have you numbered the hairs on your head? Not just counted them, have you numbered them? 'Oops, there goes 476, I'm going to miss you.' You hardly do that; God has *numbered* the hairs of your head. That is part of God being infinite; He is an infinite person, and He is infinitely personal. There is not a day, there is not a moment of your life, there is not a thought that crosses your mind that God is not caring about. You should care about it, too, to see whether these thoughts are pleasing to God; this should always be on our minds. Examine them to see whether there is self-life there or whether it is God's life. We cannot shrug our shoulders; there is no escaping; we are in the hands of God.

HOLINESS IS NECESSARY TO SEE GOD

We need to learn holiness; "without holiness no one will see the Lord" (v. 14b). God chastens us so that we might be partakers of His holiness.

---

4. *Luke 6:27–28.*

5. *Romans 12:14.*

6. *Matthew 5:44.*

7. *Romans 12:18.*

He does it for our good. If we do not recognize that God is chastening us for our good in all the trials that come into our lives, we will come short of the grace of God, we will settle for less, and God, who loves us, does not want us to settle for less. A root of bitterness *will* spring up. There will not be that joy in the Lord, that peace, that hope in God. In the position in which I am, as pastor, I have had opportunities to talk with people and hear their stories. Not only how they came to the Lord but also how God has continued to work. There are deep, deep struggles when God is doing a deeper work. There are long-term concerns and issues. God knows, He knows our every thought, and He is working on these trials to get down and take that out. The universe is rational, and there is nothing so eminently rational as God's dealings. God's omniscience and infinite love stand in contrast to our way of thinking, our limited vision, where we cannot make sense of it, and we become discouraged and let our hands hang down. With respect to the work of the kingdom of God, loving and serving God, we let our hands hang down, our knees become weak,[8] and we turn aside. **"See to it that no one misses the grace of God and that no bitter root grows up to cause trouble and defile many"** (v. 15). See to it, because you will not be the only one involved, your life will be a witness. Others will see your life, what you say and do, and instead of being a blessing to others, you will cause stumbling and will **"defile many."**

Consider Esau

What did we want? Some scrap of sensuality, indulgence? Like Esau, who was sexually immoral. We sell ourselves out for that, a moment of self-indulgence. The way Esau did with his food.[9] Food and sex, is that what it is all about? Gratifying those desires when the itch occurs? Some bit of honor from the world? Some form of worldliness? **"See to it that no one misses the grace of God"** (v. 15a), that we do not cling to some bit of worldliness, some creaturely thing that cannot last, will not last; that we do not cling to some bit of idolatry; that we do not cling to silly, vain, empty desires which hold on to us, like Esau—desires that cause us to come short, because we are not ready to give them up.

---

8. *Ezekiel 21:7* NKJV.

9. *Genesis 25:27–34.*

We are clinging to them, and we are not learning holiness in the midst of our trials. **"See that no one is sexually immoral, or is godless like Esau, who for a single meal sold his inheritance rights as the oldest son"** (v. 16). God has given us the promise of this kingdom that cannot be shaken. This is our blessing. Are we going to settle for less? Will we let God do His work in our trials and lives? Are we going to keep looking to God and asking God to teach us and instruct us concerning holiness? Or will we indulge ourselves and come short of the grace of God? What will it be? Every one of us, moment by moment, face this choice in our lives: living unto God or unto self; learning holiness or hardening in our sin. Some of us have come around a mountain of trials. We are sitting down at the base of it, sulking, steaming in anger, feasting on that carrion comfort we call despair, indulging our despair and finding some comfort.[10] 'I will never be disappointed again because I will not hope again. I will settle down, and this is my spot forever.' Yes, you should not hope again in any worldly hope but put your hope in God. Everyone has their spot. It is a place where we feel comfortable and at ease. Carlos Castaneda, when he was going through his apprenticeship in sorcery with Don Juan, found his spot where he could settle and be at peace.[11] What is your spot? Is your spot in despair, or is it in true hope in God? Do not come short of the grace of God. Do not come short of the fullness that there is in God.

The interesting thing about Esau is that he had this mix of worldliness and teaching in God. Afterward, when he wanted to inherit the blessing, he was rejected. It is not that he wanted something and could not have it. There is no conflict in God between what we want and what we have. Here it seems to say that afterwards, when Esau wanted to inherit the blessing, he was rejected. But what he did not want to do was to change his mind. There is a want and a conflict; he wants the blessing but cannot have it because he does not want to change his mind. It says, **"Afterward, as you know, when he wanted to inherit this blessing, he was rejected. He could bring about no change of mind, though he sought the blessing with tears"** (v. 17). We cannot

---

10. Foundation, Poetry. 2021. "Carrion Comfort by Gerard Manley Hopkins." Poetry Foundation. November 20, 2021. https://www.poetryfoundation.org/poems/44392/carrion-comfort.

11. Carlos Castaneda, *The Teachings of Don Juan: A Yaqui Way of Knowledge* (New York: Washington Square Press, 1985).

have the blessing without holiness. We cannot have the blessing with worldliness. We cannot indulge our self-life and think we will see the beauty of the Lord. There is no way; it does not work that way. God is eternally wise. He has created us in such a way that unless we deliberately seek Him, we cannot find Him, and we cannot understand. Unless we see the sin and death in our own lives and have the fear of the Lord, we will not seek Him; we will not find Him. Esau did not seek God, he was a profane person, a godless person. Here is another level of despair and cynicism; we might say, 'I'm not even a Christian, I'm a profane person, I'm godless. Yes, that is what I am, I know that I'm not saved. God is just using me to make a point. Look, everyone who passes by, behold and wonder. Look at someone who doesn't know God, who is near to it and doesn't see it!' We find ways to joke about it and pass it on. You cannot even settle down as being 'non-Christian', for God will not relent; He will not leave us in our sin. We are in the hands of God. He's got the whole world in His hands, He's got the tiny little baby in His hands,[12] in every detail. If God has to break your heart so that you might bow your head for your good, He will do it. Let us not be stiff-necked, let us not be resentful against God's dealing, let us recognize God's gracious dealings in our lives and bow before Him and worship Him.

CONTRAST:
The Grace of God at Sinai and at Mount Zion

This epistle is written to the Hebrews who wanted to settle down at a level of comfort and not press on. They had come out of the Old Testament; these were Hebrew Christians. They went so far, and they did not realize that it was going to be this rough. 'Oh, you didn't realize that. You thought it would be the Red Sea experience all the way, God will drown the evil.'[13] No, we have sin. Forgiveness is not the same as cleansing. We have the self-life, and God wants to cleanse us from this. They did not think they would have to go without water, and learn to trust God for water. No one has said to me, 'I don't have any water, I

---

12. "He's Got the Whole World in His Hands." Hymnary.org. 2011. https://hymnary.org/text/hes_got_the_whole_world_in_his_hands.

13. *Exodus 14.*

need water to drink.' No one here has had to struggle in this way. Our needs are of a lesser degree, primarily financial. The Israelites in the wilderness had to look to God and trust God for their very daily sustenance. Day by day, they collected the manna. It was not "the tasty food," the leeks, the garlic, and the onions they had in Egypt. We think that all of our desires will die in God. 'I will shrivel up and become a nothing, just a dry stick, no desire. Is that what godliness is about? Being a dead dry stick, eating manna in the morning and manna at noon and manna at nighttime, too? All the time?' Oh, but it is heavenly food. Let it do its work. Suffer in the flesh, be done with sin, and come into the joy that is in God.

There is an in-between place, a 'no man's land.' It is a bad place to be. Why did you ever go there? Why are you trying to have it both ways? Get rid of the one and come to God, be with the people of God, and enjoy His way. Forget about the manna experience, the longing for the worldly desires of Egypt; you are not going to die, and it is going to be the best thing for you. It is just what you need, better than anything human you can imagine. Be like Daniel who, though he was in the court of the king and had all the wines, meats, and provisions, wanted vegetables and water. This is not a self-imposed asceticism; I am not advocating that, but in God's providence, if it is this way, then eat the vegetables, eat the rice and beans, drink water, and be thankful. Set your heart on God. Do not be like Esau, selling out his soul for a morsel of food, which is self-indulgence that lasts for a short time in this world. Let us give ourselves to godliness in learning.

The Israelites came to a mountain where God tried to make clear the reality of sin and death that there is if we do not obey His Word. **"You have not come to a mountain that can be touched and that is burning with fire; to darkness, gloom and storm"** (v. 18). That mountain was one that burned with fire, **"God is a consuming fire"** (v. 29). God has not changed. This is a contrast in the sense of 'all the more.' There we had a mountain burning, here we have **"God is a consuming fire."** If we come into God's presence with chaff, with the odiousness of the self-life, it will be consumed by the fire. Self-life cannot come into the presence of God. Think about our Lord Jesus, who did not hold on to His self-life in any way. He endured the cross, and we are to be like Him. If we are going to be seated with Him, reign with Him, and be in the presence of God, we must be holy. We must put our self-life aside; there is no turning back. Determine in your mind that you will take up your cross daily and follow the Lord, whatever it is, knowing that God is good. We have in us the deceitfulness of our sin, and God will work with it. No matter what happens, be looking to God, trusting in Him, and persevering in Him, knowing that He will bring about holiness, without which no one will see the Lord.

"No discipline seems pleasant at the time, but painful. Later on, however, it produces a harvest of righteousness and peace for those who have been trained by it" (v. 11). Let us go through training. Some of you know about training in the armed forces, starting with boot camp, but there is a lot more to learn after that. This is a training that God puts us through so we might love and serve Him. That mountain burned with fire, and God is a consuming fire. There is darkness and gloom, there is a lake of fire, spiritual death, the second death forevermore, if we do not heed. Let us not come short of the grace of God and lose it forever and ever. Let us not be in a no man's land where we lose out on good deeds of service to God forever and ever. We may be saved, but we have lost out on opportunities and the pleasure that there is in serving God through serving His people, serving in the body of Christ.

"You have not come to a mountain that can be touched and that is burning with fire; to darkness, gloom and storm" (v. 18). There is darkness, gloom, and storm on that mountain, and a trumpet blast and a voice saying, **"If even an animal touches the mountain, it must be stoned"** (v. 20b). What is spoken here is that God is holy. This is impressing upon people that God is holy and that in our sin, we must submit to God to learn the way of holiness. Keep this in mind: **"If even an animal touches the mountain, it must be stoned"** (v. 20b). Something so inadvertent, an animal without understanding may wander in its natural instinct, and in fulfilling its instinct, it may transgress. Yet that animal must be stoned. The point is not so much against the animal; the point is in regard to the holiness of God. When God descended on Mount Sinai and made His presence visible, that whole area became holy because God is holy. God said to Moses, "Do not come any closer . . . Take off your sandals, for the place where you are standing is holy ground" (Ex. 3:5). We cannot come into the presence of God without holiness. We cannot just remove our shoes and come in; this is not enough. Many places put this into practice; at best, taking off one's shoes is symbolic when one goes into a holy place. I remember visiting mosques in India and the extensive washing you must go through before entering. This is merely symbolic, for our hearts must be washed, and they must be cleansed. Our hands and what we do, the works that we give, must be washed. We must do the works of God, not be hearers only, and deceive ourselves. **"If even an animal touches the mountain, it must be stoned"** (v. 20b). **"The sight was so terrifying that Moses said, 'I am trembling with fear'"** (v. 21). Moses, who enjoyed the presence of God more than anyone else; Moses, with whom God spoke face to face, said this. When there was a deeper revelation of the grace of God and of the presence of God, Moses came in fear and trembling. Job, the most righteous man on all the earth, had reached a level of comfort and peace in God, but God wanted to come nearer to Job, and Job went through the chastening. To come into the presence of God, the fullness of His presence, we must be holy. We must put away our sin. There is no turning back. If you come this far and turn back, there is only judgment ahead, only the spiritual death that is due to sin.

"But you have come to Mount Zion, to the heavenly Jerusalem, the city of the living God" (v. 22a). We have come to Mount Zion, the Church, the people of God, where God dwells, where God is present. It is called the heavenly Jerusalem, not the earthly. For those who believed, the city always signified and was a picture of the presence of God. In Jerusalem, the temple was the place where God dwelt. God dwells in the midst of His people, so we come to the heavenly Zion, the heavenly Jerusalem, Mount Zion, the city of the living God. The people of God is the city of God, an organic unity—complete. We learn what it is to live in relation with one another, to live at peace with fellow believers, not to be offended by sin, and to recognize our own sin. We are not to be offended by how someone else's sin may have affected us and distressed us, but we are to be at peace with all men. To recognize these things are coming from the hand of God. **"You have come to thousands upon thousands of angels in joyful assembly"** (v. 22b), these are spiritual beings created by God, a third of which turned aside and became demons in their turning aside. But many remained faithful, **"to thousands upon thousands of angels in joyful assembly."** They are present; they are surrounding the city of God; they are looking on; they are beholding what is going on in the city of God, in the lives of the people of God. They are beholding the grace of God, the magnificent, secret, powerful, holy work of the Spirit of God causing His Word to be applied deep down into our lives. Penetrating between that which is of the self and that which is of the Spirit of God. The angels are looking at this, joyful in God and celebrating God's holiness. Remember the cry of the Seraphim, the angel of a high order. There are orders among the angels, we learn, angels and archangels. Cherubim and Seraphim cry out, "Holy, holy, holy is the LORD Almighty; the whole earth is full of his glory" (Is. 6:3). They see His glory, and that is why they are joyful. They see God, the One who has created heaven and earth and rules in all things. Let us reckon with this, that they are looking on, they are watching what is happening in Zion, the people of God, the details of our lives, and they are celebrating the grace of God, the truth of God, the righteousness and the holiness of God, and the wisdom of God. We have come to:

> **. . . the church of the firstborn, whose names are written in heaven. You have come to God, the judge of all men, to the spirits of righteous men made perfect, to Jesus the mediator of a new covenant, and to the sprinkled blood that speaks a better word than the blood of Abel** (vv. 23–24).

We are not on the mountain, we do not have the mountain that is burning with fire and comes with the warning that if an animal touches the mountain, it must be stoned. God coming nearer requires greater holiness on the part of the people of God. All of this means greater grace and greater nearness, and the Holy Spirit is poured out in greater abundance. Remember Ananias and Sapphira,[14] who lied about their money. They were indulgent in this way, and God is concerned with how we handle and spend our money; it often reflects our self-life. It is not the only way, but God wants us to honor Him in everything. Ananias and Sapphira, when they lied to men about this, had already lied before God, but it became manifest, and God took their lives. We do not believe that they died as unbelievers, but God is holy. He wants us to be holy in everything we do.

> On that day HOLY TO THE LORD will be inscribed on the bells of the horses, and the cooking pots in the LORD's house will be like the

---

14. *Acts 5:1–11.*

sacred bowls in front of the altar. Every pot in Jerusalem and Judah will be holy to the LORD Almighty, and all who come to sacrifice will take some of the pots and cook in them (Zech. 14:20–21a).

In our kitchen, God wants us to be holy; in our cars, God wants us to be holy. When you get cut off in traffic, respond by uttering, 'Blessed be the name of the Lord!' God wants us to be holy in the reckoning of our time. I struggle with this; I do not want to waste my time. But who says it is our time? It is not our time. Every second God gives us is a second from Him. Every breath I draw is from Him. I have to learn that and do what the Lord would have me to do. We come to the Father, Son, and Holy Spirit, **"to Jesus the mediator of a new covenant, and to the sprinkled blood that speaks a better word than the blood of Abel"** (v. 24). Always better, more than, more grace, more holiness, and more responsibility. When God is scourging us, He is treating us as sons. You may say, 'Oh, that manna experience, I can handle that!' And God brings other trials into our lives, and we respond, 'Oh, I wasn't ready for this, Oh, that hurts, Oh, I'll never be the same, I'll die a dry stick. My hope is gone now.' No, God is teaching us holiness, that we might see Him.

DO NOT REFUSE:
There Is No Escape (Indulgence)

See to it that you do not come short of the grace of God, see to it that you are not like Esau, and in verse 25, **"See to it that you do not refuse him who speaks."** This warning came very early in the Book of Hebrews and this theme is continuing and deepening throughout. **"If they did not escape when they refused him who warned them on earth, how much less will we, if we turn away from him who warns us from heaven?"** (v. 25b). The Israelites who were warned did not escape when they refused Him—how many of them died in the wilderness? How many of them died in their casual response at Mount Sinai when they worshiped the golden calf? How many defiled themselves with the Moabites?[15] They complained about the food, missing the comforts of Egypt; they complained about lack of honor. This attitude even

---

15. *Numbers 25:1–18.*

penetrated Aaron and Miriam,[16] and even Moses, when he struck the rock instead of speaking to it.[17] They did not escape.

Even a believer who is under the hand of God and wrath of God, will not escape. **"If they did not escape when they refused him who warned them on earth, how much less will we, if we turn away from him who warns us from heaven?"** (v. 25b). The Holy Spirit was sent from heaven and poured out upon us abundantly, and Christ Himself has come down from heaven. It is not that Hebrew believers were looking forward to the fulfillment of the Old Testament—Christ had come, He had poured out His Spirit, and there was a greater manifestation and fullness of the grace of God. We have had the example of the apostles' lives. We have had the Book of Revelation, which speaks about the consummation of the ages. We have all of this—God has spoken from heaven in His Word. This New Testament revelation came not with a burning fire from heaven, it came with flaming tongues resting upon the believers at Pentecost,[18] and they spoke the Word of God and declared the wonderful works of God. God has come, He has spoken. If we ignore this Word, turn back from this promise, this fullness, and settle back for less than all that God has, we will not escape. How much less will we not escape if we turn away from Him who warns us from heaven? I have referred to this turning away as a turning back, coming short, settling for less, and settling down. We are to give ourselves to holiness, to be rid of the self-life completely, and not compromise the way the Israelites did when they conquered Canaan and let others live and dwell among them. They settled back for less, and the Canaanites were thorns in their flesh and in their eyes, and they had bitter, hard experiences. Let us give it up, let us go all the way, let us not settle back for less, let us not come short.

A KINGDOM WHICH CANNOT BE SHAKEN

"At that time his voice shook the earth, but now he has promised, 'Once more I will shake not only the earth but also the heavens'" (v. 26). This is not referring to the creation, because we know there

---

16. *Numbers 12.*

17. *Numbers 20:10–13.*

18. *Acts 2.*

will be a new heaven and a new earth and the creation will no longer groan under the curse. He is speaking about the works of man done apart from God, which will not stand. God will shake it all. In our entertainment, in those times when we want to kick back, relax, and just settle back for what is comfortable, we are not responding faithfully to God. Even in the literature we read, the articles, and news we listen to, will we settle back and come short? Do we go to the antinomies of conservatives and liberals without the kingdom of God in the forefront? We are settling for less, stopping short, and God does not want us to stop there. We cannot refuse Him who spoke from heaven to bring in this greater fullness. God is going to shake it; He is going to shake everything. **"The words 'once more' indicate the removing of what can be shaken—that is, created things—so that what cannot be shaken may remain"** (v. 27). What will remain is the kingdom of God. What will remain are the works that we have done in keeping with the kingdom of God. Everything else is going to go. If we waste our lives, and our time, and do not give it for service in the kingdom of God, all of our work will be like wood, hay, stubble; it will go up in smoke.[19] We have one short life, relatively speaking, 40, 50, 60 years to serve the Lord. It is so short; the night will soon come, old age and sickness and death will soon come. We are then less and less able to serve the Lord. For 60 years, such a short time, let us give ourselves to serving the Lord and not works that will be burned with fire, works that will be shaken and fall apart.

"**Therefore, since we are receiving a kingdom that cannot be shaken, let us be thankful**" (v. 28a). Be thankful in the midst of trials, receiving the trials as part of the way in which God works so that we may receive cleansing. Without holiness, no one shall see the Lord. "**Therefore, since we are receiving a kingdom that cannot be shaken,**" let those things that are shaken by the trial fall apart—let them go. Let us be thankful in those circumstances. We should say, 'Thank you, God, for taking away this idol of my heart that I so loved and delighted in.' Manna is the best thing for us as God continues His work. Let it do its work and let us come into what God has for us. "**We are receiving a kingdom that cannot be shaken.**" We should study history to know how many major kingdoms and civilizations there have been. We should study

---

19. *1 Corinthians 3:10–15.*

them and know what has happened to all of them; we should know the fundamental structure of all of them and how all of them collapsed, every one of them. All the kingdoms of man have collapsed, and all the glory of man faded away. **"We are receiving a kingdom that cannot be shaken,"** so when God shakes our lives apart, let us be thankful. Let us not be bitter and resentful, **"let us be thankful, and so worship God acceptably with reverence and awe"** (v. 28b). Let us bow before Him as Job did when God shook his life apart. He was an example for us. Let us be thankful because God is bringing us into something that cannot be shaken, that will last forever. Bow before God as Job did, all the way, when he said, "The Lord gave, and the Lord has taken away; Blessed be the name of the Lord" (Job 1:21 NKJV). God is giving so much more; even in this trial, we are receiving a kingdom that cannot be shaken. We thank God, we fear God, we understand sin and death, we have reverence in our lives, and we bow before God in awe.

"For our 'God is a consuming fire'" (v. 29). There is an eternal reality of holiness that cannot be compromised in the least. It is the very nature of holiness not to be compromised, not to settle for less, not to come short. It is because God is holy that the earth is full of His glory. He rules in everything that comes to pass for the revelation of His glory. Holiness is the antithesis to compromise, to settling, to coming short; **"our 'God is a consuming fire.'"** He will consume everything that is not holy. If an animal touches the mountain, it must be stoned. The one who comes before God, into the presence of God, must be holy. The holiness of God is seen in Christ as He hung on the cross and cried out, "My God, my God, why have you forsaken me?" (Matt. 27:46b). Nevertheless, He said, "Father, into your hands I commit my spirit" (Lk. 23:46). "Therefore God exalted him to the highest place and gave him the name that is above every name, that at the name of Jesus every knee should bow, in heaven and on earth and under the earth" (Phil. 2:9–10). We have come **"to Jesus the mediator of a new covenant"** (v. 24), and we come to remember Him in the Lord's Supper.

15

Exhortations to Life

Hebrews 13:1–25

¹Keep on loving each other as brothers. ²Do not forget to entertain strangers, for by so doing some people have entertained angels without knowing it. ³Remember those in prison as if you were their fellow prisoners and those who are mistreated as if you yourselves were suffering.

⁴Marriage should be honored by all, and the marriage bed kept pure, for God will judge the adulterer and all the sexually immoral. ⁵Keep your lives free from the love of money and be content with what you have, because God has said,

"Never will I leave you;
never will I forsake you."

⁶So we say with confidence,

"The Lord is my helper; I will not be afraid.
What can man do to me?"

⁷Remember your leaders, who spoke the word of God to you. Consider the outcome of their way of life and imitate their faith. ⁸Jesus Christ is the same yesterday and today and forever.

⁹Do not be carried away by all kinds of strange teachings. It is good for our hearts to be strengthened by grace, not by ceremonial foods, which are of no value to those who eat them. ¹⁰We have an altar from which those who minister at the tabernacle have no right to eat.

¹¹The high priest carries the blood of animals into the Most Holy Place as a sin offering, but the bodies are burned outside the camp. ¹²And so Jesus also suffered outside the city gate to make the people holy through his own blood. ¹³Let us, then, go to him outside the camp, bearing the

disgrace he bore. [14]For here we do not have an enduring city, but we are looking for the city that is to come.

[15]Through Jesus, therefore, let us continually offer to God a sacrifice of praise—the fruit of lips that confess his name. [16]And do not forget to do good and to share with others, for with such sacrifices God is pleased. [17]Obey your leaders and submit to their authority. They keep watch over you as men who must give an account. Obey them so that their work will be a joy, not a burden, for that would be of no advantage to you.

[18]Pray for us. We are sure that we have a clear conscience and desire to live honorably in every way. [19]I particularly urge you to pray so that I may be restored to you soon.

[20]May the God of peace, who through the blood of the eternal covenant brought back from the dead our Lord Jesus, that great Shepherd of the sheep, [21]equip you with everything good for doing his will, and may he work in us what is pleasing to him, through Jesus Christ, to whom be glory for ever and ever. Amen.

[22]Brothers, I urge you to bear with my word of exhortation, for I have written you only a short letter.

[23]I want you to know that our brother Timothy has been released. If he arrives soon, I will come with him to see you.

[24]Greet all your leaders and all God's people. Those from Italy send you their greetings.

[25]Grace be with you all.

INTRODUCTION

THE BOOK OF HEBREWS CALLS US TO fix our eyes on Jesus, who is the author and finisher of our faith.[1] What was begun by God in the Old Testament was completed by our Lord Jesus Christ in the New Testament. He is the One who will bring in the Sabbath rest that was promised.[2] He is the One who is a priest forever after the order of Melchizedek.[3] He is the One who brought into effect the new covenant. He is the One who has been given the name above every name, who will bring about the completion of the work God has given to us.

---

1. *Hebrews 12:2.*

2. Gangadean, *The Biblical Worldview,* 125–146.

3. *Hebrews 7.*

He is the One who is the heir of all things, and we are heirs to Jesus Christ. We are inheritors of the kingdom of God, which God has prepared for us from the foundation of the world. Christ is the One who is able, and He will complete the work of God so that we do not settle back and do not settle for less. We do not go so far in our growth and then say, 'Now I am comfortable,' and remain there. We do not allow ourselves to drift away from the hope set before us. Our hope is an anchor, the city of God to which the men and women of past ages were looking forward. They have died, they have not received the thing promised, and they, without us, will not be made complete.[4] We build on what they have done, and we continue the work. In the midst of all the things that He uses to prepare us to do the work, amid the discipleship, in the scourgings that come in order that our self-life may be put aside—a deeply rooted, subtle, enticing but death-filled self-life—under Jesus Christ our Lord, Christ will free us from it and make us holy for the praise of His Father.

This is the context of the Book of Hebrews, written to the Jews who had become believers but were without patience and, under trial, were tempted to settle back to their comfort level. It is written to them and us to not settle back or settle for less. It is written to us that we are not to settle for anything less than the holiness for which our self-life is stripped from us. We are pressing on to take hold of that for which Christ took hold of us.[5] We are pressing on to take hold of the Lord's kingdom. We are running a race that is set before us. We will strip ourselves of everything that hinders us from running this race.

The Word of God has come to us in greater fullness, and because it has come to us in greater fullness, there is greater responsibility. The warnings do not come as they did on Mount Sinai, that even if an animal touches the mountain, it must be put to death. God is holy, and we must live in holiness, but the warning is even greater: "Our God is a consuming fire" (Heb. 12:29). God will consume everything that is not pure and right, and He will purify all the dross out of the gold and silver. He will have people who are like jewels: pure and clear and reflecting His glory. Our God is a consuming fire. He will burn every work that is not in Him, and those who are outside of Him will be

---

4. *Hebrews 11:39–40.*

5. *Philippians 3:12–14.*

consumed in spiritual death. They will be consumed in the pit of darkness and burning and gnawing of conscience forever and ever. Let us give heed to God.

We believe the apostle Paul is the writer to the Hebrews, though I know others have thought otherwise. In closing, the apostle is exhorting believers in a still more practical way. Exhortations have been mixed with doctrine throughout. As we get near the end of the book, the exhortations become greater and greater, from more general to more specific. As we come to Hebrews 13, we come to the most specific forms of appeal. It is always the case that doctrine is to be accompanied by life, and doctrine without life really means no doctrine. If the doctrine is true, if the doctrine is vital, then life will be present. There is no split between the Word of God and life. The Word of God brings life to us. Let us give heed to this Word, every word of God, including these exhortations.

KEEP ON LOVING EACH OTHER AS BROTHERS

We are to **"keep on loving each other as brothers"** (v. 1). I think this is difficult for us. Think about having a brother; how many of us here have brothers who are really what you may think of as *real* brothers or sisters? Many of us have brothers and sisters, but they are not brothers and sisters in the faith under the same Father. It is really a different father, so we do not know that closeness, and I do not think we know experientially what it is to love as brothers. Sometimes, you hear the talk about 'the brotherhood.' Islam has a kind of brotherhood in which the Islamic faith comes before national identity. There is also a brotherhood in the mafia, but these are not the brotherhood that is being exhorted here. Even though that type of brotherhood has something to it, we need to pray that God will help us understand what it is to have brothers and sisters in Christ. We have sometimes had to become alienated from our natural family, but this is family in God, and we are brothers and sisters forever. I am afraid that self-life and worldliness have not allowed us to come into this true brotherhood.

Do you know how we will come into that brotherhood? We live together, we grow up together, we share together. We grow up together, and perhaps we are in the process of becoming brothers; we go through a lot together, and after it has been proven over a period of time we know we can go through difficulties, but they are not going to break us. We know the other person will be there, and we will go on together forever. That is the beauty of it. We are going to go on together forever. We have been there with each other, shared and contributed to each other, and lived together, which is a kind of brotherhood. We love each other as brothers. Even young children know their brothers and sisters; they play with each other and enjoy each other's company. It is a natural thing that happens, being able to share together in the Lord, where we find pleasure, ease, comfort, and delight.

Entertain Strangers: Wisdom

"Do not forget to entertain strangers, for by so doing some people have entertained angels without knowing it" (v. 2). This is not the only reason to entertain strangers. God comes to us, sometimes directly as He did to Abraham as an angel, and we might have the privilege of entertaining God. If God does not come to us so directly, He nevertheless comes to us through others. "I tell you the truth, whatever you did for one of the least of these brothers of mine, you did for me" (Matt. 25:40). This is not just speaking about brothers, but strangers, that we are to be hospitable to strangers. Remember how Lot entertained strangers,[6] they were angels, and how Abraham entertained the angels.[7] There is a need for a certain kind of wisdom in entertaining strangers, and Scripture warns us about this. We have to use a certain amount of discretion; not everyone has faith, and we can at times be in a vulnerable position. How we do this is a matter of judgment and wisdom. We are to be careful that we do not become so "wise" or so "careful" in our wisdom that we avoid it. We have to pray and ask God for grace and wisdom to know how to entertain strangers. But we are to show this kind of hospitality. If we are to show this hospitality to strangers, how much more to brothers? This does not mean we 'sponge' off of each other. When persons come to our house, we should offer them refreshments and food. Whatever nice things the Lord has given us we can offer to them and be good to others. These kinds of touches

---

6. *Genesis 19.*

7. *Genesis 18.*

are remembered, and they are remembered for a long time. So keep on loving each other as brothers, and do not forget to entertain strangers.

Imprisoned and Mistreated

As part of this love, we are to love our neighbors as ourselves, and those who are in prison because of their witness to God. **"Remember those in prison as if you were their fellow prisoners, and those who are mistreated as if you yourselves were suffering"** (v. 13). In one kind of prison or another, as fellow prisoners, we feel with them, we should be compassionate. Some use the expression, 'I *feel* your pain,' and it has become a matter of mockery. It becomes a mockery because at times some people say this without really, truly feeling. But this is what compassion is: feeling with others, rejoicing with those who rejoice, and weeping with those who weep. We need to know both. Paul calls us to remember those in prison as if we are fellow prisoners. Paul himself was in prison, and what a feeling it is for Paul and others in prison to know that those who are outside are feeling what they are feeling. It is a strength and a comfort to those within that they are not forgotten. It is not that they are just occasionally remembered, but that people are *with* you, care about you, and appreciate that this witness has led you to suffer for Christ in this way. They benefit; they share in the suffering and the glory also. If one member suffers, we all suffer. If one rejoices, we all rejoice. We are knit together. Some of us are mistreated for the sake of the gospel. Remember those who are so mistreated.

When we feel and think others are feeling with us in this way, there is comfort in knowing that we are not alone. This is part of what knits us together as brothers and sisters in Christ. So *love* each other as brothers. This is how the body of Christ is built up, as each part does its work. It is a vital unity, not a mere verbal unity. As we contribute to each other, we appreciate one another. We can laugh with one another, and we can sorrow with one another. We are going to be *there*; we are going to be faithful and remain committed. This is the sort of thing that builds up the family of God. Let us be the family of God. Let us keep on loving each other as brothers. Get to know one another, get to know your brother, get to know your sister. I am going to remind you that at the end of this chapter, when it says, **"Greet all your leaders and all God's people"** (v. 24a), to salute and embrace. Do not just say 'hi' to those people you know and like; it is easy to say hi to them. Say 'hi' to *all* God's people. Be warm and outgoing and express your feelings. In some churches, before the service starts, they have a time to 'stand and greet,' and they turn around, greet each other, and shake hands. The Episcopal Church is that way. What they are getting at is derived from what is mentioned here, be able to move around and connect with each other. Some of you have not said 'hi' and greeted others for months, but you have been in the same church. That is not what it says to do; it says to greet *all* God's people. Do not just say, 'Hi, you all.' Well, this is better than nothing, and it would be great if some persons could just say, 'Hi, you all.' Some of us may say, 'Well, I'm a little bit shy, and I don't do that.' The Bible says to greet one another. So let us do it. It is part of loving each other as brothers.

MARRIAGE SHOULD BE HONORED BY ALL

This exhortation is in contrast to the self-life. **"Marriage should be honored by all"** (v. 4a). Those who are married and those who are not should honor marriage. It speaks of the relationship between God and His people, Christ and His Church. We are created male and female. Both of these aspects are in God. God gave them to us; male and female are equal in power and equal in glory but different, and we are to relate in such a way as to manifest the glory of God. **"Marriage should be honored by all"** (v. 4a). Marriage is a wonderful estate. We should not disesteem it; we should be on our guard to watch over and protect it, not in and of itself or for itself, that would be a bit of self-life, but in God, of God, for God, and for the blessing that God will give to us. **"Marriage should be honored by all, and the marriage bed kept pure"** (v. 4a). One of the ways we turn aside, most often left to ourselves, is by turning aside to relationships with others in trying to find our satisfaction. King David certainly did.[8] **"God will judge the adulterer and all the sexually immoral"** (v. 4b). God wants us to be holy, to be pure, and love is holy; true love is holy. Sex is not to be separated from love. With sex and love, there is a full union, physical and spiritual. This is

---

8. *2 Samuel 11.*

with *one* other person and it is lasting. A full union with one person that is lasting *is* marriage.[9]

There is not to be any sex in any way outside of marriage. Nothing that we think approximates sex, but is not quite sex; there are all kinds of quibbles that people make about this. It is uncleanness; it is *porneia*; it is a form of fornication. God does not want this for His people; He wants us to truly love, not simply use others for our gratification and leave. God wants us to be pure, He wants us to be holy, He wants us to love as He loves, and He does not want any uncleanness in us regarding sexual matters. It goes without saying this includes what we see, not only explicit pornography but the stuff that gets in before you can blink. If occasions for lusting are accessible, put them aside. If your TV causes you to stumble, if it is an occasion to sin, throw it out, trash it, do not watch it again. There is a lot of stuff on TV that is sick, that is sexually immoral, and a lot of jokes that are immoral. God wants His people to be pure.

Warning Against the Love of Money

Sex and money tend to go together: Marx and Freud, sound familiar? Whatever way you cut it, there is violence and corruption, as in the days of Noah, it is always there; this is how it goes. Money and the power it affords—watch out for the love of money. **"Keep your lives free from the love of money"** (v. 5a). This will creep up on us without us knowing it. Our vision of the goal dims; it becomes far off. We plan to do this in a reasonable way, in a comfortable way, getting the stuff that we need, and then we find we are not pressing on for the goal. We switch from the priority of seeking first the kingdom of God and His righteousness, and we become concerned about what we will eat, what we will drink, and how we will pay the bills.[10] I know we have to pay the bills, and it seems reasonable that we often are willing to put this first, but Scripture says otherwise; our Lord Jesus said, no, "seek first his kingdom and his righteousness, and all these things will be given to you as well" (Matt. 6:33). Watch out for the love of money and what

---

9. Gangadean, *Philosophical Foundation*, 245–254.

10. *Matthew 6:31–33.*

it represents, a way of life coming short of the goal and finding satisfaction in the natural things apart from God.

"Be content with what you have, because God has said, 'Never will I leave you; never will I forsake you'" (v. 5b). What a promise. I may have said this before, but I'll say it again: there is one promise that is unqualified in Scripture, at least one that I know of: "And we know that all things work together for good to those who love God, to those who are called according to His purpose" (Rom. 8:28). You may say, 'Ah, there is a catch, it is for those who love God, I don't know if I love God, I don't know if I'm called according to His purpose.' Well, then, simply obey God and love Him. Do you want to love Him? Do you want to obey Him? Certainly we can do that if it is our desire. So this is not really a qualification. "All things work together for good." Sometimes, this involves having the breath knocked out of us with regard to our own ideas about the good. But in an unqualified way, you can say, "all things work together for good," even the bad things. Say it to yourself, and it may sound like a mantra, but get this deep in your mind, 'this too works together for good; God knows it, and God will bring it to pass.' All the things that floor you, which you cannot understand, God's Word says, "we know that all things work together for good to those who love God, to those who are called according to His purpose" (Rom. 8:28). An unqualified, 100%, ironclad promise. No lawyer, philosopher, ontologist, epistemologist, sophist, or casuist can break that promise—it is unqualified. There is a place of rest. I have been looking for a place of rest, and this is the place of rest I have found. **"Never will I leave you; never will I forsake you"** (v. 5b). Nothing can separate us from the love of God that is in Christ Jesus our Lord.[11]

Christ our Lord has shown by His life that God causes the things that are evil to praise Him, the wrath of man to praise Him. There was evil done to Joseph and God worked it together for good.[12] How much more the evil that was done to Christ Jesus our Lord? It was worked together for good, for the salvation of the world. God worked together the greatest evil for the greatest good. Is that the pattern? It surely is. No matter what or how bad it seems, we can rest in this. When it says, **"Never will I leave you; never will I forsake you,"** this is the same

---

11. *Romans 8:38–39.*

12. *Genesis 50:20.*

promise. We can be content; we can learn to submit to the providence of God, and in the providence of God, this trial or challenge has come. All kinds of things come to us time and again in the providence of God. **"So we say with confidence, 'The Lord is my helper; I will not be afraid. What can man do to me?'"** (v. 6). Or animals, or spirits, or extraterrestrials, if you are concerned about that. Do not worry about it; the Lord is your helper, so do not be afraid.

REMEMBER YOUR LEADERS

We have this call to live holy lives and to be content because God is with us, and all things work together for good. We have another exhortation. **"Remember your leaders, who spoke the word of God to you"** (v. 7a). Do you know that you have leaders? We do not like to think this way because 'we live in a democracy!' There is no one who is leading. The Church is thought to be a democracy, but it is not. It is a theocracy; God rules, and you do not vote on it. There are some things you vote on, like the pastor's salary; you get to vote on that, but there are a lot of other things you do not vote on. We are led by the Word of God and we are called here to **"Remember your leaders, who spoke the word of God to you. Consider the outcome of their way of life and imitate their faith"** (v. 7). Notice, the leaders are those who spoke the Word of God to you. God has given us leaders, established the Church as an institution, and told us, not in so many words but in many more basic ways, to attend church. Some have asked, 'Where does it say in Scripture to go to church?' Followed by, 'Where does it say to go to church on Sundays?' Then, 'Where does it say to go to *your* church?' There are ways to answer these questions, and we will.[13] The assumption is that God has established the Church. He has given to the Church the pastor-teachers for works of service,[14] and you are to remember that those who are in that position are leading. They spoke the Word of God to you.

---

13. Gangadean, "Paper No. 134: Worship, the Sabbath, and the Church," in *The Logos Papers,* 679–682; Gangadean, *The Westminster Confession,* 385–386.

14. *Ephesians 4:11–13.*

I read in Phillip Johnson's newest book, *The Wedge*,[15] about Wentworth, who went to Harvard in the 1920s. It was about how he drifted away from the faith, and how his old pastor knelt with him and prayed and warned him about going to Harvard. What Phillip Johnson was showing is how Harvard had been so affected by the naturalistic, scientific spirit that when they taught a naturalistic interpretation of the world, this young man crumbled under it, was absorbed into it, saw what he took to be the reasonableness of it, and did not really fight that much against it. His pastor had warned him against going there and told him to go to the local college instead. The young man did not listen to his leader, his pastor, who had spoken the Word of God to him. He lost his faith. The article on Wentworth's life appeared in the *Atlantic Monthly*. Phillip Johnson read and analyzed this to illustrate how the spirit of naturalism has worked and is currently working in science.

As elders speak the Word of God to you, you are called to pay attention, consider their lives, and imitate their faithfulness. When you enter the last stage of life, you are an elder. I am almost on my last leg; I will be 65 in a few years. It should be that the elders have lived their lives and you can see it and consider the outcome of their way of life. You have to consider that, think about it carefully, and what we are to do is to imitate their faith. They are men susceptible to weakness; imitate their faith, not when they come short, not their folly; imitate their faith. There may be times, and it is sad, when those who are in leadership yield to some folly or other. God may forgive and restore. The person in the office of elder is to be blameless, not faultless, not sinless, but blameless, living a life walking in the light, and that life should yield fruit. God calls us not only to follow Christ, but as Paul says, follow me as I follow the Lord.[16] He wants to make it concrete in our witness. In this situation, you are asked to follow your leaders. Imitate their faith. We have a higher standard, a longstanding standard. It is not a question about what this way of life should be. It is, **"Jesus Christ is the same yesterday and today and forever"** (v. 8). God's purpose remains unchanging, His way of achieving His purpose remains unchanging, and the law of God remains unchanging. Men and women

---

15. Phillip E. Johnson, *The Wedge of Truth: Splitting the Foundations of Naturalism* (New York: Intervarsity Press, 2002).

16. *1 Corinthians 11:1.*

have lived this through the centuries, illustrating the way God would have us live. If there is any question about their way of life and what it has been, it ultimately goes back to our Lord and His way. **"Remember your leaders."** More will be said about the Church and the leaders of the Church in a few verses hence.

GRACE VERSUS CEREMONY (WITHOUT FAITH)

We are exhorted to have our lives established by grace and not by ceremonial foods and rituals which *signify* grace. It is not that ceremonies are of no value, but the ceremony only, in and of itself, without grace, is empty. Scripture says, **"Do not be carried away by all kinds of strange teachings"** (v. 9a). In this context, **"It is good for our hearts to be strengthened by grace, not by ceremonial foods, which are of no value to those who eat them"** (v. 9b). Here, he is speaking particularly of the ceremonial foods of the Old Testament which have now been done away with in Christ, and going back to those and thinking that the correct way is by partaking of them. It could be the Passover. It could be the Mass. I was with some persons recently who attend Mass, but I do not think they consider the significance of why Christ died. They have accepted the openness of the Second Vatican Council, that men can be saved anywhere if they live according to the light they have.[17] Yet, these persons have the ceremonial food of the Mass; they may go several times a week to partake of it. The Mass becomes the answer to the Passover; it is possible to eat the ceremonial food of the Passover without understanding what it signifies, and therefore to not feed on Christ by faith. We can take the Lord's Supper, not by faith, and think our hearts are strengthened by it rather than by the grace it represents.

We are warned, **"Do not be carried away by all kinds of strange teachings"** about this and that and the other, but **"It is good for our hearts to be strengthened by grace, not by ceremonial foods."** These mere ceremonies are of no value. Earlier, Paul spoke about faith, pleasing God by faith, understanding, having the certainty and the evidence of things and the grace that comes and enables us to hear the truth of

---

17. Healy, Nicholas J., and Jr. n.d. "Vatican II and the Universality of Christ's Saving Mission." https://www.catholicworldreport.com/2022/11/03/the-universality-of-christs-saving-mission-the-teaching-of-vatican-ii/.

God; this is how we are strengthened, this is how we are transformed, this is how we are renewed, by understanding God's Word that reveals Christ. **"We have an altar from which those who minister at the tabernacle have no right to eat"** (v. 10). Those who continue with the tabernacle as if Christ had not come—and thereby say 'Jesus is not the Christ' and deny Christ—do not have the right to eat from the Lord's Table, which is where we eat. The Hebrews, remember, were tempted to go back to the old way; they were accustomed to that way, it was comforting. He says, go by grace and not by the ceremonies. He enlarges us further, not only to live this life and not go back to that old way, but let us go *out* to Jesus. We are not to go back into the city; we are to go out of the city. There is a double emphasis here of not turning back, not settling down, not settling for less, not going back to the level at which you are comfortable. Press on to the fullness. We are not to go back to eat that food but rather look to Christ.

> **The high priest carries the blood of animals into the Most Holy Place as a sin offering, but the bodies are burned outside the camp. And so Jesus also suffered outside the city gate to make the people holy through his own blood** (vv. 11–12).

This is how we become truly holy, not by these ceremonies. **"Let us, then, go to him outside the camp, bearing the disgrace he bore"** (v. 13). There is an antithesis here. Sometimes, people generally want to look 'cool'; the way we dress, our manners, the way we salute others, we want to look cool. We like the praise of men. Sometimes, people think it is even cool to be a Christian, to be 'rad,' to be 'anti.' We want to be cool, we want to be accepted, and we like the praise of men. We want others to think of us as being a cool thing, being on the cover story of a magazine, and that Christians can have so much fun, and this is the place to hang out. No, that is not it. It says, **"Let us, then, go to him outside the camp, bearing the disgrace he bore."** When we have the grace of God, we have the *disgrace* of the world. We are disgraced in the eyes of the world because they do not understand the grace of God. There is a close connection between grace and disgrace. When we are with Christ, we turn our backs on the things that are prominent, the things that men hold up as high, as beautiful, as the 'in-thing,' the acceptable thing, and we go outside of the city bearing the disgrace of

Christ. We leave the pomp and glory of Egypt. We leave the pomp and glory as Paul says, the things that were gained to me, I now count as rubbish, that I may be found in Him, that I may know Christ.[18] Let our hearts be established by grace. We feed on Christ; He is our life. Let us not go back to the old way and those who would minimize and undermine the truth of who Christ is.

The Catholics have the splendor of the Mass and the Cathedral, and what a place to be as you hear the music rise. I once sat in the Cathedral of Cologne. It is magnificent, and 'that is enough to make you a Catholic forever.' Sometimes, we go to a storefront church. It is not very glorious, but the truth of Christ, the Lord's Supper and what it means, are being observed properly. So we go outside the city, we go outside of the world with its pomp and glory, and we bear the disgrace of Christ. We are not trying to look cool and be accepted, and so on. If need be, we suffer disgrace. You know how hard it is to say in front of a guru, 'I am a Christian.' Because they have all the 'straw man' arguments, all this muck and mire that they are going to heap on you. Before you know it, you will be the scum of the universe—exactly, scum of the universe. That is how Paul describes it; the Apostles were set forth last as the scum of the universe, the offscouring of all things.[19] That is how he puts it. You want to be cool? Be the scum. Is that what you want to be? We cannot indulge our self-life and compromise. Someone may say, 'You're a Christian, aren't you?' 'Yes, I love Jesus.' Just think about that. Let us go outside of the city bearing the disgrace He bore because He loved us, and we love Him. Jesus laid down His life for us, and we lay down our lives for Him. Jesus is the lover of our souls and our souls love Him. We will go out leaning on Him, leaning on our beloved, Christ Jesus our Lord, the King of kings and the Lord of lords, who is rejected by this world but who nevertheless is the King of kings and Lord of lords. **"For here we do not have an enduring city, but we are looking for the city that is to come"** (v. 14). Do not settle for less; do not settle for what is here now. This is not the City of God we are waiting for; this is not the diamond city, nor the completion of the work. We have lots of work to do. We are looking for a city that is to come. Let us work for that city; let us run the race for that city.

---

18. *Philippians 3:7–8.*

19. *1 Corinthians 4:9.*

SACRIFICE OF PRAISE:
The Fruit of Lips That Confess His Name

Let us offer sacrifices to God. Here is another exhortation: "**Through Jesus, therefore, let us continually offer to God a sacrifice of praise—the fruit of lips that confess his name**" (v. 15). There is something about our very lips, the physicality of it, and having on our lips the name of Jesus. That our lips could utter it, that our voices could utter His name and affirm that God is the God of glory, justice, goodness, and mercy. Christ is the glorious king. We take His name upon our lips. Our lips confess His name, praise God, rejoice in God, and thank God. This is an offering, a sacrifice raised up to God. Sometimes I let the lifting of my hands be as an evening sacrifice, lifted in prayer and praise. There is a bodily aspect of worship. We can worship anywhere, in spirit and in truth, but God wants us to worship with our whole being. We bow down on our knees and on our faces, at times, in worship. We can have the form and the reality.

Let us offer the sacrifice of praise to God, but this sacrifice is to be accompanied by other sacrifices, too. It is a sacrifice, an offering. It costs us something to get to that point, to know the Lord. The glory that was revealed was revealed to us through suffering. Now that we have the knowledge of that glory, we offer it up to God. Blessed be your name, O Lord, gracious and holy forever. This is our sacrifice that we offer up to God. But there is another sacrifice that goes along with this. Paul says, "**And do not forget to do good and to share with others, for with such sacrifices God is pleased**" (v. 16). There is a sacrifice of service, of good works, to do good and to share with others. Let us learn to share; let us watch out for our love of money; let us learn to share. It is a blessing to share in this way; it is a sacrifice, and with this, God is well pleased.

Again, another exhortation, "**Obey your leaders and submit to their authority**" (v. 17a). Earlier, it said, "**Remember your leaders**," and "**imitate their faith**." Here it says, "**Obey your leaders and submit to their authority.**" There are times when the leaders have to speak a word to you. Do you know why they have to? They keep watch over you. God has put them there; they are shepherds, and they must watch. "**They keep watch over you as men who must give an account**" (v. 17). If a sheep is going astray, they must speak to that sheep and warn them. If they do not warn them, they will have to give an account. God will require the blood of that sheep at the hand of that shepherd if he has not warned them. They have to give an account in this way. God has placed them in that position. They do not like to have to be calling you back from your self-life, especially when it is a 'dug-in' form of the self-life. They warned you against following the way of your particular desire and you have been 'miffed' by that correction. You have given the cold shoulder to those who would speak the Word of God to you. This is not a joyful thing.

The leaders want to see you thrive in God. They must give an account, they must warn you, they must speak the Word of God. Sometimes, as an elder, it is the case that you just have to do it! Make yourself do it, pick up the phone, call that person, and speak a certain word to them; no matter how much you do not want to do it. You do not want to have to confront someone, and you also know that the person could go further away as a result. This is not what is being called for here. **"Obey your leaders and submit to their authority"** (v. 17a). When your leaders say to you, 'Don't go, stay.' Obey them. When they say, 'Don't go there now, this is not wise, this is not safe for you.' Listen to them. When they say, 'Don't continue doing that, don't pursue that relationship, give it to God.' Listen to them. When they say, 'Don't go so far away that you are away from the Word of God and will become vulnerable. Seek first the kingdom of God. Be with God's people.' Listen to them. When they say, 'Don't hold on to that particular thing. Don't neglect the reading of the Scriptures. Have family devotions. Be in the church. Call if you will not be here.' Little things like that. Obey your leaders, be in the church, call if you are not here. **"Obey your leaders and submit to their authority. They keep watch over you as men who must give an account. Obey them that their work will be a joy and not a burden"** (v. 17a). That word 'burden' in Greek means constrained and narrow conditions. Being in a limited space, like being under a house in the crawling space. Once I had to go into the crawling space under the house and Patricia heard me groan, I said to her, 'Stay with me, stay with me.' Sometimes it is like that when you are giving oversight, a strained condition. Elders shrink from having to bring oversight, so obey.[20]

---

20. The closing remarks for Hebrews 13:18–25 were not preserved in the Archive records. Rather than reconstruct what Pastor Gangadean may have said, we will leave it as is to not alter the historical accuracy of his work.

———

PART II

THE FOUNDATION
2001 SERMON SERIES

———

16

SIN AND THE NEED FOR CHRIST

Hebrews 6:1–3

¹Therefore let us leave the elementary teachings about Christ and go on to maturity, not laying again the foundation of repentance from acts that lead to death, and of faith in God, ²instruction about baptisms, the laying on of hands, the resurrection of the dead, and eternal judgment. ³And God permitting, we will do so.

THE CITY WITH FOUNDATIONS
Revelation 21

W E ARE GOING TO CONTINUE FROM where we left off in the sermon series on the Book of Revelation: the vision of the city of God, the city with foundations. The city is pictured and symbolized as 1,400 miles long, 1,400 miles wide, and 1,400 miles high, which is a big city. This city is shining with the glory of God, like jasper; it is clear as crystal, like a diamond. Through this city, all the glory of God is refracted in its many colors. This city has foundations. The first foundation is described as jasper, and we want to speak about the foundation of this city.

The Church is still quite divided.¹ Each church is still struggling a great deal with sin in the lives of its members. We need to overcome these divisions if we are to be that glorious city. This is not just a city on a hill that the pilgrims dreamt of when they came to this country;

---

1. Gangadean, *The Unity of the Church*.

that was one small reflection of this city. This is *the* city. It is the city of God for which Abraham sought, the city that Adam was given to build through all of his offspring; the city of God. The city has foundations and the work of building this city remains before us. In the vows of membership and baptism, we ask, "Do you purpose to seek first the kingdom of God and His righteousness in all the relationships of your life?"[2] We are speaking about the work of the kingdom of God, the city of God. This foundation must be laid if we are to come into maturity in Christ and fruitfulness. In the Letter to the Hebrews, Paul contrasts those who are children in Christ (young in Christ), and those who go on to maturity. It says of some, in Hebrews 5:12, "In fact, though by this time you ought to be teachers, you need someone to teach you the elementary truths of God's word all over again." That is, they need someone to teach them the *stoicheia*, the foundational principles, all over again.

> You need milk, not solid food! Anyone who lives on milk, being still an infant, is not acquainted with the teaching about righteousness. But solid food is for the mature, who by constant use have trained themselves to distinguish good from evil (Heb. 5:12b–14).

The matter of this foundation has to do with maturity. It also has to do with whether one is in Christ or not, but in essence it has to do with maturity. The apostle bids us in Hebrews 6:1–3,

> **Therefore let us leave the elementary teachings about Christ,** [the *stoicheia*, the foundational principles] **and go on to maturity, not laying again the foundation of repentance from acts that lead to death, and of faith in God, instructions about baptisms, the laying on of hands, the resurrection of the dead, and eternal judgment. And God permitting, we will do so.**

We want to speak about this first foundational truth: "repentance from acts that lead to death," repentance from sin and death. There are two responses to hearing the Word. The first is of those who hear and do the Word of God—those who hear, not outwardly, but with understanding, and put it into practice.

---

2. Gangadean, *The Westminster Confession*, 387.

Therefore everyone who hears these words of mine and puts them into practice is like a wise man who built his house on the rock. The rain came down, the streams rose, and the winds blew and beat against that house; yet it did not fall, because it had its foundation on the rock (Matt. 7:24–25).

The second response is that of the foolish builder, those who hear the Word outwardly, without faith, and do not put it into practice. Our Lord said:

But everyone who hears these words of mine and does not put them into practice is like a foolish man who built his house on sand. The rain came down, the streams rose, and the winds blew and beat against that house, and it fell with a great crash (Matt. 7:26–27).

WHAT IS SIN?

This message has application for all, for those who are in Christ and those who are not in Christ. We want to make this one point in the message: *If we do not have sin, we do not need Christ, but if we have sin, we need Christ.* We will be looking at what sin is to understand this better, to see whether we have sin, and to see whether this sin is such that we stand in need of Christ. We will be looking at examples of sin within and outside the Church to see how close you can come to understanding sin and the need for Christ and still not have it. I want to exhort all who are present to search their hearts as we speak about this, to consider the reality of sin. Those who have been raised in the church, those who have come into the church, and those who are not in the church, consider the reality of sin, death, and our need for Christ.

Clarity and Inexcusability (Romans 1:18–20)

What is sin? The apostle Paul tells us very clearly in Romans 1. If Romans 1:18–20 is undermined, then everything falls, but if this passage stands in place, then we believe everything else stands. If you want to know a certain position on which to stand or fall, here it is. We will see many attempts to get around the truth of clarity and inexcusability,[3] but the truth is such that you cannot get around it. You cannot go around it; you cannot go under it; you cannot go over it; you must go *through* it; you must acknowledge this truth. What is this truth?

> The wrath of God is being revealed from heaven against all the godlessness and wickedness of men, who suppress the truth by their wickedness, since what may be known about God is plain to them, because God has made it plain to them. For since the creation of the world, God's invisible qualities—his eternal power and divine nature—have been clearly seen, being understood from what has been made, so that men are without excuse (Rom. 1:18–20).

God has created the world and has made it *clear* so that unbelief, in every form, is without excuse. This is the one truth that establishes the reality of sin. We cannot speak of sin unless it is clear—objectively clear, not necessarily subjectively clear, but objectively clear—that God has created the world. His eternality and divine nature is clearly revealed so that all humanity stands guilty for all our distortions of God. All of the distortions about God are without excuse because God has made it clear. What we must do when thinking about our own lives and the lives of those to whom we witness, when evaluating what others are saying and doing, is come back to this one truth. If there is no sin, there is no need for Christ. We are not speaking about Christ as a teacher but about Christ dying on the cross. If there is no sin, there is no need for Christ as the One who came and died on the cross. If there is no clarity, there is no sin. The existence and nature of God is clear so that we are without excuse. This truth is the seal; this is necessary to establish inexcusability for our unbelief. What may be known of God, His invisible qualities, His eternal power (we specify His eternal power and divine nature), and the rest of His attributes,[4] that He is wise, holy,

---

3. Gangadean, "Paper No. 3: The Principle of Clarity," 15–20; "Paper No. 35: The Clarity of General Revelation (Applied to GR-SR-HC)," 195–200; "Paper No. 95: Rational Presuppositional Apologetics," in *The Logos Papers*, 503–506; "Paper No. 102: The Clarity of General Revelation," 527–529; "Paper No. 120: Contra Voluntarism," in *The Logos Papers*, 611–647.

4. Gangadean, *On Natural and Revealed Theology*, 213–222, 149–165; Gangadean, *The Westminster Catechisms*, 119–122; Gangadean, *The Westminster Confession*, 1–13.

just, good, infinitely powerful—all of these are clearly revealed so that men are without excuse.[5]

The Law Is Written on the Heart (Romans 2:12–15)

This is not the only point on which men are without excuse. Romans 2:12–15a says,

> All who sin apart from the law will also perish apart from the law, and all who sin under the law will be judged by the law. For it is not those who hear the law who are righteous in God's sight, but it is those who obey the law who will be declared righteous. (Indeed, when Gentiles, who do not have the law, do by nature things required by the law, they are a law for themselves, even though they do not have the law, since they show that the requirements of the law are written on their hearts.

This is the other point that is clear from general revelation. God's law is written on the heart of each and every single human being.[6] Believers and non-believers, who do not acknowledge and live according to the moral law, show that they have come short of the glory of God. What has been mankind's response, according to Scripture, to this clear revelation of God? Romans 3:23 says, "all have sinned and fall short of the glory of God." Notice that word "all." Each and every one has sinned and come short of the glory of God. This establishes the universality of sin, and we will go into this in greater detail as we proceed.

The Universality of Sin (Romans 3:10–11, 23)

Romans 3:10–11 says, "As it is written: 'There is no one righteous, not even one; there is no one who understands, no one who seeks God.'" If human beings had been seeking God, since the revelation of God is clear, they would have seen and would have agreement. The failure to see it and all the disagreements about God go back to this root doctrine. There is no one who seeks God, no one who understands, no one who

---

5. *Romans 1:20.*

6. Gangadean, *Philosophical Foundation*, 171–284; Gangadean, *History of Philosophy*, 61–69; Gangadean, *The Westminster Catechisms*, 215–267; Gangadean, *The Westminster Confession*, 207–221; Gangadean, *On Natural and Revealed Theology*, 127–139, 166–178.

is righteous. If we had been seeking God, we would have seen what is clear because it is clear. What is clear is clear to our understanding. The Scripture says, "his eternal power and divine nature—have been clearly seen, being understood from what has been made" (Rom. 1:20). Here are some examples of divisions on this point:

Materialists—atheists—say that the material world is eternal.[7] There is no God the Creator. Matter has always existed and will always exist. They explain the world in terms of a Big Bang oscillating universe. They explain human life in this way: the brain is the same as the soul. There is no mind or soul separate from the brain. They explain the origin of life by way of evolution. Have you heard of such a thing? It happens to be the dominant paradigm in Western culture. It is based on a claim to a scientific, rational experience, and what have they come up with? That all is eternal, and it is matter. Scripture says it is clear that God is eternal, and only God is eternal, so that materialism as a form of unbelief is without excuse. It should be clear to us that the soul exists, and that the mind, or the soul, is not the same as the brain. Yet, many people have questions, 'How can we know that?'

Spiritual monists[8] and dualists[9] believe that the soul exists and that the soul is eternal. It existed before this life and has always existed; it was not created. It is clear, according to Scripture, that the soul is created by God. If the soul is eternal, and I am going through life after life after life by way of reincarnation, the question is raised: why are we not released yet? We have had an infinite amount of time. It does not make sense; it is clear that the soul is not eternal. We do not have infinite knowledge. If we had an infinite amount of time, being eternal, we would have had infinite knowledge by way of growth, but we do not have infinite knowledge.

There are those who say matter is eternal, and it is clear that it is not. There are those who say the soul is eternal, and it is clear that it is not. There are some who say nothing is eternal; all is temporal. Siddhartha

---

7. Gangadean, *Philosophical Foundation*, 71–100; Gangadean, *History of Philosophy*, 81–85; Gangadean, "Paper No.78: Material Monism," 405–411; "Paper No. 90: Christianity and Secular Humanism," 473–477; "Paper No. 130: Major Secular Ethical Theories," in *The Logos Papers*, 671–672

8. Gangadean, *Philosophical Foundation*, 101–127.

9. Gangadean, *Philosophical Foundation*, 129–137; Gangadean, *History of Philosophy*, 87–105, 111–114.

Gautama, the Buddha, said all is *dukkha*, all is impermanent, transitory, all is suffering. He gave an explanation of suffering in the world. He had a vision of old age, sickness, and death. He gave an explanation of that in the context of reincarnation. Scripture teaches that it is clear the soul is created by God, it is not eternal. This teaching, that it is clear from the creation that God's eternal power and divine nature are clear so that men are without excuse, stands; unless we can come back and show that it is not clear. What would we have to do in order to show that it is not clear? We would have to neglect, we would have to avoid, we would have to resist, and we would have to deny reason, which God has put into our lives.[10] What we have read in John 1:4, "In him [the Logos] was life, and that life was the light of men." The life of God comes into all human beings as reason, and we have to neglect, avoid, resist, and deny reason to avoid seeing what is clear. There are some consequences that follow.

The Scripture says there is *no one* who seeks God, *no one* who understands, and *all* have sinned and come short of the glory of God. It is of such a nature that we need Christ, and Christ only can provide the remedy for sin. We have to start with the doctrine of sin. Sin is universal, not a cultural phenomenon. We will examine more distortions of the doctrine of clarity and inexcusability, as well as the clarity of the moral law written on our hearts because our hearts are given to excuse ourselves from it. Paul says it is clear so that men are without excuse, and guess what we do on a regular, ongoing basis, day and night, in and out? We excuse ourselves from saying it is clear that God and only God is eternal and everything else is created. We are obligated to honor and worship Him as our God, our Creator. We should expect excuses to multiply through the centuries, through the brightest of religions that raise themselves up against the knowledge of God, for failure to see that God and only God is eternal.

THE WAGES OF SIN IS DEATH
Romans 6:23

Sin is universal, and what are the consequences of sin? Scripture teaches in Romans 6:23 that the wages of sin is death. "For the wages of sin is

---

10. Gangadean, "Paper No. 103: The Noetic Effect of Sin," in *The Logos Papers*, 531–528.

death, but the gift of God is eternal life in Christ Jesus our Lord." This death is spiritual death. It is a death that is present in us now. Ephesians 2:1 says, "you were dead in your transgressions and sins." When a child comes for baptism, we speak about this death. Baptism signifies regeneration, being brought from spiritual death to life.[11] It is to have one's reason turned on at the basic level to see that what you formerly believed does not make sense, and only in God as Creator and in Christ as redeemer does the world makes sense. It is to see the reality of sin. All of us who have been touched by the work of the Spirit have come to see the emptiness of our lives without God, and we have come, by His grace, to acknowledge Him. Without God, we continue to thirst. Jesus said, "Everyone who drinks this water will be thirsty again, but whoever drinks the water I give him will never thirst. Indeed, the water I give him will become in him a spring of water welling up to eternal life" (Jn. 4:13–14). We are made to know God. When we neglect, avoid, resist, deny, and excuse ourselves by saying 'It is not clear,' and that 'We require so much time to know it', or 'This is the best we can do,' we are denying the clarity of general revelation and we are inexcusable on that basis. We will thirst again. There will be guilt when our failure to see God is addressed. We will excuse it. We will neglect, avoid, resist, and deny what is clear.

What is this sin? What does sin do? Sin resists the light. John 1:4 speaks about all men having this light, it is the light of God, and because we resist this light, we are in spiritual death. The light of reason is shining in us. "The light shines in the darkness, but the darkness has not understood it" (Jn. 1:5). Though we resist it, we cannot overcome it. The demands of reason are still there in our lives, asking us to make sense of the world. Sometimes, when we neglect reason, someone from outside comes in and asks, 'Where are you?' How do you answer this? What is our response then? Do we engage? Do we seek? Do we try to give an answer? Do we try to show that the belief that we are holding is clear? That it must be so? Our failure to do this is a clear indication that we are not seeking, we are avoiding and resisting reason to avoid what is clear; God has created us in this way.

We resist reason within us, and we turn it off. Remember some of the great meditators who would empty their minds of all thought and

---

11. Gangadean, *The Westminster Confession*, 299–305.

consider this the highest wisdom. Can you truly, honestly, live without thought? Is this the height of wisdom, to have a mind empty of all thought? Is that what knowing God is? This is not what Paul is speaking of here. The whole earth is full of His glory, and we need to come to know that glory. It involves understanding. Sin not only resists the very reason that is in us, but it resists the Logos in the world because it says, "He was in the world, and though the world was made through him, the world did not recognize him" (Jn. 1:10). Though His glory is revealed in the world, the world did not know Him. This is the world as a whole, across the board, each and every one left to themselves. Everyone is in this condition: "the world did not recognize him."

What else happens? How do we respond to this Word of God that comes to us? "He came to that which was his own, but his own did not receive him" (Jn. 1:11). What did we do when it came to us in the Scriptures through the prophets? We resisted the prophets, we avoided them, and sometimes, we stoned and killed the prophets. More often than not, we kill the prophets who bring the Word of God to us. This is what sin does; it resists God.

Last of all, when the Word of God comes to us incarnate in Jesus Christ,[12] what do we do to that Word? We crucify the Word; we kill the Word of God incarnate. Christ's death on the cross revealed mankind's true heart response to God in sin. It is a rejection of God as personal as it was in the crucifixion of Jesus Christ on the cross. "Away with him, away with him, crucify him" (Jn. 19:15). We will not have God to be ruler in our hearts and lives. There is no way we can try to minimize this. This is the very essence of sin. But here, the grace of God triumphs over sin: In the very act of crucifying Christ, in that very act, Christ absorbs into Himself the punishment for our sin that was due to us, and He bears the penalty away. And it *must* be borne away. God is holy and just; He cannot neglect, avoid, and resist sin; He cannot overlook it; it must be punished. Our sin was punished in Christ. "Salvation is found in no one else, for there is no other name under heaven given to men by which we must be saved" (Acts 4:12). That is why all the religious teachers of the world who come short of acknowledging Christ and Him crucified, who come short of acknowledging sin, are

---

12. *John 1:14.*

still under the power of sin and the curse as a call back from sin. They still have not seen God.

What does sin do? Sin is a rejection of God. As the revelation of God comes to us in our very inmost being as reason, in the world as general revelation, in the Scriptures given through the prophets, and in Christ.[13]

What does sin deserve? If sin is a personal rejection of God, what sin deserves is that we would be rejected by God. This is what Christ experienced on our behalf as He hung on the cross—when He cried out, "My God, my God, why have you forsaken me?" (Matt. 27:46b). He was forsaken because the sin of the world was placed upon Him. "God made him who had no sin to be sin for us, so that in him we might become the righteousness of God" (2 Cor. 5:21). God is holy, and God is just; this is clear from the way He has created and ruled the world. Failing to see and acknowledge this is inexcusable. If there is no sin, there is no need for Christ. But if there is sin, the only way we can come to God is through Christ. We have to deal with sin, clarity, and inexcusibility. This is the most basic teaching.

EXAMPLES OF SIN

Adam

There are a few examples of sin for us to consider in case we have misunderstood it. The first example is Adam and Eve. This is the paradigm of sin.[14] God created Adam in His own image, called him to exercise dominion over the creation and rule in the creation so as to fill the earth with the knowledge of God. This knowledge of God is eternal life. The whole earth is full of His glory; God intends that the earth shall be full of the knowledge of the glory of God as the waters cover the sea.[15] All mankind, everyone descended from Adam, together would do this work. This was God's purpose, and Adam was our representative head. Talk as you will, as mightily and as learnedly as you want to

---

13. Gangadean, *The Westminster Confession,* 121–135; Gangadean, *The Westminster Catechisms,* 144–152, 113–114

14. Gangadean, *The Biblical Worldview.*

15. *Isaiah 11:9; Habakkuk 2:14.*

appear about evolution; evolution is dead wrong.[16] It is not the case that we evolved from lower life forms over a long period of time. We were created in the image of God.[17] Evolution cannot explain the difference between the mind and the brain. It is right there in our very inmost consciousness. The mind cannot evolve; the mind is not eternal. All the scientific hindrances you might have about the creation account and all the propaganda we have had in the name of science do not stand up against the clarity of general revelation. If there is any desire for discussion about how it is clear that God has created (and it is clear that God created), I think just about anyone in this room who confesses Christ will be ready to give an answer and to show this.[18] You should be able to show it, and if you stumble, you need to do some work. Talk to Stephen Jay Gould, the golden boy of paleontology, and give an answer. Many of you have come out of believing in evolution. When we come to this story in Genesis 1–3, I know you have been saturated with evolutionary thinking and teaching, but we are saying it is clear that God created the world, created man in His own image, and created him to have dominion. God placed him in the Garden and placed the way of life and death before him; life represented in the tree of life, and death represented in the tree of the knowledge of good and evil, and He said to Adam, "In the day that thou eatest thereof, thou shalt surely die" (Gen. 2:17b KJV).

What did Adam do? What did Adam, as representing us, mankind, do? What do we do characteristically in the face of this choice between life and death, and good and evil? In Adam, it was clearly represented. The tempter came to Adam and said,

> "Did God really say, 'You must not eat from any tree in the garden'?" The woman said to the serpent, "We may eat fruit from the trees in the garden, but God did say, 'You must not eat fruit from the tree that is in the middle of the garden, and you must not touch it, or you will die.'" "You will not surely die," the serpent said to the woman. "For God knows that when you eat of it your eyes will be opened, and you will be like God, knowing good and evil" (Gen. 3:1b–5).

---

16. Gangadean, *Philosophical Foundation*, 90–96.

17. Gangadean, *The Biblical Worldview*, 109–124; Gangadean, *The Westminster Confession*, 79–83; Gangadean, *The Westminster Catechisms*, 133–135.

18. *1 Peter 3:15.*

Adam was created and placed in the Garden, crowned with honor and light to know God. Was Adam seeking God and knowing God? When he was tested, and this word came to him, "You shall not surely die . . . you will be like God, knowing good and evil," did Adam understand God, who God is, and how God knows good and evil? Did he understand the nature of good and evil? No, he did not. God knows good and evil, not by discovery; God knows good and evil by determining it through creation. God created us with our natures, and given the natures we have, 'good' for us is according to the nature that God has created for us. This very basic truth is that we are created by God with a certain nature, and 'good' for us is according to that nature, and God *determines* good and evil by creation; they were tempted on this point. Understand this. Do you understand that you are created by God, or do you think you can be like God, knowing good and evil? What did Adam and Eve do in the Garden? They believed the falsehood, "you will be like God, knowing good and evil" (Gen. 3:5b). What does this show? It shows that they did not understand the first truth that distinguishes God from man. God is infinite and eternal, and we are finite and temporal, created by God. We are the creature, God is the Creator. We cannot know good and evil the way God knows good and evil. God knows it by creation; we are creatures and cannot create. Is that clear to reason? It should be. Is it objectively clear? It is. The sin of Adam and Eve is failing to know God as He has clearly revealed Himself; the very same sin that all of us experience, the very same sin of all mankind. If it is true of our first father and mother, should we say it is true of the rest of us? Yes, it is. We have an example of sin in Adam.[19]

Israel

We have an example of sin in Israel, the people of God, the covenant people in the Old Testament, and it equally applies to the covenant people in the New Testament. You that say someone should not steal, do you steal?[20] You that say we should honor God, do you dishonor God? You that say man should not sin, do you fail to see what is clear? Has the Church failed to engage with the clarity of general revelation

---

19. Gangadean, *The Biblical Worldview*, 159–195.

20. *Romans 2:21.*

in its witness? Has the Church been fideist, believing 'by faith?' Yes, it has. This failure to live according to the moral law is true of those in the Church, too. Emptying belief of meaning can take the form of both ends of the Church. It could take the form of a Nicodemus, who is an older gentleman, kind, charitable, wise, and a teacher in Israel.

> He came to Jesus at night and said, "Rabbi, we know you are a teacher who has come from God. For no one could perform the miraculous signs you are doing if God were not with him." In reply Jesus declared, "I tell you the truth, no one can see the kingdom of God unless he is born again" (Jn. 3:2–3).

Unless you experience what is signified in baptism, what is signified in circumcision, you cannot be born again. Nicodemus, who was a master in Israel, missed the meaning of circumcision. I do not know how many children Nicodemus may have circumcised, where he engaged in the ritual of circumcision, but he missed it—characteristic of sin, it empties our lives of meaning. Nicodemus did not understand the need to be born again, though he should have, on the basis of circumcision. Or it could be someone like Saul of Tarsus, who became Paul the Apostle,[21] the writer of most of the New Testament, who was zealously engaged for the Word of God to the point of persecuting others. You know what? Saul, too, missed it. Or it could be Israel historically. Their most holy day is Yom Kippur, and they are waiting for the Messiah; they have not made the connection between the Day of Atonement and the Messiah who will atone.[22] To this day they are looking for a Messiah, but not one who will atone for sin by His death. How close can you get and not be there? It is also true of Islam.

Islam

Islam professes to build on Judaism and Christianity. The central truth of Judaism and Christianity is the atonement, and in Islam, what happens to the atonement? It is completely gone. Allah is compassionate and merciful, but is Allah just and holy? Must sin be paid for? What is the concept of God in Islam? What is the acknowledgment of sin

---

21. *Acts 9.*

22. Gangadean, *Philosophical Foundation*, 193–194.

and the need for Christ? It is not there.[23] There are over a billion Muslims who believe this distortion. Just as Saul of Tarsus, who was zealous for the law of God, did not see the need for Christ. If there is no sin, there is no need for Christ, but if there is sin, there is a need for Christ. We can have a defective view of sin that is not grounded in the clarity of general revelation and the death that comes from that, and we can miss Christ.

Deism and Liberal Christianity

Thomas Jefferson rewrote the New Testament, leaving out the death of Christ and all the miracles. He wanted the ethics of Christ, he wanted Christ as a great teacher, but not as one who died on the cross—Thomas Jefferson, President of the United States. Many others have followed in his footsteps. Liberal Christianity has done this, too; it has removed Christ from the cross. This is a defective view of sin. These persons did not consider the clear revelation of God.

GOD'S CALL BACK:
The Curse and the Promise

God calls us back to Himself through the curse and the promise. What is the curse? It should be clear to us that when God created the world, it was very good.[24] At the end of Genesis 1, after having it said six times that "it was good" (Genesis 1:4, 10, 12, 18, 21, 25), it says:

> And God said, "I give you every seed-bearing plant in the face of the whole earth and every tree that has fruit with seed in it. They will be yours for food. All the beasts of the earth and all the birds of the air, all the creatures that move on the ground—everything that has the breath of life in it—I give every green plant for food." And it was so. God saw all that he had made, and it was very good. And there was evening, and there was morning—the sixth day (Gen. 1:29–31).

---

23. Gangadean, *Philosophical Foundation*, 191–192; Gangadean, *The Westminster Confession*, 21–27, 37–41, 67–69, 129–130, 236–238; Gangadean, "Paper No. 91: Christianity and Islam," in *The Logos Papers*, 479–484.

24. Gangadean, *The Biblical Worldview*, 91–108.

The animals did not devour each other; the world was good, just as God intended, without natural evil. It should be clear to us, as it should be clear to the deists, that there is physical death in the world. It should be clear to each and every one of us that there is physical death in the world. It should be clear that God is Creator and there is physical death, and it should be clear to us that God did not make the world this way with physical death. The reality of physical death says something is wrong. It speaks of the reality of sin. If anyone tries to acknowledge God the Creator, they must deal with the reality of physical death. My father died this year, and in February, I went to his funeral. The one truth that came through during the funeral is that death is natural. The one truth that comes through Scripture is that death is not natural. Whom shall we believe? We were not a spirit that existed before, that happens to be in a body, as in dualism or Mormonism; we were created a body/soul unity. Death is a rending of our very self, a splitting apart of our soul and our body, and it is the most unnatural thing. The *whole world* will try to teach that death is natural; it just happens. This is another piece that should be clear to all mankind, but mankind left to itself, every last one, has turned away from this truth. The curse is in the world: animals devour each other, the weather conditions are very different than they once were, the excesses of nature, the calamities of nature, the terrible storms and earthquakes. This was not the way God made the world, including physical death—old age, sickness, and death. Through the curse, God is calling us to stop, think, remember Him, and recognize the reality of sin.

Our resistance to recognizing what is clear is what caused God to impose a curse upon us. Adam was called through the inner call of conscience, and he resisted and covered himself. He was called outwardly through the voice, "Where are you?" He justified himself and blamed another, so God imposed the curse.[25] If we say God the Creator exists, we have to deal with the reality of death in the world. This is not the way an infinitely powerful and infinitely good God made the world. The curse is there, but with the curse, at the very time the curse came, the promise came, too. The promise was given: The seed of the woman shall crush the head of the serpent.[26] Something must now be done.

---

25. Gangadean, *The Biblical Worldview*, 55–68, 275–294.

26. *Genesis 3:15.*

The sin that Adam did, which is a sin of all mankind that all of us continue to repeat, that sin must be atoned for. The penalty of sin must be paid. The essence of sin is a rejection of God, and the consequent result is God giving us up to go our own way,[27] to go into the darkness of meaninglessness and not understanding, to go into every desire without satisfaction, and to go into a torment of guilt. Our sin deserves the rejection by God, and we cannot come before God in our sin; our sin must be punished.

The promise was given by God in calling us back. The seed of the woman will crush the head of the serpent; the serpent will strike His heel.[28] I remember seeing a picture of Krishna in a textbook. Krishna is standing on the head of a serpent; in another drawing, that serpent is striking his heel. On the cross, there was a striking against Christ, but Christ was raised from the dead. There seems to have been a remnant of the original Edenic revelation that was passed on to the nations.[29] China also has references to this. Immediately after the Flood, that revelation was carried to all the nations. If you go into the very heart of these scriptures, in the most ancient form, you see reference to the one who will come and redeem. The '10-fingered one' who will come and redeem. 10-fingered means he is a human being and He is also divine. He will come and redeem. Someone will come, and there will be a sacrifice for sin. The nations have forgotten the sacrifice, abused the sacrifice, and engaged in human sacrifices and other sacrifices, but there was an original sacrifice, the Lamb of God, that takes away the sin of the world.[30] This is the only way in which we can come before God.

There are many who want to improve the world, change the world, but they do not begin with the reality of sin and death. Many attempt to address the curse that is on the world, starvation and diseases, but they do not want to come back to the reality of sin, from which the curse was imposed. Those who would do this make light of the cross of Christ. It is only through Christ that we, mankind, can have life. We need Christ not only to die for our sins, but we need Christ. The word Christ comes from the word *christós*—the Anointed One. It is

---

27. *Romans 1:21–32.*

28. *Genesis 3:15.*

29. Alexander Hislop, *The Two Babylons* (London: Crossreach Publications, 1857).

30. *John 1:29.*

the same word in Hebrew that is Messiah—the Anointed One. Christ is the Anointed One; He is anointed with the Spirit; He is the One who will send the Spirit to give us a new heart and to illuminate our minds so that we can understand the Scriptures and come to know the truth, and that truth will set us free.[31] We cannot have the Spirit apart from Christ. We cannot have forgiveness apart from Christ. Those of us who witness to others in this world and consider the witness of others must ask, where is Christ and the cross of Christ in this world? Without sin, there is no need for Christ. With sin, we can have forgiveness only through Christ.

The biblical foundation calls us to repent of sin that leads to death. In the name of God, in the name of Christ Jesus, I must ask you, have you repented of sin that leads to death? Have you acknowledged the curse as God's curse?[32] Old age, sickness, and death is God's curse imposed on us to call us back from sin and death. Have you come through Christ, the One promised, who would die for our sins and who would send the Spirit upon all mankind? May the grace of Christ be with you to enable you to repent of sin and acknowledge Him.

---

31. *Ezekiel 36:26; John 8:32.*
32. Gangadean, *The Biblical Worldview,* 37–54, 275–294.

17

REPENTANCE AND FAITH

Hebrews 5:11–6:3, 11:1–6

[11]We have much to say about this, but it is hard to explain because you are slow to learn. [12]In fact, though by this time you ought to be teachers, you need someone to teach you the elementary truths of God's word all over again. You need milk, not solid food! [13]Anyone who lives on milk, being still an infant, is not acquainted with the teaching about righteousness. [14]But solid food is for the mature, who by constant use have trained themselves to distinguish good from evil.

6:1Therefore let us leave the elementary teachings about Christ and go on to maturity, not laying again the foundation of repentance from acts that lead to death, and of faith in God,

[2]instruction about baptisms, the laying on of hands, the resurrection of the dead, and eternal judgment. [3]And God permitting, we will do so.

11:1Now faith is being sure of what we hope for and certain of what we do not see. [2]This is what the ancients were commended for.

[3]By faith we understand that the universe was formed at God's command, so that what is seen was not made out of what was visible. [4]By faith Abel offered God a better sacrifice than Cain did. By faith he was commended as a righteous man, when God spoke well of his offerings. And by faith he still speaks, even though he is dead.

[5]By faith Enoch was taken from this life, so that he did not experience death; he could not be found, because God had taken him away. For before he was taken, he was commended as one who pleased God. [6]And without faith it is impossible to please God, because anyone who comes to him must believe that he exists and that he rewards those who earnestly seek him.

INTRODUCTION AND REVIEW:
Sin and Death

AT THE END OF THE BOOK OF REVELATION, we saw how that beautiful city of God was descending from heaven upon earth. It was a city with foundations, and the foundations were glorious.[1] This was the city for which Abraham sought, he was looking for a city with foundations.[2] This is the city of which our Lord Jesus Christ spoke when He said, "Repent, for the kingdom of heaven is at hand."[3] The kingdom of God is represented to us as a city, a city with foundations, and we have been speaking about the foundations of this city. We spoke about the reality of sin and death. *If there is sin, there is need for Christ, and if there is no sin, there is no need for Christ.* Clearly, there is sin; God has made a clear revelation of Himself; men are without excuse for failing to see, know, and acknowledge God.[4] Physical death is in the world as a reminder of spiritual death and, with it, the curse. God did not make the world with the curse in it; He made it very good, and the curse is a call back from sin and death.[5] We experience the curse as toil, strife, old age, sickness, and death in every degree. If we acknowledge God in any way, we must acknowledge the curse present in the world as a call back. All human beings are aware of suffering, and we all have to deal with it.

The First Foundation Is Repentance from Dead Works and Faith in God

We have to understand the notion of works and the notion of dead works. The New King James Version says, **"repentance from dead works"** (v. 6:1b). There is certainly death in the lives of people, spiritual death because of sin, but there is also death remaining in believers in that sin remains in believers. It does not dominate; it is not the central core of their being, but it can influence enough to cause there to be dead

---

1. *Revelation 21.*

2. *Hebrews 11:10.*

3. *Matthew 3:2, 4:17; Mark 1:15.*

4. Gangadean, "Paper No. 102: The Clarity of General Revelation," 527–529; "Paper No. 41: What Is Clear About God," 225–229; "Paper No. 112: Why General Revelation Is Basic in the Christian Worldview," in *The Logos Papers,* 583–585.

5. Gangadean, *The Biblical Worldview,* xxvi.

works. We believe it is concerning this that Paul the Apostle speaks in 1 Corinthians 3:10–15. Let us look at that for a moment and notice how this is connected with foundation and foundational truths. "By the grace God has given me, I laid a foundation as an expert builder, and someone else is building on it" (1 Cor. 3:10a). Notice that the building starts with the foundation; there is a city with foundations. If this foundation is in place, we can individually go on to maturity, and corporately—the city of God, the kingdom of God, the Church, the people of God—can come into the unity of the faith and the fullness that there is in Christ.[6] Paul says, "But each one should be careful how he builds. For no one can lay any foundation other than the one already laid, which is Jesus Christ" (1 Cor. 3:10b–11).

There is so much in that statement, "Jesus Christ." We may take the minimal, truncated view, but we can and should take the maximal view; Jesus is the Christ, God with us, God the Son incarnate who has come to *undo* what Adam did and to *do* what Adam failed to do. He is the Messiah, the Anointed One who sends His Spirit upon the Church to enable it to do the work of calling all people to God. Foundation is Jesus Christ. "If any man builds on this foundation using gold, silver, costly stones, wood, hay or straw, his work will be shown for what it is, because the Day will bring it to light" (1 Cor. 3:12–13a). That "Day" is the day that is dawning, since Christ's coming and the gospel, the light of the gospel going into all the world, "the Day will bring it to light."

> It will be revealed with fire, and the fire will test the quality of each man's work. If what he has built survives, he will receive his reward. If it is burned up, he will suffer loss; he himself will be saved, but only as one escaping through the flames (1 Cor. 3:13b–15).

If our works are not according to the foundation that God has set, they will be works that lead to death,[7] works that will be burned. We are speaking now about Christians whose works are not according to the foundation, who, though they themselves are saved, their works will be burned. This is another dimension of sin, death, and dead works. We were dominated by it before we came to Christ, and sin still remains

---

6. *Ephesians 4:13.*

7. *Hebrews 6:1.*

in us after we come to Christ. We have to be sanctified and cleansed of sin. Sin remaining produces dead works which will be burned up. The first foundation has to do with sin and death, dead works, and repentance from works that lead to death. We are focusing on this: repentance from dead works that lead to death.

Dead Works: Five Passages

Dead works are contrasted with *good* works, and we should keep in mind five biblical passages in addition to 1 Corinthians 3:10–15. (1) Hebrews 6:1 speaks of the foundation, which says, **"repentance from dead works,"** and introduces the notion of works: dead works and good works. (2) 1 Corinthians 3:15 speaks of the idea that the dead works of Christians may be burned up. (3) Ephesians 2:10: "For we are God's workmanship, created in Christ Jesus to do good works, which God prepared in advance for us to do." He prepared us in advance from before He laid the foundation of the world. He had in mind that we, His people, will do good works. Notice how this plays on the original idea of creation. We were created to do good works from the very beginning; when God blessed Adam upon creation, He said, "Be fruitful and multiply; fill the earth and subdue it; have dominion" (Gen. 1:28 NKJV). Through dominion in the creation, we are to come to the knowledge of God. Creation is revelation.[8] The whole earth is full of His glory, and we are to come to the knowledge of God. This work was set before man; he was to work for six days, and the seventh day was the Sabbath. He is to remember the purpose of his life.

From the beginning, we were created to do good works. Those are not tossed aside now because Christ has come; rather, Christ has come in the place of Adam to *do* what Adam failed to do. Remember, Ephesians 2:10 says, "For we are God's workmanship, created in Christ Jesus to do good works, which God prepared in advance for us to do." Instead of doing good works for which we were created to do, we were doing dead works. We have to repent of dead works that lead to death and do good works. We are trying to present this to you in a particular order. We are created for good works. We are recreated in Christ for good works, and Scripture is given to prepare us for good works. (4)

---

8. Gangadean, *The Biblical Worldview*, 21–36, 91–124.

2 Timothy 3:16–17 says, "All Scripture is God-breathed and is useful for teaching, rebuking, correcting and training in righteousness, so that the man of God may be thoroughly equipped for every good work." We are created for good works, and the Scripture is given that we may be thoroughly equipped for every good work.

How do we bring together our original purpose, our redemptive purpose, and the purpose of reading Scripture? (5) Ephesians 4:11–12 is again speaking of good works: "It was he who gave some to be apostles, some to be prophets, some to be evangelists, and some to be pastors and teachers, to prepare God's people for works of service, so that the body of Christ may be built up." On the Novitiate,[9] we have one section about works of service: at home, at church, and at work, how are we doing in these areas? God has created us for works of service. In the church, the works of service are "so that the body of Christ may be built up." Each one is to do this, and they are to do it through the preaching of the Word. We are created for this purpose, Scripture is given for this, and the pastor-teachers who expound the Scripture are to prepare us for good works, every good work, "to prepare God's people for works of service." The outcome of the works of service is this: "so that the body of Christ may be built up." And in verse 13, "until we all reach unity in the faith and in the knowledge of the Son of God and become mature, attaining to the whole measure of the fullness of Christ." Through works of service that members of the body of Christ do, we attain the unity of the faith. Through works of service, the body of Christ is built up, we attain to the unity of the faith, and—not apart from everyone doing his work—we attain to the whole measure of the fullness of Christ. In contrast, Ephesians continues:

> Then we will no longer be infants, tossed back and forth by the waves, and blown here and there by every wind of teaching and by the cunning and craftiness of men in their deceitful scheming. Instead, speaking the truth in love, we will in all things grow up into him who is the Head, that is, Christ. From him the whole body, joined and held together by every supporting ligament, grows and builds itself up in love, as each part does its work (Eph. 4:14–16).

---

9. Gangadean, *The Westminster Confession*, 389–390.

We cannot come into the unity of the faith without each member of the body of Christ doing its work. The first foundational truth is that we are to repent of works that lead to death and have in their place good works that have the fullness of Christ as their purpose.

THE FIRST PRINCIPLES:
The *Stoicheia* and *Arche*

Yet, something is causing a problem. It says in Hebrews 5:12a, "**In fact, though by this time you ought to be teachers, you need someone to teach you the elementary truths of God's word all over again.**" The *stoicheia* are the elements, the rudiments, the rudimentary things, the elementary things. They need to be taught the principles, the *arche,* the structures, the first beginning structures of the things of Christ. I want to bring this word to you, and I hope it becomes riveted in your attention: the *stoicheia*, the elements. We have misunderstood the foundational principles. We have to ask: Why are these elements, the *stoicheia*, not in place? Why is it that "though by this time you ought to be teachers, you need someone to teach you the elementary truths of God's word all over again."

Keep in mind that these are the first principles. These things are *milk*, not meat. "**You need milk, not solid food!**" (v. 5:12b). We have reversed the order; we have tried to say the first principles, or elementary truths, are deep truths, and that they are only for the mature, but we have reversed this truth. These are the foundational things: the rudimentary elements, the *stoicheia,* the *arche* principles of Christ. It is like milk for infants. Paul in Hebrews 5–6 spoke about the high priesthood of Christ and the Melchizedekian priesthood that abides forever; these are deeper things that we should know. We cannot go on to learn about deeper truths unless we have the foundation in place. We cannot go on to maturity and cannot teach as we should. "**Though by this time you ought to be teachers, you need someone to teach you the elementary truths of God's word all over again**" (v. 5:12a). This is what we are trying to do in preaching the Word of God, to prepare God's people for works of service, to continually go over these foundational principles until they are well-established in the lives of the people, that we may go on to maturity, that each part may do its work. In this, we will no longer be doing works that will result in death, works that will be burned up, but we will do works that will last and bring glory to God. There is resistance to this foundation being laid because there are other foundations, other elements, and other *stoicheia* in place in our lives. Let us look at these other foundations in Scripture.

Human Tradition: The *Stoicheia* of the World

Colossians 2:8 says, "See to it that no one takes you captive through hollow and deceptive philosophy, which depends on human tradition and the basic principles [*stoicheia*] of this world rather than on Christ." See to it that no one takes you captive. Instead of us taking the world captive, they are taking us captive through the *stoicheia* of the world, the rudimentary principles of the world. We will either have the rudimentary principles of the kingdom of God in place in our lives, or we will have the principles of the world—and one foundation resists the other. We have to tear out one in order to have the other laid, and in doing so, we have to repent. That is why it speaks of repentance from works that lead to death. Where and how we will, or have, or might encounter this hollow, deceptive philosophy depends on "human tradition." Notice the word "tradition." Everyone in this room has a tradition. We have been brought up in a particular way; we have a particular background, and these traditions have been passed on through our upbringing and background. We took it in as we took in our mother's milk; to extend that metaphor, we took it in by osmosis without even noticing.

Tradition is deeply rooted, deeply laid in our lives, and we have to come to recognize it and root it out. Our parents, our grandparents, the mass media, the songs that go through our minds again and again, our teachers, the books we have read, the movies we have watched are of the world. The world has reinforced certain basic ideas, and we hardly have time to stop, think, and analyze them. We take it for granted, and it is there. These elements of the world hold us captive; they are received by tradition. 'That's how I've been brought up, and I've always done it that way and never thought to question it.' Well, we must begin to think, question, and recognize it. And because we have gotten the world's foundation in this way, by human tradition, received from our parents and culture, we do not notice it all the more. Saying that we receive it from our fathers is a general term for the whole cultural upbringing, particularly as it comes through family. "See to it that no one takes you captive through hollow and deceptive philosophy, which depends on human tradition and the basic principles of this world rather than on Christ" (Col. 2:8).

This is not a slam against philosophy; this is a slam against philosophy based on worldly *stoicheia*, worldly elements, rather than on Christian truth, philosophy based on Christ and the first principles of Christ.[10] We have an antithetical *stoicheia*, an antithetical basic principle, one that we have gotten by tradition. The first principles of Christ we have to get in regeneration and a new life in God. Continuing on to Colossians 2:18a: "Do not let anyone who delights in false humility and the worship of angels disqualify you for the prize." Remember, your works can be burned, and you can lose your reward, though you may be saved.[11]

The Church is very badly divided, which is an indication that there is a lot of worldliness. Remember, worldliness is the incarnation of the self-life. We all have self-life in various ways, and we have picked it up in the world and brought it in to the Church. This will disqualify us for the prize, the high calling that is in Christ Jesus. We are to take every thought captive, come to the knowledge of God, and see the earth filled with the knowledge of God. These traditions we have been brought up with are deeply rooted and uncritically held and hold us captive. We are warned twice, "See to it that no one takes you captive" in verse 8 and in verse 18, "Do not let anyone . . . disqualify you for the prize." Going on to verse 20, "Since you died with Christ to the basic principles of this world, why, as though you still belonged to it, do you submit to its rules . . . ?" We submit to and go along with many worldly ways and customs. How do we educate our children? What sorts of programs do we allow our kids to watch? How do we relate to our work and future? What do we consider true wealth? Why do we still submit to worldly rules? It is the basic principles and rules that enforce and carry out these principles. Why do we do this? We have died with Christ[12] and to the basic principles/*stoicheia* of this world.

10. Gangadean, "Paper No. 20: Christianity, Philosophy, and Public Education," in *The Logos Papers*, 127–133.

11. *1 Corinthians 3:15.*

12. *Galatians 2:20.*

The Word of God Will Overcome the Worldly *Stoicheia*

There are other passages that speak about this. 1 Peter 1:18–19 speaks about the traditions with which we were brought up: "For you know that it was not with perishable things such as silver or gold that you were redeemed from the empty way of life handed down to you from your forefathers, but with the precious blood of Christ, a lamb without blemish or defect." This should help us see how important it is that we have been redeemed and that Christ has shed His blood for us. What a contrast it is. Unless we say He shed his blood in vain. There is an antithesis between the kingdom of God and the kingdom of this world. There are traditions handed down to us by our fathers, and there are hundreds and hundreds and hundreds of human traditions. The Hindu tradition is not the same as the Chinese; the French are not the same as the English; the Moroccans are not the same as the Ecuadorians; the Hopi are not the same as the Navajo, the Apache, or the Papago. Each nation has its own tradition. We all have our traditions, but they are each based on some form of self-life. Particular rules that carry the self-life as we conceive of it. This is an empty way of life, it is the way of death, works that lead to death. We have been redeemed from this by the precious blood of Christ. Let us not say Christ shed His blood in vain and continue on in self-life.

2 Peter 3:9a: "The Lord is not slow in keeping his promise, as some understand slowness." The Lord is not 'slack,' in the way that word is used today, as those who are 'slackers.' They do not get with it and they lack drive; they drift aimlessly. God is not a 'slacker' concerning His promise. He wants everyone to repent from dead works and have faith in God. The Lord is not slow or slack in keeping His promises, as some understand it. Peter continues, "He is patient with you, not wanting anyone to perish, but everyone to come to repentance" (1 Pet. 3:9a). This is repentance from works that lead to death. "But the day of the Lord will come like a thief. The heavens will disappear with a roar; the elements [*stoicheia*] will be destroyed by fire, and the earth and everything in it will be laid bare" (1 Pet. 3:10). As the people of God witness faithfully and the pressure builds, there will come a time when all of a sudden the world system on which it is built will collapse. It will come in a moment, like a thief in the night. Suddenly, it happens; the systems and paradigms that this culture is ruled by will

collapse. Think about a paradigm shift;[13] a whole new order of things will come into place. There is a shift in the paradigm through crises that the world goes through from time to time. It comes rather quickly, suddenly, and we do not expect it. What happened before World War II and after World War II? There was a shift. A new way of looking at things. There was still a significant shift *within* the world. How much more when there is a shift from the world to the kingdom of God?

How about a shift within the kingdom of God from premillennial dispensational to postmillennial? That is a significant shift, a paradigm shift. Just as the Reformation came in relatively quickly. There was a major shift, like an earthquake. An earthquake is a good figure of speech; it is quick, devastating, and widespread, and everything changes in a few seconds. That is how it will come, "The heavens will disappear with a roar; the elements will be destroyed by fire" (2 Pet. 3:10), the elements, the *stoicheia*. We tend to think in terms of the physical elements, but these are moral and spiritual elements. This is the *stoicheia* on which the world is built, being replaced by the *stoicheia* of the kingdom of God. These are the foundational principles that we should have in place if we have been properly taught and if we have repented.

"Since everything will be destroyed in this way, what kind of people ought you to be? You ought to live holy and godly lives as you look forward to the day of God and speed its coming" (2 Pet. 3:11–12a). We speed the day of God by our faithful proclamation of the gospel, the *stoicheia*. "That day will bring about the destruction of the heavens by fire, and the elements will melt in the heat" (2 Pet. 3:12b). This is the preaching of the Word. In Acts 2:1–4, a mighty wind and the tongues of fire rush as the people of God speak and are faithful witnesses.[14] We are not to be slack and sloppy witnesses, but to know God's truth. We are to have taken the time and effort to seek diligently to know, and to speak those truths that will melt the elements of this world—the foundational principles.

We can melt the element of 'neutrality' based on science and observation if we can point out how experience is being interpreted from a

---

13. Borrowing from Thomas Kuhn's terminology in *The Structure of Scientific Revolutions* (Chicago: Chicago University Press, 1996).

14. This is explained in chapter 19, *The Doctrine of Baptism: Part II.*

particular framework.[15] Pressure is building against this, and if we remain faithful and each one continues doing his work and we all, in so many ways, support and encourage this, there will come a time when the whole thing will collapse. The *stoicheia* of the world is in place and is hindering the *stoicheia* of the kingdom of God from coming into place. This is why, "**though by this time you ought to be teachers, you need someone to teach you the elementary truths of God's word all over again** [the stoicheia again]" (v. 5:12a). There are two words there: (1) *Stoicheia*, the rudimentary, elementary, first principles, the basic structures. (2) And, *arche,* archetype, architecture, the fundamental structure of things. When we speak the Word of God, a change in the elements will come about and we can hasten its coming by being faithful witnesses. Peter speaks of this coming: "That day will bring about the destruction of the heavens by fire, and the elements will melt in the heat" (2 Pet. 3:12b). This is the heat of the preaching of the Word of God. The Scripture uses the word *stoicheia* to mean the elementary, foundational principles on which our lives are built, on which the kingdom of God is built, the city with foundations. This work will bring about the kingdom of God: "But in keeping with his promise we are looking forward to a new heaven and a new earth, the home of righteousness" (2 Pet. 3:13). As we do the work that God has called us to do, as we repent from dead works that lead to death, and do good works because the foundational principles are in place, we will hasten the coming of the kingdom of God.

REPENTANCE:
Active Obedience (*Metanoia*)

What we are called to do is repent (*metanoia*) of dead works, works that lead to death.[16] The word *repent* is an active verb, not a passive verb. It is something we do, not something that happens to us. It assumes the reality of sin and the need for change, not merely growth. Growth is a process that occurs differently than change; growth cannot merely be commanded. Remember, we are temporal (we grow), finite (with beginning), and we are changeable (we change)—finite,

15. Gangadean, *Philosophical Foundation*, 12–13, 20–21, 86–100.

16. *Hebrews 6:1.*

temporal, and changeable. Temporality is not the same as changeability. We will continue to be temporal in the age to come; in heaven, we will continue to grow, but we will not continue to change because all sin will have been removed, and there will be no need for repentance. Let us distinguish change from growth.

When we speak about repentance, we are not speaking about growth, we are speaking about change. Jesus' message to His people began, "Repent, the kingdom of heaven is at hand." The word for repent in Hebrew is *nacham*. It has a sense of a sigh of relief. In the New Testament, the word is *metanoia*; this word speaks more of the mind. It speaks about a change of mind, that we are to think differently, reconsider, feel compunction, and with that, a sigh may come. But here, the element of thinking is brought up, calling us to reconsider and think differently. It involves the notion of a reformation or reversal. If we are going in one direction and it is the wrong direction, we are to turn back and turn around.

The Inward Call to Repentance: Shame

In order for there to be repentance, there has to be integrity, a concern for consistency, a concern for truth. In the case of Adam and Eve, when they sinned, they experienced the inner call of God to repentance; they experienced shame and guilt. Shame is subjective, and guilt is objective.[17] When the judge pronounces you guilty, you do not all of a sudden feel ashamed. But you are objectively guilty, whether you feel ashamed or not. Shame is the subjective part. I know the words may be used variously, but that is the basic use of it. Adam and Eve experienced shame, which was God's call to repentance. God has structured us in this way. What did they do? They avoided it; they avoided it by covering it up. They put what was reminding them of their sin out of sight and paid no attention to it. When we ask why there is no repentance of works that lead to death, we have to address the pattern that was in Adam and Eve. We have to address the lack of integrity in us and what the result of it might be, because we have been called to repentance and have not always repented of works that lead to death.

---

17. Gangadean, *The Biblical Worldview*, 241–257.

The Outward Call to Repentance: Where Are You?

The second call came to Adam after he resisted the first call.[18] Adam and Eve had covered up; they mutually agreed, and they were going around with these leaves hanging on them, whereas before, they had nothing there. You can cover up one thing, but you cannot cover up the cover-up. It is logically impossible to cover up the cover-up because what you are covering up with is always manifest. Even if you put ten layers on it, the last covering will be there. They can see what they are using to cover up, which should remind them. They have to deal with it. There is a form of self-deception going on, but instead of repenting, we try to cover it up. When God came near to them and said "Where are you?", it was another call to repentance, an outward, external call through someone coming to them. "Where are you?" What did Adam do? He blamed the woman, he blamed God, and he justified himself.

When we are called to repentance, inwardly and outwardly, we may not repent. We may not wish to be consistent; we may hide it from ourselves, deceive ourselves, justify ourselves, and dig ourselves in. Our Lord Jesus Christ encountered this when He came preaching to the Jews. The Jewish leaders continued to resist the call to repent, despite the many works He did, and in the end, the Lord pronounced judgment upon them. The judgment was this: "Woe to you, teachers of the law and Pharisees, you hypocrites!" (Matt. 23:23). Hypocrisy is the opposite of integrity,[19] which is necessary for repentance. What we have to do, as our Lord did, is recognize the reality of hypocrisy and treat it as such. We are not to participate in another person's sin by failing to recognize hypocrisy as hypocrisy. We are not to participate in another person's sin by failing to recognize a lack of integrity: the failure to see what is clear and to know what is clear, the failure to seek God diligently, to know and acknowledge what is clear. We are to keep it ever in our minds and call each to keep it before us. That is why I say in the classroom, somewhat facetiously but with a measure of truth, if you are not committed to using reason to see what is clear, stand up before everyone, tell everyone, 'Hey, I want you to know this, I'm not concerned about reason, I'm not concerned about truth!' And then sit down and shut up for the rest of your life. If you had any concern for

---

18. Gangadean, *The Biblical Worldview,* 259–273.
19. Gangadean, *Philosophical Foundation,* 199–205.

consistency, you would do that. Of course, a person who is not concerned for consistency will not do that. But we are to remind others that they have failed to see what is clear. And where is the integrity in that? We are to remind others that they fail to show concern for truth and ask how we can continue talking about this. I have to treat you as a human being with dignity and hold you responsible for seeing what is clear.[20] I have to treat you as a human being capable of seeking the truth and being called by God to diligently seek Him. We are not to be casual about it and let it slide by and not read the Scriptures. We are to be as the Bereans were and search the Scripture every day to see if it is so.[21]

We should not say, 'We are going to agree to disagree, agreeably.' 'I'm okay, you're okay, everybody's okay, Adam and Eve were okay, maybe even the devil is okay.' In his self-life, his lack of concern for truth. How can you pick on the devil when you are a child of the devil? The lack of concern for the truth; there is no truth in him.[22] Do not get down on the devil's case when you are believing his lie. We are to hold ourselves accountable, hold each other accountable, and repent. We will not repent unless we have integrity. If we do not have integrity, we should have the integrity to recognize we do not have integrity, which I know will not happen. If you do not have a concern for integrity, then we have to do as our Lord Jesus, we have to watch ourselves and say, 'That is hypocrisy, that is a lack of integrity.' This is the external voice saying, 'Where are you in relation to what is clear? Where are you in relation to the work of the pastor-teachers in Church history? Have you considered that and searched the Scriptures? If you have not, why do you talk the way you do, as if you are concerned about the truth when you are not concerned about *stoicheia*, the first truths? Surely, if you kid yourself, I do not want you to kid me. Surely, I should not participate in your self-deception. Why are you calling me to participate, the way Adam and Eve called each other to do it? We are called to repent, and there is some point at which we must repent. We must repent at the basic level of autonomy of determining good and evil for ourselves.

---

20. Gangadean, *Philosophical Foundation*, 231–243.

21. *Acts 17:11.*

22. *John 8:44.*

SIDE BY SIDE:
Repentance and Faith

We are called to repentance: to humble ourselves, give up our pride, and say, 'I am a creature, utterly dependent on God for all good. More than that, I am a *sinful* creature. I have taken it upon myself to determine good and evil. I need help, I need serious help.' We are to acknowledge that side by side with repentance comes faith, **"repentance from acts that lead to death, and of faith in God"**(v. 6:1b). **"Without faith it is impossible to please God"** (v. 11:6b). **"This is what the ancients were commended for"**(v. 11:2).

What is faith? What kind of repentance do we need? As long as we come short in faith, our faith is lacking, and there is a need for repentance. Is our faith lacking? Should it be more than it is? Should it be growing and changing our understanding? Should we be getting rid of the old elements of the world? Yes, we should. Repentance should be an ongoing process. If sin is ongoing in us, repentance needs to be ongoing. Because sin leads to death. We want to have good works that will lead to the building up of the body of Christ and the praise of God. **"Without faith it is impossible to please God."**

What do you think has happened to 'faith' defined by the world as against faith understood according to the Bible? Christians have bought in, by and large, to 'faith' as it is understood by the world. The world has forced their definition upon Christians, and we do not have the foundation in place, so we cannot teach as we should. The Bible says this about faith: **"Now faith is being sure of what we hope for and certain of what we do not see"** (v. 11:1). The King James Version says, **"Now faith is the substance of things hoped for, the evidence [or proof] of things not seen."** It is the underlying reality. You see the color of this podium, but you do not see the atoms themselves; they do not have color. The atoms, out of which this is made are a material substratum, the substance. So faith is a substance, the surety of things hoped for. What is hoped for? In this context, the kingdom of God, the certainty that the city with foundations will come. If we understand good and evil, we will know for sure that this will come about.[23] If we

---

23. Gangadean, *Philosophical Foundation*, 207–219; Gangadean, "Paper No. 104: Eschatology (Twelve Points)," 539–544; "Paper No. 118: Eschatology (Seven Points)," 603–607; "Paper No. 119: Pauline Eschatology," in *The Logos Papers*, 609–610.

understand God's purpose in creation, we will know for certain that it will come about. If we knew the meaning of the Sabbath, we will know for certain that this will come about.[24] This is so fundamental, so basic to God's purpose: to glorify Himself and that the whole earth will be filled with the knowledge of God's glory. This is so basic; it is underlying everything. That the material substratum of this podium is there is certain. As it is said in philosophy, secondary qualities may come and go, and we may be uncertain about them, but the primary underlying substratum is there.[25] One may be appearance, the other is reality. Faith is the reality of things hoped for, the proof of things not seen.

Do we need proof? The Bible teaches that we need proof. Does faith need proof? Yes, it needs proof. What kind of proof? Sight? No. It is proof of the invisible, it is not proof by sight, it is proof by reason.[26] Proof by the Word of God which lightens every man that comes into the world. Proof by the *logos*, which is most often translated as *reason*. By the Word of God understood as reason, the Word of God in all men, is how we see and know. What does Romans 1 say? "Being understood from what has been made." There is a process of understanding, reasoning, and thinking. We have proof of these things that we hope for, what will come about; we have proof of what the good is and how the good will come about, and what it will look like when the good comes about. The good is the knowledge of God, this is for sure.[27] What will it look like when it comes about? "For the earth will be full of the knowledge of the LORD as the waters cover the sea" (Is. 11:9b). No ferocious beast will be there, "The wolf will live with the lamb" (Is. 11:6a). There will be a highway, it will be a highway that no unclean thing will walk in; the way of holiness. By faith, we understand.[28]

---

24. Gangadean, *The Biblical Worldview*, 125–146.

25. Gangadean, *History of Philosophy*, 139–149.

26. Gangadean, *Philosophical Foundation*, 71–161; Gangadean, *History of Philosophy*, 47–58; Gangadean, *The Westminster Confession*, 1–13; Gangadean, "Paper No. 3: The Principle of Clarity," 15–20; "Paper No. 39: Clarity," in *The Logos Papers*, 217–220.

27. Gangadean, *Philosophical Foundation*, 171–177, 208–211; Gangadean, *The Westminster Catechisms*, 109–111, 321–325; Gangadean, *On Natural and Revealed Theology*, 33–39, 127–139.

28. For a fuller exposition of faith as understanding, see: Gangadean, *The Biblical Worldview*, 3–20; Gangadean, *Philosophical Foundation*, 32–45, 121–127; Gangadean, *History of Philosophy*, 3–12, 163–167; Gangadean, "Paper No. 21: Faith and Reason in Christianity," 135–138; "Paper No. 28: Prepare the Way of the Lord," 171–173; "Paper No. 98: Faith

18

THE DOCTRINE OF BAPTISM
PART I

Matthew 28:16–20

¹⁶Then the eleven disciples went to Galilee, to the mountain where Jesus had told them to go. ¹⁷When they saw him, they worshiped him; but some doubted. ¹⁸Then Jesus came to them and said, "All authority in heaven and on earth has been given to me. ¹⁹Therefore go and make disciples of all nations, baptizing them in the name of the Father and of the Son and of the Holy Spirit, ²⁰and teaching them to obey everything I have commanded you. And surely I am with you always, to the very end of the age."

REVIEW:
Foundation, Sin, and the Need for Christ

WE FINISHED A SERIES ON THE BOOK OF REVELATION and saw that the consummation of the work of dominion is the city of God, where the river of life flows. God has sent Jesus Christ, our Lord, so we might have life and have it more abundantly. We have this life in the city of God, a city with foundations. We saw the beauty of this city spoken of in Revelation 21, in the vision of John the Apostle. There are foundations to this city, and there are foundations in the lives of the people of God.[1] Hebrews 6:1–3 speaks of the foundation.

---

and the Word of God," 511–514; "Paper No. 128: Abraham's Faith," 665–666; "Paper No. 129: Faith and Reason in the Life of Abraham" in *The Logos Papers*, 667–669.

1. Gangadean, "Paper No. 43: My Last Lecture," in *The Logos Papers*, 237–253.

Therefore let us leave the elementary teachings about Christ and go on to maturity, not laying again the foundation of repentance from acts that lead to death, and of faith in God, instruction about baptisms, [doctrine or teachings] the laying on of hands, the resurrection of the dead, and eternal judgment. And God permitting, we will do so.

In this passage, we have, among the things that are foundational, the teachings about baptism. In the first sermon in this Foundation series, we spoke about our need for Christ, the reality of sin, and how sin manifests. We spoke about our need for Christ crucified, specifically Christ and His atoning death on the cross. If there is no sin, there is no need for Christ; we must establish this. But if there is sin, our only way out of this sin is through Jesus Christ and Him crucified. We spoke about clarity and inexcusability. We will speak further about autonomy, which is the other side of sin. One side is not seeking, and the other is going our own way and determining good and evil for ourselves. In autonomy, we determine good and evil, which is idolatry; we set up idols in the place of God and all that goes with idolatry; it is an attempt to be in control, and not to see that God is in control. It is the extent that we go in order to be in control of our lives, rather than seeing that we are mere creatures, that we are dependent on God. We should submit to God's rule in our lives and His control.

Three Forms of Baptism: Sign (Water), Reality (Regeneration), and Suffering (Sanctification)

We will go through the doctrine of baptism, see how we need to have the teaching of baptism laid in our lives, and how the Church is so severely divided on this one point. We will go over the three forms of baptism: (1) the outward sacramental sign administered through water, and (2) the inward work of regeneration, where we are united to Christ through repentance and faith, and (3) the baptism we hesitate to speak about, and that is the baptism of suffering. This is called the 'baptism of fire,' which we will be immersed in. Not much is said about it, but it is a reality, and we should speak about it. Christ is the one who baptizes us with the Holy Spirit and with fire.[2] We should

---

2. *Matthew 3:11.*

expect this fire and understand how it comes. Jesus spoke about the baptism that He was to undergo as He approached the cross, suffering for the sake of righteousness.

DIVISIONS REGARDING BAPTISM

We do not wish to reinvent the wheel. Much work has been done on baptism, and I will be reading to you from the Westminster Confession of Faith on baptism. But to help you see where we are going, sometimes we have to understand that God allows opposing ideas to be raised in the history of the Church. Because of our lethargy, our slackness, and our slothfulness with respect to truth, God causes opposing views to be raised up and presses us that we might stop and think more deeply about it. In the history of the Church, there have been opposing views on the subject of baptism.

The Church has longstanding divisions in understanding baptism. One way is the Roman Catholic Church and its sacramental theology. In Protestantism, there is a conflict regarding covenant theology raised up by Baptist and Anabaptist theology, whose views have become widespread in the Church. We need to understand why it has become so widespread and see that a whole teaching system goes along with a particular practice and understanding. Here are divisions that have been raised up, and we want to think about them. We want to think about covenant theology, how dispensationalism has been raised up, and how it is an outgrowth of failing to see the nature of the covenant, the unity between the Old and New Testament. Coupled with this is Arminian theology. Some Arminians practice baptism outwardly correctly, but many who do not practice baptism of infants hold to Arminian theology.

We have to see how we understand the meaning of baptism and what it is to be born again, something so simple and so basic. How do we understand regeneration and circumcision, what do they mean, and what is God doing through them? We are to understand whether we do see the mighty work of God in what is signified in baptism, whether we see the resurrection from the dead, whether we see how people are dead, and what it means to say, "As for you, you were dead in your transgressions and sins" (Eph. 2:1). This goes back to the very first foundation of sin and death, how we understand sin, and how we understand death and the reality that is around us. Do we understand how we are to engage in proclaiming the gospel, how we are in the world, how we are to teach, and what we see the needs to be? There is a whole system of theology connected with this. These truths are foundational, and we should be aware of where divisions have occurred.

There is sacramental theology, dispensationalism versus covenant theology, versions of dispensationalism, Arminian theology, and most recently, open theism. Open theism is a view that God does not know everything. The future is open to God. If God knew everything, that would eliminate our freedom, and it would not be consistent with other things that are said about God. Open theism is a renewal and development of a failure to understand sin and death and the nature of freedom, and this is connected with the failure to understand baptism.

If we start with sin and death and understand what these are, we will easily understand baptism, but we must remark that this is not yet in place. We have a certain level of understanding sin, which has to deepen. "By faith we understand" (Heb. 11:3); faith is not antithetical to understanding, but rather, "faith is the substance of things hoped for, the evidence of things not seen" (Heb. 11:1 KJV). "This is what the ancients were commended for" (Heb. 11:2), and if we had an understanding of sin and death, and what it is to seek God diligently, we would see this established. Remember, our concern is the city of God, and through this city, the glory of God. And through this, the nations of the earth, the kings of the earth, will bring their glory into this city.[3]

The work of the pastor-teachers, past and present, is:

> to prepare God's people for works of service, so that the body of Christ may be built up until we all reach unity in the faith and in the knowledge of the Son of God and become mature, attaining to the whole measure of the fullness of Christ (Eph. 4:12–13).

We will continue to work on these teachings and ever increase our understanding. We will see that repentance is connected with lack of faith, and faith has to do with progressive understanding, so repentance is progressive. It is not a one-time deal. As God reveals more to us about His nature and our condition, the more we repent. We have

---

3. *Revelation 21:24.*

to see what repentance is. It is not enough to take note of these truths; we have to acknowledge that we have not thought about the foundational truths, and we must repent.

THE WESTMINSTER CONFESSION OF FAITH:
Of Baptism

Without reinventing the wheel, what is the teaching concerning baptism? Chapter 28 of the Westminster Confession of Faith addresses baptism, and we would like to read this. If we read it, we will have to talk about sacraments; if we talk about sacraments, we will have to talk about the covenant. All of these are given deliberate attention in the Westminster Confession of Faith. To fail to know this is to fail to be grounded in the work of the pastor-teachers, which is necessary to become established. We will see how so much is summed up so quickly in this section.

> Baptism is a sacrament of the New Testament, ordained by Jesus Christ, not only for the solemn admission of the party baptized into the visible church, but also to be unto him a sign and seal of the covenant of grace, of his ingrafting into Christ, of regeneration, of remission of sins, and of his giving up unto God, through Jesus Christ, to walk in newness of life: which sacrament is, by Christ's own appointment, to be continued in his church until the end of the world (WCF 28.1).

"Baptism is a sacrament of the New Testament." You have to know what a sacrament is; you have to understand the idea of the testament, the covenant, and covenant theology. "Baptism is a sacrament of the New Testament, ordained by Jesus Christ." Matthew 28:19 says, **"Therefore go and make disciples of all nations, baptizing them."** We have the direct, immediate command of Jesus Christ, our Lord, to baptize. The Westminster Confession of Faith continues: "not only for the solemn admission of the party baptized into the visible church; but also, to be unto him a sign and seal of the covenant of grace." So much is contained in those words, "sign and seal of the covenant of grace." It is not merely a sign, and it is not just a seal; it is a sign and a seal, in different ways, and it is a sign and seal of the covenant of grace. There is so much misunderstanding of the simple concept of the covenant of grace. The Old Testament is mistakenly treated as if it is the covenant of works. Arminians and popular evangelicals say: 'We are not under the covenant of works under the Old Testament, but under grace in the New Testament.' That is such a big misunderstanding. "It is to be a sign and seal of the covenant of grace, of his ingrafting into Christ." Christ is our representative head in the covenant of grace and we are ingrafted into Christ. We are not in Adam; we are in Christ. There is a new covenant head, "of regeneration," and all of these things are signified by baptism: being born again and being brought from death to life. This is a work of recreation, another mighty work of God, "of remission of sins," forgiveness of sins, and the washing away of sins. "Of regeneration, of remission of sins, and of his giving up unto God, through Jesus Christ, to walk in newness of life." This is by our union with Christ, buried with him in baptism in our sin; we are raised with Him to walk in newness of life. We are to die to the old and live unto the new. All of these things so quickly, easily summarized in this statement.

This passage reminds me of the Church's work in the Council of Chalcedon, when it summarized that Christ "acknowledged in two natures which undergo no confusion, no change, no division, no separation." Oh, the work that went into those words. The decades that went into those words. The fighting back and forth that went into those words. The Westminster Confession later synthesized this understanding even further. Without *conversion,* one nature does not become another nature; without *composition*, it is not half and half; and without *confusion,* each nature acts and does what is appropriate to it yet is indissolubly united together in one person.[4] So, too, these words: "sign and seal of the covenant of grace, of his ingrafting into Christ, of regeneration, of remission of sins, and of his giving up unto God, through Jesus Christ, to walk in newness of life." This could not be summarized better. "Which sacrament is, by Christ's own appointment, to be continued in his church until the end of the world." Continued until the end of this age, when the work is completed. Everyone who comes into the Church, the visible Church, has to have this sacrament applied.

---

4. Gangadean, *The Westminster Catechisms,* 31.

> The outward element to be used in this sacrament is water, where-with the party is to be baptized, in the name of the Father, and of the Son, and of the Holy Ghost, by a minister of the gospel, law-fully called thereunto (WCF 28.2).

We will be giving attention to this when we come to the laying on of hands and what constitutes divine authority in the Church. We will see how Paul addresses problems raised about his ministry. It is "in the name of the Father, and of the Son, and of the Holy Ghost." The work of God the Father, God the Son, and God the Holy Spirit, are all manifest in our coming to Christ. This is recognized when we are baptized in the name of the Father, and of the Son, and of the Holy Spirit. The Father elects, the Son dies and is raised again, and the Spirit regenerates and comes to dwell in us, to sanctify us. What a summary of the work of God.

"Dipping of the person into the water is not necessary; but baptism is rightly administered by pouring, or sprinkling water upon the person" (WCF 28.3). The mode of baptism has been discussed and divisions have occurred over this. "Not only those who do actually profess faith in and obedience unto Christ, but also the infants of one, or both, believing parents, are to be baptized" (WCF 28.4). But the infants of those who do not believe are not to be baptized. This has been a mal-practice in the Roman Catholic Church, given the assumption, an un-warranted assumption, that unbaptized infants perish. Every attempt was made to baptize infants, whether their parents were believers or not. They did not see that the sign is not the reality. It was pushed to the point of baptizing infants who were not infants of believers. Some deny that baptism is to be applied to infants at all. This is one of the great points of division within the Church as the Baptist theology has been adopted by many.

> Although it be a great sin to contemn or neglect this ordinance, yet grace and salvation are not so inseparably annexed unto it, as that no person can be regenerated or saved, without it; or, that all that are baptized are undoubtedly regenerated (WCF 28.5).

You can be regenerated and saved without baptism, but it should not be neglected because there is a teaching and a grace that is conferred in it. "Or that all that are baptized are undoubtedly regenerated." This statement addresses another problem, as if baptism is a seal and not a sign. Some churches have practiced *baptismal regeneration*, thinking that when an infant is baptized, they are automatically regenerated by the pronouncements of those words, understood as the remission of original sin. Anabaptists and Baptists have reacted to this position. We have not had faith/understanding. We have not understood the reasons for baptism, or had the evidence for it. We have not had the faith that is pleasing to God, so we have gone astray to the left and right.

Please note this next section carefully. Some of you have had children baptized recently, and others have children who were baptized in the past. Sometimes, we wonder about our baptized children.

> The efficacy of baptism is not tied to that moment of time wherein it is administered; yet, notwithstanding, by the right use of this ordinance, the grace promised is not only offered, but really exhibited, and conferred, by the Holy Ghost, to such (whether of age or infants) as that grace belongeth unto, according to the counsel of God's own will, in His appointed time (WCF 28.6).

It was always understood that grace is *conferred*, not by man, but by the Holy Spirit, to those who are the elect, and in God's own time. That must be kept in mind whenever we baptize; there is an ordinary connection, but not an inexorable connection. It is an ordinary connection but not a necessary connection. Certain conditions come upon any child who is appropriately baptized. That is, the child is a covenant child and will always be treated by God as a covenant child, for better or for worse, and it could be either. Israel will *always* be treated as a covenant people, for better or for worse, and it may be either. You are never the same when baptism is conferred upon you. It does not mean that automatically, inevitably, that child will become a believer.

"The sacrament of baptism is but once to be administered upon any person" (WCF 28.7). It is on this point we have the great division in the Church between baptizing once and the Baptist position, which is really called 'Anabaptist'—baptizing again. Some baptisms are not according to the Word of God. It is administered by a group professing itself to be a Christian church, which is not a Christian church. It is not a Christian church in that its official teaching would not be the basis on which anyone could be saved. They may call themselves

Christian, but it is not a Christian church. It is not a Christian church if they teach salvation by works and not by grace alone. Baptism by such a church is not legitimate, no matter what. It is not just the individual intent of the person baptizing or the individual church but the church's standards. Secondly, the right church may baptize someone who should not be baptized. That is not legitimate, either. That is, if you are an infant and your parents are not believers, no matter what, that baptism should not occur; that is not the right use of this ordinance. In those cases, we do not say that this is Anabaptism, baptizing again, but rather baptism proper. Baptism is offered once and only once.

Baptism is a sign and seal of the righteousness that comes by faith. First of all, baptism puts a distinction between those who belong to the visible Church and those who do not. Children are baptized on the basis of their parents' profession of faith. Adults are baptized in light of their profession of faith being credible. We do not know the hearts of people, but if they have a credible profession of faith, it is believable that the person may be baptized. Once a person has the mark of baptism, they are regarded as in the covenant, for better or for worse. Israel took a covenant oath; at Mount Sinai, both the blessings and the curses were pronounced, and Israel was never the same after that. To this very day, God regards them under His covenant.

Baptism is not to be entered into lightly; it distinguishes between those who belong to the visible Church and those who do not. Baptism is a sign and seal of the covenant of grace; it is a sign, not the reality. One may have the sign (baptism) without the reality (regeneration), and one may have the reality (regeneration) without the sign (baptism). Romans 4:11 speaks of Abraham, who received the sign and seal: "And he received the sign of circumcision, a seal of the righteousness that he had by faith while he was still uncircumcised." We, too, have righteousness through faith. Circumcision was a sign and seal of the righteousness he had by faith. It is not a sign and seal of something secondary, a merely temporal people with outward physical blessings, as dispensationalists have tried to argue concerning Israel in the past. Circumcision is a sign and seal *of faith*. Notice the connection between circumcision and the reality of faith, which reality we have, also. We have a righteousness by faith, which should be enough to settle the whole question. Attempts are made to divide and distinguish the rest of the Scriptures in dispensational periods, but there is another side of it.

The righteousness that we have by faith, we have by faith in our Lord Jesus Christ as our representative head. This is a sign and seal of the righteousness of faith that comes to us through our union with Christ according to the covenant that God has made. A testament is like a covenant but has to do particularly with the death of the person, the last will and testament, and the inheritance that comes with the death. The ideas of covenant and testament are interchangeable, one being larger and inclusive of the other. The righteousness that we have by faith is in the covenant of grace. Anyone on the face of the earth who has ever been saved has been saved by the covenant of grace. They have been saved through faith in Christ. Whether Christ is taught by signs and symbols, they are still pointing to Christ. Abraham was saved by the faith in Christ to come. Adam was saved, and we believe, according to Scripture, that God covered him with the coats of skin, which signified the righteousness of Christ imparted to him. Adam wore those skins day in and day out, and this spoke to him continually. The coats of skin stood in contrast with the covering of leaves that he had made and his sin and the need for a covering of sin. God Himself provided the covering.[5] So, the one covenant of grace goes all the way back to the Garden of Eden.

If we understand the covenant of grace, we can understand the covenant of works. The covenant of works was established with Adam; upon his obedience, he and all with him would have been established in righteousness. This is the covenant of works. Adam failed, and Christ came to *do* what Adam failed to do. There was not another covenant, it was the same covenant of works, but Christ came to fulfill it, and He also came to *undo* what Adam did, according to the covenant of works, that is, Christ paid the penalty for sin and death. We cannot understand the covenant of grace apart from the covenant of works, because the covenant of grace is a fulfillment by Christ of the covenant of works. If we understand this, we will see that there is one covenant of grace, administered differently under the Old Testament and the New Testament, but one and the same covenant of grace. As a matter of fact, this one covenant of grace has had two sacraments. In the Old Testament, it had circumcision, which becomes baptism in the New

---

5. Gangadean, *The Biblical Worldview,* 295–309.

Testament, and Passover, which becomes the Lord's Supper. Both of these sacraments are fulfilled and continue into the New Testament.

There is one covenant of grace and baptism is a sign and seal of that covenant of grace. This is why the Confession speaks of "ingrafting into Christ," because this covenant of grace is no longer in Adam. We are all born in Adam; everyone that is born on earth has been represented by Adam, and Adam sinned, so we all sinned. Christ has come in the place of Adam and has perfectly obeyed. When we come into the covenant of grace by the working of God's Spirit, we come into Christ. When we are ingrafted into Christ, we are no longer in Adam. We must understand this to properly observe the sacrament of baptism and understand this as foundational. We have to understand the covenant of works and the covenant of grace—Adam and Christ—and how the covenant of grace fulfills the covenant of works. As believers, we are in Christ. This is a basic truth. It is foundational. The teachings about baptism are foundational. I dare say that in the professing Christian Church today, these things are not taken into account, and it is characteristic of our condition of being in sin and death. In sin, we fail to seek and understand, and in death, we lack understanding of the meaning of baptism; it has been emptied of meaning, and it is often a mere ritual and devoid of meaning. This is a manifestation of spiritual death, and we can do this very thing with the sacraments of God. We are not to participate in baptism without understanding its meaning. This is why our parents must be believers. "And without faith it is impossible to please God" (Heb. 11:6a). As we repent of our sin, more and more, we come to greater and greater understanding of this. This is how a believer becomes established in Christ, and this is how the city of God has foundations, a city shining and clear as crystal, that diamond city, the city of God. This is how we come to that city. The city that we sang of in Psalm 48 is a praise and a joy for the whole earth. These are the truths that we must know and speak faithfully.

Ingrafting into Christ presupposes the covenant of works and the covenant of grace. Baptism is a sign and seal of regeneration. "As for you, you were dead in your transgressions and sins" (Eph. 2:1), and God, the Holy Spirit, made us alive in Christ. We must ask ourselves and our fellow believers, do you believe you are dead in your trespasses and sins? And do you understand what this death means? Do you think you can do anything to bring yourself and turn yourself to God? Does physical death signify anything like spiritual death? Does the use of the term spiritual death, even as when we are physically dead, mean we can do nothing? When we are spiritually dead, we can do nothing to bring ourselves to God. Do we understand that we are dead in trespasses and sins and must be made alive in God by the work of the Holy Spirit for us even to hear the gospel? Until we are made alive, we cannot hear. We do not have what is called the 'effectual calling.'[6] We have an outward call; we hear outwardly but not inwardly with understanding. It is not until we are restored to life, the life of understanding, the life of the Word of God in all men, the life of the Logos, the life of reason that God has put into all men, which distinguishes us from animals, that we can hear and understand.

How many have quickly said as soon as you start talking about reason, 'Oh you think you can reason your way to God, and this is your own work that you are doing!'? They are not seeing that the very use of reason is the supreme work of the Holy Spirit. They are not understanding that our sin is the failure to see what is clear and that it is so clear that without the work of the Holy Spirit, we will continue not to see it. We truncate the gospel, and we are being blasted left and right, and the walls of Zion are being torn down because we cannot speak what is clear. Baptism is the sign and seal of regeneration, we are being brought out of sin and death. And what do people say? 'If I cannot do it outwardly, how can I be held responsible for it?' This raises the whole question of freedom and responsibility. Listen, listen people of God. Is Christ the Lamb of God, slain from before the foundation of the earth? Were the very words of Christ, that He would later speak on the cross, known and spoken by the psalmist in Psalm 22? "My God, my God, why have you forsaken me?" (Ps. 22:1). The psalmist also spoke of the groanings of Christ, the piercings, and the gambling for His clothes. Is God omniscient? Does God know all these things before they come to pass? Does that hinder the freedom of Christ? "No one takes [my life] from me, but I lay it down of my own accord" (Jn. 10:18). God cannot lie. Does this mean He is not free when He speaks the truth? Why do we raise up this folly of a false view of freedom and then hold it up against God and say, 'The future must be open, God must not know everything, He cannot plan.'

---

6. Gangadean, *The Westminster Confession,* 143–148.

ORDO SALUTIS:
The Order of Salvation[7]

If we understood sin and death and the need for regeneration, we would know that regeneration is the work of the Holy Spirit and that conviction of sin and death comes out of regeneration. We are speaking now about the *ordo salutis*, the order of the application of redemption to the people of God, the effectual calling. And then conversion comes upon conviction of sin and death; that is, we recognize that our lives are empty without God. Our lives are empty, and they are empty because we are without God and we are justly liable for being without God and failing to recognize our Creator. We deserve to be cast off from God. This is the convicting work of the Holy Spirit that comes *after* regeneration. Only when our minds are turned on can we see the contradictoriness and meaninglessness of what we formerly believed. We see the meaninglessness and death, continue to hold on to it, and respond properly to it. Non-believers can see this existential condition, but whether they turn to the Word of God or not is another matter. God not only restores us to life but sustains us in life so we cannot get away. By the grace of God, we respond in faith; this is the irresistible grace of God. Up to the time of regeneration, we are resisting, but from the time of regeneration, when God works inwardly in us to recreate us in knowledge, holiness, and righteousness, we no longer resist. We have to ask ourselves, are we going to object now to the fact that God has restored reason in us, restored us to our right minds? "Shall what is formed say to him who formed it, 'Why did you make me like this?'" (Rom. 9:20b). Can we say, 'I do not think it is reasonable, God, that you made me a reasonable creature'? Is that statement made with thought? The thing formed cannot say to the one that formed it, why have you made me so? Some things are given, and some things are not only given, they are taken. We assume the reality of our being when we question God, including the reality of our rational being and our responsibility for rationality.

Out of regeneration comes conviction of sin and death; out of that comes repentance and faith in Christ, which is conversion. Out of

---

7. Gangadean, *The Westminster Confession*, 143–206; Gangadean, *The Westminster Catechisms*, 191–207.

repentance and faith comes justification. Upon this justification, we are adopted into the family of God and treated as children. Then we have the Holy Spirit coming into our lives to call upon Him, 'Abba, Father.' Being adopted as sons, we have the working of the Holy Spirit to conform us to the image of Jesus Christ our Lord. We have the hope of glory in us. Through all the terrible, terrible conflicts with sin and death that will continue to rage in our lives, we have the hope that Christ has died, that He is the one who baptizes us with the Spirit, and that He sent the Spirit to overcome sin in ourselves and ultimately in the world. We have hope that we may be dashed against the rocks again and again,[8] and by the grace of God we will overcome. We may be dashed against the Holy One, again and again, so that God's Word will remain in us, that we would call upon the Lord, and in due time, the Spirit enables us to overcome. We have the hope of glory in us. One day, we shall be like Him, we shall see Him as He is, and as we behold His glory, we will be transformed into the same image day by day.

CIRCUMCISION AND BAPTISM MEAN REGENERATION

Baptism is a sign and seal of our ingrafting into Christ, our regeneration, and the remission of sins. Our sins are forgiven on the basis of the work of Christ—Christ and Him crucified. If we are cut off from our old life, we are buried with Christ in baptism, and we are raised to live in newness of life. Baptism and circumcision signify the same thing. In Philippians 3:3, we have another line of thought to help us to see who is to be baptized and how we are to be baptized. "For it is we who are the circumcision, we who worship by the Spirit of God, who glory in Christ Jesus, and who put no confidence in the flesh— though I myself have reasons for such confidence" (Phil. 3:3–4). Paul directs this letter to his brothers, the Philippians, who are Gentile believers. He says, "we who are the circumcision." What circumcision signifies has come now upon the Gentiles. The reality of salvation is here; what is intended and what is taught by it has come now. What does circumcision signify? It signifies having a new heart. Circumcise your hearts and not your flesh. He speaks about the circumcision done by the hands of men, and the circumcision that is done by the Spirit,

---

8. *Psalm 137.*

the reality applied to the heart.[9] Circumcision signifies regeneration. Nicodemus should have known this when Jesus declared, "I tell you the truth, no one can see the kingdom of God unless he is born again." "How can a man be born when he is old?" Nicodemus asked. "Surely he cannot enter a second time into his mother's womb to be born!" (Jn. 3:3–4). "You are Israel's teacher," said Jesus, "and do you not understand these things?" (Jn. 3:10). It is possible to miss the meaning. Baptism signifies being born again; it signifies regeneration. With regeneration will come faith, and so baptism is a sign and seal of faith, the righteousness of faith that you have in Christ.

In Colossians 2:11, this connection is made more specific: "In him you were also circumcised, in the putting off of the sinful nature." This is what circumcision signifies. This is spoken to the Colossians, who were Gentiles. They were circumcised, not literally, physically, but they were circumcised in reality in that they put off the sinful nature by the work of regeneration and being born again. One and the same thing signified by both one and the same covenant, one covenant of grace.

> In him you were also circumcised, in the putting off of the sinful nature, not with a circumcision done by the hands of men but with the circumcision done by Christ [through His Spirit], having been buried with him in baptism and raised with him through your faith in the power of God, who raised him from the dead. When you were dead in your sins and in the uncircumcision of your sinful nature, God made you alive [regeneration] with Christ. He forgave us all our sins, having canceled the written code, with its regulations, that was against us and that stood opposed to us; he took it away, nailing it to the cross (Col. 2:11–12).

Circumcision and baptism signify the same thing. This underscores further the unity of the covenant in that Christ is our Passover; mentioned in 1 Corinthians 5:7, the Passover is fulfilled in Christ; Christ is our testator, the one who dies on our behalf. What are we to conclude from this? If circumcision and baptism signify the same thing, do we need an explicit command in the New Testament to baptize infants? The assumption behind that position is that there are two covenants and things have changed, rather than there is one covenant of grace

---

9. *Colossians 2:11–12.*

and there is continuity. We should not expect a command in the New Testament saying we should baptize infants since it is the same as circumcision, and circumcision has been applied to infants in the one covenant of grace by which we are all saved. So those who would deny the unity of the Old and New Testament, and the sameness in meaning of circumcision and baptism, are the ones who are dividing the body of Christ by holding to and teaching this false teaching. It is a failure to understand sign and reality, the covenant of grace, regeneration, and the *ordo salutis* in which God applies salvation.

19

THE DOCTRINE OF BAPTISM
PART II

Acts 1–2; Ephesians 4

CHRIST HAS ACCOMPLISHED REDEMPTION BY HIS LIFE, DEATH, RESURRECTION, ASCENSION, AND SESSION

CHRIST HAS SENT THE HOLY SPIRIT TO APPLY redemption to the hearts of His people. This redemption has been applied from the beginning, from when sin entered the world in Adam. God was the first to proclaim the gospel to Adam in connection with the Word spoken to the serpent. God said, "I will put enmity between you and the woman, and between your offspring and hers; he will crush your head, and you will strike his heel" (Gen. 3:15). Adam believed the promise was certainly going to take place because of the work of the Holy Spirit. He believed that it was certain that the seed of the woman would come and would accomplish redemption. The One to come will *undo* what Adam did by dying on the cross and paying the penalty for sin. He will come as the Lamb of God to take away the sin of the world.[1] This One to come will *do* what Adam failed to do. Adam was called to be fruitful, multiply, fill and rule the earth in such a way as to fill the earth with the knowledge of God.[2] Jesus comes as the Lamb of God to take away the sin of the world and He is the Christ, the Anointed One, the Messiah, the One who is anointed with the Holy Spirit, who

---

1. *John 1:29.*
2. *Isaiah 11:9.*

will send the Spirit upon a people that were to come from Adam, who was to increase in number and multiply.

The redemption of those in Christ comes through the work of the Spirit in regeneration, that His people will be enabled to do the work God had given Adam to do: to fill the earth, disciple all the nations, and fill the earth with the knowledge of God. Jesus, the Word of God, the Son of God incarnate, has come to make God known. Jesus has accomplished redemption, and He sends His Spirit to apply redemption. Redemption was applied before Christ was crucified. The Holy Spirit regenerated men from the beginning. He regenerated our first parents, Adam and Eve, by turning their hearts back to God. The work of regeneration is the work of the Holy Spirit. The Holy Spirit has also worked through the ages to sanctify men, to illumine their minds so that they understand the Word of God and serve God in holiness and righteousness all the days of their lives. No one has begun this life, nor has grown, apart from the work of the Holy Spirit, the giver of life.

JESUS IS THE CHRIST, THE MESSIAH, THE ANOINTED ONE:
He Sends the Holy Spirit in Fullness

Something new has happened since Christ died and ascended. He said, **"Do not leave Jerusalem, but wait for the gift my Father promised, which you have heard me speak about. For John baptized with water, but in a few days you will be baptized with the Holy Spirit"** (Acts 1:4b-5). This is why He is called the Christ, the Messiah, the Anointed One. We use these words, Jesus Christ, again and again. We should use them with understanding: Jesus, the Anointed One; Jesus, anointed with the Holy Spirit, who being anointed with the Holy Spirit, will send the Holy Spirit upon His people to accomplish God's purpose, which was intended from the beginning. Through the Holy Spirit's work, Jesus Christ will accomplish what Adam failed to accomplish. He will have a people, an entire human race, that will live before God under God's Word, exercise dominion, rule in the creation, and develop all the powers latent in the creation in such a way as to reveal the glory of God, who is revealed in everything He has made and every way in which He rules. Christ will accomplish this, and He will accomplish this through the Spirit of God, the blessed Holy Spirit, whom He sent.

Being baptized with the Holy Spirit, we are being immersed in the Holy Spirit. The Holy Spirit is coming upon His people in fullness, which is a difference between the Old and New Testaments. In the Old Testament, He came upon all His people, but not in the fullness with which He comes in the New Testament. It is a difference between being young and not yet of age and what happens when you come of age. There are privileges and responsibilities that are ours when we come of age. Many people look forward to when they are 18 or 21 years old. They can drive a car, do all the important things adults do, and exercise responsibility. They can be married, have a job, and vote. But now, this is coming into full citizenship in the kingdom of God and with it, all our privileges and responsibilities.

MORE THAN REGENERATION AND ILLUMINATION:
You Shall Be Witnesses

Christ has spoken of a twofold purpose in connection with the coming of the Spirit. First, "when he, the Spirit of truth, comes, he will guide you into all truth" (Jn. 16:13a). Oh, what fullness there is in those words "all truth." We begin to see this fullness if we pay attention to God's work in the history of the Church and see what it means that the Holy Spirit will lead the Church, the people of God, into all truth. The leading of the Spirit is more than the illumination and sanctification that is going on individually in the Church. Second, in connection with leading us into all truth, we will be witnesses in all of the world.[3] The Church in the Old Testament did not go into all the earth to make disciples; rather, people came to Jerusalem. There was protection, and a hedge was built around the Church. For centuries, the Church matured in the truth of God and lived with such truth that became indelible. Passover, circumcision, and the Day of Atonement were kept alive by the Church in the Old Testament, and they have become very much a part of the truth of the people of God, indelibly written in the hearts of the people of God through the ages, and we observe these truths.

The Church has come of age, and God wants the Church to go into all the earth and make disciples as Jesus said, "All authority in heaven

---

3. *Matthew 28:18–20.*

and on earth has been given to me. Therefore go and make disciples of all nations" (Matt. 28:18b–19a). That is, *exousia*: the power to act, authority. The Holy Spirit comes upon the Church to give power, *dunamis*, power, might, and strength to exercise the authority given to Christ to make disciples of all nations. This is why the fullness of the Spirit must come upon the Church now, enabling us to do the fullness of the work that we have been called to do.

There is a teaching of Scripture, a foundational teaching, concerning the baptism of the Holy Spirit. We can expect the glorious truths in this teaching that we need to hold on to in order to see clearly if we are to accomplish the work that God intends us to do. This is the positive side. We need this doctrine well laid in our lives. We still have a tremendous amount of work to do, and we will accomplish it as we understand the teachings of the baptism of the Holy Spirit. We can equally expect that a lot of sin will come in, distorting this doctrine, and many will turn aside. We must understand this teaching in order to avoid the error that is so widespread in the Church today concerning the baptism of the Spirit.[4] These are reasons why we need to understand the teaching of baptism, the baptism of the Spirit, and the fullness of the Spirit.

Christ has accomplished redemption. He will *undo* what Adam did, and He does so as the Lamb of God, dying to take away the sins of the world. He will *do* what Adam failed to do. He does so as Christ, the Anointed One, who sends His Spirit upon His people to enable them to be witnesses in all the earth.

THE BEGINNING WORK OF THE HOLY SPIRIT

We can distinguish between the beginning work of the Holy Spirit and the continuing work of the Holy Spirit. This is a distinction that has not been made, and this distinction needs to be made.[5] We should understand the teaching regarding regeneration; it is universal and common throughout the Church in all ages. In John 3:3, Jesus said to

---

4. Gangadean, "Paper No. 122: Contra Charismatic Distinctive," in *The Logos Papers*, 651–653; Gangadean, *On Natural and Revealed Theology*, 223–228.

5. Gangadean, "Paper No. 16: The Historic Christian Faith," in *The Logos Papers*, 103–114; Gangadean, *The Westminster Confession*, xix–xxix, 349–351, 107–118.

Nicodemus, "I tell you the truth, no one can see the kingdom of God unless he is born again." This was spoken of in ages past through the sign of circumcision. The need for a new heart continues in the Church today through the sign of baptism.[6] Water baptism in the name of the Father, Son, and Holy Spirit, signifies regeneration. Regeneration is the work of the Holy Spirit and has been with us through the ages. God, the Holy Spirit, has illumined His people through all ages but now will illuminate us in a greater, fuller way as we engage in a greater, fuller work.

In John 16:5–15, Jesus speaks about the coming of the Holy Spirit. He knew that the work of the Holy Spirit has been there in history, but He speaks about Himself sending the Spirit.

> Now I am going to him who sent me, yet none of you asks me, "Where are you going?" Because I have said these things, you are filled with grief. But I tell you the truth: It is for your good that I am going away. Unless I go away, the Counselor will not come to you; but if I go, I will send him to you. When he comes, he will convict the world of guilt in regard to sin and righteousness and judgment: in regard to sin, because men do not believe in me; in regard to righteousness, because I am going to the Father, where you can see me no longer; and in regard to judgment, because the prince of this world now stands condemned (Jn. 16:5–11).

The work of regeneration is manifested in conviction of sin, righteousness, judgment, repentance, and faith.

THE CONTINUING WORK OF THE HOLY SPIRIT

Jesus continued,

> I have much more to say to you, more than you can now bear. But when he, the Spirit of truth, comes, he will guide you into all truth. He will not speak on his own; he will speak only what he hears, and he will tell you what is yet to come. He will bring glory to me by taking from what is mine and making it known to you. All that

---

6. Gangadean, *The Westminster Confession*, 299–305; Gangadean, *The Westminster Catechisms*, 283–286.

belongs to the Father is mine. That is why I said the Spirit will take
from what is mine and make it known to you (Jn. 16:12–15).

Jesus speaks about the Spirit coming and convicting the world; this
does not mean that the Spirit has not convicted before being sent out.
There is a distinction between the conviction working in the hearts of
covenant people in the Old Testament and those of the world. They,
too, needed conviction of sin, and they, too, needed regeneration because circumcision was applied. But now He said, "he will convict the
world," those outside the boundaries of the covenant, of the same reality of sin and death and the need for faith in Christ. This is the work
of regeneration, and what accompanies regeneration, at the beginning,
which has been going on through the centuries. First within the covenant people and now beyond. There is an enlargement of the work of
the Holy Spirit, and the specific point on which it is being enlarged is
that He will convict the world.

Think about this: How much of the world remains to be convicted
by the Holy Spirit? Jesus came to bring this about. He will do this in
connection with the preaching of the Word. Jesus said, "But when he,
the Spirit of truth, comes, he will guide you into all truth" (Jn. 16:13a).
He will guide us, lead us, into all truth. Jesus had much to share with
the Church, but we could not bear it then. Think about all the Church
has learned through the centuries and how it has come to learn. Jesus
knew all this. He knew the Church needed to learn these things, but
we were not able to bear it. The Holy Spirit will come, did come, abides
with the Church, and guides us. Notice, He did not just deliver the
Church all at once; He guides us, the people of God, the Church, into
all truth. This has been the work that has been going on throughout
the centuries, the work of the Holy Spirit, and it is still going on and
still needs to go on. As we understand the teaching of the baptism of
the Holy Spirit and how this works, how the Holy Spirit is guiding us
into all truth and making us witnesses to all the world (those two are
intimately connected), we will see how we can benefit from the work
of the Holy Spirit and how the work of the Holy Spirit can and must
continue in us and through us. We will give ourselves to this work and
not be tossed back and forth by every wind of doctrine as has been the

case in much of Church history.[7] Instead, we will come into maturity, the maturity of the sons of God, and we will come into the unity of the faith as the people of God. This is part of the work of the Holy Spirit and we will be witnesses unto the ends of the world. Jesus came to *undo* what Adam did and to *do* what Adam failed to do. He does so as the Anointed One who sends the Holy Spirit upon the Church to guide us into all truth that we might be witnesses in all the world.

THE SUPERNATURAL WORK OF THE HOLY SPIRIT

Tongues at Pentecost

When the Spirit first came upon the Church, the Spirit came in a supernatural manifestation. It was a sign, and we should understand this sign in Acts 2. The Spirit came upon the Church; they were to wait for the Spirit to come, and the Spirit did come. When the Spirit came, He came with a blowing of violent wind from heaven. A certain amount of violence is connected with the work of the Spirit. There was a rushing, mighty wind, which can have tremendous force. "**Suddenly a sound like the blowing of a violent wind came from heaven and filled the whole house where they were sitting**" (Acts 2:2). It is a sign of the power of the Spirit coming upon the Church. Let us not overlook this, "**a sound like the blowing of a violent wind.**" This tells us that the Holy Spirit will come on the earth and, through the people of God, will accomplish with great power the work God intended for the Church to accomplish.

Accompanying the sound were tongues of fire. "**They saw what seemed to be tongues of fire that separated and came to rest on each of them**" (Acts 2:3). Tongues of fire. What does this speak of? The Word of God spoken will bring destruction to the kingdom of darkness. The fire will burn the chaff that is in the world. When we speak the Word of God, we will melt the *stoicheia* of this world, the foundational principles of this world. As Peter said in 2 Peter 3:10, "But the day of the Lord will come like a thief. The heavens will disappear with a roar; the elements will be destroyed by fire, and the earth and everything in it will be laid bare." The world will be destroyed with fire, which symbolizes

---

7. *Ephesians 4:14.*

destruction. It is not a literal, physical fire; it is not a literal, physical world that we destroy but the world as a system of unbelief with the self at the center and not God. This will be destroyed through the preaching of the Word of God. The Church is enabled to do this as the Holy Spirit comes upon us; there were **"tongues of fire."** This is speaking of the Word that will be spoken and how destructive it will be. The gates of hell cannot withstand the onslaught of the Church.[8] The seed of the woman will crush the head of the serpent.[9] The light shines in the darkness, and the darkness cannot overcome it;[10] cannot resist or stand up against it. Yet it does not appear that way; we seem like two small flocks of goats on the mountainside with a vast army covering the rest of the countryside, as is pictured in the days of Israel when enemies came up against them.[11] We seem so small, tiny, weak, and scattered. Yet God is always pleased to take the things that are nothing to bring to naught the things that are. Let us not go by appearances. Let us go by the truth of Scripture and the truth concerning the baptism of the Spirit and what is intended.

We are pushed back to the wall in many ways, but this is not the end of the story. Through that very being pushed back, we will be enabled by the Holy Spirit to understand truth more fully. God will use even this pushing back to guide us into all truth. Let us not be discouraged or despair about this when we are being pressed back, especially when we are still pressed back and see no end in sight. There is an end. There are foundations already in place. There is work that God, the Holy Spirit, has done in the Church, and we will come back to what has already been accomplished and go further. We will speak with tongues of fire, and that Word will be like a rushing mighty wind. We will accomplish the purpose that God has intended. Ezekiel was asked, "Son of man, can these bones live?" (Ez. 37:3a). Ezekiel was taken, in the Spirit, to a vision of a valley of dry bones. This is pretty desperate and desolate, isn't it? Yet the Spirit came upon those bones, and they came to life. The bones were rattling and coming together. These bones, these dry bones, all 206 bones of the body gathering together; they will come

---

8. *Matthew 16:18.*

9. *Genesis 3:15.*

10. *John 1:5.*

11. *1 Kings 20:22–29.*

together by the work of the Holy Spirit. There are at least 30,000 denominations in Christianity, yet they will come together. Individual congregations will come together, and the people of God will come together, because this is the express intended purpose of the work of the Holy Spirit through the work of the pastor-teachers. We will not go back to the early, beginning work of the Holy Spirit and remain immature, but we will build on the work of the Holy Spirit through Church history. Many of you have come from charismatic, Pentecostal backgrounds in which you were raised. Much is made there of the baptism of the Spirit, but it is a teaching of baptism that has distorted the work of the Holy Spirit. Therefore, we have to guard against this teaching. We have to see positively what the work of the Holy Spirit is and guard against misunderstanding it.

The Spirit came in this way, **"All of them were filled with the Holy Spirit and began to speak in other tongues as the Spirit enabled them"** (Acts 2:4). Speaking in tongues, too, is a sign of what God will do. There was one other major event like this in world history. It was the Tower of Babel, where the tongues of men were confused. The language of mankind, the one language, was confused and became many languages, and the people were scattered over the face of the earth.[12] Pentecost is the beginning of the reversal of that whole process. The Spirit of God came upon men, enabled them to speak in other tongues, and men from all parts of the earth could understand them. **"Now there were staying in Jerusalem God-fearing Jews from every nation under heaven. When they heard this sound, a crowd came together in bewilderment, because each one heard them speaking in his own language"** (Acts 2:5–6). God does not continue in this particular way, but it is a sign of what is to be done. God will enable the Church to speak to all the peoples, nations, kingdoms, tribes, and languages of the earth and bring them together in the body of Christ, in Zion, that holy hill of which glorious things are spoken.[13] Tyre and Ethiopia and Babylon and Egypt, all of these nations will come because of the work of the Holy Spirit, even though our backs are being pressed against the wall. The Holy Spirit will do His work, accomplish it, and enable us

---

12. *Genesis 11:1–9.*

13. *Revelation 7:9.*

to understand more. He is the Spirit of truth who will guide us into all truth.[14]

HISTORIC CHRISTIANITY:
The Work of the Pastor-Teachers Through History

We see in Acts 15 how the Holy Spirit guides the Church into all truth. This is the characteristic way in which the Holy Spirit accomplishes His purpose. "Some men came down from Judea to Antioch and were teaching the brothers: 'Unless you are circumcised, according to the custom taught by Moses, you cannot be saved'" (Acts 15:1). These were Jews who had come to believe in Christ. Then in verse 5, "some of the believers who belonged to the party of the Pharisees stood up and said, 'The Gentiles must be circumcised and required to obey the law of Moses.'" What is going on here is typical of the conflict and struggle that we have throughout Church history and it must be expected. Those who were in the Church, the Jewish people who came to believe that Jesus is the Christ incarnate, brought with them understanding and misunderstanding from their past. They brought their historical practices, an admixture of understanding and misunderstanding, and their cultural baggage. This is exactly the process we will find as we go into all the world, into all the nations. When they come to Christ, every nation will bring their cultural baggage, too. Hindus will bring it, Muslims will bring it, Marxists will bring it, and everyone will bring their baggage.

The Greeks came and brought their cultural baggage. It is still with us, and we are still fighting it off: Greek dualism, Greek otherworldliness that emphasizes the vision of life of the soul apart from the body.[15] It has affected some of the leaders in the Church, Augustine and Aquinas, as they brought into the Church the teachings of Plato and Aristotle and built on their work.[16] Particularly, they built on their epistemology, their theory of knowledge (how we come to know). The process of taking thoughts captive is part of the Holy Spirit guiding us into all truth. We need to deal with this baggage and overcome it. This baggage

---

14. *John 16:13.*

15. Gangadean, *On Natural and Revealed Theology,* 9–32.

16. Gangadean, *History of Philosophy,* 87–105, 111–114, 121–126.

contains falsehood that needs to be worked through. God, the Holy Spirit, will guide the Church into all truth by enabling us to struggle with this baggage until we overcome it, come into unity, and go forward with it. This is the plan.

It is understandable that the first group that were brought in would be those from the Old Testament, the party of the Pharisees who converted, who had practiced circumcision and did not see and understand exactly how this transition would go. They were saying that circumcision was required for salvation, not seeing how Old Testament practices were types and shadows pointing to the New Testament, how there can be continuity of the truth but change in outward form from circumcision to baptism—that was not seen. It was as if all believers were to continue to come up to Jerusalem to observe Passover rather than the Church going into all the world. Instead, now we observe the Lord's Supper. They did not understand this, so the challenge came, and the Church had to struggle to respond to it.

What happened in Acts 15 is the standard for the Church through Church history.[17] Who came together? It was no longer just the Apostles, but now the Apostles and elders. It was Apostles and elders sharing in authority and decision-making. That authority continues now in the elders and the work of the pastor-teachers in the Church and through Church history. From time to time, as the Church is faithful in its witness and going out against the world, the world strikes back with its falsehood, trying to mix truth and falsehood, and the Church is going to have to overcome. The work of the Holy Spirit will guide us into all truth, that we might be witnesses in all the world, to bring all the world together. Do you see how this work is very much before us? The extraordinary supernatural work of the Holy Spirit in the beginning and the continuing work of the Holy Spirit through Church history is before us.

Notice how this work goes: In Acts 15, they met to consider the nature of God's work in history, "The apostles and elders met to consider this question. After much discussion, Peter got up and addressed them" (Acts 15:6–7a). "After much discussion," Peter got up and spoke; James got up and concluded it, and the assembly agreed. The assembly,

---

17. Gangadean, "Paper No. 16: The Historic Christian Faith," 103–114; "Paper No. 60: The Spiritual War (Part II)," in *The Logos Papers*, 329–330.

sometimes called the synod, is another word for the Church's general assembly of the elders. This is why we are Presbyterian; this is why we believe in Church councils and assembly. Not that these have ultimate authority over the Word of God, but this is the way God, the Holy Spirit, works through Church history.

After much discussion, they came to agreement. We should expect *much* discussion. Why? This is the process by which God, the Holy Spirit, leads us into all truth. There is still much truth to be discovered because there is much falsehood out there in the world, and those falsehoods have to be taken captive.[18] It will not be easy in one way, but it will be easy in another way. It will not be easy because of sin in us, but because of the Holy Spirit in us and the foundational truth, it will be easy. If we build on the work of the Holy Spirit through Church history, if we build on the Westminster Confession of Faith, which is the high-water mark of the work of the pastor-teachers through Church history, we can do it! The opening words of the Westminster Confession of Faith are:

> Although the light of nature, and the works of creation and provi-
> dence do so far manifest the goodness, wisdom, and power of God,
> as to leave men unexcusable; yet are they not sufficient to give that
> knowledge of God, and of his will, which is necessary unto salva-
> tion (WCF 1.1).

What are these opening words speaking of? The clarity of general revelation.[19] Where is the Church in relation to this? Not noticing it. Not speaking of it. There are other such truths in the Westminster Confession of Faith. I should say that in some ways, the truth is taken for granted, and it is going to be challenged. Since the Westminster Confession of Faith was written in 1648, it has been challenged for the past 350 years, and we have been pushed back against the wall in terms of the following: The Church has 'faith,' and the world has 'reason.' The world has science and says, 'In the name of science, reason, and experience, we claim this ground. You have blind faith; you cannot show

---

18. *2 Corinthians 10:4–5.*

19. Gangadean, "Paper No. 102: The Clarity of General Revelation," 527–52; "Paper No. 41: What Is Clear About God," 225–229; "Paper No. 112: Why General Revelation Is Basic in the Christian Worldview," in *The Logos Papers,* 583–585.

it; you can only keep it private. Privatize your religion, keep it personal and for yourself, and do not bring it to this public arena unless you can show this is so. Unless you have some authority to back up what you are saying, do not bring it or try to sneak it in through the back door or window. You come through the front door or do not come at all.' The world will despise any attempt of Christians who try to be sneaky in their witness.

We must come through the front door and boldly, yet graciously, speak the Word of God, and the Holy Spirit will guide us into all truth. That means we, the people of God, will continue to be pressed against the wall until we learn to respond to the challenges that God has brought, just as the Church did in Acts 15. When they concluded the Council of Jerusalem, they sent men out with the letters of the requirements, and in verse 28, they said, "It seemed good to the Holy Spirit and to us not to burden you with anything beyond the following requirements." They sent the men out with letters to speak the truth to overcome the things that were dividing in the Church. The baptism of the Spirit entails that He will guide us into all truth so that we might be witnesses to all the earth to make disciples of all the nations. This is the ordinary way in which this work is done.

THE WORK REMAINING TO BE DONE

Let us turn to Ephesians 4:1–3.

> As a prisoner for the Lord, then, I urge you to live a life worthy of the calling you have received. Be completely humble and gentle; be patient, bearing with one another in love. Make every effort to keep the unity of the Spirit through the bond of peace.

Maintain the *unity of the Spirit,* get along with one another, be humble, and do not think of ourselves more highly than we ought, but let us esteem one another highly.[20] This is part of the work of the Holy Spirit. Maintain the unity of the Spirit, care for one another, say 'hello' to one another, and encourage one another. Do simple things like this; do not be so self-centered that you cannot see the other, our brothers

---

20. *Romans 12:3.*

and sisters in Christ. This is why it says, "Be completely humble and gentle; be patient, bearing with one another in love."

> Be completely humble and gentle; be patient, bearing with one another in love. Make every effort to keep the unity of the Spirit through the bond of peace. There is one body and one Spirit—just as you were called to one hope when you were called—one Lord, one faith, one baptism; one God and Father of all, who is over all and through all and in all (Eph. 4:2–6).

The diversity and the purpose of this is unity through which there is diversity. "But to each one of us grace has been given as Christ apportioned it. This is why it says: 'When he ascended on high, he led captives in his train and gave gifts to men'" (Eph. 4:7–8).

Another part of the doctrine of the baptism of the Spirit is that He "gave gifts to men." At the beginning of the Church, some of the gifts were supernatural, but there is an ordinary way that these gifts work. "What does 'he ascended' mean except that he also descended to the lower, earthly regions? He who descended is the very one who ascended higher than all the heavens, in order to fill the whole universe" (Eph. 4:9–10). To fill everything in every way.[21] Adam was to fill the earth with the knowledge of God by filling everything in every way.

"Jesus came to them and said, 'All authority in heaven and on earth has been given to me'" (Matt. 28:18). All authority. Every knee shall bow, and every tongue confess, that Jesus Christ is Lord.[22] His lordship in every area of life is to be established. He gave gifts to men so that the fullness of all things might be accomplished. The gifts of the Holy Spirit are to accomplish the purpose of filling everything in every way, to fill the whole universe.

> It was he who gave some to be apostles, some to be prophets, some to be evangelists, and some to be pastors and teachers, to prepare God's people for works of service, so that the body of Christ may be built up until we all reach unity in the faith and in the knowledge of the Son of God and become mature, attaining to the whole measure of the fullness of Christ (Eph. 4:11–13).

---

21. *Ephesians 1:23.*
22. *Isaiah 45:23; Romans 14:11; Philippians 2:10.*

This is why we have the baptism of the Holy Spirit. This is why we have the Holy Spirit fully poured out on the people of God, that we may attain to the whole measure of the fullness of Christ. Christ says the Holy Spirit will guide us into all truth.[23] By dealing with each nation, each people, each falsehood, and each division we must wrestle with, after much discussion, we will come to a common understanding, declare that word, and come into the *unity of the faith.* We will do this through the work of the Holy Spirit, the purpose for which the Spirit was given, the baptism of the Spirit. Then we will become mature.

> **Then we will no longer be infants, tossed back and forth by the waves, and blown here and there by every wind of teaching and by the cunning and craftiness of men in their deceitful scheming. Instead, speaking the truth in love, we will in all things grow up into him who is the Head, that is, Christ. From him the whole body, joined and held together by every supporting ligament, grows and builds itself up in love, as each part does its work (Eph. 4:14–16).**

We no longer have apostles and prophets, and there is no new revelation of the Spirit; the revelation is completed. Tongues and prophecies ended when the Scripture was completed.[24] The Scripture was to give revelation of the One to come. Unless you say this, you are opening up the whole Bible to new revelation. This revelation has been closed; it has been completed. The work of the Holy Spirit continues in various ways in the Church that we might be built up as each part does its work. There is no extra part in your body. God has made the body in His wisdom and with unity, nothing extra, nothing lacking. Each part does its work, the work of the Holy Spirit.

How does this apply to us? We are to benefit from the work of the Holy Spirit through Church history as the Spirit leads us into all truth. We are to know how men have contended earnestly for the faith as Jude says: "I felt I had to write and urge you to contend for the faith that was once for all entrusted to the saints" (Jd. 1:3b). People will come into the Church and bring with them their damnable heresies, and this is one of the places where we must contend for the faith, not

---

23. *John 16:13.*

24. Gangadean, "Paper No. 11: From General Revelation to Special Revelation," in *The Logos Papers,* 69–73.

just outside of the Church but in the Church. Right now, a teaching called 'open theism' says God does not know the future. In the name of freedom, a false understanding of freedom, they say, 'God does not know the future; He is learning, too, and He is not compromising human freedom.' Open theism is bringing damnable heresies into the Church, and we have to contend with this. But if we build on the work of the Holy Spirit that has gone before us, we will be able to handle these challenges. Behind this doctrine of open theism is a root doctrine and assumption of the nature of freedom that has not been discussed and dealt with.[25]

The Holy Spirit wants to guide us into all truth. It is the ordinary process to engage after having much discussion. Do not claim to be a simple Christian and avoid the discussion process. It does not mean you rush into it either, but we are to go into it building on the work of the Holy Spirit through the pastor-teachers in Church history in the Westminster Confession. Christ wanted to guide us into all truth, but we were not able to bear it then. The Holy Spirit will guide us into all truth through Church history. We must respond to this and come into the unity of the faith in the Church so that we might be witnesses in all the world. Jesus prayed that they might be one that the world might believe.[26] We have the teaching of the baptism of the Spirit, the Spirit given to us to lead us into all truth, with greater fullness, that we might be witnesses in all the world. God has been doing this work and will continue this work as we understand, believe, and embrace with our whole heart the baptism of the Spirit and the work of the Holy Spirit through the pastor-teachers through Church history.

We will give ourselves to more fully contending for the truth of God, but we cannot do so unless we build on the basics. Those who want to go back to the New Testament Church bypass all of Church history. They are bypassing the work of the Holy Spirit through Church history. The charismatics who think that the Holy Spirit comes as a second experience apart from conversion do not see the transitional role of the gifts, a separate experience given to those who were believers under the Old and came to the New. Those who say the gifts continue do

---

25. Gangadean, *Philosophical Foundation*, 155; "Paper No. 18: Salvation by Grace," in *The Logos Papers*, 119–122.

26. *John 17:21.*

not see that the Scripture has been completed. Those who expect to witness through miracles do not understand that miracles were signs of the Apostles of their apostolic authority. They do not understand the clarity of general revelation. Those who want, through the Holy Spirit, miracles of healing, are not understanding God's love and the way the curse works.[27] A whole system of teaching goes along with a charismatic/Pentecostal teaching that keeps the Church in a state of immaturity.[28] It is not the fullness intended by God in giving the Holy Spirit to lead us into all truth. This teaching has not built on the work of the pastor-teachers in Church history, which is the way we should come into the greatest truth in the fullness that God has for us. We have to understand the teaching of the baptism of the Spirit. He will guide us into all truth, and we will be witnesses in all the earth. May God enable us to take to heart the baptism of the Spirit to accomplish the work that God has given His Church.

---

27. Gangadean, *The Biblical Worldview*, 55–68, 275–294.

28. Gangadean, *On Natural and Revealed Theology*, 223–228.

20

LAYING ON OF HANDS

John 2:12–22

¹²After this he went down to Capernaum with his mother and brothers and his disciples. There they stayed for a few days.

¹³When it was almost time for the Jewish Passover, Jesus went up to Jerusalem. ¹⁴In the temple courts he found men selling cattle, sheep and doves, and others sitting at tables exchanging money. ¹⁵So he made a whip out of cords, and drove all from the temple area, both sheep and cattle; he scattered the coins of the money changers and overturned their tables. ¹⁶To those who sold doves he said, "Get these out of here! How dare you turn my Father's house into a market!"

¹⁷His disciples remembered that it is written: "Zeal for your house will consume me."

¹⁸Then the Jews demanded of him, "What miraculous sign can you show us to prove your authority to do all this?"

¹⁹Jesus answered them, "Destroy this temple, and I will raise it again in three days."

²⁰The Jews replied, "It has taken forty-six years to build this temple, and you are going to raise it in three days?" ²¹But the temple he had spoken of was his body. ²²After he was raised from the dead, his disciples recalled what he had said. Then they believed the Scripture and the words that Jesus had spoken.

REVIEW:
God's Continual Call to Repentance through the Curse

PREVIOUSLY, WE SPOKE ABOUT REPENTANCE from works that lead to death. God calls us to repentance, and God's continuing call to repentance is through the curse.[1] When we did not respond to the inward call of shame or the external call of self-examination, "Where are you?" (Gen. 3:9b), God imposed the curse. In the daily trials of life of experiencing the curse, we should consider this and take it to heart: God is calling us to repentance. He uses the curse to restrain us from going as far away from Him as we might. God uses the curse of toil, strife, old age, sickness, and death in many forms and intensities to call us back to Himself and to restrain and recall us. For those who have come back to Him, He uses the curse to sanctify further. We see this clearly working in the case of Job. Job, though he was the most righteous man in all the earth, had still come short, and God used the curse to call him even further to Himself. So there are many levels at which the curse works, and we are being called back. Particularly, we should remember that we have been called back from self-deception about our seeking God. Sin is manifested in not seeking, not under-standing, and not doing what is right.[2] Not seeking is manifested in the fact that we do not know what is clear about God.[3] We have not acknowledged what is clear about God. If we had been seeking God diligently, we would have seen what was clear.[4] How many would have seen what is clear? Anyone who was seeking. There is a lot of self-de-ception in the world; there is a lot of self-deception in us about seeking God. The call to repentance is the call to acknowledge our self-decep-tion, deal with our self-justification, turn and seek Him diligently, and acknowledge Him as He is.

---

1. Gangadean, *The Biblical Worldview,* 55–68, 219–294.

2. *Romans 3:10–11.*

3. Gangadean, *Philosophical Foundation,* 71–161; Gangadean, *History of Philosophy,* 47–58; Gangadean, Gangadean, *The Westminster Confession,* 1–13; Gangadean, "Paper No. 3: The Principle of Clarity," 15–20; "Paper No. 39: Clarity," in *The Logos Papers,* 217–220.

4. Gangadean, "Paper No. 102: The Clarity of General Revelation," 527–529; "Paper No. 41: What Is Clear About God," 225–229; "Paper No. 112: Why General Revelation Is Basic in the Christian Worldview," in *The Logos Papers,* 583–585.

ORDINATION:
Set Apart for the Work

The next topic in the sermon series on foundation is the laying on of hands. Literally, hands are laid on people for particular purposes. Hands are laid on them to set them apart for the work to which God has called them. One of the first manifestations of this is in Acts 13:2. If we look at this in context, we see how it came about.

> In the church at Antioch there were prophets and teachers: Barnabas, Simeon called Niger, Lucius of Cyrene, Manaen (who had been brought up with Herod the tetrarch) and Saul [that is, Paul]. While they were worshiping the Lord and fasting, the Holy Spirit said, "Set apart for me Barnabas and Saul for the work to which I have called them." So after they had fasted and prayed, they placed their hands on them and sent them off (Acts 13:1–3).

God, the Holy Spirit, called the Church to separate and set apart, or ordain, Barnabas and Saul for work, and this was done through the laying on of hands through fasting and prayer, which was in the context of worship.

We should know that this did not happen without context, and as we go back to Acts 11:19, we see the prior context:

> Now those who had been scattered by the persecution in connection with Stephen traveled as far as Phoenicia, Cyprus and Antioch, telling the message only to Jews. Some of them, however, men from Cyprus and Cyrene, went to Antioch and began to speak to Greeks also, telling them the good news about the Lord Jesus. The Lord's hand was with them, and a great number of people believed and turned to the Lord. News of this reached the ears of the church at Jerusalem, and they sent Barnabas to Antioch. When he arrived and saw the evidence of the grace of God, he was glad and encouraged them all to remain true to the Lord with all their hearts. He was a good man, full of the Holy Spirit and faith, and a great number of people were brought to the Lord (Acts 11:19–24).

We are seeing how it is that men are set apart when hands are laid on them. Barnabas had shown his commitment and dedication to the Lord's work earlier when he gave his land. He was a son of consolation; he was an encourager. Barnabas had also been in contact with Saul earlier. The church in Jerusalem sent Barnabas up to Antioch to further the work, and when he saw how God was working, he thought of Saul of Tarsus.

> Then Barnabas went to Tarsus to look for Saul, and when he found him, he brought him to Antioch. So for a whole year Barnabas and Saul met with the church and taught great numbers of people. The disciples were called Christians first at Antioch (Acts 11:25–26).

It was in the context of Saul's conversion and witness and Barnabas' ministry that he was sent to Antioch, and the work prospered under Barnabas. Barnabas brought Saul of Tarsus, and the work prospered further under their joint ministry. Saul and Barnabas were ministering at Antioch for an entire year, and in this context, Barnabas and Saul were set apart, and hands were laid on them. They had a *proven* ministry, which must be kept in mind when we speak about authority and the laying on of hands. They had a proven ministry, and it is in this context that it says, "Set apart for me Barnabas and Saul for the work to which I have called them" (Acts 13:2b).

The Hebrew word for 'consecrate' is translated as ordination, as Aaron was ordained. It is the Hebrew word *yad*. It is a primitive term referring to the hand that is open, as the hand that is open is being laid on the person in the ordination. The context of the open hand being laid on someone is showing that a gift is being given to the person. Paul spoke about this gift that is given in 1 Timothy 4:14: "Do not neglect your gift, which was given you through a prophetic message when the body of elders laid their hands on you." Here is the Hebrew term *yad*, an open hand being laid on, and a gift is imparted.

Imparting of a Gift and Recognition of Authority

There are two aspects of this teaching about the laying on of hands. One has to do with the gift being imparted, and secondly, the setting apart, in a public way, for the work to which God has called us. This is a foundational truth, and the question is: Is this just for some in the ministry, or is it for all? The practice has not been laying hands on each and every one in terms of imparting gifts. There is a good reason for this because gifts are given to *all* by the Holy Spirit. As they stir up that gift that is given to them by the Holy Spirit (and it is not always by the laying on of hands), they come into a position of ministry and service. As the church recognizes the members' ministry and service, they are set apart for that particular work. There is an intimate and necessary connection between these two aspects of the teaching of the laying on of hands: (1) imparting of the gift, and (2) recognition and setting apart.

All members of the body of Christ have gifts. Each and every member has a gift according to the teaching of Scripture. Is there some sense in which each and everyone is set apart for a particular work, and is there some sense in which that setting apart for their particular work may be recognized by the rest of the church? We can, by good necessary consequences, infer both, even though it has not been the practice to lay hands on each and every one. In a sense, the church may recognize the varying gifts that there are, and make room for, allow, encourage, and receive the activity of various gifts operating. Once we connect this to the body of Christ, that we are all members of the body, we see that we all have some particular function. We all have a particular gift, and we are to recognize it, make room for it, and honor people according to their gifts and abilities. As this becomes explicit, we may speak of this as a setting apart—recognizing and laying on of hands—for a purpose.

The laying on of hands is to be done with care. In 1 Timothy 5:22, Paul says, "Do not be hasty in the laying on of hands, and do not share in the sins of others. Keep yourself pure." "Do not be hasty in the laying on of hands." The church was not hasty in the laying on of hands on Paul and Barnabas. Barnabas had a proven ministry, and Paul had a proven ministry; they bore fruit. They showed that they could do this, and the results proved it: there was increase in the church as they witnessed an entire year. Before someone is set apart or recognized in any particular way by the church, they must show by their lives, by the stirring up of the gift that is within them, by its exercise, and by ministering according to the proportion of faith that God has given them, that they have this ability. Then, the church recognizes what God is doing and honors it.

The laying on of hands is a foundational doctrine. It is the recognition of the gifts that God has given to the church and the authority that the church has to recognize the existence and exercise of those gifts. We might put it this way more technically: the Holy Spirit endows the church with gifts, power, and *dunamis*. This is said in Acts 1:8, "But you will receive power when the Holy Spirit comes on you." In having this power, we exercise it, the church recognizes it, and we are in positions of authority (*exousia*). There is a connection between having a gift and having authority and the recognition of that authority by the laying on of hands.

Let us look at another Scripture in 2 Timothy 1:6, where Paul exhorts Timothy, "For this reason I remind you to fan into flame the gift of God, which is in you through the laying on of my hands." There is a gift in Timothy, and he was to fan it into flames, and when he did this, it became manifest. When *we* do this, when we exercise ourselves in the particular area of gift and ability that God has given us, it becomes manifest. Then, in connection with the continual manifestation of ability in this area, the church recognizes the gift and sets persons apart. The doctrine that a gift is given to every one is plainly taught in Scripture.

As we go into this message, we are going to come head-on—clashing—with a faulty view of authority. That is why I read the passage in Matthew 21:23, "By what authority are you doing these things?" This was asked of Jesus as He was questioned by the authorities. Sometimes, those in a position of authority but lacking a certain gift and ability may question those who do have the gift and ability, which have been proven. We have to be alert that from the very beginning, gifts are imparted, the gifts are exercised, and then it is recognized in terms of the fruit that is borne by being set apart through the laying on of hands. Keep this basic context in mind so we can work through many problems people have had about how we come into and exercise authority.

Gifts Are Given to Every Member of the Body

The fact that a gift is given to every one is stated in a number of places. The two primary passages are 1 Corinthians 12 and Romans 12. Let us look at both of these passages.

> Now about spiritual gifts, brothers, I do not want you to be ignorant. You know that when you were pagans, somehow or other you were influenced and led astray to mute idols. Therefore I tell you that no one who is speaking by the Spirit of God says, "Jesus be cursed," and no one can say, "Jesus is Lord," except by the Holy Spirit. There are different kinds of gifts, but the same Spirit. There

are different kinds of service, but the same Lord. There are different kinds of working, but the same God works all of them in all men. Now to each one the manifestation of the Spirit is given for the common good. To one there is given through the Spirit the message of wisdom, to another the message of knowledge by means of the same Spirit, to another faith by the same Spirit, to another gifts of healing by that one Spirit, to another miraculous powers, to another prophecy, to another distinguishing between spirits, to another speaking in different kinds of tongues, and to still another the interpretation of tongues. All these are the work of one and the same Spirit, and he gives them to each one, just as he determines (1 Cor. 12:1–11).

Scripture teaches that everyone in the Church has a gift, and this is made more explicit in the following verses:

The body is a unit, though it is made up of many parts; and though all its parts are many, they form one body. So it is with Christ. For we were all baptized by one Spirit into one body—whether Jews or Greeks, slave or free—and we were all given the one Spirit to drink (1 Cor. 12:12–13).

All the diverse backgrounds make no difference with respect to having a gift in the body of Christ. Male or female, slave or free, covenant children or non-covenant children, we are all in the body of Christ, we are each a member of the body, we have a particular function, and that is our individual gift. The body is not made up of one part but of many, and here, the diversity of the body is being expressed. We tend to have a monolithic view of gifts, but there is great diversity in the body and many gifts. Each one has a gift. We need not emphasize this further.

Let us look at Romans 12:3–8, "For by the grace given me I say to every one of you: Do not think of yourself more highly than you ought, but rather think of yourself with sober judgment, in accordance with the measure of faith God has given you" (Rom. 12:3). Having understanding and discerning needs and concerns in relation to Christ in particular areas is the measure of faith that God has given us. We have different sensitivities, we notice different things, and we have to learn to work together as a body.

Just as each of us has one body with many members, and these members do not all have the same function, so in Christ we who are many form one body, and each member belongs to all the others. We have different gifts, according to the grace given us. If a man's gift is prophesying, let him use it in proportion to his faith. If it is serving, let him serve; if it is teaching, let him teach; if it is encouraging, let him encourage; if it is contributing to the needs of others, let him give generously; if it is leadership, let him govern diligently; if it is showing mercy, let him do it cheerfully (Rom. 12:4–8).

In this message, we are not elaborating on particular gifts; we are saying that each one has a gift given by the Holy Spirit, and we are to exercise that gift.

Let us open this up further. There is a connection between the Spirit giving gifts, the exercise and recognition of these gifts (its authority), and the work of service that God has called us to do. This is how the body of Christ is built up as each part does its work. Each one has a work to do. No one can say, 'Well, I don't know. I can't say anything. I'm just in the church and glad to be here.' You should not only be in the church but also be aware of your service and be diligent in stirring up the gift that is within you. Learn how to use your gift, and be encouraged and exhorted by others to do so "that the body of Christ may be built up" (Eph. 4:12b). We are not going to be built up as a body apart from each one doing its work, this is why the doctrine of the laying on of hands is foundational. After the doctrine of baptism, we have the teaching about diversity in the body of Christ, the gifts we have, the exercise of these gifts, their recognition, encouragement, and our receiving one from another. It is a beautiful thing when we see these gifts working together in the body of Christ.

Though God gives gifts to the Church, these gifts are not always recognized. In this context, we are talking about three laws working together. There is the law concerning authority,[5] there is the law concerning talent,[6] and there is the law concerning integrity.[7] These three together, when recognized, cause the body to work as it should, to the

---

5. Gangadean, *Philosophical Foundation*, 185–198.

6. Gangadean, *Philosophical Foundation*, 255–265.

7. Gangadean, *Philosophical Foundation*, 199–205.

glory of God. When these commandments are not recognized and understood, then we have disaster in the Church.

THE AUTHORITY OF CHRIST QUESTIONED:
Seven Instances

Jesus' authority was questioned in John 2 and I will be listing seven instances of the struggle to recognize and deal with authority appropriately.

First: Cleansing the Temple

> When it was almost time for the Jewish Passover, Jesus went up to Jerusalem. In the temple courts he found men selling cattle, sheep and doves, and others sitting at tables exchanging money. So he made a whip out of cords, and drove all from the temple area, both sheep and cattle; he scattered the coins of the money changers and overturned their tables. To those who sold doves he said, "Get these out of here! How dare you turn my Father's house into a market!" (vv. 13–16).

Passover was to represent coming out of the world, getting rid of all leaven, getting rid of everything that represents the world and worldliness, and in the temple, the Most Holy Place, this worldliness is being manifest in the buying and selling of sheep and birds. They turned God's holy place, the meeting place with God, into a marketplace. They desecrated it and turned it into a place of self-interest and a source of making money.

Jesus was doing what the religious leaders should have been doing. They should have been watching out. The priest particularly should have been watching out that the teaching about Passover would not be misunderstood or desecrated. They should have been watching to see that the temple was not desecrated. But both of these were desecrated; the temple and the whole notion of the holiness of God being taught through Passover were desecrated. Jesus corrected this and taught by His actions; those who should have been watchful were not. What happened is that those who saw Jesus cleansing the temple questioned Him on His right and His authority to do this. You see how the reversal has occurred. "**Then the Jews demanded of him, 'What miraculous**

sign can you show us to prove your authority to do all this?'" (v. 18). 'Who set you apart for this?' Those who had been set apart for this were not doing their job; Jesus did it, and those who were not doing it questioned the authority of the One who was doing it. How ironic? This is a pattern that has occurred again and again in history and in each of the following examples.

Jesus gave them *the* sign. Were they recognizing the Aaronic priesthood and all the ministry that went with it? In Numbers 16, there was a dispute when this priesthood was being set up in the wilderness. Korah, Dathan, and Abiram came and said that Moses and Aaron took too much upon themselves.[8] But God answered those who said this, and they and all those who joined them perished. Then, the people grumbled and thought they would all be killed; they did not understand how God worked. Then God gave them a sign. A staff from each tribe was brought before the Lord with their names on it, and the following morning, their staffs were brought out, and the staff with Aaron's name on it budded, blossomed, and bore fruit. This was the miraculous sign God had given; it is exactly the miraculous sign that Jesus was giving. What is this a sign of? The sign of the resurrection life. The One who will be raised from the dead is the One who will have the priesthood.[9] He is the One who is holy, who will be the Passover, who will give His life, and because He is perfectly righteous, He will be raised again from the dead. The One who is raised from the dead is the One whom God has set apart with authority, the One who pleased God. Jesus connected perfectly the question that they were asking Him and what He was doing; He was doing the priestly work to maintain the holiness of God.

"'What miraculous sign can you show us to prove your authority to do all this?' Jesus answered them, 'Destroy this temple, and I will raise it again in three days'" (vv. 18–19). This is interesting. *You* destroy this temple, not *I* will destroy this temple, but *you* destroy this temple, and *I* will raise it in three days. Those who lack insight in positions of authority were going to oppose Him to the point of destroying Jesus. What an ironic sign. They will kill Him, and He will be raised from the dead in three days, and this will be the sign of His authority that God has appointed Him to cleanse the temple. They should have

---

8. Gangadean, "Paper No. 64: Aaron's Rod," in *The Logos Papers*, 341–352.
9. See: Sermon 7, "Christ: A Priest Forever."

known that what Jesus was doing was right from Scripture and that they were delinquent. When they asked for a sign, they should have known immediately that this was wrong. The selling of sheep and birds in the temple place was wrong. They should have known what Passover meant. They should have known how the temple was set apart, and it was not for the purpose of making money. Jesus' very act was the teaching, and they could not receive it. The sign of His authority is that He will be raised from the dead. He is the high priest, the One appointed by God who will uphold God's holiness and accomplish His purpose.

Second: Nicodemus

> Now there was a man of the Pharisees named Nicodemus, a member of the Jewish ruling council. He came to Jesus at night and said, "Rabbi, we know you are a teacher who has come from God. For no one could perform the miraculous signs you are doing if God were not with him" (Jn. 3:1–2).

Jesus taught Nicodemus; He spoke to the point, and He saw exactly where Nicodemus was. Remember, God asked the question, "Where are you?"[10] Jesus could discern where Nicodemus was, and the fact that Nicodemus had come at night was an indication. Why did he not come during the day? He had seen Jesus in some ways, but not for who He is, not to come and bow before Him in worship. He did not yet recognize that Jesus is the Son of God, the Lord and Savior of the world. He had not seen what he needed to see. "In reply Jesus declared, 'I tell you the truth, no one can see the kingdom of God unless he is born again'" (Jn. 3:3). Nicodemus did not understand. Nicodemus was close, very close. This raises the question of how close one can get without having a clue. Nicodemus takes the cake.

Nicodemus was a covenant child raised in the covenant and stayed within the boundaries of the covenant, but he did not have the inner meaning. He was a teacher in Israel, a teacher of the covenant people, and he still did not have a clue; he did not see it. He had a very high regard for Jesus as coming from God, but he still did not see it. Nicodemus went further; he came to Jesus, though he came at night. Many people have a high regard for Jesus but do not see it or have a

---

10. *Genesis 3:9.*

clue. Furthermore, Jesus instructed him, but he still did not get it. He instructed him twice! Nicodemus was in a position of authority but without insight, not in the same open, opposing way as those questioning Jesus in John 2, but still in a position of authority without understanding and insight. "'You are Israel's teacher,' said Jesus, 'and do you not understand these things?'" (Jn. 3:10). "You should not be surprised at my saying, 'You must be born again'" (Jn. 3:7). 'Nicodemus, did you understand circumcision and what it taught about sin and death and the need for salvation? Did you understand the person and work of the Messiah? Did you understand that the Scripture spoke about this?' Nicodemus had seen the signs and knew they were miraculous, but he did not understand what they pointed to. They pointed to Christ. "Jesus is the Christ, the Son of God, and that by believing you may have life in his name" (Jn. 20:31b). All Nicodemus knew was that there was something miraculous in Christ; it was God acting, no man can do these miracles except God be with him. But it was more than this; these signs pointed to Jesus as the Son of God, the Messiah. It showed that Nicodemus had a regard for the signs, he had a regard for the Passover, he kept the Passover, but he did not understand its meaning. He lacked faith.[11]

Nicodemus could be born and raised in the covenant, be a teacher, be in a position of authority, and have a high regard for Jesus, but not have faith. Then Jesus instructed him, and Jesus exercised His true authority in instructing Nicodemus. At this point, Nicodemus still had not gotten it. Later, Nicodemus gets it, and by the time Jesus dies on the cross, Nicodemus has gotten it. It was he who went with Joseph of Arimathea (and we believe this was an act of faith); he no longer comes at night, but he openly identifies with Jesus in going and taking the body down off the cross with Joseph of Arimathea to prepare it for burial, he now identifies with Jesus in His death. He sees that Jesus is dying for the sins of the world. Nicodemus comes to thank God for His grace.

Third: Teaching in the Temple

What is legitimate authority? What is the doctrine of the laying on of hands? How do we recognize it? "Jesus entered the temple courts,

---

11. Gangadean, *The Biblical Worldview*, 3–20.

and while he was teaching, the chief priests and the elders of the people came to him. 'By what authority are you doing these things?' they asked. 'And who gave you this authority?'" (Matt. 21:23). 'Who laid hands on you?' No one laid hands on Jesus at this point, that is why they are asking, "who gave you this authority?" Notice that Jesus was in the temple, and He was teaching, which is an exercise of authority. Authority is exercised in teaching, as parents teach children and pastors teach in the Church. The question came, "By what authority are you doing these things?" they asked. "And who gave you this authority?" It seems as if they are really concerned about authority, and in a way, they are, but it is more in jealousy of their own position rather than a legitimate question of authority. Jesus exposes this when he replied, "I will also ask you one question. If you answer me, I will tell you by what authority I am doing these things" (Matt. 21:24). Here is the third law, about integrity. Were they really concerned for consistency?

> "John's baptism—where did it come from? Was it from heaven, or from men?" They discussed it among themselves and said, "If we say, 'From heaven,' he will ask, 'Then why didn't you believe him?' But if we say, 'From men'—we are afraid of the people, for they all hold that John was a prophet." So they answered Jesus, "We don't know." Then he said, "Neither will I tell you by what authority I am doing these things" (Matt. 21:25–27).

He exposed the motive behind their question, which was self-serving and attempting to protect their own interests and privileges rather than the legitimate authority of God.

The fact that John was sent indicates what was going on in Israel. Teaching had broken down. The ordinary way is that those in authority should be teaching, and the hearts of the fathers will turn to the children in instructing them, and the hearts of the children will turn to the fathers.[12] This had not happened; things had broken down. John was sent, without any hands being laid on him by anyone. But God sent him in a broken-down situation to restore it by preaching. The content of John's message is according to the Word of God, and therefore has authority. You can ask questions about the authority of so and so, but you have to notice how authority works in a broken-down situation,

---

12. *Malachi 4:6.*

as in the situation into which John was sent. When the teachers of the law and the Pharisees asked questions about authority, it was in this way: 'We didn't recognize you, so you can't be here doing this!' Well, what about John? Were they really concerned about that? Authority comes first from the Word of God and the teaching of that Word. Those in positions of authority will raise questions about those who exercise legitimate authority.

Fourth: The Apostles vs. the Authorities

In Acts 4, the Apostles were being forbidden to teach in Jesus' name. Verses 18–19 say, "Then they called them in again and commanded them not to speak or teach at all in the name of Jesus. But Peter and John replied, 'Judge for yourselves whether it is right in God's sight to obey you rather than God.'" There it is: to obey you (man), or to obey God. "For we cannot help speaking about what we have seen and heard" (Acts 4:20). There is an element of basic truth here. How can it possibly be illegitimate to speak what you have seen and heard and to testify to it? We cannot do anything but speak and testify to it. God would have us to do this. God would have us speak the truth. If you say 'no,' then you are putting yourself in authority over and against God. "Judge for yourselves whether it is right in God's sight to obey you rather than God." From where does authority come? Authority comes from knowing and speaking the truth.

Later on, they were forbidden again in Acts 5:27–29:

Having brought the apostles, they made them appear before the Sanhedrin to be questioned by the high priest. "We gave you strict orders not to teach in this name," he said. "Yet you have filled Jerusalem with your teaching and are determined to make us guilty of this man's blood." Peter and the other apostles replied: "We must obey God rather than men!"

The authorities did not recognize hands being laid on these persons for the exercise of authority, but God revealed truth to them, and that carries an authority that must be spoken, and it cannot be wrong to speak the truth. If necessary, we may have to oppose those who are in positions of authority in order to be submitted to the authority of God. The Apostles are exercising authority in that they are teaching.

Fifth: Saul Persecutes the Church

Acts 9:1–2 says,

> Meanwhile, Saul was still breathing out murderous threats against
> the Lord's disciples. He went to the high priest and asked him for
> letters to the synagogues in Damascus, so that if he found any there
> who belonged to the Way, whether men or women, he might take
> them as prisoners to Jerusalem.

Saul went to the high priest and asked for letters to the synagogue
in Damascus, and all of this was done by the book. 'We have got the
letters! We have the authority!' But it is illegitimate because it is not
based on truth.

Sixth: Paul's Authority—Letters of Recommendation

Later on, Paul is going to have to deal with the question: 'Paul, where
are your letters in the church? Where are your credentials?' In 2 Corinthians 3:1, after speaking about his ministry, he says, "Are we beginning to commend ourselves again? Or do we need, like some people,
letters of recommendation to you or from you?" He is addressing the
question of authority. 'Where is your letter of recommendation to show
that you can be in this position?'

> You yourselves are our letter, written on our hearts, known and
> read by everybody. You show that you are a letter from Christ, the
> result of our ministry [the fruit of our ministry], written not with
> ink but with the Spirit of the living God, not on tablets of stone
> but on tablets of human hearts (2 Cor. 3:2–3).

Paul had letters at the beginning, but they were not legitimate because
they were written for a wrong cause. Then, in a right cause, he is asked
for letters and says, 'You know what? You Corinthians should not need
letters because you are the result of the ministry God has given me.'
They are the credentials, the fruit that is borne, the exercise of the gift;
it is proven and seen, and this constitutes the authority that Paul has.
The general principle is that a gift exercised and recognized puts one
in a position of authority. You could be put in a position of authority
without gifts, or without exercising them, or without fruit, which is not

legitimate. This is laying hands on someone suddenly or too quickly, and there must be fruit for there to be a ministry.

Seventh: Apostolic Authority—By Succession or Historically Cumulative Insight

The Roman Catholic Church has made much of apostolic authority by claiming to be the one, holy, catholic, and apostolic church with the line of authority coming down from Peter. 'Hands have been laid on successively through the generations, and we have legitimate authority.' What did the Reformers do? The Reformers objected to the official teaching of the Roman Catholic Church; hands were not laid on them. Luther was a monk, but he was excommunicated. What about Calvin? Hands were not laid on him. Where are his credentials? Where is his authority in terms of laying on of hands? Theirs was an unusual situation: the Church had gone astray during the Reformation, and the Reformers challenged the Church in the name of apostolic truth, not succession, but apostolic truth, the Apostles' teachings. This is where authority resides, in the teaching of the truth. If they do not engage, it shows that their authority is illegitimate. Those who continue in the apostolic tradition, in the Apostles' teachings as they have been developed through history, are the ones who are in legitimate positions of authority.[13] One could be in a position of authority by tradition without understanding, and in doing so, oppose the truth. This has been encountered by the Lord, by the disciples, by the Apostles, and in Church history. Or one could have insight/understanding into the truth, the exercise of which shows the blessing of God in bearing of fruit, and that constitutes authority. Those who have built on the Westminster Confession of Faith as a summary and continuation of the apostolic teaching, not merely in a traditional way but in a historical way, Historical Christianity (not traditional Christianity), are the ones who are truly continuing the apostolic teaching. They are continuing in the Word of God. It is the truth of God, the Word of God, that is of ultimate authority, and those who abide in that truth and live according to it exercise legitimate authority.

---

13. Gangadean, "Paper No. 16: The Historic Christian Faith," 103–114; "Paper No. 38: The Holy Catholic and Apostolic Faith: Given for the Unity of the Faith," in *The Logos Papers*, 583–585; Gangadean, *The Westminster Confession*, xix–xxix, 349–351.

We hope that you can see this truth through these examples from Scripture. There may be a discontinuity of persons because of sin in the Church, but not discontinuity of the teaching. The Word must come all the way down, given from the beginning in Adam to the present time. The way to protect against false teachers and prophets is not by saying, 'So and so had hands laid on them.' This has been in the Church; there has been simony and all kinds of corruption of the worst sort in the Church. The way to protect against false teachers is not by appealing to apostolic succession, but by appealing to the apostolic teaching, which is the Word of God that has been continued from the Apostles.

CONCLUSION

There is a teaching about the laying on of hands and works that are exercised when gifts are given to bear fruit for God, all in the context of the Word of God. When things are working as they should be, hands will be laid on individuals to recognize their authority. The ultimate authority that we build upon is the apostolic teaching, not apostolic succession in an outward form. May God give us ears to hear and understand and believe and obey His teaching concerning the laying on of hands.

21

RESURRECTION OF THE DEAD

1 Corinthians 15:12–28

¹²But if it is preached that Christ has been raised from the dead, how can some of you say that there is no resurrection of the dead? ¹³If there is no resurrection of the dead, then not even Christ has been raised. ¹⁴And if Christ has not been raised, our preaching is useless and so is your faith. ¹⁵More than that, we are then found to be false witnesses about God, for we have testified about God that he raised Christ from the dead. But he did not raise him if in fact the dead are not raised. ¹⁶For if the dead are not raised, then Christ has not been raised either. ¹⁷And if Christ has not been raised, your faith is futile; you are still in your sins. ¹⁸Then those also who have fallen asleep in Christ are lost. ¹⁹If only for this life we have hope in Christ, we are to be pitied more than all men.

²⁰But Christ has indeed been raised from the dead, the firstfruits of those who have fallen asleep. ²¹For since death came through a man, the resurrection of the dead comes also through a man. ²²For as in Adam all die, so in Christ all will be made alive. ²³But each in his own turn: Christ, the firstfruits; then, when he comes, those who belong to him. ²⁴Then the end will come, when he hands over the kingdom to God the Father after he has destroyed all dominion, authority and power. ²⁵For he must reign until he has put all his enemies under his feet. ²⁶The last enemy to be destroyed is death. ²⁷For he "has put everything under his feet." Now when it says that "everything" has been put under him, it is clear that this does not include God himself, who put everything under Christ. ²⁸When he has done this, then the Son himself will be made subject to him who put everything under him, so that God may be all in all.

INTRODUCTION:
The Diamond City, the City with Foundations

WE ARE SEEKING A CITY WITH FOUNDATIONS. It is the city that is clear as crystal: "It shone with the glory of God, and its brilliance was like that of a very precious jewel, like a jasper, clear as crystal" (Rev. 21:11). We seek the diamond city, a city of the people of God. In this city, the glory of God is refracted in a billion ways, in and through each and every one of His people. Each person is uniquely human and manifests some unique aspect of the image of God, and it takes all people to show forth the glory of God in its fullness. His glory can never be shown in its exhaustiveness, but it will be shown in its fullness in terms of all that we can expect.

When I was on the waters of Prince William Sound off the coast of Alaska, I was impressed by the sheer immensity of the waters and how it saturates. It just covers as fully as anything can cover. I was reminded that the earth shall be full of the glory of God as the waters cover the sea.[1] I often meditated on this as I was on the waters and saw the high mountains all around us, high and lifted up. As we traveled from the air, ocean, and roads, and saw these mountains, I asked, 'Will this be? Will this come about? Will it indeed be so?" I was reminded of that Word of Scripture, which says, "Truly I tell you, if you have faith as small as a mustard seed, you can say to this mountain, 'Move from here to there,' and it will move" (Matt. 17:20). These mountains that seem so vast are the cultures, the many cultures, the many groups that are in the world, these chains of mountains. These mountains will melt before the clarity of general revelation and the faithful testimony of God's people. These mountains will be hurled into the midst of the sea.[2] Nothing will be raised and stand up against the knowledge of God.

FOUNDATION (BASICS AND MILK) AND MATURITY

We come today, in the preaching, to the hope of the resurrection of the dead. When we understand the implications, we will see that the fundamental teaching concerning the resurrection of the dead is a

---

1. *Habbakuk 2:14; Isaiah 11:9.*

2. *Psalm 42.*

Christian doctrine of the hope of the glory of God. The resurrection signifies the last enemy to be destroyed; it signifies the completion of the work, and it signifies good not only triumphing and being achieved but also good being achieved in the presence of evil. Good overcoming evil. You cannot have any greater fullness of the good than in the context of spiritual war where good overcomes evil. Remember, in Adam, before the Fall, we would have had the good had he been preserved, but God chose to reveal His glory by allowing evil in its many forms to come in.[3] In the conflict between good and evil, good will overcome evil: **"The last enemy to be destroyed is death"** (v. 26). The resurrection of the dead has always been the hope of the Church. We must give attention to this.

We are looking for the diamond city, which reflects God's glory in every way. I have often thought about the Diamond Sutra of the Buddhists. I like that name, the Diamond Sutra. I am particularly drawn to images of light and vision. I tend to be very visual in that way. Diamonds and light and the effect of light are especially attractive to me. Well, here we have the diamond city—vast—1,400 miles long and wide and high.[4] This is the city of God. I think we should, and I encourage you to do so, think of it and call it the diamond city, a city with foundations. This is what we are considering. Today, we are considering one aspect of the foundation.

By way of review, let me remind you of the other aspects that we have covered in the order in which it is stated in Hebrews 6:1–3.

Sin and Death

We have spoken about sin and death. We spoke about sin, clarity and inexcusability, as well as the spiritual death that comes from sin in the denial of what is clear. We did not yet emphasize the idea of spiritual death versus hell.[5] This is another big piece that needs to be in place in the Christian community. When we speak about hell as something

---

3. Gangadean, *Philosophical Foundation*, 145–161; Gangadean, *On Natural and Revealed Theology*, 141–147; Gangadean, "Paper No. 7: The Problem of Evil," in *The Logos Papers*, 33–39; Gangadean, *The Biblical Worldview*, 219–239.

4. *Revelation 21:16.*

5. Gangadean, *The Biblical Worldview*, 37–54, 97–217; Gangadean, *Philosophical Foundation*, 195–197.

literal, future, and imposed, and we fail to see hell as spiritual death, which is present, not future, much is amiss. We must get these basic truths in place; these are foundational truths; it is milk that we must have to go on to maturity.[6]

Repentance from Dead Works and Faith Towards God

In connection with this, we spoke about sin and death. Concerning sin, we spoke about clarity and inexcusability. We spoke about repentance, especially from the *stoicheia,* the elements of this world, and what it takes to deal with the baggage we brought into the kingdom of God. We spoke about the need for deep-seated cleansing. Also, the problem of integrity is connected with repentance, and what we repent of is not just sin. We are to repent of our self-deception, self-justification, and sin, starting with the sin of not seeking God diligently. We need to take much to heart if we are to be faithful witnesses and call others to repentance. We have to back up and keep backing up until we come to the question of integrity and hypocrisy regarding seeking, because if it is clear, then men are inexcusable for failing to see and acknowledge it. We must bring out root sin in our witness, which is why the curse is upon us, calling us back.[7] We spoke about repentance in this context.

We spoke about faith as involving understanding, evidence, proof, and support; it is the substance[8]—the underlying support—of things that we see, just as matter is the underlying support of the color that we see. Matter in itself has no color. Atoms and energy have no color, yet the atoms manifest themselves with color, texture, and so on. Substance is the underlying support—that in which these qualities inhere. Faith involves "the substance of things hoped for," notice the connection between faith and hope, and "the evidence of things not seen," particularly the future that is not seen (Heb. 11:1 KJV). In speaking about repentance and faith, we see that this is very different from the popular view, and the historical view needs to be developed further. We are speaking about the basics and the foundation of the Christian faith from which we go on to maturity. In Hebrews 5:11–14, Paul wanted to

---

6. *Hebrews 5:11–14, 6:1.*

7. Gangadean, *The Biblical Worldview,* 55–68, 275–294.

8. *Hebrews 11:1.*

speak about the priesthood of Melchizedek further, but it was hard to speak about this because the foundation was not in place. Let us keep this in mind: We must have some things in place to understand others.

Baptism

We spoke about the doctrine of baptisms: water baptism, regeneration and the *ordo salutis*, and the baptism of the Holy Spirit. His work is to lead us into all truth and enable us to be witnesses in all the world. There is a connection between knowing the truth and speaking to the whole world. The work primarily speaks to the falsehoods that the Church has to struggle with, the falsehoods that, at the time of conversion, people bring with them into the Church. The Church has had to deal with these falsehoods in the form of challenges and heresies, and the pastor-teachers have summarized responses in the creeds and councils.[9] This is part of the work of the Spirit leading us into all truth and enabling us to be witnesses in all the world. Please notice how much greater and larger this is than is commonly thought in terms of the baptism of the Spirit, often individualistically conceived, narrowly conceived. If we are going to see the city built, the diamond city, we must have the foundation, and this is the foundation. If there are any doubts after this preaching, this is the time to raise those questions. Do not shrug it off. We cannot shrug off our differences on basic matters. We must engage with it. I exhort you, encourage you, and invite you to do so in the discussion to follow if you have any questions.

The Laying on of Hands

Laying on of hands concerns the imparting of gifts and the authority connected with it. Again, notice the interconnection between these: gift, empowerment, and authority. In this laying on of hands, we have the doctrine of the Church in that the working of these gifts together builds up the body. Those who have authority in the body, those in oversight, elders, are to teach, so that the members develop their gifts and stir up the gifts within them to serve God. The doctrine of the Church is manifested in this particular way: using our gifts to serve God and others, and those in oversight encouraging and leading us in this way.

---

9. Gangadean, "Paper No. 16: The Historic Christian Faith," in *The Logos Papers,* 103–114.

With these things in place, we can now go on to the resurrection of the dead, the hope of the Christian, or the doctrine of eschatology. The Church at large is badly divided on eschatology. Even those professing postmillennialism have not kept in mind the connection between the kingdom of God, taking thoughts captive, the nations being converted, and the earth being filled with the knowledge of the glory of God as the waters cover the sea.[10]

If eternal life is knowing God and we are to have the fullness of this life, then we are not asking people too much to have this foundation in place and to exercise their minds. Where did we ever get the idea that Christianity was for the 'mindless,' that Christianity is for the 'simple' who will not exercise their minds? It is faith that is pleasing to God, faith that involves seeking God diligently and understanding His revelation. God wants us to have this understanding. If we knew and understood that the goal is for the earth to be filled with the knowledge of God, we would see how much it is that God is calling us to exercise our minds to understand, because this life is connected with faith, or understanding. We are to understand these things that divide us.

We come to the doctrine of our hope, eschatology, and this becomes concrete for Christians in the teaching concerning the resurrection of the dead. The resurrection is something that we look forward to in the future. We will first speak about the resurrection in general, in contrast to other views that may minimize and avoid it. Then, we will speak about the necessity of the resurrection, Christ's resurrection, and then the resurrection of all, particularly as a summation of our hope.

THE RESURRECTION OF THE DEAD IN GENERAL

Versus No Afterlife

The resurrection is versus non-resurrection in many forms; it is *a* versus *non-a*, if you will. What is *non-a*? *Non-a* is that there is no resurrection. Simple, is it not? That is almost brilliant. There is no resurrection. What do you mean by that? There is no resurrection at all. The Sadducees believed that there was no resurrection and no spirit or angels. They seem to deny the spiritual reality of life. Maybe God is spirit, but some

---

10. *Isaiah 11:9; Habakkuk 2:14.*

people hold a strange view of Christian materialism. It surfaces here and there, and it has been around in philosophical circles. The Sadducees were a group in Israel, a prominent group, a leading group, and they denied the resurrection of the dead. This is to say that some deny the resurrection altogether.

Materialists say there is no afterlife whatsoever. So you can be closer to belief in God, as the Sadducees were, and deny the resurrection, or you can be a materialist and deny it. Paul recognizes that the most common way of denying the resurrection is to say there is no afterlife at all. There are other ways of denying the resurrection and affirming the afterlife; we will look at those and how this works. How does Paul recognize this? He speaks of it this way in 1 Corinthians, "If the dead are not raised, 'Let us eat and drink, for tomorrow we die'" (1 Cor. 15:32b). How many people do you know that think, 'When you're dead, you're dead. That's it. You only go around once, so just enjoy yourself now'? The logic of this is compelling, and many people, practically speaking, operate this way, believing that there is no resurrection. This teaching of the resurrection is in contrast to that belief. The belief is that 'there is no future, no hope, no point in life, you just get what you can and you go on.' As they go through certain crises in their lives, many people begin to think, 'What's the point? What's the hope? Why go through this struggle?' The resurrection is not a common belief. And if it is held, it is seen as a theoretical and distant belief that does not affect us vitally from day to day.

Versus Heaven

Consider the view of dying and going to heaven. I have often asked in class, 'Well, that's it, that's the whole story?' They say, 'Yeah, what more?' And I ask, 'Don't you want your body back?' They look at me strangely and say, 'Why would I want my body back?' Furthermore, when they think about getting their body back, they think of it as some decaying corpse. 'Why would I want to have that back? I will be rid of it, gone, left, free of it, free at last.' They, too, operate as if there is no resurrection. It is a very deficient view of the nature of man and God's purpose. Ask yourselves, what do you think happens to us when we die? Do you say, 'We go to heaven.' What happens then? 'Well, we receive all the blessings.' And what about the resurrection? 'Well, Christ was raised from the dead.' What about your resurrection? Then you get some hemming and hawing, and maybe they come around and say, 'Oh yeah, oh yeah.' The resurrection is seen as an addendum: why have it? This view shows that it is *individualistic* rather than seeing the corporate nature of our life. Remember, **"For as in Adam all die, so in Christ all will be made alive"** (v. 22). The view of dying and going to heaven is *dualistic*, split between matter and spirit, and the essential 'you' is the spirit, as if we were angels and not a body/soul unity. It is *escapist*. Heaven is basically an escape from natural evil. We can understand the desire to escape from natural evil, but if we have the fear of the Lord, we want to escape moral evil, not just natural evil.

Versus Reincarnation

Many are attracted to reincarnation.[11] A lot of people say, 'Well, why not?' Here is why not. First, reincarnation is not any kind of immortality. The only immortality worth noting is personal immortality, and reincarnation is not personal. No memory continues, and no personal identity continues. Maybe karmic influence continues, but there is no personal identity. Individuality is ephemeral, froth in the ocean that disappears and ultimately must fully disappear. There is no personal immortality. If it is not personal, what kind is it? We melt back into some ocean, and we lose all our identity. No, the kind of identity we speak about is personal, and reincarnation is against this, even at the level of the soul, not apart from the body.

Reincarnation focuses on natural evil. The Buddha taught that old age, sickness, and death is a punishment of karma that we have to keep repeating. The Buddha's account is opposed to the biblical worldview and our understanding of the nature of sin and death, as well as clarity and inexcusability. If we had clarity and inexcusability, we would never go the way of reincarnation because one life would suffice to know what is clear. The question is, why are we not seeing what is clear? Reincarnation also confuses the temporal and the eternal by taking a temporal soul to be eternal, but in doing so, it destroys hope because we have to ask: how long have we been reincarnating? What hope is there to get out of an eternal cycle? If we understood the difference between

---

11. Gangadean, *Philosophical Foundation*, 101–105.

eternal and temporal and sought and used our minds to think about this, we would never go the way of reincarnation, which rejects the resurrection. It attempts to explain why things happen, but it ends up blaming people. Why were you born crippled? 'Because of your karma in your previous life.' It blames someone when no blame should be brought because the curse is not punishment. The belief in karma oppresses people; whole groups of people may be kept in certain stations because they are born into that karma. The Dalit class in India, the untouchables, are oppressed because of their station in the reincarnation process. What it does is it excuses us rather than explaining and calling us to be responsible. Think about people who say, 'These things happen because of my karma,' rather than seeing that your failure to exercise responsible action leads to negative consequences.

(1) When you are dead, you are dead. (2) You die and go to heaven. (3) There is no resurrection, just reincarnation. All of these doctrines set themselves over and against the resurrection of the dead. All of them fail to make sense upon analysis. We will speak further about dying, going to heaven, and receiving the blessing.

THE NECESSITY OF THE RESURRECTION

When Paul spoke in 1 Corinthians 15, some were saying that 'since there is no resurrection of the dead, Christ is not raised.' They reasoned from the general to the particular. 'If there is no resurrection of the dead, then Christ is not raised.' In responding to this, we must show the necessity of the resurrection. We must show that Christ *must* be raised and that we, too, will be raised. We must show that the work that God has given will be completed so that we may have hope. "Now faith is the substance of things hoped for, the evidence of things not seen" (Heb. 11:1 KJV). It is the proof; it is the support. It should be clear, especially as we deal with what is basic: the milk, the most basic things of Christianity. If we get the foundation in place, our hope will be firmly set. Our hope must be firm because hope is an anchor. Without this hope, we would be drifting about.

Let us think more on this and get the teaching about the resurrection more clearly in focus. Against those who say there is no resurrection in a general way, we say there *must* be a resurrection, Christ *must* be raised, and we, too, will be raised in Christ. All of this implies that the last enemy will be destroyed and the work will be completed. We are looking for a city, the diamond city, the city with foundations. These teachings and doctrines are in Scripture, declared to be affirmed as foundations. Let us get these in place.

God Is Creator, God Is Good, and Original Creation Was Very Good

We know that God is the Creator; it is clear from general revelation.[12] In understanding that God is the Creator, the only eternal being, we understand the goodness of God. He has created us with a moral sense; God is not morally indifferent, and God cannot be morally evil. If He were morally evil, He would be infinitely evil, which is an impossibility. It is impossible to be infinitely opposed to oneself. God must be good. And being good, the original creation was very good; it was a revelation of His glory. There was no natural evil, that is, no physical death, in the original creation. We can know this much if we understand God's goodness as Creator. I ask you, I urge you, to think about this. If you have any questions or reservations about that inference, please ask.[13]

Physical death is not original, and physical death is not inherent in sin. It is spiritual death that is inherent in sin. There is nothing about Adam and Eve's sin that brought about physical death, but there is something about their sin that brought about spiritual death. Physical death is in the world; there is no question about that, and it is therefore present in the world, not because it was original or inherent, but because it was imposed by God. It was imposed by God because of our sin, not arbitrarily. It was imposed but not as punishment for sin; it is not in any way a matter of justice. Physical death and natural evil are not proportionally distributed. Psalm 73 speaks about how the wicked often flourish and the good suffer. If physical death and external, circumstantial suffering were justice, then it would be proportional because justice must be proportional. In addition, physical death is not lasting; all will be raised from the dead, the just and the unjust.

---

12. Gangadean, "Paper No. 102: The Clarity of General Revelation," 527–529; "Paper No. 41: What Is Clear About God," 225–229; "Paper No. 112: Why General Revelation Is Basic in the Christian Worldview," in *The Logos Papers,* 583–585.

13. Pastor Gangadean's ministry commonly encouraged engagement in discussion to find meaning and settle disputes. He consistently invited discussion in his ministry and classroom.

Furthermore, all of the punishment of our sin was carried by Christ. If we say physical death is punishment, then we are denying that Christ has carried all of our sins, and we open the door to the doctrine of purgatory, where we pay for some of our sins.

There are many reasons why we say physical death is not punishment; it is imposed as a call back from sin, particularly the sin we use to cover: our self-deception and self-justification.[14] It is a call back from the sin of not seeking God, not understanding, the sin of autonomy, determining good and evil for ourselves, and the sin of unbelief regarding what is eternal: 'you shall be like God.' You are a temporal creature. You are a creature who is necessarily temporal because creatures are created and come into being. The temporal creature is vastly different from the eternal. To blur this distinction, to forget that God is the Creator and all that this implies, is evil; it is sinful. We are being called back not only from the sin of failing to seek and understand and determining good and evil for ourselves, but we are being called back from how we have covered this up. Perhaps the first thing we are to repent of is our hypocrisy, our self-deception, and our blaming others for what is going on in us. It is so prevalent; let us watch for it in ourselves.

God imposes physical death and, with it, the curse—toil and strife, financial struggles, illnesses that we all have, strife with others in various forms of intensity, individually and collectively. God imposes the curse as a call back. This call back from sin assumes redemption and a redeemer. In Scripture, we have the revelation of the One who will redeem us: the seed of the woman, someone in place of Adam, who will *undo* what Adam did and *do* what Adam failed to do—the work of dominion. When redemption is completed—and it will be completed, we cannot imagine it not being completed; God accomplishes it—death *will* be removed. Death *must* be removed because it is imposed as a call back from sin. When sin is removed, the continuation of death makes no sense whatsoever. Therefore, we conclude death *must* be removed. We are a body/soul unity, and death is unnatural. Death must be removed and death will be removed by the resurrection of the dead. Therefore, we teach with certainty that there must be a resurrection of the dead. Not that there *might* be; not that there *can* be; we do not infer our resurrection from Jesus' resurrection which we believe based on Scripture

---

14. Gangadean, *The Biblical Worldview*, 241–294.

and testimony. That would be reasoning from the possibility to actuality. Instead, we argue from the *necessity* of the general resurrection to the *actuality* of it. There must be a resurrection of the dead.

We know that physical death was imposed sovereignly, immediately and directly by God, so that it will be removed sovereignly, that is, immediately and directly by God. Death was the last thing imposed; it is the last call back, a continuing call back, and it will continue until it has done its work. It is the last enemy, but as an enemy, it, too, will be destroyed.

THE RESURRECTION OF CHRIST

There is not only the necessity for the resurrection but the necessity for the resurrection of Christ. In Acts 2:24, it says, "But God raised him from the dead, freeing him from the agony of death, because it was impossible for death to keep its hold on him." Romans 1:4 says, "and who through the Spirit of holiness was appointed the Son of God in power by his resurrection from the dead: Jesus Christ our Lord." He is declared to be the One whom God has anointed and appointed to be the heir of all things. He is declared to be the Son of God, who claimed He was in this life to bring redemption. Romans 4:25 says, "He was delivered over to death for our sins and was raised to life for our justification." Christ, as the redeemer, must overcome all enemies. He cannot be subject to death itself if He is the one to overcome the enemies. He must be raised from the dead. Notice the word "impossible"; it is a logical term; it is impossible for death to hold Him. There is no possibility of it because of His righteousness, who He is, His perfection, and His paying the price fully. He has overcome sin, and with overcoming sin, He has overcome all that accompanies sin. This includes physical death; notice I use the word 'accompanies.' It is not punishment, but it certainly accompanies sin in God's purpose.

Christ overcomes all of this, and His authority is affirmed through overcoming. Remember the teaching about Aaron's rod that budded.[15] The One whom God has appointed is the One who is holy, who, being holy, will overcome sin if He is going to *undo* what Adam did and *do* what Adam failed to do. So, He is raised from the dead, and

---

15. Gangadean, "Paper No. 64: Aaron's Rod," in *The Logos Papers*, 341–352.

it is necessary for us to know this if we affirm that we are justified in Christ. If Jesus had not paid the penalty fully, He could not be raised from the dead, He could not justify us. Jesus was perfect, absolute in His holiness, and perfect in His obedience. He satisfied the justice of God, and death could have no power over Him because of His perfection. He was declared to be the One whom God has appointed, His very Son whom He sent, and He was slain for our justification. It is impossible for death to hold Him; He is declared with power to be the Son of God by His resurrection, and He is raised again for our justification. We should expect that Christ, who will reign forever, will be raised from the dead, will be seated at the right hand of God, and will send the Spirit. He is God and man, fully man, body and soul, and continues to be God and man forever, overcoming sin and death, and being raised from the dead. Jesus has ascended into heaven, He sits at the right hand of God, and He sends the Spirit to accomplish what Adam failed to accomplish. He, the Anointed One, sends the Spirit and will bring this about; the Spirit will lead us into all truth. The Spirit will regenerate us; the Spirit will sanctify us with the Word and bring us into the truth of God.

It must be the case that Christ is raised from the dead; we should expect this, and if He was not raised from the dead, we should say He is not the Christ. We must expect that He would be the Messiah in terms of the teaching of the Lamb of God that takes away the sin of the world.

THE RESURRECTION OF ALL:
The Last Enemy (Death) and Our Hope

There is the necessity for the resurrection and the necessity for the resurrection of Christ. There will also be the resurrection of each and every one of us from the dead. Each and every one of us! Not just the believer but the non-believer. Remember, physical death is not punishment; it is a call back. There will come a time when that call back is ended for the believer and the non-believer. The process of sanctification will be ended for the believer. At death, there is no more sanctification going on. The saints are made perfect in glory and holy, with no sin remaining. This is the state of glorification. Death is no longer operating on them to call them back. We expect that we will be raised from the dead because we are a body/soul unity.

There will be a resurrection of all, and it is necessary for there to be a resurrection of all. The resurrection is necessary for *continuity* between this life and the next. There is not an escape from this life to the next, but a continuity. Continuity is in terms of body/soul existence, and continuity is in terms of the labor that we accomplished. It is not that we are leaving this life behind and going to another realm altogether. Our labor in the Lord is not in vain. The acts of this life continue into the next, and we will continue in a way that we will enjoy the work of dominion that is done. Without this, we have a radical discontinuity and naturally drift towards the view of questioning, 'Why should we get involved in many of these cultural activities in the world? Why not save as many souls as we can for heaven, where we achieve the full blessedness?' Many of you have encountered this sort of thing in popular evangelical circles. 'Evangelism is the main thing. Doctrine that would distract us from evangelism (getting people saved and going to heaven) must be minimized and put aside.' This is not the view that God calls us to; there is much more work to be done. If we do not see the work to be done, we will naturally emphasize the salvation of souls and reduce the Christian life to evangelicalism to get as many people saved as we can. You know what? Even believers cannot live such a narrow life; there is a fullness that we desire. Popular evangelicalism has a narrow spirituality, and then the rest of life is said to be 'neutral,' which leads to a dualism. If we are to have hope regarding our labor and life, we must have continuity, and there must be the resurrection. If we are to hope that this will be completed, there must be consummation. There must be a time when the dead are raised, when the work is completed, the good is achieved, and evil is overcome.

Redemption Applied

Redemption is accomplished when Christ says, "It is finished" (Jn. 19:30). Now, we have the application of redemption. We are speaking about the *completion* of the *application* of redemption in the resurrection from the dead; the last enemy to be destroyed. This hope is based on faith. Paul speaks about this in Acts, and I will draw attention to it in several places. In Acts 22:21, Paul says, "Then the Lord said to me,

'Go; I will send you far away to the Gentiles.'" Verse 22 continues, "The crowd listened to Paul until he said this. Then they raised their voices and shouted, 'Rid the earth of him! He's not fit to live!'" What is the point here? The promise God made to Abraham was: "in you all the families of the earth shall be blessed" (Gen. 12:3b NKJV). When that promise was being fulfilled, the Jews—who misunderstood their election and did not see that this favor was not just for them but for all men—could not stand it. They shouted out, "Rid the earth of him! He's not fit to live!" Here is where the hope that all the families of the earth will be brought in is misunderstood by the Church.

In Acts 23:6, Paul says, "'My brothers, I am a Pharisee, descended from Pharisees. I stand on trial because of the hope of the resurrection of the dead.' When he said this, a dispute broke out between the Pharisees and the Sadducees, and the assembly was divided" (Acts 23:6b–7). In Acts 24:21, When Paul was on trial before Felix, he said, "It is concerning the resurrection of the dead that I am on trial before you today." Acts 26:6–8 says:

> And now it is because of my hope in what God has promised our ancestors that I am on trial today. This is the promise our twelve tribes are hoping to see fulfilled as they earnestly serve God day and night. King Agrippa, it is because of this hope that these Jews are accusing me. Why should any of you consider it incredible that God raises the dead?

Notice how Paul connects the resurrection of the dead with the hope. It is the hope in the consummation of all things. Romans 8 says, "For the creation waits in eager expectation for the children of God to be revealed" (Rom. 8:19), "that the creation itself will be liberated from its bondage to decay and brought into the freedom and glory of the children of God" (Rom. 8:21). Again, the hope is there.

> By faith he made his home in the promised land like a stranger in a foreign country; he lived in tents, as did Isaac and Jacob, who were heirs with him of the same promise. For he was looking forward to the city with foundations, whose architect and builder is God (Heb. 11:9–10).

If they had been thinking of the country they had left, they would have had opportunity to return. Instead, they were longing for a better country—a heavenly one. Therefore God is not ashamed to be called their God, for he has prepared a city for them (Heb. 11:15–16).

Abraham was looking for a city, he was hoping, there was a *longing*. It is what they were longing for. Longing is connected with hope. Our hope is the consummation of all things.

This hope is based on faith and is fulfilled in love. These three remain: faith, hope, and love. Our understanding is the basis and the certainty of our hope. This hope is described in Hebrews 6:18–19 as an anchor for our soul. It is a motivator, and it keeps us steady; it keeps us steadfast and keeps us from drifting away. This is what we want; there is no alternative! Dying and going to heaven is not going to do it. Dying and going to heaven will leave us waiting for this hope, even as others are now waiting. This is an anchor amid all the work we are called to do. It is also a helmet. Ephesians 6:17 says, "Take the helmet of salvation and the sword of the Spirit, which is the word of God," and 1 Thessalonians 5:8 says, "But since we belong to the day, let us be sober, putting on faith and love as a breastplate, and the hope of salvation as a helmet." Putting those two together, we come up with the notion that the hope of salvation is a helmet. Think about this figure of speech; hope is an anchor and a helmet. You do not want to go into battle without being covered. Faith is described as a shield, the breastplate of righteousness, and the love that comes with doing what is right is there on us, and hope is a helmet. Faith, hope, and love. It is used in this way: faith is the ground of hope, and hope enables us to be steady in obedience, righteousness, and love. "And now these three remain: faith, hope and love. But the greatest of these is love" (1 Cor. 13:13); love is a consummation. This doctrine must be in place to be established in God and bear fruit for Him.

22

ETERNAL JUDGMENT

John 15:1–8

¹I am the true vine, and my Father is the gardener. ²He cuts off every branch in me that bears no fruit, while every branch that does bear fruit he prunes so that it will be even more fruitful. ³You are already clean because of the word I have spoken to you. ⁴Remain in me, as I also remain in you. No branch can bear fruit by itself; it must remain in the vine. Neither can you bear fruit unless you remain in me.

⁵I am the vine; you are the branches. If you remain in me and I in you, you will bear much fruit; apart from me you can do nothing. ⁶If you do not remain in me, you are like a branch that is thrown away and withers; such branches are picked up, thrown into the fire and burned. ⁷If you remain in me and my words remain in you, ask whatever you wish, and it will be done for you. ⁸This is to my Father's glory, that you bear much fruit, showing yourselves to be my disciples.

THE TWO WAYS:
Life and Death

IN THIS SECTION ON THE FOUNDATION regarding eternal judgment, we come to the teaching about life and death. In the judgment of God, there are two ways—life and death. It has been that way from the beginning; it will be that way in the end. It has always been that way and will always be that way because it *must* be that way. With God, there is life. Without God, there can be no life; there is death. God has made us with choice, and we can go in the way of life or in the way of death. Scripture teaches in Romans 6:23, "For the wages of sin is death, but the gift of God is eternal life in Christ Jesus our Lord." Here, we have a contrast between wages, what we earn/deserve, on the one hand, and on the other hand, a *gift*, which is a matter of grace, which is not something earned. It is a gift because it is given to us in Christ Jesus, who is the gift of God to us.

Christ—the Second Adam

On the one hand, we are in Adam, and we inherit his sin; we live in this sin, and we die in this sin. On the other hand, we are in Christ, in the covenant of grace, and have the life that comes with Christ the Lord. Christ is the second Adam, the last Adam, the One who *undoes* what was done by Adam, and the One who *does* what Adam failed to do. The One who is the Lamb of God who takes away the sin of the world,[1] and the One who is the anointed of God, anointed with the Spirit, who sends His Spirit on His people that we may be fruitful, multiply, make disciples of all nations, and do the work that God called Adam to do.

The Reward of Knowing God

We can speak here about the reward in connection with life. It is not a reward of works, something we earn; it is a reward of an effort we make but an effort we make because of God's grace working in us. "But without faith it is impossible to please Him, for he who comes to God must believe that He is, and that He is a rewarder of those who diligently seek Him" (Heb. 11:6 NKJV). Coming to God is a work of God's grace; without this grace, we would all be left in the condition of sin and death, going our own way. We came because God elected us in Christ and sent His Spirit in due time to work in each of our hearts to regenerate us and bring us to life so that we may know the reality of sin and death, repentance, and faith in Christ.[2] So when we say that He is the rewarder of those who diligently seek Him, we must believe that God is—this is of God's grace. Not only coming to God but also continuing on in God. Not only coming out of Egypt but continuing

---

1. *John 1:29.*

2. Gangadean, *The Westminster Confession*, 143–206; Gangadean, *The Westminster Catechisms*, 191–207.

into Canaan. It is of God's grace: "the gift of God is eternal life in Christ Jesus our Lord" (Rom. 6:23b).

GOD'S ETERNAL JUDGMENT:
Timeless, Eternal, Permanent, Fixed, Always Present, and Inherent

God's judgment is called an eternal judgment. We should give some attention to what this means. Some may think of this eternal judgment primarily in terms of the Last Judgment, which we spoke of in Revelation 20.[3] It certainly includes this, but it includes more than this. God's judgment is not only an event in the future, yet to come; it is going on now. Life and death are operating now, and life and death manifest the judgment of God. When we speak about eternal judgment, we should not think only of a future judgment, continuing forever. God's eternal judgment is eternal; in a sense, it is timeless, it is permanent, it is fixed, it is final, it is always present, and it is inherent. God's eternal judgment is in the order of a law or a principle, not only, or simply, an event in the future. When we come to this teaching of eternal judgment, we are to think not just of the Last Judgment in the future but God's recurring judgment at all times now and brought to consummation in the future in the Last Judgment.

How Eternal Judgment Has Been Understood

In the context of foundation, we have to consider—by way of contrast and challenge and alternative and distortion—ways this teaching has been misunderstood. We are to consider to what extent one's thinking constitutes a misunderstanding in a significant way. We speak of this judgment of God in terms of death and life, "For the wages of sin is death, but the gift of God is eternal life in Christ Jesus our Lord" (Rom. 6:23). Something happens to us when we think about the eternal judgment. We generally imagine it in the future as the Last Judgment merely, and we make it out to be something that will transpire after death. The Scripture says, "the wages of sin is death, but the gift

---

3. Surrendra Gangadean, *The Book of Revelation: What Must Soon Take Place—Doxological Postmillennialism*, (Phoenix, Logos Papers Press, forthcoming 2025).

of God is eternal life." We *must* think about God's eternal judgment in terms of life and death—from the beginning of the Garden it was so. God placed the tree of life and the tree of death, the tree of the knowledge of good and evil, before Adam. God said of that tree, "for in the day that you eat of it you shall surely die" (Gen. 2:17b NKJV). It was so from the beginning; it could not have been otherwise. These trees merely made manifest outwardly what was inherent. Even though we do not eat of that tree in an outward act as Adam did, we are involved in exactly the same sin, blurring the distinction between God and man, putting ourselves in the place of God to determine good and evil.

The tree of the knowledge of good and evil did not cause sin; it made sin manifest. Adam and Eve were in unbelief when they heeded the words of Satan, "you will be like God, knowing good and evil" (Gen. 3:5b), *before* they ate, and the eating simply made it manifest. What I am saying is that life and death are inherent in the way God has made things. We cannot speak about just one way; we cannot simply speak about life without conceiving of death. At least, conceptually,[4] we must also think about non-life or death and the reality of death. We can speak of neither life nor death apart from each other. God made us in His image, with understanding; we cannot avoid the notion of life and death.

Life and death are present from the beginning to the very end of the Bible. Life is depicted through the *river of life* and the *tree of life*, while death is through the *lake of fire*, which is the second death. These terms are used to the very end. What has happened? We have to see foundation laid again in regard to eternal judgment, seeing the judgment in terms of life and death instead of heaven and hell. We have to ask ourselves: What is death? How are we to understand death? Not only theoretically in general, but how is it manifested in our lives? How is it manifesting in the lives of those around us? This is part of what we will try to bring into focus as we understand the eternal judgment in terms of death and also seek to do the same for life.

---

4. Gangadean, *Philosophical Foundation*, 10–15; Gangadean, *History of Philosophy,* 25–35.

Spiritual Death within a Person: Meaninglessness, Boredom, and Guilt

We have spoken about death as, first of all, foremost within the person, and then we speak about it within relationships between two persons and in groups of persons. Within a person, it connects with how God has made us in our thoughts, feelings, and will. All of these are affected by death. Concerning our thoughts, we come into a darkened state of mind where we do not understand or we lack understanding, and the meaning of things ceases, drains out, and becomes emptied of meaning. We have summarized this by saying spiritual death involves meaninglessness, starting with the mind being darkened when it is turned off from seeing what is clear about God.[5] Notice the inherent connection between sin—not seeking God, not seeing what is clear, not engaging our minds, turning off our minds—and the darkness that comes in. This is part of what we mean by the permanence of God's judgment—the timelessness of it.

There is a necessary connection between sin and death. The Bible speaks about it as the mind being darkened.[6] Ecclesiastes brings out the point of meaninglessness. "'Meaningless! Meaningless!' says the Teacher. 'Utterly meaningless! Everything is meaningless'" (Ecc. 1:2). Meaninglessness in Ecclesiastes is understood as emptiness. Things that are in vain, without purpose or end—a waste. We may begin with the element of thought and the mind being darkened, but the word *meaningless*—the focus in Ecclesiastes—is encompassing more than just philosophical or intellectual meaninglessness. As we go on, we will see other applications, too.

In addition to meaninglessness in the mind, death comes into our feelings and affections. How does death enter into our soul? How does it enter the aspect of our soul that we speak of as *feeling*? There is a deadness in our feeling. We do not *feel* anything; the thrill is gone. Life is not satisfying; it is boring and empty. Where does this death come from? How do we respond because of the first aspect of death, the meaninglessness, the darkness of the mind, and the failure to see

---

5. Gangadean, *The Biblical Worldview*, 37–54, 177–195; Gangadean, "Paper No. 146: The Biblical Worldview (Part VI)," in *The Logos Papers*, 741–745; Gangadean, *The Westminster Catechisms*, 144–15; Gangadean, *The Westminster Confession*, 99–110, 369–376.

6. *Ephesians 4:8.*

and understand? We do not understand the significance of things; we take things as given, and they are just there. We do not see how all that exists gives glory to God. There is no longer pleasure or satisfaction, and it is experienced as boredom. In the spiritual death that comes with sin, there is boredom. We have boredom, not independently of the mind, but because the mind is first darkened, we do not see and understand the meaning of things. The more we see and understand, the more thrilling life becomes. Notice I use a process word, *becomes*. There is a whole process of life and death, and we want to see this, too. We want to see that in understanding God's eternal judgment there is a whole process of life and death going on. We are temporal creatures, and for us, life and death operate in time. It begins, it grows, and it increases. Bear in mind that it is not static.

Besides this condition of meaninglessness and boredom, there is guilt. We are in a condition of misery because we have not done what is right. There are several levels of guilt. I want to spend some time speaking particularly about guilt because I am becoming more aware of how guilt operates and manifests in people's lives. I will only begin to talk about this; there is much more to say.

Using a False Moral Standard

When our lives are empty of meaning and when our lives are boring, we often go to excess, and in going to excess, we transgress. We seek wealth more as a way to get things to satisfy the emptiness in us, and we cannot get enough; we need more wealth. We do wrong things, we cheat, steal, and practice oppression to feed the emptiness in us, and then guilt comes in that way. But there are many other ways in which guilt comes in. Let us say we find things boring, we are not excited, and we deal with this by going to excess in drinking. This is not uncommon; a lot of people have been involved with drinking to the point of getting drunk, and we might still do it to get a buzz, and our lives are kind of flat or as Hamlet puts it: "How weary, stale, flat and unprofitable, Seem to me all the uses of this world!"[7] We try to get thrills in various ways, get into dangerous situations or relationships, and go into excess in many ways. There is a guilt that comes with this, but I

---

7. "Hamlet - Act 1, Scene 2 | Folger Shakespeare Library." n.d. www.folger.edu. https://www. folger.edu/explore/shakespeares-works/hamlet/read/1/2/.

want to go to a deeper level of guilt. Guilt where we feel worthless, we feel bad about ourselves, and we develop low self-esteem and an inferiority complex. Some people have struggled with this for years and years on end. It has become a very basic part of their lives; they have grown accustomed to this sense of guilt; they would not know what to do without it. It has become a way of life, and they beat themselves up like those who exalt themselves. These are two responses to the same thing. It just does not go far enough.

We think we are bad; we have missed the mark; we have come short; we do not measure up to this standard or that standard, the other standard, my mother's standard, my father's standard, or the standard of society. We may drive and push ourselves to keep trying to measure up and feel worthy, but we feel guilty. We feel we come short in life; it is just a strain of misery and feeling bad about ourselves—connected with guilt that runs through our life. You think you are not measuring up, you think you have come short, you feel bad about it, feel bad about yourself, and get down on yourself. Well, cheer up; things can get worse. You are not nearly as bad as you think you are; you are much, much worse. We are using a fake standard. We are far worse than others may think of us.

The Lord's Standard

We are to measure up to the standard the Lord sets: "For he who comes to God must believe that He is, and that He is a rewarder of those who diligently seek Him" (Heb. 11:6b NKJV). How do we process what our sin deserves? When we put sin in those terms, along with not seeking God, and add to it self-deception, guess what? We think we are seeking God; we think we are seeking God more than we really are. How much do we confess that as our sin and repent of that as our sin? If we do acknowledge this, how much do we see clearly enough to repent of it as opposed to just beating ourselves up about it? This is what we are to do with sin. If we think that we can pay for our sins by beating ourselves up, we are wrong. Christ paid for our sins. What our sin deserves is not to beat up on ourselves; it is to be forsaken of God forever.

We will break out of this antinomy of pride and self-abasement when we see sin clearly and truly. We are fooling ourselves if we are mucking around with either of these. Guilt (spiritual death), even false guilt because of false standards, limited guilt, or distorted guilt because of the distorted standards, is still part of death. We are to come back to seek God, to know God, to recognize sin for what it is, and to repent of it, not to just beat up on ourselves and think that is what we deserve. Do not think, 'If I go to purgatory for 10,000 years, that is what I deserve.' No, no, you do not deserve that; you deserve hell forever and to be left in that condition. Do not let us kid ourselves with a secondary level of guilt.

The inferiority complex comes short just as the superiority complex in pride comes short, and it is really, in essence, a form of pride. We are still not seeing ourselves quite the way we are; we are thinking of ourselves more highly than we ought.[8] Let us judge by the true standard; let us have this foundation well laid so that we may *overcome* these feelings about ourselves that have plagued us for so many years. Let us come to the truth of God, the truth about the nature of sin and what it deserves, and our need for Christ. Then we thank God for His love for us in Jesus Christ our Lord. Come to Him. Because of spiritual death, meaninglessness, boredom, and guilt, we punish ourselves in so many ways. We do ascetic acts of self-control; we think, 'I can do it; I can bring this body under control; I can exercise six times a week, two hours a day. I can make this body look like I want it to. I can control it, I can get my appetites under control, I can fast for two weeks!' This is to get back a sense of, 'I'm in control, I'm not so bad, I'm okay.' God does not call us to ascetic self-control. He calls us to be controlled by the Spirit of God and not to set up our own standards and go our own way. Many people are afflicted—one side with self-abasement and low self-esteem, and the other side with pride. But they are two sides of the same coin. We do not have to be in death if we come back, if we seek the Lord and see sin for what it is and see forgiveness for what it is.

Spiritual Death: Increased Meaninglessness

Spiritual death manifests itself in the Church. It manifests itself in coming to church as a matter of duty without diligently seeking God. It manifests itself in reading your Bible daily without seeking God diligently. It manifests itself in ritual obedience, where the act is progressively

---

8. *Romans 12:3.*

emptied of meaning—emptiness and meaninglessness. Everything we touch becomes emptied of meaning. Meaninglessness enters in and we do not have to go too far down to see it. When challenged by the decay of the culture, we lose sight of the meaning that has a basis in the moral law. We cannot name sin for what it is. We use words without meaning, and they become meaningless. When we do not seek God diligently, it is sin; the reward of knowing Him is not present. It is not life; instead, there is death. There is no love, joy, and peace, but something that masquerades as love, a substitute for joy and often a restlessness in our lives. It is death, which we cannot avoid.

LIFE IN CHRIST VERSUS SPIRITUAL DEATH

The only way to have life is in God through Jesus Christ our Lord. We have the forgiveness of sins, the beginning of life, and being born again, justified, and forgiven, but God has much more for us. Jesus has come that we might have life and have it to the fullest, and have it more abundantly.[9] He wants us to take the full measure of the stature of Jesus Christ, who is to fill the universe in every way.[10] That is why He has been given a name that is above every name.[11] All authority in heaven and earth has been given to Him[12] that he might fill everything in every way.[13] God wants us to come into this fullness. Without diligently seeking Him, we will not come into fullness, and there will be restlessness even in the lives of believers. This is the glorious blessing of sanctification. Not only does God forgive us and justify us in Christ, but sanctification is one of the blessings accompanying justification. It is the progressive deliverance from the power of sin and self-life that has worked its way into all of our thinking and relationships. God wants to cleanse us from all this so we might be holy before Him. He wants us to have life; He wants us to have faith, which involves understanding, which comes in connection with diligently seeking Him. He wants us to have hope as we understand the good and the promise of God. He

---

9. *John 10:10.*

10. *Ephesians 4:13, 1:23.*

11. *Philippians 2:9.*

12. *Matthew 28:18.*

13. *Ephesians 1:23.*

wants us to have love as we give ourselves in obedience to serve Him patiently and perseveringly, not being pulled this way and that way by every wind of doctrine, not being tripped up, but growing from strength to strength in Christ. In evaluating our lives this past week, we should see a progression of God's work in us. This is what we are looking for.

Death comes in relationships. Not all relationships are what they should be. We settle down in them. It is not just settling for a person but settling for less in that relationship because you no longer have hope to overcome. We fail to believe that God's Word can help us to see what is lacking. The Word, by the power of the Spirit, can be effectual in our lives. We should pray to this end, work to this end, and witness to this end. We settle for less when death is present. Sometimes, death may progress to such a point that the relationship breaks altogether. Some could be in the midst of the congregation of the people of God for some time, they could be raised as covenant children; they could hear outwardly and think they understand and miss the meaning. There is death in this way of life. This happens in groups, churches, nations, and civilizations; they can die, and they appear to survive and go on, but then, as it is challenged more and more, it cannot hold up. It is exposed, and they die. Some civilizations may have a measure of common grace; they may limp along, but they eventually die. Churches die, and individual churches die because they have not sought the Lord and have not lived by faith. Death overtakes them.

We need to learn the fear of the Lord. We will learn the fear of the Lord as we understand spiritual death. There is a connection with meaninglessness, boredom, and guilt in its many forms and not seeking the Lord diligently so as to understand and overcome. When the fear of the Lord is worked in us, it will deliver us from the fear of hell. Many people are moved by the fear of hell, something future and imposed, 'I don't want to go to hell. I may be in spiritual death, but I don't want to go to hell!' Some people are moved by the fear of the police, it is a real fear. We have the fear of the curse. Job said, "What I feared has come upon me; what I dreaded has happened to me" (Job. 3:25). He feared the loss of so many of the blessings of God, temporal blessings. But we are not to fear the curse. We can have a fear of man that brings a snare. We care what others think of us, and we want to fit in and belong. We can have the fear of Satan, but Satan cannot do anything beyond what God will allow him. He could not touch Job beyond what God would allow him. We have the fear of spirits and what they may do. We have the fear of God as a big foot in the sky, ready to drop on you. 'When is God going to strike me dead for this?' We do not understand eternal judgment. We do not understand spiritual death. We do not understand its current presence now. We do not understand that the fear of God as a big foot in the sky ready to drop is a distortion, and it is a manifestation of spiritual death in our lives.

We need to have the fear of the Lord well laid in our lives. Where did this teaching of hell come from? How are we to understand it? Romans 1:18 says, "For the wrath of God is revealed from heaven against all ungodliness and unrighteousness of men, who suppress the truth in unrighteousness" (NKJV). The wrath of God is revealed; that is a judgment of God. Every time that we turn away, at that time, the wrath of God is revealed. It is not God's emotion that changes when we turn away; God is permanently set against sin. His wrath is manifest not after it happens, not before it happens, but from the very way in which He has created us. He structured this into the creation; He is timelessly, eternally angry with sin. His wrath is manifest in this way. How is it manifested in Romans 1:24, 26, and 28? Three times, the wrath of God is manifested in these words, "He gave them up, He gave them up, He gave them up." Go! That is the wrath of God, not some big foot in the sky ready to drop. All those who speak about the big foot in the sky ready to drop and crush never get to the darkness of mind that is operating. They fail to see the darkness of the mind; they fail to see what is clear and the lack of meaning that is there.

DISTORTION OF THE FUNDAMENTAL TEACHING OF LIFE AND DEATH

We distort this basic, fundamental teaching. Scripture says that their foolish hearts were darkened, "For although they knew God, they neither glorified him as God nor gave thanks to him, but their thinking became futile and their foolish hearts were darkened" (Rom. 1:21). Elsewhere, it speaks about being cast into outer darkness.[14] Are these two different things? To be given up to the foolish heart? Is this a physical casting into darkness? He gave them up to a darkened mind; this is

---

14. *Matthew 22:13.*

what it means to be cast into darkness. They "burned in their lust one toward another" (Rom. 1:27 KJV). God gave them up to do those things that are unseemly. Men with men, women with women, doing things about which we are ashamed to speak. They cannot have satisfaction; they go to excess, doing things that cannot even be uttered. This is the fire that is not quenched,[15] we continue to burn in our lusts, burn in our desires. There is no satisfaction apart from God. "Although they know God's righteous decree that those who do such things deserve death, they not only continue to do these very things but also approve of those who practice them" (Rom. 1:32). Their conscience is striking out against them. It is gnawing at them; it is tormenting them. It is the worm that Jesus spoke of that does not die.[16] He spoke of hell in all these terms: the wrath of God, to be cast into outer darkness, where the fire is not quenched, and the worm does not die. This is to be understood in a spiritual sense.

Jesus spoke about hell as a bottomless pit.[17] Why a bottomless pit? Because you do not hit bottom, you keep going down into that pit. Just as we can grow and increase in life more and more, in this lifetime and in the afterlife, so those who are in death will grow in death more and more. This is too horrible to contemplate. But it is inherent in the way that God has made us; we are temporal beings. We never cease to grow in one way or the other, in life or in death. There is a bottomless pit.

Spiritual death is also spoken of as a lake of fire. "Then Death and Hades were cast into the lake of fire. This is the second death" (Rev. 20:14). If you think about it, you can see that it is not a literal lake of fire. Those who think the soul goes to hell do not understand that the soul cannot be affected by a literal fire. Those who think that the body is cast into hell do not understand that the body cannot last forever and ever in a fire. Those who try to make it so that the body is restored moment by moment so it can burn forever and ever have a distorted picture and commit themselves to a physical fire; but then Satan is cast into the lake of fire, and Satan is a spirit without a body. So they have to back up and try to go back to a spiritual fire. What is a spiritual fire? And if that is not enough, Death and Hades are cast into the lake of

---

15. *Mark 9:44–48.*

16. *Mark 9:44–48.*

17. *Revelation 9:2.*

fire, and they are neither spiritual nor physical. The lake of fire is a way of speaking about destruction, not cessation of being, but destruction. Things are turned inside out, they are not functioning as God intended them. We were once dead in our trespasses and sins, and God has quickened us. He has brought us by regeneration from death to life.

The eternal judgment of God—the timeless, permanent judgment—is being left to ourselves in spiritual death. It is not the case that there will be nothing after this life; there is an afterlife, body and soul, and this condition that is present now (spiritual death) will continue forever. The Bible speaks about it as *Gehenna*, the place where there are fires. *Gehenna* was like a garbage dump where fires burn. Combustible gas, methane gas, is produced in dumps; it is figurative of a life wasted. A life that was not fruitful, an empty life, that did not accomplish its purpose. It did not serve its purpose, at least positively, in one way, though it did serve its purpose to manifest the glory of God, but not in the sense of coming to *know* the glory of God.

Eternal judgment has to do with death, and death is, we believe, as it is spoken of in the Bible, in spiritual terms, spiritual death. "The gift of God is eternal life in Jesus Christ, our Lord" (Rom. 6:23b). Life consists not in heaven, where after this life, we die and the soul goes to heaven. Rather, life is, as Jesus said, knowing God: "Now this is eternal life: that they know you, the only true God, and Jesus Christ, whom you have sent" (Jn. 17:3). Now, think about this, to what extent is this the understanding of God's judgment, to what extent is this the understanding of life in the Church? If you are already persuaded of this, and many of you are, think about being able to persuade others of this; ways in which you can raise questions and engage people's understanding. That takes a certain wisdom, a certain guidance, seeking the Lord in relation to a particular person, wisdom to know how to engage and be a witness to them. The more you think about how to seek and understand God, the more you will know how to easily witness, not in a strained and uncomfortable way.

We know God in all that by which He makes Himself known, in all His works of creation and providence, in all of history.[18] Scripture teaches in Isaiah 6:3, "the whole earth is full of his glory," and in Habakkuk 2:14, "For the earth will be filled with the knowledge of the glory of

---

18. Gangadean, *The Westminster Catechisms*, 100.

the LORD as the waters cover the sea." This is life. In order to achieve this fullness, you must be fruitful. In John 15, Jesus speaks about the vine and the branches and He says, **"By this My Father is glorified, that you bear much fruit"** (v. 8a). "Man's chief end is to glorify God, and to enjoy him forever" (WCF 1.1). Glorifying God is through bearing fruit, fruit that will remain, fruit that will last, fruit that is spoken of in John 15:16. It takes a great number of people a long time to uncover this revelation, this life. God made it so in the beginning when He said to Adam, "Be fruitful" (Gen. 1:28). He reiterated this when He said, "Therefore go and make disciples of all nations, baptizing them in the name of the Father and of the Son and of the Holy Spirit, and teaching them to obey everything I have commanded you" (Matt. 28:19–20a). Is this our understanding of life? Is this the life that we seek? Remember, coming out of Egypt, we were relatively passive; we did not have to exercise the faith expressed in the Passover, but coming into Canaan, we had to fight and engage. When we do so in the strength of God, by the power of God, it is still a matter of grace.

Are we giving ourselves to seeking life in this way, or are we settling for less, getting discouraged, not knowing how to go on because we are not seeking to know how? Are we engaging in something less than this that will be burnt up according to 1 Corinthians 3? Paul says, "For what is our hope, our joy, or the crown in which we will glory in the presence of our Lord Jesus when he comes? Is it not you? Indeed, you are our glory and joy" (1 Thes. 2:19–20). Our crown, our life, our blessing, our fruit is in seeing sons and daughters of God, who in turn, not only come to know God but serve to make God known.

This is the life that God has called us to. Let us not turn aside to the doctrine of the intermediate state in heaven. The intermediate state is where we are *until* the work is completed, *until* we have the resurrection of the body, *until* every name is subdued to Christ. It is where we are waiting, and we shall see Him as He is. It is not the beatific vision.[19] It is seeing God, without sin, in all that whereby He makes Himself known in His works. It is continuing to see that revelation unfold as the Church on earth, the Church militant, does its work. Those who

---

19. Gangadean, *On Natural and Revealed Theology,* 9–39; Gangadean, "Paper No. 106: The Good and Heaven," 547–556; "Paper No. 116: The Knowledge of God vs. The Hope of Heaven," in *The Logos Papers,* 597–598; Gangadean, *Philosophical Foundation,* 40–41, 71–73.

have gone on will not be made complete apart from those who remain. When this work has been completed, we will enter into the fullness of the blessing of God. The teaching of God's eternal judgment, this foundation teaching, stands before us. If we have this, we will go on to maturity. If this is in the Church, it will be the city of God that will last forever, full of beauty and glory. Amen.

INDEX

Aaron, 67-72, 81, 99, 106,
    110-111, 121, 131, 137-138,
    232, 324, 330, 350
Abel, 13, 53, 167, 175-176, 179,
    191-193, 208, 219, 230-231,
    271
ability, 326
Abraham, 12-14, 20, 32, 38-39, 73,
    83-84, 96-99, 102-110,
    123-126, 146, 155, 167-168,
    180-185, 191-197, 208, 213,
    220, 239, 254, 272, 287n28,
    295-296, 353-354
Acts 15, 312-315
Adam, 26, 45, 60, 73, 140,
    262-264, 273-274, 282-284,
    296-297, 303-306, 309,
    349-350, 356-358
    and Eve, 188, 204, 262-264,
    282-284, 304, 358
Allah, 265
Ananias, 230
angels, 3-4, 15-22, 25, 29, 32-33,
    229-230, 239
apologetic(s), 48
Aquinas, Thomas, 312
Arminian(ism), 169n3, 289-290
atonement (see also vicarious
    atonement), 20, 33, 36, 76, 131,
    138, 155, 169n3, 175, 199, 265
    vicarious, 199
attributes, 256
Augustine, St., 14, 312

autonomy, 87, 188, 216, 284, 288,
    349

Babel, 104, 107n9, 181, 311
beatific vision, 91, 368
boredom, 89, 360-364
born again, 13, 169, 193, 265, 289,
    292, 301, 307, 363

Calvin, John, 6, 14, 336
causes, 80, 215, 222, 242-243, 289
Chalcedon, council of, 292
charismatic, 311, 319
chastening, 189-190, 220-221, 224,
    229
Christian, 93, 192, 206, 210, 248,
    294-295, 341
    faith, 342
Christianity, 77, 157, 173,
    265-266, 336, 344
church, 244, 255, 291, 294-295,
    325-326
    the, 325
City of God, the, 229, 237,
    253-254, 272-273, 287, 290,
    297, 341, 369
clarity, x, 197, 256, 259, 346
    of God's existence, 171, 191
common sense, 171n10
concept(s), 47, 69, 265, 292
conscience, 10, 131, 139-140, 145,
    150-152, 159-161, 177,
    236-238, 267, 366
context, 58, 323-324

contextual, x-xi, xiv
  interpretation, xi
covenant, 18, 33, 53, 101, 111,
  115-116, 120-138, 145-147,
  150-151, 160, 164, 221, 236,
  264, 289-297, 301-302, 308,
  331
  children, 182, 327, 364
  of grace, 291-292, 295-297,
    301-302, 356
  of works, 60, 292, 296-297
  theology, 289-291
creation, 27, 51, 177, 191,
  262-264, 274, 304, 348, 353
  and providence, 314, 367
  original, 177, 348
curse, the, 32, 78, 81, 144,
  266-269, 272, 322, 349, 364

David, 13, 17, 51, 59, 68, 71-72,
  95n23, 112, 121, 155, 171n9,
  186, 192, 200-201, 208, 241
death, 20, 29-33, 77-79, 87-89,
  107, 140, 144-145, 176, 198,
  254, 260, 263, 267-269,
  272-274, 279, 290, 296-299,
  341, 348-351, 355-367
  physical, 267, 348-350
  spiritual, 260, 272, 298, 341,
    348, 364-367
decree(s), 366
devil, the, 20, 32, 36, 210, 284
diligence, xv, 23, 55, 61, 83, 95-97,
  136
dispensationalism, 289-290
divine justice, 147
division(s), xiii, 65, 253, 258,
  289-290, 293
doctrine, xi, 238, 259, 288, 306,
  318, 328, 343-344
dominion, 274

work of, xvi, 58, 73, 287, 349,
  352
Dort, 169n3
doxological
  focus, x
  postmillennialism, xv, 162

elect, the, 31, 294
election (see also unconditional
  election), 353
empiricism, 159, 171n9, 192
epistemological, 170, 171n9
Esau, 12, 109, 183-185, 196, 214,
  219, 224-227, 231
eschatology, 53, 91, 171, 344
eternal, 17, 38, 71, 132, 144-146,
  190, 256-260, 346, 349,
  355-358, 367
  life, 38-39, 45, 142, 260-262,
    344, 355-358, 367
evangelical(s), 292, 352
Eve, 264, 282-284
evil, 24, 73, 81, 86, 97, 176, 181,
  243, 263-264, 285, 288, 341,
  346-349, 358
  moral, 14, 38, 65, 74-75, 79, 93,
    103, 149, 155, 177, 187,
    190, 194, 197, 206-208,
    211-212, 226, 250, 284,
    298-299, 307, 341, 355, 364
  natural, 346-348
evolution, 213, 258, 263
Ezekiel, 224n8, 269n31, 310

faith, xiv-xvi, 12-14, 48, 57-58, 83,
  86, 90, 93-95, 124-125, 128,
  160-161, 167-188, 191-201,
  204, 211, 238, 245-246, 271,
  275, 285-290, 294-296,
  299-301, 314-317, 327, 332,
  339, 342-344, 354-356

Fall, the, 61-62, 93, 233, 255

father, 13, 106

female(ness), 28, 125, 241, 327

fideism, 159, 168n2, 171-172

foundation, xiv-xvii, 86, 92, 191, 253-254, 273-274, 277, 343

free will, 169n3

freedom, 44-45, 290, 298, 318, 353

fruit, 77, 94-95, 165, 197, 263, 335-336, 355, 368

fruitfulness, xiv, 27, 254

fullness, xiv, 39-41, 53-54, 65, 101-102, 107-108, 112-113, 125, 133-134, 148, 186, 198, 221, 232, 237, 275, 305-306, 316, 319, 340, 363

Galatians, 10, 12n13, 76n15, 123-125, 175n24, 278n12

Garden of Eden, 296

Genesis, 12, 38, 239, 266
1-3, xivn7, 38, 263

good and evil, xvi, 43, 81, 86-87, 92, 140, 174, 181, 188, 204, 217, 263-264, 284-285, 288, 341, 349, 358

good and necessary consequence, 195

good, the, xvi, 45, 56, 152, 204, 286, 341

grace, 29, 109, 164, 179, 197, 221-224, 246-247, 291-297, 356

Greek, 6, 58, 63, 125-126, 195, 250, 312

guilt, 89, 161, 260, 268, 282, 307, 360-364

hardship, 203-207, 214, 217, 222

heaven, 10, 16, 103, 115-116, 119-120, 132, 147, 219, 230-233, 272, 282, 309, 333, 345-347, 352-354, 367

Hebrews, the, xiii, 5-7, 14-16, 22, 85, 101, 134, 152, 226, 238, 254

hell, 77, 92, 143, 310, 341-342, 358, 362-366

hermeneutic(s), xi

Hinduism, 27

history, x, 9, 41, 133, 181, 191, 289, 311-314, 318, 336

holiness, 17, 31, 68-71, 107n9, 138, 141-143, 157, 189, 198, 203, 216-234, 237, 286, 299, 304, 329-331, 350-351

Holy Spirit, 24-26, 40-42, 91, 133, 157, 293, 298-300, 303-319, 323-326

human nature, 17, 68

humility, 278

image of God, 263, 340

incarnation, 144-145, 278

inexcusability of unbelief, 191

intellectual, 359

irresistible grace, 299

Isaac, 38, 96, 109, 167-168, 180, 183-185, 195-196, 212, 353

Isaiah, xvn11, xvin18, 31, 41n7, 42n11, 56n11, 77, 91n19, 138n12, 166n17, 178, 194, 200, 262n15, 303n2, 316n22, 340n1, 344n10, 367

Islam, 77, 87, 88n8, 142n15, 157, 173, 175n23, 238, 265, 266n23

Israelites, 22, 41, 46-48, 53-54, 58, 62, 77, 123, 146, 177, 185, 196, 227, 231-232

Jacob, 12-13, 38, 167, 180, 183-185, 196, 353

Jefferson, Thomas, 266
Jephthah, 186, 200
Jeremiah, 45, 75n12, 111, 121-123, 126, 158n10
Jerusalem, 7-8, 11n10, 109, 139, 146-147, 158, 219, 229-231, 304-305, 311-315, 321-324, 329, 334-335
Jesus, 11n10, 13, 19, 23, 31-32, 35-42, 45, 49, 52-53, 57-58, 65, 68-71, 79-81, 84, 98-101, 113-120, 125, 134-135, 141-145, 148, 153, 156-157, 175, 189, 205, 211-213, 234-237, 243, 247-249, 260-261, 265, 273-274, 287, 291-292, 300-301, 304, 307-308, 316, 321, 326, 329-333, 351, 357, 363, 366-368
Jewish, 6-9, 12-14, 39, 53, 101, 116, 121, 134, 175, 182, 283, 312, 321, 329-331
Jews, 7-10, 13, 37-39, 142, 237, 283, 311-312, 321-323, 327-329, 353
Job, 13, 46, 75, 160, 229, 234, 322, 364
Joseph, 11n10, 185, 196-197, 243, 332
Judaism, 8-10, 77, 157, 173, 265
   post-biblical, 175
justice, 23, 92, 143, 348
   infinite, 92
   of God, 351

king, 99, 103-105, 109
King James Version, 187, 212, 272, 285
king(ly), 99, 103-105, 109

kingdom, the, 10, 18, 38-40, 61, 146, 162, 166, 193-194, 220, 233-234, 237, 242, 254, 272, 279-281
   of God, ix, 38-40, 43, 61, 92, 105, 148, 162, 165, 191-193, 199, 207, 220, 224, 233, 237, 242, 250, 254, 265, 272-273, 277-281, 285, 301, 305-307, 331, 342-344
   of heaven, 10, 272, 282
knowledge, x, xiv, 48, 56, 75-76, 107n9, 172-174, 178, 258, 262, 274, 278, 286, 316, 344, 358
   of God, x, 48, 56, 75, 174, 178, 262, 274, 278
   of the Lord, 26, 286

law, 8-11, 15, 38, 99-105, 112, 119-125, 152, 157-159, 257, 328
   ceremonial, 38, 102, 105, 120-121, 151-152
   civil, 38, 102, 152
   moral, ix, 127
   of God, 158-159
liberty, 200
Locke, John, 171n9
love, 27-28, 95, 160-164, 168, 240-243, 248, 275, 316-317, 354, 363
Luther, Martin, 14, 152, 336

male(ness), 28, 106n9, 125, 241
man, 25, 68-69, 172, 351
   the image of God, 263, 340
materialism, 192, 209, 258, 345
matter, 97, 139, 258, 295
Matthew, xv, 43, 57

maturity, x, xiv, 83-85, 89-91, 112, 133, 253-254, 271-273, 276, 288, 309, 342, 369

meaningless(ness), 89, 129, 177, 268, 299, 359-364

mediator, 16, 115, 124, 132, 141-142, 145-146, 151, 154, 219-221, 230-231, 234

mercy, 138

metaphysical, 170

Modern(ity), xiii, 5n4

moral evil (also ME), 14, 38, 65, 74-75, 79, 93, 103, 149, 155, 177, 187, 190, 194, 197, 206-208, 211-212, 226, 250, 284, 298-299, 307, 341, 355, 364

moral law, ix, 127

Mormonism, 267

Moses, 9-13, 16, 24-25, 35-39, 48, 53, 62, 99, 115, 119-124, 132, 146-147, 150, 153, 163, 174, 185, 194, 197-199, 208, 212, 219, 228-229, 232, 312, 330

much discussion, 313-314, 317-318

Muslims, 96, 142-143, 266, 312

natural evil (also NE), 24, 176, 267, 346-348

naturalism, 171, 192, 245

Noah, 104, 107n9, 167, 174, 179-180, 183, 191, 208, 242

obedience, 22, 79, 177, 187, 200

ontological, 26, 88

ordination, 324

ordo salutis, 90, 299, 302, 343

original sin, 294

oversight, 250, 343

pastor-teachers, 26, 56, 128, 133, 244, 275, 284, 290-291, 311-314, 318-319, 343

perspicuity, x

Pharaoh, 198

Plato, 312

post-biblical Judaism, 175

Postmodernism (also Postmodernity), ix, xiii

power, 32, 71, 174, 256, 306, 309, 326, 351

prayer, 23, 80, 95, 137-138, 189n2, 249, 323

presuppositional, 159

priest, 20, 24, 30-36, 40, 43-44, 52, 65-73, 76-81, 84-86, 91-92, 98-100, 103-118, 121, 129-150, 153, 156, 160-161, 221, 235-236, 247, 329-331, 334-335

priestly, 75n13, 139, 330

promise, xvi, 12-13, 21-23, 34, 43, 47, 107-109, 121-125, 160, 167, 180-183, 187, 197, 201, 243, 267, 279, 353

Promised Land, 167, 180-182, 353

prophet, 68, 73, 84, 116, 200, 333

prophetic, 324

providence, xi, xvi, 59-60, 174, 227, 244, 314, 367

Psalms, 28n6, 64n19, 75n13, 194

purgatory, 349, 362

purpose, 21, 36, 42-44, 97, 179, 186, 208, 243-245, 275, 286, 316, 331, 367

God's, 21, 36, 42-44, 97, 107n9, 168, 186, 245, 262, 286, 304, 345, 350

rapture, the, 181

Rational Presuppositionalism, ix-x,
   xv
rationalism, 159
realism, 171n10
reason, 6, 33, 88, 106n9, 155, 163,
   171, 259-260, 283, 286, 298,
   314
Red Sea, 62, 185, 199, 226
redemption, 156, 303-304, 349,
   352
   accomplished, 156-157,
     304-306
   applied, 299, 303-304, 352
reformation, 282
repent, 269, 281-284, 342, 361
repentance, 83, 87, 90, 93, 254,
   274, 279, 282-285, 288-290,
   322, 342
representation, 3, 15, 20, 90, 117
representative head, 262, 292, 296
revelation, x, 101, 257, 262,
   266-268, 317, 348, 368
righteousness, 3, 10, 18, 105, 118,
   140, 179, 198, 242, 254,
   295-296, 307, 354
Roman Catholic(ism), 11, 152-153,
   157, 175, 289, 293, 336
   church, 11, 152, 157, 289, 293,
     336
Romans, 125-127, 174, 223,
   255-259, 350, 365
root sin, xi, 63-64, 77, 87, 161, 342

Sabbath, 11, 41, 54, 60, 147, 151,
   236, 244n13, 274, 286
Saul of Tarsus, 64, 76, 79, 140,
   144, 177, 265-266, 324
seed of the woman, 155, 267-268,
   303, 310, 349

seeking, xvi, 46, 74-78, 173, 178,
   188-190, 322, 342, 361-363,
   368
self-deception, xi, 78, 88, 136, 140,
   189, 223, 283-284, 322, 342,
   349, 361
self-examination, 322
self-justification, xi, 78, 88, 137,
   223, 322, 342, 349
Shiva, 27
sin, 30-33, 42-44, 55-57, 64,
   68-69, 73, 77-80, 87-90, 114,
   140-145, 148, 153-155, 175,
   198, 204, 210, 222, 226, 229,
   255-269, 272, 288-290,
   296-299, 303, 307, 341-342,
   348-351, 356-358, 361-363
   actual, 64, 77
   consequences of, 259
   original, 294
   root, xi, 63-64, 77, 87, 161, 342
Sinai, 121-123, 220, 226-228, 231,
   237, 295
skepticism, 48, 159, 171-172
Son, the, 3, 15-18, 31, 37-39, 71,
   106, 142, 293, 332, 350
soul, the, 21, 41, 51, 63-65, 84, 89,
   97-98, 104, 133, 155, 171, 177,
   206, 227, 258-259, 267, 312,
   346, 349-354, 359, 366-367
sovereign, 174, 216
   grace, 174
Spirit, 18, 24, 71, 133, 157, 164,
   175, 230, 269, 293, 298-300,
   303-319, 323, 326-327, 343,
   351, 356
spiritual death, 138, 187, 195,
   228-229, 238, 260, 272,
   297-298, 341-342, 348,
   359-367
spiritual warfare, xvi, 55, 166, 341

substance, 47, 127, 170-172, 187, 285, 290, 342, 347
sufficiency, 156

tabernacle, 30, 33, 38, 53, 115-120, 131-132, 135, 138-143, 147, 151, 154, 235, 247
Talmud, 11
temptation, 34, 39, 95, 151
temptations, 34
Ten Commandments, 102, 121, 152
Tertullian, 14
testament, xi, 141, 145, 291, 296
  new, 141, 145
testimony, 5-6, 150, 163, 197, 340, 350
theology, 87, 289-290
  covenant, 289-291
tongues, 232, 280, 309-311, 327
Torah, 11
translation(s), 6
TULIP, 169n3

unbelief, 49, 76, 133, 256
unbelievers, 230
United States, 266
unity, xiv, 101, 240, 275, 315-317

Van Til, Cornelius, 14
vicarious atonement, 199

wilderness, the, 44, 62, 163, 227, 231, 330
will of God, xv, 69-71, 151, 165-166
Word of God, xi, 23-25, 38, 57, 62-65, 76, 84-86, 94, 98, 102, 108, 111, 135-137, 142, 159, 166, 175, 179, 197, 201, 205-206, 213, 221, 232, 237-238, 244-245, 250, 254, 261, 265, 276, 279-281, 286, 287n28, 294, 298-299, 304, 309-310, 314-315, 333-337
work of dominion, xvi, 58, 73, 287, 349, 352
work of the Spirit, 230, 260, 304, 309, 343
world, the, 25, 28, 111, 145, 148, 155, 174-176, 179, 192-193, 198-199, 204, 210-213, 247, 256, 260-262, 267-268, 272, 277, 280, 285, 303, 308-309, 313-314, 318, 329, 343, 348
worldview, xvi, 47, 107n9, 168, 171, 180-182, 191-193, 199, 346
  biblical, 346
worship, 17, 135, 152, 189, 249
wrath, 45, 73, 142, 232, 243, 256, 365-366

Yom Kippur, 265

ABOUT THE AUTHOR

DR. SURRENDRA GANGADEAN (1943–2022) was a Professor of Philosophy at Phoenix College and at Paradise Valley Community College for 45 years. Additionally, he taught from the pulpit at Westminster Fellowship for almost 30 years and taught courses at Logos Theological Seminary for over 25 years. Courses he taught include: Introduction to Philosophy, Logic, Ethics, Philosophy of Religion, Eastern Religions, World Religions, Introduction to Christianity, Introduction to Humanities, Philosophy of Art, The Great Books, Philosophical Theology, Biblical Worldview, Biblical History, Church History, Systematic Theology, Biblical Hermeneutics, and Existential Hermeneutics. He received an M.A. degree in Literature from the Arizona State University, an M.A. degree in Philosophy from the University of Arizona, and a Ph.D. in Natural Theology from Reformed International Theological Seminary. He presented academic papers and public lectures on Natural Theology and the Moral Law. Dr. Gangadean was the organizing Pastor of Westminster Fellowship Church, and President of The Logos Foundation, which serves academic education in Liberal Arts and Theology.